REYNER BANHAM

The MIT Press   Cambridge, Massachusetts   London, England

REYNER BANHAM
Historian of the Immediate Future

REYNER BANHAM
Historian of the Immediate Future

Nigel Whiteley

This book was set in Frutiger by Graphic Composition, Inc.
Printed and bound in the United States of America.

Library of Congress Cataloging-in-Publication Data

Whiteley, Nigel.
    Reyner Banham: historian of the immediate future / Nigel Whiteley.
       p. cm.
    Includes bibliographical references and index.
    ISBN 0-262-23216-2 (hc.: alk. paper)
      1. Banham, Reyner—Criticism and interpretation.   I. Title.

  NA2599.8.B36 W48 2002
  720'.92—dc21

                                         2001030605

To my father, Eric, and the memory of my mother, Peggy, with much love and gratitude

CONTENTS

ILLUSTRATIONS

PREFACE

One of Reyner Banham's most quoted sentences reads: "Our accession to almost unlimited supplies of energy is balanced against the possibility of making our planet uninhabitable, but this again is balanced, as we stand at the threshold of space, by the growing possibility of quitting our island earth and letting down roots elsewhere."[1] It comes from the introduction to his seminal *Theory and Design in the First Machine Age,* published in 1960, and it is usually quoted to demonstrate the extent to which Banham was a child of his times and, therefore, supposedly ecologically reckless, technologically naïve, and politically innocent. An optimism toward the future could seem to be more important to him than conventional social responsibility and conventions of academic propriety.

As a child of his time, Banham was suitably precocious, and during the 1960s, the enfant terrible was accorded the status of a guru-like figure in progressive architectural circles. The fall from grace began in a general sense in the turbulent year of 1968, when a new political radicalism revealed the old Modernist radicalism to be more a part of the Establishment than it would have believed. In the 1970s, the fall, for Banham, was accelerated by the seeming anachronism of his unflinchingly pro-technological books such as *The Architecture of the Well-tempered Environment,* and was hastened by energy crises and the widespread loss of faith in progressivism as the binding myth of Western industrial society. Banham himself acknowledged that, by a form of apostolic succession, the child of his time appeared to have become yesterday's man: the new enfant terrible was Charles Jencks with his theory of Post-Modernism.

In 1979, about the time when his reputation had fallen to its lowest point, Banham reviewed a book by Michael Thompson titled *Rubbish Theory: The Creation and Destruction of Value.* He was fascinated by Thompson's notion that (as Banham paraphrased it) "all transient consumables slide slowly down the parallel scales of social esteem and actual cash value until they bottom out as absolute rubbish. At that point, however, they are not necessarily discarded, but may suddenly leap to the top of both scales."[2] It would have been very characteristic of him to translate Thompson's remarks about consumables into terms of professional reputation, wondering when—his incurable optimism would deny any anxiety about "if"—his own leap back into the scales of academic esteem and actual historical value would occur. The great leap forward began before his death in 1988. Critical acclaim greeted the publication of *A Concrete Atlantis* in 1986 and, a year later, he was appointed to the prestigious Solow chair at New York University, polevaulting himself back into the top architectural history league.

Earlier in the decade, a selection of Banham's writing had been published under the title *Design by Choice* (1981). Prior to that, some of his design criticism had appeared in *Arts in Society* (1977), a collection of essays by writers who contributed to *New Society.* Following his death, the splendid anthology *A Critic Writes* (1996) has made available a wide range of his essays. The present book is an attempt to move into a phase of critical examination of Banham's theories and ideas. His writing is now ripe for reassessment because we are historically distant enough from the period he was writing in, the issues he was affected by, and (most of) the names that he was discussing. Banham's ideas and values were largely formed by the conditions of the Second Machine Age; I would argue we are now in the Fourth, and so have as clear a view of the Second as Banham himself had of the First.[3]

I have been a Banham enthusiast since I first encountered *Theory and Design* in the very early 1970s, as an undergraduate. By the mid-1970s I had become aware of the range of his writing and marveled at the way he could write so eruditely and compellingly about such a range of topics. In a period when obfuscation became de rigueur in academic writing, Banham remained a model of clear and direct communication. I personally witnessed— and somehow survived—that *very* clear and *very* direct communication at my PhD orals in the summer of 1982.

In researching this book, I have heard many anecdotes about Banham's "bluffness" and unwillingness to "suffer fools gladly"—these are oftrepeated tales. Almost every architect or architectural or design historian over the age of forty has a Banham recollection: sometimes fond, sometimes hostile, sometimes fondly remembering a hostile put-down at someone else's expense. What has intrigued me is how each casts light on one aspect of Banham's output, and the speaker sometimes assumes that aspect typifies the whole. Knowledge of his body of work, in other words, is patchy: to one reader, Banham is *Theory and Design;* to another, *Los Angeles;* or

Megastructures; or his *New Society* articles. Indeed, I remember a sociologist commenting on Banham's *New Society* articles, but expressing surprise when I told her that he wrote architecture books, too! This is understandable when you realize Banham wrote a dozen books and over seven hundred articles.

The current volume attempts to examine the complete body of work and analyze the commonalities of value, as well as the contradictions which, by declaring that "the only way to prove you have a mind is to change it occasionally," Banham accepted and even relished. This book will disappoint those seeking an insight into what made the man tick. It is not a biography nor is it particularly biographical, and Banham's presence is not conjured up. My aim has been to outline his ideas, provide critical analysis, offer interpretation and attempt evaluation. I have used a large number of quotations to give a flavor not only of what he said but also of how he said it. In the end, however, this is a critical reader's guide to Banham's writing, the first to try to make sense of the full oeuvre. One of his favorite quotations was Moholy-Nagy's aphorism "Man, not the product, is the end in view." I might paraphrase it in relation to this book by claiming that "The writing, not the man, is the end in view." A biography is under way, and I look forward to its appearance to learn about the man and his life.

The structure I have adopted is a mixture of the chronologically thematic and the thematically chronological, with some exceptions. The introduction outlines Banham's career and discusses some of the values he reacted against in his early professional years. Chapter 1 analyzes his contribution to our understanding of the Modern Movement of the First Machine Age. Chapter 2 discusses the importance of the Independent Group for his thinking, and his growing interest in an *architecture autre* and New Brutalism in the 1950s. The third charts his attitudes to technology and his arguments in the 1960s for an architecture of technology of and for the Second Machine Age. The fourth explores his fascination with mechanical services and the liberatory potential of technology in the late 1960s and 1970s which heralded the Third Machine Age and could have brought about the demise of architecture and urban design as they were customarily recognized. Chapter 5 addresses Banham's enthusiasms for James Stirling's buildings and attitude and for High-Tech architecture, and assesses his beliefs and values in the post-1968 world of changing paradigms, including the rise of Post-Modernism, alternative technology, and architectural Traditionalism. Chapter 6 discusses his writing about design—the "dreams that money can buy"—in the Second Machine Age, and analyzes his views about the role of the critic. The conclusion attempts to identify and historicize his key values and assumptions, including his architectural relationships with his *lieber Meister* Nikolaus Pevsner and his doctoral student Jencks.

ACKNOWLEDGMENTS

Charles Jencks is one of a number of people who have read drafts of chapters, discussed ideas, contributed information, or shared anecdotes. I would like to thank him along with others, including George Baird, Paul Barker, Gill Chitty, Adrian Forty, Kenneth Frampton, Tony Gould, Richard Hamilton, the late Ron Herron, Victor Margolin, Robert Maxwell, Martin Pawley, Cedric Price, the late Colin Rowe, Peter Smithson, Penny Sparke, Gavin Stamp, the late James Stirling, David Watkin, and Michael Wilford. The staff of the Getty Museum made my stay there to consult the Banham archive an enjoyable and productive one. Funding, for which I am most grateful, was provided by the Getty Trust, the Arts and Humanities Research Board, and the Faculty of Arts and Humanities at Lancaster University. Acknowledgments are due *Architectural History* and *Oxford Art Journal,* in which sections from some of the chapters first appeared, and Valerie Bennett at the Architectural Association slide library. Thanks, too, to those at in the Graduate School of Design at Harvard University and in the Design History Society who commented on papers I presented.

I am indebted to Mary Banham for allowing me to use Reyner Banham's photographic archive, which is now housed at the Architectural Association slide library, London. Other photographs are taken by the author unless otherwise stated.

I would also like to thank Roger Conover at the MIT Press for his commitment to this project, Deborah Cantor-Adams and Beth Wilson for their assured and sensitive editing, and to Emily Gutheinz for her excellent designing. My wife, Diane Hill, and children, Daniel and Ella, have acted with convincing interest or, at least, quiet dignity during the writing of this book. However, my greatest debt is to Mary Banham, whose helpfulness and generosity have been unstinting, and whose insights have been invaluable.

REYNER BANHAM

INTRODUCTION

"The only way to *prove* you have a mind," Banham was wont to remark, "is to change it occasionally." Professionally, he changed his mind possibly less than he cared to imagine, but without the first and extremely significant change, he would be unlikely to be the subject of a book.

Formations

"I never really thought of doing anything else but engineering even when I was at school . . . all the Banhams before me were technology men."[1] School was the King Edward VI Grammar School in Norwich, and Peter Reyner Banham, born in 1922, duly moved on, in 1939, to Bristol Technical College, where he began training as a mechanical (aero-) engineer before working at the Bristol Aeroplane Company as an engine fitter.[2] But all was not well. He failed his HNC (Higher National Certificate)[3] and suffered from stress: "Well you can't go on doing 24 hour shifts one after another forever and just before the end of the war I was invalided out. The weakest went to the wall and I was a very callow youth . . . I was turned down by the services, too."[4] On leaving the Bristol Aeroplane Company, Banham claimed that "I decided to recycle myself as an intellectual."[5] It was not a career move that either the recast "Reyner Banham"[6] or the audiences for his books, articles, broadcasts, and lectures were to regret, although some members of the architectural and design professions were to think otherwise.

The recollection about his unsuccessful attempt at engineering presents a Banham that few of us would recognize. Other anecdotal recollections provide us with insights into a more readily identifiable, certainly comprehensively recycled, intellectual. The first, written in 1964, which recalls the provincial culture of the 1930s in which he grew up, emphasizes the centrality of popular culture in his life. His early life was amid neither "high" nor "aspirational" culture, but "American pulps, things like *Mechanix Illustrated* and the comic books (we were all great Betty Boop fans) . . . the penny pictures on Saturday mornings . . . [and] the speedway."[7] Popular culture was Banham's staple diet during his childhood and youth. As a young adult he discovered high culture, but it did not *replace*—*dis*placed—popular culture in his life—Banham was to use a similar phrase to describe the effect on his thinking of Buckminster Fuller's approach to architecture. He relished the postwar American mass media, "pop culture" boom in the

Reyner Banham, working-class intellectual, early 1960s (courtesy Mary Banham)

Reyner Banham, the pop professor, early 1970s (anonymous)

Reyner Banham, the cowboy, 1980s (courtesy Mary Banham)

1950s: "We returned to Pop of the early 'fifties like Behans going to Dublin or Thomases to Llaregub, back to our native literature, our native arts."[8] Banham and those like him were "back home again."[9] This explains not only his enthusiasm for the Independent Group activities in the early 1950s, but also his continuing interest in pop cultural artifacts—from car styling through surfboard decoration to paperback book covers.

The second recollections from the perspective of 1960, is one of his apprenticeship days, and relates to how he discovered architectural history. He describes being in a bus queue in 1943, but missing the bus because he had been transfixed by Nikolaus Pevsner's *Outline of European Architecture* (1943),

still smelling of fresh ink. . . . I can still see the back of that blasted bus as it pulled away, graven in my mind's eye as a marker for the moment when I became an architectural historian. . . . We were the first generation to come to the live study of architectural history uncorrupted by previous contact with Banister Fletcher. For us it was never the embalmed death-roll of mislabelled styles that old BF made it; for us it was always a snap-crackle-pop subject. The *Outline* changed the outlook, *for good*.[10]

The original paperback edition was "a sharp-edged weapon, like J. M. Richards' *Introduction to Modern Architecture* [1940] or C. H. Waddington's *Scientific Attitude* [1941]—all sharp enough to slice through fatigue, mental staleness, the noise of war and transport, the hostile atmosphere of barracks and digs."[11] Here is Banham the enthusiast, influenced by texts which stimulated the "live study" of architecture: something at which he was to succeed so completely in his own writing.

Books played an important part in Banham's formative years. Indeed, his undelivered inaugural lecture for the Solow Chair of the History of Architecture at New York University, in the year before his death, assessed the importance of particular texts—the importance, even, of particular editions of those texts which became "a set of actual monuments"[12]—in communicating received wisdom about the Modern Movement.

In his own case as a schoolboy and then apprentice, his third recollection testifies to the impact of a number of books available around the time of the Second World War or soon after: in addition to the books already mentioned, Moholy Nagy's *The New Vision* (originally published as *Von Material zu Architektur* in 1928, it was translated as *The New Vision* and published in 1930, and republished in 1938 and 1946) was paramount, nothing less than "a sacred text";[13] but other major works included *Mechanisation Takes Command* (1948); the catalogs of the Museum of Modern Art's *Cubism and Abstract Art* (1936) and *Bauhaus 1919–1928* (1938) exhibitions; the British Constructivist-influenced collection *Circle* (1937); Nikolaus Pevsner's *Pioneers of the Modern Movement* (1936: reprinted by the Museum of Modern Art as *Pioneers of Modern Design* in 1949); and Sigfried Giedion's *Space, Time and Architecture* (1941, republished in 1949).[14]

These texts were important to Banham in three ways. First, they provided information about, and fueled his commitment to, the Modern Movement. Second, by presenting what Lawrence Alloway was to describe as "fact condensed in vivid imagery,"[15] they evoked a *spirit* of modernity which Banham enthusiastically imbibed. Third, they provided the basis for his own revisionist writing as a historian, which was stimulated, he recalled, by a BBC radio talk by Bruno Adler "some time in the Forties"[16] that argued that the de Stijl movement "had considerable influence on the Bauhaus. Reference to the pages of *Bauhaus 1919–1928* produced ample visual justification for this proposition, but it also produced a positive statement that de Stijl was of little consequence in Bauhaus history. Such patent contradictions between fact and propaganda certainly stimulated my earliest researches into the history of the Modern Movement." Banham discovered what he was to term a "Zone of Silence" about the Futurist and Expressionist tendencies that Pevsner ignored or dismissed in *Pioneers.* "By the beginning of the Fifties, the existence of the Zone of Silence was widely noticed, its contents the subject of interest and speculation."[17]

The texts were important, but so were relationships with key individuals. After reading *An Outline of European Architecture,* Banham tracked down its author, whom he saw "in the flesh, for the first time, when he lectured on [Balthasar] Neumann at the Courtauld."[18] This takes us to the point of Banham's formal education at the Courtauld Institute of Art in London. Successful on his second attempt to gain admission, and with aspirations, initially, to be an art critic, "I wormed my way into the undergraduate course [in 1949] . . . and did 20th century architecture—which was very rare—so really anybody who did it got a certain amount of grooming for stardom."[19] In 1952, when he completed his B.A., three events made the year memorable. First, Banham joined the staff of the *Architectural Review,* part-time, as "literary editor"; second, he commenced studying for his doctorate, also part-time; and, third, he saw, for the first time "in the chrome," a contemporary American automobile, a Chevrolet. Banham's response ran counter to the received wisdom of the older generation, including Pevsner, who dismissed such design as "extremely un-British, indeed un-European" in its vulgarity and showiness.[20] Banham recollected: "I saw that, on one level at least, it *wasn't* badly designed, that tremendous visual skill went into it and that the detail was of a quality which very little European design could equal."[21] By the mid-1950s, he was applying art historical techniques to this type of contemporary popular design, acknowledging in particular his debt to the Courtauld's emphasis on iconography.

Banham's doctorate at the Courtauld took six years, largely under the "eagle eye" of Pevsner,[22] and formed the main body of what was to become *Theory and Design in the First Machine Age* (1960)—the first and last chapters were postdoctoral additions. Banham may have acquired a broad outline of Pevsnerian Modernism at the Courtauld but, in the final recollection, he admitted that he "hadn't got on to the Futurist thing" when he commenced work on his doctorate. The rediscovery and reinterpretation of Futurism was to be one of Banham's major contributions to architectural history in the later 1950s and the 1960s. He acquired an intellectual understanding of the movement by reading Futurist texts, and greater interest was sparked by a visit to the exhibition "Modern Italian Art" at the Tate Gallery in 1950 that included paintings by Umberto Boccioni and Giacomo Balla.

However, the feeling for the Futurist *sensibility* initially came not from the texts but from a less obvious source—a suburban London railway station. Traveling to an evening class from his North London home, Banham changed trains at Willesden Junction, then a two-level wooden station: "Standing on the platform, one night a week, and at a certain point . . . the Flying Scot or something used to hurtle through underneath, and the whole building would shake and steam would come up through the platform. And at the same time an electric would come through at the high level, bursting through the steam . . . And suddenly I got the message . . . about the actual kind of experience that Futurism was all about, and it suddenly began to hang together from then on."[23] He had discovered the Futurist sensibility, and his attitude not just to the Modern Movement, but to architecture in general, would be permanently affected. An attraction to the Futurist sensibility, combined with respect for the "set of actual monuments" of Modernism—whether texts or buildings—belief in modernity; commitment to architectural history as a vital and alive discipline; and enthusiasm for American popular culture characterizes Banham's output from the mid-1950s on.

The Futurist spirit, however much in evidence at Willesden Junction, did not reflect the domestic architectural scene in general in the early-to-mid-1950s, and Banham's views were not typical. They were, however, largely shared by, and at times derived from, a small circle of progressive young architects and artists—including James Stirling, Alison and Peter Smithson,

Richard Hamilton, Eduardo Paolozzi, Robert Maxwell, Alan Colquhoun, Colin St. J. (Sandy) Wilson, Nigel Henderson, and Sam Stevens—who met regularly at the Banhams' North London flat at this time.[24] Banham has testified to the importance of these regular gatherings, which were like "an invisible college of a remarkable kind. . . . these people were a big part of my education . . . [M]ost of my indoctrination into the Modern Movement in architecture came from the Sam Stevens/Bob Maxwell/Jim Stirling/ Sandy Wilson network. That was a fantastic body of conversation—the whole period of constant competitions, from Coventry Cathedral to Sydney Opera House."[25]

Those conversations ranged widely, but three of the issues from them that arose in Banham's writing were, first, a vehement opposition to any parochialism of value (usually associated with a call for national identity or Englishness); second, a comprehensive rejection of revivalism or architectural historicism; and third, a deeply unsympathetic attitude to preservation and the conservation lobby. All these positions were justified in terms of a commitment to modernity and progress. Banham's position on them did not significantly change during his lifetime: indeed, they represent assumptions underlying much of what he wrote, and thus we will be be discussing them in this introduction.

Oppositions: 1. Englishness and the Picturesque

At the time Banham widened his research scope to international Modernism, other architects and writers were preoccupied with national characteristics and the idea of "Englishness" in architecture and design. Banham was an internationalist in architectural terms and deeply suspicious of a self-conscious concern with supposed national characteristics—which was, in his opinion, more than likely to lead to a "failure of nerve and collapse of creative energy."[26] Important buildings should compete on international, not national, grounds, and should avoid a gentlemanly and compromised Modernism "justified" by supposed Englishness, as had often happened in the prewar period. His essay that directly dealt with this issue in terms of the postwar/1950s architectural scene was a retrospective one. Significantly, it was published in *Concerning Architecture* (1968), a collection of essays honoring Nikolaus Pevsner. Banham's academic relationship with his mentor was a complex one, as we shall see at various places in this book, including the conclusion: at this point, however, it is instructive to analyze Banham's reaction to Pevsner's notion of Englishness, because it shows the two historians at their greatest point of disagreement about contemporary architectural thought.

All the essays in *Concerning Architecture* maintained a tone of dignified respect toward Pevsner, except for Banham's, which not only placed Pevsner in the "enemy" Modernist camp of the early-to-mid-1950s, but also accused him of nothing less than "betrayal." The message came across that Pevsner's Modernist thinking was hopelessly compromised by his respect for "Englishness," and fatally flawed in his understanding of what made the Modern Movement a vital force. Banham's invective started with a claim that "those of my generation who interrupted their architectural training in order to fight a war to make the world safe for the Modern Movement" resumed their studies after demobilization "with sentiments of betrayal and abandonment" because two of "the leading oracles of Modern Architecture" appeared to have contradicted their own, prewar principles and "espoused the most debased English habits of compromise and sentimentality."[27]

The lesser oracle was J. M. Richards, whose "highly persuasive" *Introduction to Modern Architecture* was undercut by his *The Castles on the Ground* (1946), an apology for English suburbia. The greater oracle was, of course, Nikolaus Pevsner, whom Banham castigated for deviating from *Pioneers of the Modern Movement* with its "comfortingly secure historical ancestry," international scope, and universalist aesthetics, and for publishing articles, either as author or as editor of the *Architectural Review,* "giving equally secure historical justifications for a revival of the Picturesque."[28] Pevsner stated that "the Modern revolution of the early twentieth century and the Picturesque revolution of a hundred years before had all their fundamentals in common." Banham's, "anti-Picturesque" faction found this anathema because they looked toward "Continental modern architecture and, above all, the work of Le Corbusier . . . [for] exemplars of a sane and rational design method (as they saw it) to set against the empiricism and compromises of the Picturesque."[29]

"Compromise" became an emotive word in the 1950s. The older generation of Modernists in Britain, including Pevsner and Herbert Read, upheld it as symptomatic of native good sense and lack of extremism. Read, for example, wrote in the revised edition of *Art and Industry* (1956) of the "justifiable dissatisfaction with the bleakness of a pioneering functionalism."[30] Like Read, Pevsner criticized the "dictatorial quality" of interwar Modernism, which had been an understandable aesthetic purging of Victorian historicism and overelaboration.[31] The Banham faction viewed compromise as a loss of nerve and a selling out.

A key focus of the opposition between the two views was the Festival of Britain in 1951. Described as "a tonic to the nation," it was intended as a celebration of survival and epitomized the vision of a future Britain "made safe for the Modern Movement." But it was a version of the movement that typified British Modernism. That is not to say that the Festival was a complete embarrassment to Banham's generation. In his main essay on the Festival, written to commemorate its twenty-fifth anniversary, he refers to the "observable internationalism" of many of the architectural structures[32] which drew heavily on progressive Italian and Scandinavian architecture. But there were three aspects of it that, ultimately, located it in the enemy camp. First, part of the "humanizing" of the design was achieved through a greater use of decoration, and that could mean an aesthetic that lacked the austerity, clarity, and nobility of European Modernism.

Second, very much more self-consciously British, was the revival of Victorian letterforms, a revival that was part of a broader reevaluation of Victorian design being undertaken by the Picturesque sympathizers—in fact, Picturesque and Victorian design can be seen as different manifestations of the same set of beliefs. In 1955 Pevsner explained it thus:

The so-called Victorian Revival . . . is not another form of historicism, as it is in the United States, but, especially in the circles connected with or influenced by *The Architectural Review,* an antidote. It is never overall, as neo-Georgian tries to be, it is no more than spice added to a modern setting. Its effect is contrast and surprise, in the sense in which Uvedale Price asked for it. Overdo it, and it defeats its object. All the same, it remains *Ersatz.* It is an admission that the twentieth century cannot invent its own fancy, or not

Festival of Britain litter bin, 1951 (courtesy Mary Banham)

enough of it. That is where the exteriors and interiors on the South Bank in 1951 were so revealing, and indeed epoch-making. For here for the first time it was demonstrated how much of fancy can be done within the modern style and with only very occasional and limited Victorian borrowings and how much strictly modern fancy, without any Americanisations will be enjoyed by all and sundry.[33]

This is the direct link between the Picturesque and the Victorian revival: both offered contrast and surprise, irregularity, informality, and variety; they "spiced up" worthy but formal architecture and design. For Pevsner, this was British compromise at the level of a synthesis. From this point onward, Victorian design became repositioned as part of a semiofficial "British tradition." For the younger generation, the "compromise" was nothing less than a loss of resolve.

The third unpalatable aspect of the Festival of Britain was the acutely self-conscious constructing of national identity. "Englishness" was illustrated not only in art by Gainsborough, Constable, Turner, and Paul Nash, but also by the eccentric Far Tottering and Oyster Creek Railway and the Lion and Unicorn pavilion that included a gallery of British eccentrics, with pride of place given to the White Knight from *Through the Looking Glass,* who represented "the fantastic genius in the English character." There was, undoubtedly, an overall tone of "English whimsicality,"[34] as Mary Banham described it, pervading the Festival. Both popular culture and folk art interests (as well as the revival of Victoriana) emphasized a nationalism and love of tradition that did not endear them to the Banham faction. Pevsner may have seen these interests as feeding into a rejuvenation of Modernism, but others saw them, at best, as a reestablishment of an insular, "little Englander" mentality which took refuge among corn dollies and Morris dancing in an Arcadian, Picturesque, anti-industrial fantasy island not unrelated to the Utopian *News from Nowhere.*

The Festival had, in Pevsner's opinion, been an "epoch-making" event that helped to galvanize English creativity into producing a softened Modernism which expressed national identity. If so, the epoch was a short-lived one. Banham was skeptical that its influence endured: Basil Spence's Coventry Cathedral may have "carried the Festival Style deep into the surprised sixties, but this was less an example of long-term influence than a fossilised survival."[35]

Pevsner continued his investigation of English characteristics in art and design, eventually presenting his findings as the *Englishness of English Art,* the Reith Lectures for 1955. By that time, Banham, stimulated by the Independent Group activities we will discuss in chapter 2, was writing articles on Erich Mendelsohn, Antonio Sant'Elia, and the flaws in the "selective and classicising" Machine Aesthetic as part of his ongoing research, praising the avowedly anti-Picturesque "New Brutalism" associated with the Smithsons, and iconographically interpreting contemporary American autos.[36] He had nailed his colors to a mast that did not display the emblem of the British architectural establishment. By that time, Banham's generation was making its mark.

His joining the staff of the *Architectural Review* in 1952 was seen by some of his circle—as Banham anecdotally recalled nearly twenty-five years later[37]—as akin to defecting to the enemy camp, or at least appeasing the enemy, even though the journal's editorial policy was considerably more tolerant and inclusive than its Picturesque polemics might suggest. In his early days there, he may have written about subjects that seem more *Review* than Banham,[38] but long-term compromise was never a serious possibility. Apart from providing a regular income, working there was an opportunity too good to miss because it afforded him personal contact with many of the architects and designers he was to write about in *Theory and Design in the First Machine Age.* Also, in the 1950s alone, the *Review* provided an outlet for research-centered articles on, amongst others, Le Corbusier, Adolf Loos, Piet Mondrian and de Stijl, Paul Scheerbart, Finnish Modernism, Louis Sullivan and Frank Lloyd Wright.[39]

Oppositions: 2. Revivalism

With the completion of his doctorate and its conversion into a book and, from 1959, the full time post of assistant executive editor, Banham was able increasingly to turn his attention to contemporary architecture at the turn-of-the-decade. One of the premises which underlies not only his turn-of-the-decade writing, but also his architectural writing in general, is his passionate rejection of revivalism or architectural historicism. Banham was typical of Modernists of all generations in this respect. Whereas he and Pevsner may have been opposed about Englishness and the Picturesque, they were in almost total agreement about the irrelevance—and the danger—of period styles in contemporary architecture.

Pevsner defined historicism as "the trend to believe in the power of history to such a degree as to choke original action which is inspired by period precedent."[40] The word "choke" is a telling one, its intent confirmed by his assertion that "all reviving of styles of the past is a sign of weakness." Historicism or revivalism can be divided into two aspects: revivalism of traditional styles and revivalism of the Modern Movement, of which Art Nouveau can be classed the starting point, in that it rejected historicism. The former can be dealt with summarily because Pevsner and Banham demonstrated the standard, unambiguous Modernist response to historicist styles. Pevsner passed over contemporary architecture by "Georgian-Palladian diehards" because it could self-evidently "be left to die of old age."[41] It represented that choking of originality.

Throughout his career, Banham held almost identical views about traditionalism, regarding historicism, at the beginning of the 1960s, as nothing less than "architectural irresponsibility."[42] At the end of that decade, Banham was praising the environmental management of the turn-of-the-century Royal Victoria Hospital in Belfast (see chapter 4), but berating its "depressingly unmodish" historicist styling, which demonstrates "with painful clarity the total irrelevance of detailed architectural 'style' to the modernity of the functional and environmental parts."[43] In the next decade he was still railing against "gutless" or "pompous" historicism:[44] for Banham, like Pevsner, "historicist defeatism"[45] was nothing less than a drying up of creativity, a diminution of belief, a denial of relevance, and a dearth of guts. Here was an uncompromising, unchangeable attitude which linked Banham and Pevsner as unambiguous Modernists.

The idea of a revival would always be anathema to Banham. A revival may be viable if you think in terms of form and style, but if, like Banham, you commit yourself to the idea of an attitude or spirit, determined by the conditions of the day, then a revival can be contemplated only in unusual circumstances: "The only conceivable justification for reviving anything in the arts is that the reviver finds himself culturally in a position analogous to that of the time he seeks to revive—a return to something like classical sophistication and affluence in Fourteenth-century Italy justifies the Renaissance architecture of the Fifteenth, the achievement of something like Athenian democratic sentiment in the early nineteenth justifies *le style neo-grec.*" However, even in these circumstances, the "justifications" may be flawed by "the presence of factors that notably were not present in the styles revived—Christianity in Renaissance architecture, industrialisation in *neo-grec*—and where these intrusive factors are too large to be overlooked, the justification must fail."[46] Any major cultural or technological change would, in his opinion, invalidate the revival.

Banham's opinions about the historicism of the Modern Movement, the second of the two aspects of revivalism, were unambiguously declared in a 1959 *Architectural Review* article on the contemporary Italian architectural tendency labeled Neo-Liberty. He included illustrations of recent work by a number of architects, among them Ernesto Rogers (to show the influence of Otto Wagner), Gae Aulenti (early Le Corbusier), and the trio of Vittorio Gregotti, Ludovico Meneghotti, and Giotto Stoppino (showing the "late" decorative style of the Amsterdam school). There was also an "attitude that produced the buildings": most notably "the polemics advanced . . . by Aldo Rossi and others." For Banham, this was not a diverting mini decorative revival. The stakes were high: "all these [buildings and polemics] call the whole status of the Modern Movement in Italy in question."[47] This was stated in the absolutist terms of the true Modernist. He then applied his general principle about revivalism to contemporary Italy:

Now a justification of Neoliberty on the basis that Milanese *borghese* life is still what it was in 1900 is indeed implied in the polemics of Aldo Rossi. But it will not wash, because that life is not at all what it was at the beginning of the century, as Marinetti, with his fanatical automobilism, already recognised *in Milan* in 1909, Art Nouveau died of a cultural revolution that seems absolutely irreversible: the domestic revolution that began with electric cookers, vacuum cleaners, the telephone, the gramophone, and all those other mechanised aids to gracious living that are still invading the home, and have permanently altered the nature of domestic life and the meaning of domestic architecture.[48]

Banham's argument is based on changed circumstances which are primarily technological—the coming of the First Machine Age. The revolution in the visual arts—Futurism, Loos, Wright, and Cubism are cited—"mark[s] a watershed in the development of modern architecture; there is a certain consistency about everything that has happened since, and a schism from what happened before. And Art Nouveau, *lo Stile Liberty,* happened before."[49]

Banham is at one with the Futurist leader about the *qualitative* distinction between the past and the present, about the clean-cut break which Futurism represented to its adherents. The lesson for Banham was crystal clear: "To revive it is thus to abdicate from the Twentieth Century—which may have purely personal attractions, like going to live on a desert island, but is no help to one's fellow-men, and architecture, for better or worse, concerns one's fellow men." Revivalism was a moral, not just a stylistic, issue,

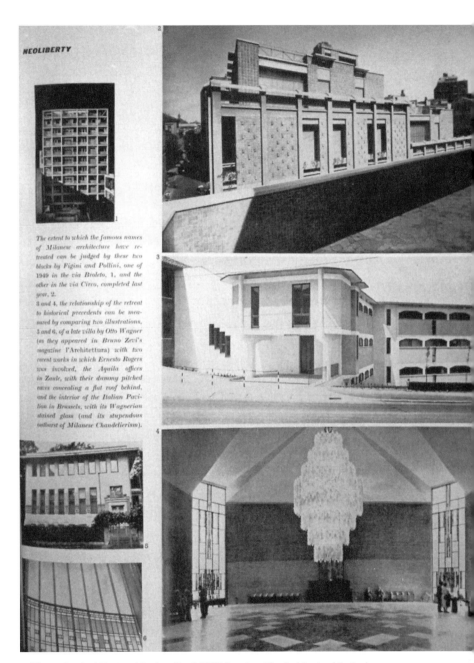

NEOLIBERTY

The extent to which the famous names of Milanese architecture have retreated can be judged by these two blocks by Figini and Pollini, one of 1949 in the via Broleto, 1, and the other in the via Circo, completed last year, 2.

3 and 4, the relationship of the retreat to historical precedents can be measured by comparing two illustrations, 5 and 6, of a late villa by Otto Wagner (as they appeared in Bruno Zevi's magazine l'Architettura) with two recent works in which Ernesto Rogers was involved, the Aquila offices in Zoule, with their dummy pitched eaves concealing a flat roof behind, and the interior of the Italian Pavilion in Brussels, with its Wagnerian stained glass (and its stupendous outburst of Milanese Chandelierism).

"Neo-Liberty," page spread from the *Architectural Review* (April 1959) (courtesy *The Architectural Review*) and to practice or encourage it was nothing short of an "abdication." The subtitle of the article itself—"The Italian *Retreat* from Modern Architecture" (italics added)—declares Banham's position and sets up a final paragraph that is redolent of the most extreme puritanical Modernist pronouncements of the 1920s:

The lasting significance of the revolution put in hand in 1907 is that it has given Western architecture the courage to look forward, not back, to stop reviving the forms of any sort of past, middle-class or otherwise. The performance of the revolutionaries may not have matched their promise, but the promise remains and is real. It is the promise of liberty, not *Liberty* or "Neoliberty," the promise of freedom from having to wear the discarded clothes of previous cultures, even if those previous cultures have the air of *tempi felici.* To want to put on those old clothes again is to be, in Marinetti's words describing Ruskin, like a man who has attained full physical maturity, yet wants to sleep in his cot again, to be suckled again by his decrepit nurse, in order to regain the nonchalance of his childhood. Even by purely local standards of Milan and Turin, then, Neoliberty is infantile regression.[50]

Here is Banham the arch-Modernist: progressivist and antirevivalist as a matter of principle; citing his hero F. T. Marinetti in order to damn his bête noire John Ruskin; committed, partisan, and condescending.

It was the sort of cocktail that anti-Modernists were to find unpalatable after the decline of Modernism in the late 1960s, but it also rankled in the late 1950s, even when Modernist values were mainstream. An outraged Ernesto Rogers, described by Banham in "Neoliberty" as the "hero-figure of European architecture in the late Forties and early Fifties," and subsequently accused of retreating on account of his historicism, passionately responded at great length to Banham's polemic in *Casabella* (1959).[51] Rogers clearly resented what he described as the "arrogant goading of Mr. Banham,"[52] and chided him for his technological progressivism, dubbing him "the *custodian of Frigidaires*"—a reference to Banham's listing of items from the "domestic revolution" that had supposedly transformed architecture after the first decade of the century. What, for Banham, could be rejected as "revivalism" or "historicism" was, in Rogers's parlance, a "critical and considered review of historical tradition." This approach might be "useful for an artist who refuses to accept certain themes in a mechanical manner. For Mr. Banham, however, determinism of forms according to an abstract line of development seems to take the place of a concept of history. From this derives his aptitude for bestowing absolutions and excommunications, which can only mummify reality."[53]

Banham's view of architecture did not respect history in the sense of national and cultural traditions and forms; rather, it upheld a post-Enlightenment commitment to a generalized notion of Western technological progress. Rogers offered this advice: "I would like to invite Mr. Banham . . . to read directly from *The Poetry of Architecture* by John Ruskin, a great Englishman, without repeating the outdated interpretation of Marinetti, a 'revolutionary' Fascist who died wearing the cap of the Academy: 'We shall consider the architecture of nations as it is influenced by their feelings and manners, as it is connected with the scenery in which it is found, and with the skies under which it was erected.'"[54]

These were, however, sentiments unlikely to appeal to Banham. Rogers is describing an architecture which is embedded in history, culture, and tradition: an architecture which, in that sense, is affirmative without, Rogers would doubtless hope, being complacent or predictable. Banham often sought an architecture—illustrated by his reaction to Neo-Liberty and his empathy for the work of the Smithsons and James Stirling—which is disaffirmative: an architecture of resistance. A few months after his exchange with Banham, Rogers presented the Torre Velasca, designed in 1957, to his international colleagues at CIAM's annual conference. Its form was determined not only by technical and functional requirements, but also by a historical analysis of the urban context, resulting in what appeared to be a medieval fortress skyscraper (arguably anticipating critical regionalism). To criticism from the then Brutalist-inclined Smithsons, Rogers replied, "There is one main difficulty that I see and that is that you think in English!"[55] Rogers had possibly identified an important tendency within English—or British—avant garde architectural thinking at this time: its lack of interest in, and even denial, of historical or cultural connectedness.

Banham did not change his mind about revivalism and Neo-Liberty: in the mid-1960s he was repeating his accusations that the "sentimental formalism" of Neo-Liberty was a "betrayal of the promise of the Italian Rationalist movement";[56] at the end of the decade he was still referring to the "years of Neoliberty nostalgia" when "the historical nerve of most Italian architects had failed almost completely."[57] It was attitudes and values like these that framed Banham's reaction against buildings which overtly confirmed the historical tradition to which they belonged: they were irrelevant to the new technological conditions of the Second Machine Age.

Oppositions: 3. Preservation and Conservation

As we will see in chapter 1, the 1914 manifesto of the Futurist City included a total rejection of the historic city: a Futurist attitude in particular, and a Modernist one in general, conditioned Banham's attitude to preservation and conservation. Simply stated, it was that an over-zealous commitment to preservation signified an inability to cope with, let alone enjoy, the "live culture of the Technological Century."[58] Preservationists were frequently "grown-up kids who can only cry when deprived of their security-blanket of ancient bricks and mortar."[59] Banham's main text on preservation and conservation appeared in 1963. Its title—"The Embalmed City"—was indicative of 1920s "high" Modernist attitudes, and there are sentences which could—almost—have been penned by Marinetti himself, such as "The load of obsolete buildings that Europe is humping along on its shoulders is a bigger drag on the live culture of our continent than obsolete nationalisms or obsolete moral codes."[60] Banham continued by asserting, "There is not one building that is not expendable; man-made, they are subject to rot and rust, worm and weather. It is time we thought of them as expendable, and made our first question: 'Which ones can we afford to keep?'"[61]

His argument was, however, more sophisticated than the apparent vindictiveness toward past architecture declared by some of the more vituperative Modernists. It had two main premises. First, that "there isn't a city in the world that wouldn't benefit from some ruthless modernisation." Most, at the time, would have agreed with him on this point, and indeed most did, because of the rapid development of the Second Machine Age with its greater affluence, including car ownership, and higher level of expectations. However, the interpretation and degree of ruthlessness would have been hotly debated. Second, that when it comes to thinking about the cities we live and work in, we "must be able to distinguish between the maintenance of the urban texture that supports the good life, and the mere embalming of ancient monuments." This was the distinction which led Banham to think of buildings as expendable, but of urban texture as relatively permanent and valuable, in that it would ensure difference and distinctiveness: "no individual building need survive. It is the in-and-out weave of men and communications among the buildings that is essential, not the buildings themselves. No monument is as important to Europe as this texture of its cities." Each city had its own texture:

. . . satin-smooth like Bath, tweed (with a silken thread) like Glasgow, broadcloth towns like Sheffield, Birmingham's bombazine conurbation. But this texture depends on the kinds of thread and their arrangement, not on the threads themselves—they can be drawn out and replaced without altering the texture. Venice and Amsterdam have been built and rebuilt where they stand, and remain themselves. The more modern buildings that go up in Venice, the more clear it becomes that it is not the style or the antiquity of the buildings that matters, but the way in which they stack up human beings within the network of canals and pedestrian ways.[62]

Banham's antirevivalism might make the reader wary that he would, in practice, not be quite so pluralist and inclusive stylistically, but the substantive point remains: it is not the individual buildings that matter but the texture, which is determined by such things as rhythm, density, and scale. Urban texture is important and should be treated respectfully by planners, but it must change if "modernisation" demands it—perhaps because the existing texture is "inefficient" or "a poor health risk," or "because it occupies ground that is needed for other urban functions that seem to have stronger human claims."[63] Modernization must almost always be given priority over preservation.

One of the key beliefs determining Banham's attitude was that, first and foremost, the city was a place to experience and a place of experience, rather than a series of architectural monuments: experience and immersion mattered more to him than the disinterested contemplation of form and style. Buildings might be an "invaluable guide" to newcomers "wishing to join the good life, to master its techniques and attitudes," but "there has always been a risk that men would mistake the buildings for the life, the stone substance for the shadow in which the life was lived."[64] Preservation, therefore, was far less important than maintaining the conditions that promote the good life. An undue concern with cultural monuments, in his opinion, was often related to cultural snobbery, and this made him suspicious of some of the motives underlying the preservation movement. His cri de coeur was that:

We are being let down by men of culture who believe that, in order to maintain what is valuable in [our] culture, you have to maintain also the rituals of gluttony, social alcoholism and conspicuously selective residence in which a bourgeois society has wrapped it. Some of my best friends are wine-and-food socialists, and I just wish that they would stop being bamboozled into defending the dwellings (or rents) of the rich on the grounds that they are Georgian, and therefore priceless monuments of our heritage of blah blah blah. Much of it is, in fact, more shoddily built and less well serviced and on occasions more overcrowded than so-called slum property in the East End; but because it is in Belgravia or Bath, it is safe from the replacement on which any sane society would insist. Men of good will are being fooled into defending privilege disguised as culture.[65]

The relationship between culture and class regularly surfaced in Banham's writings—we will discuss it fully in the Conclusion—and it was an important element in his suspicion of preservation.

For Banham, the increased listing following the Local Authorities (Historic Buildings) Act of 1962 reflected a shift of architectural politics and power from modernity to preservation, and was indicative of "how far the preservation of old buildings has strayed from the ways of reason and common sense."[66] An appetite for preservation was following directly from revivalism. Banham had chided the Neo-Liberty architects for their "*betrayal* of the promise of the Italian Rationalist movement"; now town planners were being chastised for their "*betrayal* of responsibility and leadership"[67] (italics added). By opting for preservation, town planners were adding to the "failure of urban nerve" (and were thus as guilty as turn-of-the-century historicists who suffered a "failure of nerve and collapse of creative energy," and as Italian architects whose "historical nerve . . . had failed almost completely").

One of the dangers of the preservation mentality was a sentimentalism for the past. Banham was scathing about Jane Jacobs's representation of an "urban pastoral in which a seemingly timeless background of familiar buildings supports stable human relations as effortlessly as Nature was once supposed to do."[68] This sort of attitude was leading to a reaction against innovation and modernization while establishing a desire to "spray the whole place with embalming fluid."[69] It seemed as if the living city had become a mausoleum: "fetishism replaced functionalism." The growth of the preservation lobby in the 1960s alarmed Banham, who thought its significance was not just architectural, but also cultural and psychological: "The embalmed city," he warned, "is the necropolis of the insecure."[70]

Enthusiasms: 1. Modernization and Technology

Whatever Banham's concerns about the influence of the preservation lobby, the 1960s is remembered as a decade of modernization and is reflected in the politics of the time. Banham's attitude was fully in keeping with the Labour Party's early-to-mid-1960s rhetoric about modernization: "The new Britain," Harold Wilson, recently elected leader of the Labour Party and soon-to-be Prime Minister prophesied, was "going to be forged in the white heat of this [scientific] revolution."[71] Banham firmly aligned himself with Labour's meritocratic, technologically oriented classless society, once describing himself as a "Tony socialist" in homage to Tony Crosland and Tony (Anthony Wedgewood) Benn, two key Labour modernizers of the 1960s.

The socially, politically, and culturally liberating effects of technology were not, of course, just a postwar progressive belief, but derived from the heroic period of Modernism in the 1920s and, beyond it, the pronouncements early in the century of prophets from F. T. Marinetti to Frank Lloyd Wright. Like most Modernists, he was a technological optimist, and there will be evidence of this on virtually every page of this book. His optimism stretched back to his Independent Group days of the early 1950s, his discovery of Futurism, and the seductive appeals of American popular culture. In the next decade there was the search for an "architecture of technology" that rekindled the "mechanical sensibility" but applied it to the architecture and design of the Second Machine Age. In the later 1960s and 1970s, megastructures would offer a revival of the "romantic vision of modern technology," and in the 1980s, High Tech provided "an imagery appropriate to the technological times." Banham embraced these developments as examples of a democratic architecture for the classless Second Machine Age.

Banham's main polemics about an architecture for the Second Machine Age were, as will see in chapter 3, published in the *Architectural Review* in the early 1960s. In 1964 he left the editorial staff of the journal when he was invited to join, as a senior lecturer, the Bartlett School of Architecture at University College, London (UCL), where he was given responsibility for architectural history within the reorganized program introduced by Richard Llewelyn Davies. The twelve years at UCL were the most productive ones of Banham's career, with eight solo-authored or edited books, ranging from the 1966 *The New Brutalism: Ethic or Aesthetic?* to the 1976 *Megastructure: Urban Futures of the Recent Past.* The most acclaimed was *The Architecture of the Well-tempered Environment,* published in 1969[72] and funded from 1964 to 1966 by the Graham Foundation of Chicago, which provided a fellowship to enable Banham to travel and conduct research in the United States. By the end of the 1960s he had been awarded a personal chair.

From the publication of *Theory and Design* in 1960 through the time of his departure from UCL, Banham's reputation and influence were at their greatest, and he could be described, with much justification, as "the outstanding international authority on the history and theory of modern architecture and design."[73] Such an accolade would normally allude to hardback publications. In Banham's case we need also to take into account his "expendable" criticism of pop culture and design.

Enthusiasms: 2. Pop Culture and Contemporary Design

Banham's initial enthusiasm for popular culture was, as we have seen, derived from the mass media he viewed in his youth and as a young adult. To return to it in the 1950s, in a context of enjoyment combined with the intellectual understanding provided by the informal and intellectually stimulating Independent Group (IG) discussions, must have seemed like having the best of both worlds. The IG played a role in Banham's life similar to the slightly earlier "anti-Picturesque" faction, and the idea of ongoing informal but informed discussions and arguments with new participants occasionally bringing in novel areas of expertise, clearly appealed to his temperament. Three major outcomes of these discussions were (1) an involvement with modern technology—this was an emphasis that occurred in the IG's first series of meetings in 1952/1953, of which Banham was convenor; (2) the application of Banham's Courtauld iconographical approach to the design of contemporary products; and (3) the development of a theory of design for popular culture. His achievement was, in part, to shift design thinking away from the Modernist model of abstraction with its "characteristic primary forms and colours," and toward a post-Modernist one of product semantics with forms and images rich in meaning and association. Of lasting importance was Banham's identification of expendability as the central ingredient of popular culture.

Banham had worked out his theoretical position about pop culture by the end of 1955, but almost a decade passed before he began to write the sort of criticism which did justice to the theory. Following his initial "intellectual" idea of becoming an art critic, Banham took journalism seriously and professionally. His reviews of art exhibitions for *Art News and Review* first appeared in 1950, a few months after he commenced his degree at the Courtauld, and continued until the end of 1955. As architecture became the dominant aspect of Banham's research, contributions to *Architects' Journal* appeared from 1953, but it was in the *New Statesman* (from 1958 to 1965) and, in particular, *New Society* columns (from 1965) that Banham dissected and celebrated the "noisy ephemeridae" of pop culture and contemporary society. Car styling; the design of radios and cameras; graphics on magazines, cigarette packs and potato chip bags; the decoration of restaurants, surfboards and icecream vans; cult films and TV programs—all were grist for his mill. The scope of these topics demonstrates a key aspect of Banham's contribution to contemporary design studies and cultural studies: his range of subjects was diverse, and his selection was inclusive.

Enthusiasms: 3. The United States

It was with the publication of *Theory and Design in the First Machine Age* (1960) that Banham became well known internationally. His first visit to the United States was in 1961[74]—Mary Banham recalls that it was the "realisation of a longheld dream"[75]—and he received increasing numbers of invitations to lecture there as the decade progressed. In 1963, he first attended the International Design Conference at Aspen (IDCA) in Colorado, where he met leading architects and designers of the Second Machine Age. A year later, the Graham Foundation grant funded travel, including Banham's first visit to Los Angeles in 1965, and which was to lead to *Los Angeles: The Architecture of Four Ecologies* (1971).

After he took up the full-time post at UCL, Banham remained a regular visitor to the United States, partly facilitated by being an adviser to the board of IDCA between 1968 and 1978.[76] He became a resident of the United States in 1976, when he moved from UCL to the State University of New York at Buffalo. A fascination with that city's remaining industrial buildings from the early part of the twentieth century, and with their mythological status among the masters of the First Machine Age, resulted in *A Concrete Atlantis: U.S. Industrial Building and European Modern Architecture, 1900–1925* (1981). By the time of its publication, Banham had moved on, in 1980, to a post at the University of California at Santa Cruz. Its location enabled him to indulge a love for the American deserts that found expression in *Scenes in America Deserta* (1982). In 1987, he was invited to become professor of architectural history at the Institute of Fine Art at New York University,[77] but he died in 1988, before he was able to deliver his (posthumously published) inaugural lecture.[78]

There are, therefore, three aspects to Banham's relationship to the United States: The first was the appeal of the seductively distant and exotic—the alluring and glamorous popular culture which he avidly consumed from the 1930s to the end of the 1950s. The second was the United States he came to know at first hand as a regular visitor throughout the 1960s and the first half

of the 1970s—in this period the reality largely measured up to his expectations. The third was the post-1976 period when he was a resident and able
to explore particular aspects of American culture in more depth. The permanent move there, according to Mary Banham, "had its difficult aspects,"[79]
but overall, his enthusiasm for the country remained undimmed.

Early, High, Late, and Many

Banham's career, then, from the beginning of his doctoral work in 1952 to
his death in 1988, spans thirty-six years. It subdivides into three periods relating to his places of work, each of approximately a dozen years. The first,
from 1952 until 1964—the "early" period—starts with the Courtauld but is
largely associated with the *Architectural Review* and his revisions of the
Modern Movement. The second, or "high," period is the UCL years from
1964 to 1976, a time—more accurately, in intellectual terms, from 1960—
when Banham was at his most polemical and radical about an architecture
and design of and for the Second Machine Age. This is the period of his most
influential writing. The third, or "late," period lasts from 1976 until his
death, and covers the time he was resident in the United States, where he
researched and wrote *A Concrete Atlantis* and *Scenes in America Deserta.*

Banham was a prolific writer who produced a dozen solo-authored books
and an astonishing number of articles—in excess of seven hundred. The
range and scope of his writing—from Theo van Doesburg's impact on the
Bauhaus, through the "bloody mindedness" of James Stirling's architecture,
to the design and sound of the potato chip bag—makes it seem that there
were many "Banhams" who appeared to be regularly changing their minds
or, at least, their values. The extent to which significant changes did take
place will be addressed in the chapters that follow, beginning with his revision of the Modern Movement.

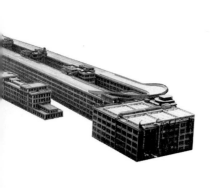

1
THE MECHANICAL SENSIBILITY

The First Machine Age Revised

In one of the articles that fed into *Theory and Design in the First Machine Age* (1960), Reyner Banham rhetorically asked:

> Why, in a word, do we have to re-write the history of the Modern Movement? Not because that history is wrong; simply because it is less than lifesize. The official history of the Modern Movement, as laid out in the late Twenties and codified in the Thirties, is a view through the marrow-hole of a dry bone—the view is only possible because the living matter of architecture, the myths and symbols, the personalities and pressure groups have been left out. The choice of a skeletal history of the movement with all the Futurists, Romantics, Expressionists, Elementarists and pure aesthetes omitted . . . was the choice of the movement as a whole. Quite suddenly modern architects decided to cut off half their grandparents without a farthing.[1]

Banham's revisionism looked two ways. Not only did it reassess the contributions of the forebears, however distant, mad, or embarrassing they were deemed to be by their respectable and aspiring offspring, but it also examined afresh the legacy handed down by Modern Movement architects, in the process contesting the will (or even the *Kunstwollen*) as interpreted by the official bookkeepers of the movement.

The contestation had begun as early as 1955 in "Machine Aesthetic," an article that was to become recognized as one of Banham's seminal texts. Banham asserts that "The 'Machine Aesthetic' of the Pioneering Masters of the Modern Movement was . . . selective and classicising, one limb of their reaction against the excesses of Art Nouveau, and it came nowhere near an acceptance of machines on their own terms or for their own sakes."[2] This chapter begins by assessing Banham's claim—and its implications—in two parts: first, that the Modern Movement was "selective and classicising"; and second, that an "acceptance of machines" qua machines was somehow crucial to a more *authentic* version of the Modern Movement. It continues by analyzing his writings about key movements and aspects of First Machine Age architecture: from Expressionism and Futurism, including the latter's central role in his highly influential *Theory and Design in the First Machine Age,* to his emphasis, after the mid-1960s, on American Modern Movement topics which culminated in *A Concrete Atlantis: U.S. Industrial Building and European Modern Architecture* (1986), published two years before his death.

Selective and Classicizing

As an example of Modernism's selective and classicizing tendency, Banham highlights the notorious example of Le Corbusier's illustrations of automobiles in *Towards a New Architecture* (1923), which he describes as "crooked": the "crookedness is disguised by the fact that the argument is partly verbal and partly visual." The verbal argument is about the virtue and necessity of standardization; the visual argument is implied through the juxtaposition of images of automobiles and the Parthenon:

. . . the totality has been read by two generations of architects and theorists as meaning that a standardised product like a motor-car can be as beautiful as a Greek temple. In its context that is how it must be read, but the *tertium comparationis* of the argument is a disingenuous pretence—none of the motor-cars illustrated is a standardised mass-produced model; all are expensive, specialised, handicraft one-offs which can justly be compared to the Parthenon because, like it, they are unique works of handmade art. Mass-produced vehicles like the Model T Ford are not allowed to sully these classicist pages.[3]

Banham's insightful criticism is hard to refute, and leads him to question whether such misleading arguments result from "naiveté? Sharp practice? Or wishful thinking?" His answer is that they are a varying mixture of all three. His revisionist writing of the 1950s was motivated by the desire to provide a more accurate historical account, and also, as we shall see in subsequent chapters, was a means of questioning assumptions about the relationship between technology and architecture in contemporary society.

The first wave of retrospective accounts and historical texts had presented a view of Modernism that stressed historical inevitability. Nikolaus Pevsner's *Pioneers of the Modern Movement,* published in 1936, had authority conferred on its account by dint of the author's firsthand knowledge of events in continental Europe. Subtitled *From William Morris to Walter Gropius, Pioneers* traced the apparently relentless developments in nineteenth- and early twentieth-century art, architecture, and design that led to the crystallization of the Modern Movement epitomized by Walter Gropius's model factory for the Deutscher Werkbund exhibition at Cologne in 1914. Gropius's buildings before the First World War—the model factory and the Fagus factory of 1911—"mark," according to Pevsner, "the fulfilment of the style of our century; entirely representative of the spirit of today."[4]

The belief in a zeitgeist was central to Pevsner's conception of history and gave rise to his argument for the authority of a version of the Modern Movement which was manifested in the classical aesthetic of order, precision, and impersonality. Pevsner draws a parallel between art and architecture: "it is no accident that the appearance of abstract art and especially of Cubism belongs to the same years as Wright's, Perret's, Mackintosh's, Hoffmann's, and Gropius's spatial discoveries."[5] However, he chastises those who claim that one of the major achievements of progressive Modern art is the extent to which artists have the freedom for complete self-expression:

To extol, in the art of Picasso or Kandinsky, their profound self-expression through the medium of abstract shape and colour, shows a wrong or at least one-sided interpretation. No doubt many of the abstract painters of today consider self-expression their principal mission; but history will decide against this. Their extreme individualism is of the past, a *reductio ad absurdum* of a conception which had been dominant for more than three hundred years. Only in so far as their art can be regarded as decoration in the service of architecture, do they work for a new ideal, the ideal of their own century.[6]

Like those progressive Modernists who equated individualism with nine-teenth-century laissez faire, and collectivism with the egalitarianism of the new age and consciousness—de Stijl was a prime example—Pevsner links self-expression and individualism as common symptoms of a bygone age. In the new age, art was to serve an architecture of reason and order. Thus, the architect who is "representative of this century of ours must needs be cold, as he stands for a century cold as steel and glass, a century the precision of which leaves less space for self-expression than did any period before."[7]

Pevsner's view of history and historicism, and Banham's relationship to them, will be discussed in the Conclusion. At this point, it is the nature of the "selective and classicising" tendencies in Modernist historiography, to which Banham so strongly objected, that concerns us. *Pioneers of the Modern Movement* ends with Gropius's *Sachlichkeit* architecture expressing the zeitgeist of the age of the machine, the era of the dominance of science and technology. The progressivist assumption and implication of the book is that the "style of the century," with its coldness, precision, and absence of self-expression, was now firmly established.

This partisan and highly selective account of the Modern Movement, with its refusal to acknowledge Romantic and Expressionist tendencies, also was preached by many of the first generation of Modernist architects themselves, Walter Gropius included. In *The New Architecture and the Bauhaus* (1935), the first English-language book about the Bauhaus and his own architectural practice, Gropius discusses the Fagus factory and the Cologne exhibition buildings, then moves directly to his involvement in the Bauhaus. Nothing is said about his Expressionist sympathies between 1914 and 1919; nor about his membership in the Novembergruppe; nor about the

Arbeitsrat für Kunst (AfK), the left-wing association of architects, artists and intellectuals in whose publication Gropius railed against the "evil demon of commercialism."[8] Instead, Gropius declares that the factory and exhibition buildings "clearly manifested the essential characteristics of my later work,"[9] implying that the war had merely caused a delay in the logical development of his architecture.

Gropius writes about the Bauhaus, as if it has a consistent program and character: "The Bauhaus workshops were really laboratories for working out practical new designs for present-day articles and improving models for mass-production. To create type-forms that would meet all technical, aesthetic and commercial demands required a picked staff. It needed a body of men of wide general culture as thoroughly versed in the practical and mechanical sides of design as in its theoretical and formal laws."[10] No reference is made to the fact that, of the nine men Gropius appointed Masters of Form between 1919 and 1924, no fewer than eight were painters who had absolutely no knowledge of or experience in design.

In the early years, the Bauhaus workshops, far from being laboratories for the development of mass-produced goods, were more like art school studios full of Expressionist-influenced ideas propounded by artists such as Lyonel Feininger, Gerhard Marcks, Wassily Kandinsky, Paul Klee, and Johannes Itten. Itten's mystic antimaterialism may have been in keeping with Gropius's AfK pronouncements, but with its accompanying physical and mental exercises, rigorous vegetarian diet, and regular purification of the system by means of fasting and enemas, it could not be farther from the mood of scientific rationalism expounded by Gropius in *The New Architecture and the Bauhaus* with chapter headings such as "Rationalisation" and "Standardisation." Gropius ignores not only the hand-made, Arts and Crafts aesthetic and values of early Bauhaus wares but also the Expressionist tone in his own output, such as the Monument to the March Dead and the villa for the timber merchant Adolf Sommerfeld in Berlin, both completed in 1921. For the first few years there was no machine aesthetic, no *Sachlichkeit* design: even the type-form did not become a conscious concern until 1923, the year the tone of the Bauhaus began to change to the one which was adopted as the "official" Bauhaus in the history books while the Expressionist, mystical ethos was rapidly written out.

The "lost" years of the war, in addition to the "glossed" years of the early Bauhaus, amount to eight "de-selected" years of Gropius's professional life and output which, if included in the histories and accounts, would undermine the smooth and orderly progression from the Cologne exhibition buildings of 1914 to the commitment to machine production at the post-1923 Bauhaus. The Gropius omissions were symptomatic of what Banham described as a "Zone of Silence," even though it was "the period when most of the Masters of Modern Architecture were perfecting their personal styles, as individuals, and the International Style, as a group."[11]

The historian's task in the Second Machine Age was, therefore, fundamentally different from that taken up by the historians of the previous generation and age. The former saw their task as converting doubters to the Modern Movement: the strategy was to trace "respectable grandfathers." Banham, on behalf of his own generation, wanted nothing less than "a psychiatric enquiry into the springs of action, the grounds of inhibition."[12] The new historian would have to be as objective as possible, even when it meant destroying favored myths and debunking established reputations: "the appointment of historians to a cure of souls, to the guardianship of the conscience, even the sanity, of the profession, places upon their shoulders a responsibility that they have not been asked to carry before."[13] Put in these rather Romantic terms, much was at stake in architectural history in the 1950s and early 1960s.

Machines on Their Own Terms

The first generation's emphasis on the classical wing of Modernism with its *Sachlichkeit* aesthetics inevitably resulted in the exclusion of Romantic tendencies with their expressive form. These were the tendencies, Banham suggested, that were committed to an "acceptance of machines on their own terms or for their own sakes." Just what he meant by this is of central importance in understanding his values. In "Machine Aesthetic," Banham exposes the architect's misunderstanding of the characteristics of engineering and machine production. The characteristics upheld by "classical"

Modernist architects in the 1920s "summed up as simplicity of form and smoothness of finish—are conditional attributes of engineering, and to postulate them as necessary consequences of machine production was to give a false picture of the engineer's methods and intentions."[14] It was hardly surprising that orthodox Modernists, given their predilection for the classical aesthetic, would uphold this belief,[15] but it was a belief that, however misguided he considered it to be, Banham does not belittle:

. . . the Machine Aesthetic was a world-wide phenomenon, nor was its mythology noxious at the time, for it answered a clear cultural need in offering a common visual law which united the form of the automobile and the building which sheltered it, the form of the house, the forms of its equipment and of the artworks which adorned it. Nor— and this is the heart of the matter—was its falsity visible at the time, for automotive, aeronautical and naval design were currently going through a phase when their products did literally resemble those of Functionalist architecture. The Intelligent Observer, turning from one set of smooth simple shapes to the other, would see apparent and visible proof of the architect's claim to share the virtues of the engineer.[16]

However, as Banham remarked, "these days were numbered." Technical developments in aeronautical design led to penetration becoming a major factor, which resulted in a change from "complex arrays of smooth simple shapes, like those of Functionalist architecture, to simple arrays of mathematically complex forms." A parallel existed in automotive design, where "the liberation of bodywork from horse-and-buggy concepts" caused a near-terminal decline in the architecturally conceived cars of the type illustrated in *Towards a New Architecture* as Manufacturers, responding to the market, adopted an approach which "led to the rapid evolution of an anti-Purist but eye catching vocabulary of design—which we now call Borax."[17] Banham goes on to discuss Borax and its appropriateness to car design. (We will return to this in chapter 2.)

What concerns us here is the basis of Banham's argument for "an acceptance of machines on their own terms." If the architecture of the pioneers paralleled the technology of the time in its "simplicity of form and smoothness of finish," then it might be assumed that the postclassical architecture of the later 1920s ought to parallel technological developments such as streamlining. This would to be to misunderstand the relationship that Banham posited between technology and architecture: architecture was not to ape the aesthetics of engineering or its visual styles, but to arrive at its own aesthetic through an active engagement with those aspects which determined twentieth-century life, including, at the center, technology. The relationship he was defining was one of attitude rather than of form; hence his comment in "Machine Aesthetic" that for the Machine classicists to accept the viewpoint of F. T. Marinetti "would have been to let go of architecture as they understood it."[18] He concludes the article by declaring: "The Machine Aesthetic is dead, and we salute its grave because of the magnificent architecture it produced, but we cannot afford to be sentimental over its passing. It is an outworn piece of mental equipment and, as Le Corbusier also said in the days of L'Esprit Nouveau: 'We have no right to waste our strength on worn out tackle, we must scrap, and re-equip.'"[19]

This typifies the "attitude" approach Banham propounded. Classical Modern buildings may be admired, or even saluted, but their quality is seen not as timeless but rather as timely, in that they reflected progressive ideas at the time they were built. This may seem like a version of zeitgeist theory; and it is, to the extent that Banham believes each age has legitimate and authentic forms of expression. However, these forms are, first, numerous and not singular, unlike Pevsner's "style of the century"; and, second, they claim their legitimacy not from the forms themselves, but from the attitude that produced them. Banham resolutely opposed a singular aesthetic or "an exclusivist standard, which is what any universal criterion of taste like the Machine Aesthetic must eventually become." Instead, over his whole professional life, he consistently favored "the enriched experience which a variety of product [or architectural] aesthetics can offer us."[20] The variety will result from an attitude which comes to terms with the permanency of technological change and which acknowledges the temporality and expendability of forms.

Expressionism and the Historian

One of the First Machine Age architects to contribute to the variety of architectural aesthetics was Erich Mendelsohn, whom Banham wrote about as
early as 1954, eight months before "Machine Aesthetic." However, before
discussing that text, we will turn to an *Architectural Review* article of 1959
on the Romantic Expressionist Paul Scheerbart, a recurring hero in Banham's
writing. Banham puts forward the case for Scheerbart, apparently "an almost spherical bohemian layabout," to be seen as one of the major prophets
of glass architecture. The case is based on Scheerbart's *Glasarchitektur* of
1914 and his direct influence on Bruno Taut, as manifested in the latter's
Glass Industry Pavilion at the Deutsche Werkbund exhibition at Cologne of
the same year. Banham thought that Taut's building was "imbued with the
homogeneity and visual certainty that Gropius's office block so conspicuously lacks, even allowing for differences of form and function."[21] However,
although its materials, steel and glass, should recommend it to Modernist
historians, its nonclassical formal properties—Banham describes it appropriately as "a primitive geodesic dome"[22]—meant that it had been excluded
from the standard histories. The resultant effect is that "the oblivion into
which Scheerbart's name has fallen suggests . . . that he is not to be numbered among Modern Architecture's respectable ancestors."[23] Yet, Banham
maintains, Scheerbart's progressive ideas, commitment to technology, and
belief in architecture's role in the new age and new consciousness—expressed in aphorisms such as "Glass brings us the new age, Brick culture does
us only harm"—should earn him inclusion in the revised history of the Modern Movement.

Banham's revisionism did not mean a complete rejection of the standard
histories, and this applied to the reevaluation of Scheerbart. He concluded:
"This is not to say that we now throw away the history of glass in modern
architecture as it has been established so far—the position of Muthesius and
Gropius among its prophets is not demolished, only diminished. We have to
find some space for Scheerbart."[24] At this stage, the question which exercised him was not *whether* Scheerbart was to be included in the histories,
but "how much space" he should be allotted.

Bruno Taut, Glass Industry Pavilion, Cologne, 1914 (courtesy *The Architectural Review*)

That question was easier to answer in regard to Erich Mendelsohn, whose work also raised issues about Expressionism and its relationship to orthodox Modernism—an attack on "selective and classicising" tendencies was, indeed, part of the opening paragraph of Banham's article. The "blanket description of Expressionist" commonly applied to Mendelsohn had, Banham argued, made a reasoned assessment of his work especially difficult: "Like *Futurist,* the term *Expressionist* has become a dirty word in architectural criticism, and it serves nowadays as a mask for our unwillingness to pay attention to a whole group of architects who lie outside the respectable genealogy of the descent of the Spirit of the Modern Movement."[25]

At this stage of the development of his writing about architecture, one might have imagined that Banham would use Mendelsohn's work as a way of attacking "selective and classicising" *Sachlichkeit* architecture, but he shows himself too good a historian to do that. Banham carefully traces Mendelsohn's career from 1914 until the early 1930s when he left Germany.

Calling on a range of sources, he charts the architect's changing attitudes and values as revealed in his buildings, designs, lecture notes and letters, and speculates on the reasons for the changes in terms of the impact of, for example, Rotterdam (early De Stijl) and Amsterdam (*Wendingen*'s "Eclectics") groupings of architects, Russian Constructivists, and his experiences in the United States.

The evidence and the analyses are too detailed to summarize here, but Banham's method and conclusions merit discussion for a number of reasons. His first priority in the article is historical accuracy—to what extent the term "Expressionist" is valid when one examines Mendelsohn's work in detail:

The term may with some certainty be applied to his work of about 1919, and the Einstein Tower is, indeed, a monument to that phase of Expressionism which reached its apotheosis in *Dr Caligari*, but the differences between the first great doctor of the German Cinema, and *Dr Mabuse*, the last, are not as great as those between the Mendelsohn of 1919 and the Mendelsohn of 1932. Like *Dr Mabuse*, the last works of his German period seem, by implication, to reject Expressionism . . . and the aim of this article is to sketch in the stages by which this transformation was effected, and to suggest some of the causes which have obliterated this change of mind from the popular mythology of Modern Architecture.[26]

Banham argues his thesis by presenting evidence in a way that seems irrefutable. One (lengthy) paragraph and a half from "Mendelsohn" will serve to indicate his method. He is discussing Mendelsohn's "second," post-rounded-form Expressionist stage:

. . . the outstanding work of this stage in his career is undoubtedly the Steinberg-Hermann factory at Luckenwald, completed in 1923. It is also the most instructive, for now, after nearly ten years of the celebrated factory projects, one can see the architect at grips with an industrial problem in reality. The product, alas, had not the *brio* quality of the Futurist dream—there is nothing very dynamic about a hat, however elliptical its plan-form—and yet the overall layout of the factory does take up the axial symmetry of the pre-1917 sketches. This is all that is taken up, however, and the meaning of the symmetrical plan is severely compromised by the fact that the main runs of the work-halls are at right angles to the axis, and therefore give no dynamic effect. The constructional material is concrete, but, far from being handled in great plastic masses, it is used structurally in precast beams and angular portal-frames, and the surfaces are largely tile-hung in a Dutch and unassuming manner. There are no visible curves externally, and the only unusual treatment of corners is that a few of them are pulled out into little storm-prows which might owe rather more to Wright than they do to *Wendingen*. The powerhouse, at one end of the central axis, is trimly cubic and rationalist, a little like some early work of Arthur Korn, but the dye-shed and drying loft in the matching position on the other side of the factory is [sic] very properly admired as one of Mendelsohn's most personal conceptions of the period. Here he was called upon to house a fairly elementary industrial function, not to express a Romantic feeling about it, and the form which the shed eventually took, though perfectly adapted to its function, reminds one so forcibly of the type of wooden cooling-tower which was then common, that any Expressionist illusions he may once have had about forms expressing generalised functions had clearly taken a hard knock. In the last analysis it was air-flows, not hats, which mattered, and therefore the form which had once served the power-station now served the hat-factory, and two years later, in the *Krasnova Snamia* scheme (Leningrad) he was to make it serve a textile mill.

Thus one sees that the contact with Holland had been instrumental in producing a fundamental change in his mode of conceiving architecture. He no longer thought in

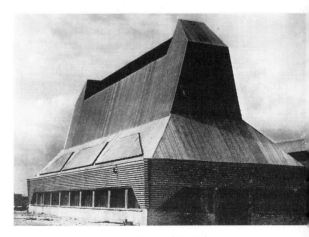

Erich Mendelsohn, Steinberg-Hermann factory, Luckenwald, 1921–1923 (courtesy *The Architectural Review*)

terms of roundly-modelled forms, broad-based like a blanc-mange, but now in terms of structural assemblies of geometrically simple units which presented themselves to the eye as tidily profiled edges, or areas of flat or vertical filling.[27]

Part of Banham's method—and undoubtedly it is a major strength—is a close analysis of particular buildings. Unlike many historians, Pevsner included, Banham relates the form to the plan, in the process noting both continuities (the axiality) and differences (the placing of the work halls), and their implications (no dynamic effect). He discusses the building materials and their particular uses and effects (concrete, which is *not* used plastically; and tile hanging), as well as particular aspects of the forms (the treatment of the corners and the cubic powerhouse), including a feature "properly admired" and associated with Mendelsohn at this time. He also notes how functional considerations (air flow) determine form, a point of significance in that it marks a move in the architect's work away from "Expressionist illusions" about forms expressing "generalised functions." Banham explains these changes (Mendelsohn's contact with Dutch architects) and generalizes on the shift in the aesthetics of the architect's work.

This type of method and analysis is based on a formal reading of architecture—as was Pevsner's of Gropius's—but it is formal investigation at a far more detailed and sophisticated level, and goes beyond mere description, or Formalism, to an investigation of sources, both of forms and of the changing practice. For example, Pevsner writes of Gropius's Fagus factory and Cologne exhibition buildings as if they are architecturally identical, which, in terms of external formal aesthetic quality, they are—both are classical, *Sachlichkeit* buildings. But Banham is more critical and perceptive, and notes, in "Mendelsohn," that

When designing a building to house a real industrial process—the Fagus factory—Gropius and Meyer make no pretensions to overall symmetry of plan, but when he was called upon to design a building to express a state of mind about machinery—the so-called factory at the *Werkbund* exhibition at Cologne—Gropius not only relapses into the Great-West-Road pretentiousness of hiding his machine hall behind an arty office block, but makes that office block symmetrical and aligns his machine hall on the axis of it.[28]

Insights of this kind are crucial to a better understanding of the determinants of form which a more Formalist historian, whether or not driven by a classicizing motivation, would be unlikely to detect.[29] What is surprising is the relative absence of footnotes giving sources of the information. At times, Banham's source of authority is anecdotal and there is no footnoted reference to whom the sources were, or what they had said, or when they had said it. Part of the explanation is that much of Banham's employment at the *Architectural Review* facilitated contact with most of the key architects still alive: "I met all the masters of the Modern Movement except one or two difficult ones like Rob van t'Hoff who needed to be winkled out; all, I think, except Mies."[30] Banham was skeptical of "official" histories and was genuinely interested in the human interrelationships, including the intrigues and personal rivalries. History for Banham was not something "academic"— to use one of his most loaded terms—but alive and vital, and part of its vitality came from its human concerns and relationships.

Banham's researches on Mendelsohn enabled him to present the conclusion that "over the period between *Dr Caligari* and *Dr Mabuse*" we see Erich Mendelsohn practicing three different styles subsequent to Expressionism, with which he had completely finished by 1922: the "Dutch manner" from 1922 to 1929, and what Banham terms the first and second *reklame* styles in parallel with it, one from 1922 to 1929, the second from 1929 until he left the country: "There is nothing here so consistently Expressionist as to justify the Mendelsohn Myth."[31] This conclusion enables him to attack other revisionists such as Bruno Zevi, whose recently published *Towards an Organic Architecture* (1950) "insists on the continuance of an Expressionist aesthetic"—a position Banham describes as "quite untenable." He postulates that "the reason for Zevi's position is easy to see. For him any stick will do to beat the dog of rationalism, and to him, as to the Rationalists themselves, it is Mendelsohn's departures from the International Style which are conspicuous, not his approximations to it. The conventional myth of Mendelsohn is much more use as a polemical weapon than is the true image of an original and changeable designer, so Zevi has a vested interest in its continuance."[32] The phrase "selective and Expressionising" comes to mind to categorize Zevi.

Banham's criticism shows that however much he wanted to redress the predominant "selective and classicising" tendencies of Modernist history, he did not want to do so at the expense of historical balance. This did not mean, as we shall see, that Banham believed the historian could operate without prejudice—the historian had to operate with a sense of timeliness rather than a quest for timelessness: "the historical victory has gone to the International Style, rather than one of the variant possibilities of the twenties, we are all now the children of Rationalism, and, noticing Mendelsohn's aberrations from our canon of form rather than his conformities to it, we tend to accept the Zevian estimate of him."[33] It depends, in other words, on the position you write from. Indeed, in the final paragraph of the article, Banham posits that, Zevi notwithstanding, the most contemporary version of the "Expressionist Myth" of Mendelsohn is the current commercial style of Borax. He writes of Mendelsohn: "His ultimate responsibility for the formal language of American product-design cannot be denied, but to hold him responsible for the enormities of its misuse is as stupid as it would be to blame Voysey for the swarming horrors which are the undoubted offspring of The Orchard, Chorley Wood."[34] That the legacy of history should not unduly shape our judgments about historical events was something that applied not only to Expressionism but also to Futurism, the movement that was pivotal between his Modern Movement revisionism and the Machine Aesthetic of the 1950s.

Futurism: The Defining Movement

An indication of the role that Futurism played in Banham's thinking comes not only from the focus he gave it directly, but also from the references to it which appear elsewhere in his writing. For example, when discussing the early work of Erich Mendelsohn, he writes that "these projects are surely attempts to realise the Marinettian vision of *immensi cantieri tumultuanti*," and describes what he sees as the "unmistakable tone of high Futurist excitement about the world of the machine" in Mendelsohn's writing.[35] When discussing Scheerbart, Banham notes that his "optimistic view of technology puts him at one with the Futurists."[36] And, of course, in "Machine Aesthetic," as well as quoting Marinetti, he presents the argument that makes an upward evaluation of Futurism inevitable. Futurism remained the symbolic core of Banham's thinking about architecture in a technological age.

Banham's first article on Futurism, published in 1955, concentrates on the Futurist architect Antonio Sant'Elia. These are early stages of his reevaluation, and Banham reviews the literature available on the Futurist, concluding that not only is it extremely sparse, but also that it often does not do justice to Sant'Elia's significance in Modern Movement theory. Indeed, he was right not only about Sant'Elia but also that Futurism in general. Mainstream Modernists either ignored or denigrated Futurism. In *Pioneers of the Modern Movement*, Pevsner allots Futurism no more than a footnote in which he quotes very selectively from Sant'Elia's 1914 Futurist manifesto, giving no indication of the full flavor of Futurism and providing the impression that Futurism is a minor offshoot of the mainstream movement. Sigfried Giedion, in his nine hundred-page *Space, Time and Architecture*, published in 1941 and with three reprintings by the early 1960s, gave Futurism four pages of text and two of illustrations, compared, for example, with over seventy pages on Le Corbusier. In *Art and Technics* (1952, reprinted frequently), Lewis Mumford dismissed Futurism as "a little ridiculous, if not repulsive."[37]

Futurism dates back to 1909, when F. T. Marinetti, the founder and chief protagonist of the movement, delivered a series of outspoken and uncompromising manifestos to provoke a reaction in the Italian art world and, as he described it, free "this land from its smelly gangrene of professors, archaeologists, *ciceroni* and antiquarians."[38] Like many other artists at the time, the Futurists believed they were witnessing the dawning of a new age of power, dynamism, and excitement. Technology was central and should not be observed with the detached air of the academic, but experienced for all its compulsive sensations. Jettisoning the aesthetic and cultural conventions of the past, the Futurists embraced the radically *new* beauty of the twentieth century, "the beauty of speed. A racing car whose hood is adorned with great pipes, like serpents of explosive breath—

a roaring car that seems to ride on grapeshot is more beautiful than the *Victory of Samothrace.*"[39]

A celebratory and romantic spirit infused the "Manifesto of Futurist Architecture," published in 1914 under the name of Antonio Sant'Elia. The "New City" would be like "an immense, tumultuous, lively, noble work site, dynamic in all its parts. . . . The house of concrete, glass and iron . . . must rise on the edge of a tumultuous abyss: the street . . . will descend into the earth on several levels."[40] The most radical Futurist proposition was the last proclamation, which included the assertion that "the fundamental characteristics of Futurist architecture will be obsolescence and transience. Houses will last less long than we. Each generation will have to build its own city."[41] Obsolescence and transience had never before been elevated to essential characteristics. The Futurists had squarely come to terms with the idea that technology is in a state of continual change, and this was largely its appeal to Banham.

Much of Banham's 1955 article on Sant'Elia is concerned with establishing the facts about the authorship of the "Manifesto of Futurist Architecture," and informing an as yet uninformed readership about the architect's output and its varied sources.[42] He points out a significant difference between the text of the "Manifesto" and Sant'Elia's drawings: the text, much expanded by Marinetti and possibly others,[43] with its references to work sites and lifts, emphasizes dynamism and energy. The imagery, "does not deal with noise, speed and physical impact, but is static, clean, subdued and essentially abstract."[44] Banham claims the staticity of the imagery "shows the change that had come over Futurism by 1914" but, given the references to dynamism in Marinetti's contribution to the "Manifesto," the contrast is less attributable to a change in the sensibility of Futurism than to different means of portraying the same end. He corrects Giedion's comment that Sant'Elia sought to "introduce the futurist love of movement into his city as an artistic element," claiming this

. . . seems now an underestimate of [Sant'Elia's] mental calibre, and a misunderstanding of his place and time in the development of Futurism. The drawings entitled *Dinamismo Architettonico* make it clear that "movement" as a quality of individual buildings

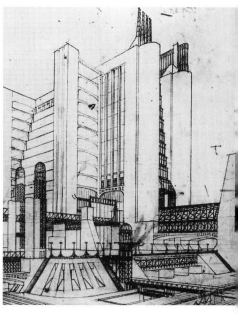

Antonio Sant'Elia, study for *The New City,* 1914 (courtesy *The Architectural Review*)

has a very special meaning in his hands, while an examination of the *Città Futurista* drawings suggests that far from trying to "introduce" movement, Sant'Elia is basing his whole design on a recognition of the fact that in the mechanised city one must circulate or perish.[45]

This rather confuses two senses of movement: the anticlassical, dynamic quality of the draftsmanship and graphic style in the drawings, with their "oblique and elliptical lines [that] are dynamic by their very nature"[46]—Futurist "lines of force" and powerful, antistatic simplicity—and the architectural vision in which physical movement is not described but implied by reference to such elements as multilayered communication networks. Whereas a classicist like Adolf Loos may end up with an antidecorative "collection of dull boxes," Sant'Elia "goes on to create forms which are exciting in virtue of their mechanistic inspiration. In fact, putting the total corpus of drawings against the text of his manifesto, we see that he was among the very first to combine a complete acceptance of the machine-world with an ability to realise and symbolise that acceptance in terms of powerful and simple geometrical form. The acceptance is more complete than Le Corbusier's, the forms more powerful than those of Gropius." Banham conclusively reasons that Sant'Elia needs to be acknowledged as a "pioneer of the International Style" who was "the first to conceive the planning of cities as fully three-dimensional structures, and his position in the family-tree of the Modern Movement is thus assured."[47]

The authorship of the "Manifesto of Futurist Architecture" was again discussed by Banham in his lecture on Futurism and Sant'Elia to the Royal Institute of British Architects in 1957.[48] By that time, the uncertainty about the authorship of contributions was largely resolved, and he acknowledges that the most radical propositions in the "Manifesto," including the one about expendability, were the ones that Sant'Elia "is recorded as disagreeing with, but—ironically—they are also the ones on which his reputation as a prophet of the New Architecture largely rests." Banham goes so far to state that if Sant'Elia's disapproval of the expendability proposition is true, "he is thereby diminished as an architectural pioneer, lacking the courage to pursue his own ideas to their revolutionary conclusions."[49]

Sant'Elia may, indeed, be seen to be less radical than was assumed, but the radicalness of the "Manifesto" as published still stands, with, logically, the real plaudits going to the author(s) of the added propositions. It was generally agreed by historians that the tone and style of the additions pointed to Marinetti, and so it is the leader of the movement, certainly not one who ever lacked the courage to pursue his ideas to their revolutionary potential or political extremes, who merits the prime place in architectural history that Banham's revisionism was establishing. Indeed, as Banham was later to note, Marinetti was to be given credit not only for creating the most radical aspects of the "Manifesto," but also for taking responsibility for drawing the attention of the wider architectural world to Sant'Elia's ideas on and images of such things as the multitowered city and fast circulation. The status which Sant'Elia acquired

. . . seems to have been almost entirely due to the energetic promotion of Sant'Elia's memory by Marinetti. It is fair to say that his reputation is largely of Marinetti's making, outside Italy at least, not only because Marinetti circulated his work to groups like De Stijl and *Der Sturm,* but also because some of the most widely admired opinions associated with [Sant'Elia's] name are only to be found in the disputed Manifesto, not in the *Messagio,* which hardly anyone outside Italy ever saw.[50]

However, praise for Marinetti's contribution raised a difficult problem about the relation of architectural and political values and attitudes that, in another context, created a real—and possibly unresolved—dilemma for Banham.

Banham is very careful to separate Marinetti's aesthetics from his politics:

It is possible, indeed commendable to be revolted by Marinetti's later politics, just as it is possible and commendable to be revolted by the later politics of William Morris. But, as Moholy-Nagy pointed out in connection with Marinetti, it is possible to have very wrong ideas on some subjects and, at the same time, very right ideas on others. Many of Marinetti's ideas were very right indeed, like many of Morris's. The one awoke a social conscience, the other a mechanical sensibility.[51]

An honest distinction between aesthetics and politics was, for Banham's (especially) Italian contemporaries, a politically sensitive issue which, had they adopted Banham's reasoning, might have appeared to make them Fascist sympathizers. The research into the authorship of the "Manifesto" that was taking place in the later 1950s was being shaped partly by political positioning. Some historians were distancing Sant'Elia from the text of the Manifesto in order to deny his involvement with Futurism because

. . . in a re-democratised Italy where men are hard at work trying to make democracy a success, Futurism is regarded with suspicion as part of the Fascist past, and many ex-Futurists are busy trying to cover their tracks. Sant'Elia's reputation as a pioneer, however minor, of the new architecture, and as the forerunner of those resolute young men who gave their lives for modern architecture and democracy in the concentration camps of the Second World War—Sant'Elia's reputation, they feel, must be kept free of the taint

of Futurism. As a democrat I feel for them, as an art-historian nurtured, however un-
gratefully, in the tradition of Pevsner, Blunt and Wittkower, I must disagree with them.[52]

Such comments reveal not only the special difficulties facing the historian of
recent events which still have a bearing on the politics of the day, but also
Banham's independence of mind.

Banham was right to disagree with those who distanced Sant'Elia from Futurism. Sant'Elia's contribution technically, may not be Futurist because the
text on which the "Manifesto" is based predates his involvement with the
movement and the word "Futurist" is, therefore, absent; but its "tone, turn
of phrase and intention"[53] make it undeniably Futurist in spirit. And it was
the spirit that formed the core of Banham's reevaluation of the Machine
Age. Banham was, of course, looking for a progressive Modern Movement
that accepted "machines on their own terms" and that was distinguished by
an attitude rather than formal considerations. In his RIBA lecture, he described the difference in terms of sensibilities, calling the "sensibility *mechanical* that Marinetti awakened, not only because this is his word for it,
but also to distinguish it from that engineering sensibility that was being in-
culcated in the same years by German writers like Muthesius and Gropius."
The engineering and mechanical sensibilities may have overlapped when it
came to appreciating such building types as covered markets and railway
stations, but the "nobility" and "monumentality" that appealed to the engineering sensibility was profoundly different from mechanical sensibility:

. . . strength might have interested Marinetti, nobility and monuments not. His discovery—and it can be fairly called a discovery among intellectuals and men of letters—was
that machines could be a source of personal fulfilment and gratification, that telephones
and typewriters, soda-siphons and cinemas, aeroplanes and automobiles had enormously extended the range of human experience at the personal, not social level. Machines work for men, a man commands his own machines, he drives his own car, no
longer has to share a train with a thousand other men. Marinetti's was the first generation of European intellectuals to be able to enjoy these new experiences, and he forcefully articulated his generation's responsive enthusiasm.[54]

Not only is Banham further articulating the difference between the classi-cizing "engineering" sensibility and the alternative "mechanical" sensibil-ity in the first twenty years of the twentieth century, but he is also declaring his own preferences and values based on the belief that "machines could be a source of personal fulfilment and gratification."[55] In chapter 3, we will be examining how that belief formed the basis of his theory of architecture and design from the 1950s on. At this point, we can see how Banham's research into the Modern Movement culminates in his first book, *Theory and Design in the First Machine Age,* which appeared in 1960.

Theory and Design in the First Machine Age

The mechanical sensibility formed a cornerstone of a qualitative change in the relationship between humans and technology at the beginning of the twentieth century. Its effect, Banham proposes in the introduction to *Theory and Design,* was that "the barrier of incomprehension that had stood between thinking men and their mechanised environment all through the nineteenth century, in the mind of Marx as much as in the mind of Morris, began to crumble. Men whose means of moving ideas from place to place had been revolutionised at their writing desks by the typewriter and the telephone, could no longer treat the world of technology with hostility or indifference."[56] This changed relationship to technology was what Banham meant by the "First Machine Age." He distinguishes "Machine" from "In-dustrial" in that "we have lived in an Industrial Age for nearly a century and a half now—the 'Industrial Age' is no less than the industrial revolu-tion." Within the Industrial Age were changing human relationships and experiences brought about by technology, and these constituted "Machine Ages." He wrote, "we have already entered the Second Machine Age, the age of domestic electronics and synthetic chemistry, and can look back on the First, the age of power from the mains and the reduction of machines to human scale, as a period of the past." Although the origins of the First Ma-chine Age could, arguably, be dated back to the availability of coal gas for heating and lighting,

. . . the mechanism of light and heat remained a flame, as it had been from the Stone Age onwards. Mains electricity made a decisive alteration here, one of the most decisive in the history of domestic technology. In addition, it brought small, woman-controlled machinery into the home, notably the vacuum-cleaner. Electrical techniques brought the telephone as well, and for the first time domestic and sociable communication did not depend on the sending of written or remembered messages. The portable typewriter put a machine under the hands of poets, the first gramophones made music a domestic service rather than a social ceremony.[57]

This was clearly a qualitative shift in human-technology relationships, and it may appear that the Second Machine Age was principally an extension of the First, merely "improved by more recent technological advances." But the broadening of the availability of technology and its increasingly personal scale had again resulted in a qualitative impact: "In the First, however, only cinema was available to a broad public, whose home life was otherwise barely touched and it was in upper middle-class homes that the First Machine Age made its greatest impact, the homes that could afford these new, convenient and expensive aids to gracious living, the homes that tend to breed architects, painters, poets, journalists, the creators of the myths and symbols by which a culture recognises itself."[58]

If the symbol of the Second Machine Age was the television, the symbol of the First, available to the elite that could afford one, was the automobile:

It was more than a symbol of power, it was also, for most of that elite, a heady taste of a new kind of power. One of the uncommented curiosities of the early part of the Industrial Age is that, in spite of its massive dependence on mechanical power, few of its elite, if any, had any personal experience of controlling that power. They could buy the use of it with money, and ride in its great ships and famous expresses, but they did not dirty their hands with the controls.[59]

Whereas a separate class of operators, such as train drivers, had operated public-scale technology, "with the coming of purchasable motorcars, it became possible, and fashionable, for the opinion-forming classes to own and personally control units of motive power up to sixty, or even a hundred horse-power." The changes of experience were "qualitative, not merely quantitative—the dynamics of the fast-moving car are different in kind to the dynamics of even a race-horse. The Man Multiplied by the Motor, to use Marinetti's phrase, was a different kind of man to the horse-and-buggy men who had ruled the world since the time of Alexander the Great."[60]

It is no coincidence that Marinetti is introduced into the text at an early stage: indeed, Futurism receives considerable attention in the book, completing the revaluation that Banham had commenced in the mid-1950s. *Theory and Design* is divided into five sections. Section 1 is an introductory assessment titled "Predisposing Causes: Academic and Rationalist Writers, 1900–1914"; the other four sections focus on particular cultural locations of architectural Modernism: Italy, Holland, Paris, and Germany. The prominence in the structure of the book given to "Italy: Futurist Manifestos and Projects, 1909–1914" is partly explained by the chronology of events, partly by the theoretical role Futurism plays in Banham's revisionist account.

Futurism was a sensibility—nothing less than an attitude of mind which, for Banham, not only characterized Futurism but also gave it value: "The qualities which made Futurism a turning-point in the development of Modern theories of design were primarily ideological, and concerned with attitudes of mind, rather than formal or technical methods—though these attitudes of mind were often influential as vehicles in the transmission of formal and technical methods which were not, in the first place, of Futurist invention."[61] This is a key quotation, for it explains much of Banham's thinking, not only during his revaluation of the Modern Movement in the 1950s but also in his subsequent writing. Form was not interesting in its own right *as form,* but as the outcome of a way of thinking, as a manifestation of a sensibility. This makes Banham an anticlassicist: form always related to an attitude of mind or a set of values, and could never be usefully detached without a loss of vitality and relevancy, and a decline into academicism.

Hence, other manifestations of the First Machine Age might have brought about formal innovations, but their forms did not reflect a wider change of attitude. For example, Banham argued that it was narrowly academic to see Futurism as an offshoot of Cubism an account of the latter's adaptation of certain formal and technical devices, because "Cubism was a

55

revolution within painting itself, and not part of a profound reorientation towards a changed world."[62] The phrase "profound reorientation towards a changed world," like the above quotation, encapsulates Banham's attitude and values, and unlocks the motivation behind his revaluation and many of his judgments.

One of the most important points made by Banham in *Theory and Design* appears only as a footnote in the chapter "Expressionism: Amsterdam and Berlin." At a point in the discussion of Mendelsohn, Banham acknowledges that

attempts to define Expressionism have been avoided so far because the term has always been so loosely used as to defy definition. The ideas quoted here can be construed as Expressionist only because they put forward a concept that is commonly associated with the work of painters like Kokoschka and Nolde, and sculptors like Barlach, but it is very doubtful if this idea of self-expression was very widely entertained even by artists such as these whose style has later become the touchstone of Expressionism. Again and again, since the word was first put into circulation around 1911, it has been used to signify, purely and simply, work that is not old-fashioned, but does not conform to the current progressive norms of the time. There is practically no other sense in which the term can be made to stick to the work of Poelzig, which seems never to have been intended to express anything personal at all, and Mendelsohn is nearly always found to be expressing something about the nature or contents of the building. Since the expression of the function of the building is taken to be one of the touchstones of the non-Expressionist approach, we may suspect that we see here, as in so much twentieth-century architectural polemics, one of those situations where an aesthetic standpoint is defended by accusing the other party of abandoning a theoretical position that is, in fact, common ground to both sides.[63]

Banham gives the example of Mendelsohn, supposedly an "Expressionist," being "rational." As an example of a "rationalist" accepting symbolism and expression, he quotes Gropius's 1923 statement that the Bauhaus's responsibility is "to educate men and women to understand the world in which they live, and to invent and create forms symbolising that world"—a statement which he describes as "revealing and surprising . . . in the context of its time, and of what the Bauhaus is often supposed to have been."[64] Perhaps the real battle was over aesthetics and form, rather than over theory. Why this point appeared in a footnote in the "Expressionism: Amsterdam and Berlin" chapter and not either in the main text or, more appropriately, the conclusion, is inexplicable, because its implications for both *Theory and Design* and the revaluation of the Modern Movement are major. Banham is collapsing the polarization of "rationalists" and "anti-rationalists" promoted by many mainstream historians, including Pevsner,[65] arguing that there are potentially equally valid alternative machine aesthetics founded on similar beliefs and ideals—a position he maintained throughout his life and applied to all Machine Ages. The real enemies of the Modern movement, he felt, were not the "anti-rationalists"/Expressionists because, following his revaluation, they ought to be regarded as part and parcel of the same Movement, but those who opposed or were out of sympathy with the characteristics and values of the First Machine Age.

Most of these are dealt with in the first section of the book, the "predisposing causes." Some of the chapters in this section discuss the "academic and rationalist writers" between 1900 and 1914 whose ideas were sympathetic to the Machine Aesthetic and who themselves became pioneers of the movement. A good example is Adolf Loos, whose contribution to the idea and meaning of undecorated architecture is well documented. Banham points out that in equating freedom from ornament with an "uncorrupted mind," and attributing that mind to peasants and engineers, Loos succeeded in "laying further foundations to the idea of engineers as noble savages (to which Marinetti also contributed) and also—and this is vital in the creation of the International Style—laying further foundations to the idea that to build without decoration is to build like an engineer, and thus in a manner proper to a Machine Age."[66] This does not, however, constitute a "profound reorientation towards a changed world," a point which Banham develops by comparing Loos to the Futurists:

. . . like many reformers, [Loos] was a Traditionalist and tended to look backward, not forward. One does not find him attacking Ruskin, as Marinetti was to do . . . He took tradition-bound English tailoring as a model of reticent good taste. Though he admired some consequences of American industry and the whole of American plumbing, he had none of the Futurists' sense of machinery as an aid to personal expression, and he mocks the ideas of a high-obsolescence, scrapping economy, such as was already appearing in the U.S., and was accepted enthusiastically by the Futurists in the next five years. He tends to see furniture and utensils as a class of possessions whose market value must be maintained, not as a class of equipment to be discarded when outmoded.[67]

Banham's values are clearly revealed in the above passage. To be a "traditionalist" obviously has negative connotations because it makes one "look backward" rather than forward, which, to Banham, makes one less progressive and therefore less Modernist. That Loos did not have a "mechanical sensibility" makes him not only different from the Futurists, but also inferior. Because he is out of sympathy with the Futurists in their commitment to expendability, Loos is, by implication, retrogressive. That it is appropriate to discuss him in relation to the Futurists is itself questionable—more tellingly, it reveals the role the Futurists were given in the book. The strength of Banham's historical writing—that it integrates fact, interpretation and significance—is also at times its weakness, especially when implicit values determine the sort of judgments that underlie the quotation on Loos. If the "selective and classicising" historians were unsympathetic and unfair to the Futurists and Expressionists, Banham, with his Futurist "mechanical sensibility," can be equally unsympathetic and unfair to Traditionalists and revivalists.

The most unsympathetic evaluations in *Theory and Design,* in fact, are accorded British architects and writers around the turn of the twentieth century. "English Free architecture"—the work of architects such as W. R. Lethaby and C. F. A. Voysey—is criticized for not achieving something that it did not seek. Such architecture, Banham adjudges, could have been "close to the mainstream of development," but "The dramatic reduction of that Free architecture to a mere provincial vernacular, in competition with a provincial version of *Beaux-Arts* Classicism, is a singular example of failure of nerve and collapse of creative energy. To some extent this may be due to muddled thinking and squeamishness—the failure to identify the Glasgow School as an ally, or to accept machine production, are examples of the squeamishness."[68] The word "squeamishness" is dubious in terms of dispassionate, historical writing—although it has to be readily admitted that Banham was always a passionate writer who wrote with verve. It is also historically simplistic in reducing the complexities and subtleties of points of view of English Free architects.

Banham is, as one would anticipate, scathing of the academic classical tradition as manifested either in Beaux Arts or in its English offshoot. Geoffrey Scott's *Architecture of Humanism* is described as "the aesthetic handbook of the neo-Georgian and Playboy phases of English architecture."[69] Although acknowledged to be "neither a trivial book nor a superficial one," it is roundly condemned for its tendency "to preach a kind of architectural irresponsibility."[70] Banham goes some way to reconsidering Scott's reputation by connecting his aestheticism with abstract theory in the 1920s. Scott's definition—that "architecture, simply and immediately perceived, is a combination, revealed through light and shade, of spaces, masses and lines"[71]—is, indeed, very close to Le Corbusier's dictum that "Architecture is the masterly, correct and magnificent play of masses brought together in light."[72] However, the differences between Scott and the Modernists are more significant and unbridgeable than the similarities (or coincidences), and Le Corbusier's rejection of stylistic classicism on the grounds that "Architecture has nothing to do with the various 'styles'"[73] is in total opposition to Scott's eulogizing of Renaissance classicism. But the link, in Banham's view, is classicism, and the way in which classical aesthetics of the late nineteenth century, under the influence of abstraction, became what Theo van Doesburg, writing of J. J. P. Oud, called "unhistorical Classicism," or what Banham termed "Academic aesthetics without Academic detailing."[74]

Tracking the development of unhistorical Classicism, Banham quotes the Cubist painter Albert Gleizes imploring his contemporaries in art and architecture to adopt classical discipline without the stylistics of Classicism: "When the ultimate effort has been made, it will not be Classicism they rediscover, but the tradition, pure and simple; that which used to permit a strict and hierarchical collaboration in the creation of works of impersonal art."[75] In his chapter on *Vers une Architecture,* Banham examines the unstructured (understandably, because it was compiled from separate articles which had appeared in *L'Esprit Nouveau*) but undoubtedly classical under-pinning to Le Corbusier's most widely known text:

Viewing the work as a whole, one sees that even if it has no argument, it has at least a motto-theme, which may be summarised as follows: architecture is in disorder now, but its essential laws of Classical geometry remain. Mechanisation does not threaten these laws but reinforces them, and when architecture has recovered these Classical laws and made its peace with machinery, it will be in a position to redress the wrongs of society. In this Le Corbusier was probably well in accord with the mood of the times as it existed.[76]

That there is a classical basis to Le Corbusier's architecture is not in dispute; nor is it in dispute that he was selective in either his arguments or the retro-spective accounts of his own practice. But Le Corbusier's "selective and clas-sicising" tendencies do not condemn him to disingenuousness or irrelevancy in Banham's account of the Modern Movement. *Theory and Design* certainly attempts to redress inaccuracies and prejudices, but the classicism in Le Cor-busier's architecture is not a major issue for Banham, for reasons which need to be fully understood if his revaluation is not to be misunderstood.

In *Theory and Design*'s conclusion, Banham states that "The architecture of the Twenties, though capable of its own austerity and nobility, was heav-

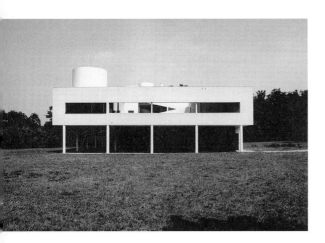

Le Corbusier, Villa Savoye, Poissy-sur-Seine, 1928–1930

ily, and designedly, loaded with symbolic meanings that were discarded or ignored by its apologists in the Thirties."[77] Finally, to demonstrate his claim and, with it, to revise the Modern Movement, he discusses two buildings to assess the extent to which the Modern Movement succeeded in its own terms in creating buildings which symbolized the age. The first was Ludwig Mies van der Rohe's German Pavilion at the Barcelona Exhibition of 1929; the second was Le Corbusier's Villa Savoye/Les Heures Claires, completed in 1930. Banham employs the same method to assess both buildings; it starts with a functional breakdown and moves on to a formal analysis because, in both cases, it is this relationship that forms the basis for the evaluation of the buildings' quality. In the case of the Villa Savoye, the visual handling is "what makes the building architecture by Le Corbusier's standards and enables it to touch the heart": "The house as a whole is white—*le colour-type*—and square—one of *les plus belles formes*—set down in a sea of uninterrupted grass—*le terrain idéal*—which the architect has called a Virgilian Landscape. Upon this traditional ground he erected one of the least traditional buildings of his career, rich in the imagery of the Twenties."[78] For example, the way the ground floor recedes visually and the upper part appears to be delicately poised in space creates something of a "material-immaterial illusionism that Oud prophesied, but that Le Corbusier more often practised."

Description is followed by interpretation and significance: the "setting back of the ground floor," Banham continues, "has further meaning." That meaning, he tells us, is to do with the way the house is planned for arrival and departure by car: there are parallel drives which join at the entrance to the house; the gap between the ground floor wall and the pilotis is the right width for a car; furthermore, according to Le Corbusier, the curve of the wall of the ground floor was dictated by the minimum turning radius of a car. For Banham, "This appears to be nothing less than a typically Corbusian 'inversion' of the test-track on the roof of . . . Matté-Trucco's Fiat factory, tucked under the building instead of laid on top of it, creating a suitably emotive approach to the home of a fully motorised post-Futurist family."[79] The Fiat factory building in Turin (to which we will be returning) was visited by Le Corbusier and is illustrated in *Vers une Architecture*, and so a direct influence is quite possible, but his description of it as a "typically Corbusian 'inversion'" makes too great a claim for something which has a commonsensical planning rationale, even if the car is accepted as a determinant of the design scheme.[80]

Banham's analysis of the interior—he draws attention to the industrial glazing, the plain balustrades of the ramp, the spiral staircase, the washbasin, and the light fittings—accurately demonstrates the "industrial or nautical" appearance: the Machine Aesthetic. He likens the internal plan to the composition of contemporary abstract paintings, composed "by jigsawing together a number of rectangles to fit into a given square plan." The abstract aesthetic is at its most pronounced where the screen wall at the top of the building

. . . is composed of irregular curves and short straights, mostly standing well back from the perimeter of the block. Not only are these curves, on plan, like the shapes to be found in his *Peintures Puristes,* but their modelling, seen in raking sunlight, has the same delicate and insubstantial air as that of the bottles and glasses in his paintings and the effect of these curved forms, standing on a square slab raised on slabs is like nothing so much as a still-life arranged on a table.[81]

This is sensitive and insightful criticism that manages a smooth transition from fact to interpretation. However, just as the claim for the test track "inversion" may be rather fanciful, so, too, is the claim that the villa, "set down in this landscape . . . has the same kind of Dadaist quality as the [figurative, traditional] statue in the Barcelona Pavilion." This is an example of Banham straining to load as much Machine Age symbolism and meaning as he could into one of the two buildings which he was using to typify the First Machine Age—methodologically, the "symbol of the age" approach has this pitfall.

Nevertheless, Banham's exegesis reveals not only that "no single-valued criterion, such as Functionalism, will ever serve to explain the forms and surfaces of these buildings," but also that "enough should also have been said to suggest the way in which they are rich in the associations and symbolic values current in their time. And enough has also been said to show that they came extraordinarily close to realising the general idea of a Machine

Age architecture that was entertained by their designers."[82] The point to note in Banham's discussion of the Villa Savoye is that the Classical aesthetic does not feature as such. Having a Classical underpinning is of interest to Banham only inasmuch as the symbolism of the Classical aesthetic is part and parcel of the Machine Aesthetic at a certain historical juncture. Banham does not accept any transcendent claims for form, but sees it primarily in visual and symbolic terms: he does not offer disinterested aesthetic analysis but deconstructs buildings' "associations and symbolic values current in their time," thereby assessing the extent to which the building expresses the "mood of the times." It is, he concludes in *Theory and Design,* "in respect of such symbolic forms that [the Modern Movement's] historical justification must lie."[83]

Thus Banham's revaluation of the First Machine Age does much more than offer Futurist and Expressionist buildings and projects in an expanded aesthetic field of formal possibilities. As we have seen, the grounds for his argument for Futurism's qualities marking a turning point were "primarily ideological, and concerned with attitudes of mind, rather than formal or technical methods." Le Corbusier's Villa Savoye earned a similar status. Alongside Mies's Barcelona Pavilion, "their status as masterpieces rests, as it does with most other masterpieces of architecture, upon the authority and felicity with which they give expression to a view of men in relation to their environment"[84]—in other words, they offered a "profound reorientation towards a changed world" in the First Machine Age. Ultimately, Banham's revaluation attacks the orthodox Modernist hierarchy that claimed the authentic zeitgeist was manifested in a superior, timeless Classical aesthetic. It is countered by an approach which disallows transcendent aesthetic claims and which sees form as symbolically loaded and historically embedded. When Banham writes that "between Futurist dynamism and . . . Academic caution the theory and design of the architecture of the First Machine Age were evolved,"[85] he is, in effect, assuming a continuum on which all outcomes and forms are potentially valid, but the potentiality can be converted into achievement only if it is derived from an attitude or frame of mind.

Intellectually and theoretically, Banham acknowledges the potentially equal worth of the "engineering sensibility" and the "mechanical sensibil-

ity" manifested in, respectively, Classical and Futurist/Expressionist buildings. However, there is little doubt where Banham's real sympathies and enthusiasms lie. In *Theory and Design* he does not revise his 1955 judgment
that Sant'Elia's "acceptance of the machine world" and his "ability to realise
and symbolise that acceptance in terms of powerful and simple geometrical
form . . . is more complete than Le Corbusier's, the forms more powerful
than those of Gropius."[86] It would seem that he feels there is evidence of a
more "profound reorientation towards a changed world" in the work of the
pioneers and masters of the mechanical sensibility.

Pevsner's Response

A revised and partly rewritten edition of *Pioneers of the Modern Movement,* titled *Pioneers of Modern Design,* was published in 1960.[87] A second
edition had appeared in 1949, published by the Museum of Modern Art in
New York, but was little different from the first. The foreword to the 1960
Pelican edition records the research of, inter alia, Banham, whose work
Pevsner of course knew not only through his articles but also through his
doctoral research. With the fundamental revisionism Banham had carried
out, it comes as no surprise when Pevsner admits that there were places in
the thesis of *Pioneers* "where I felt some slight shaking and had to do a se-
curing job." Antonio Gaudi and Sant'Elia are mentioned in this context. Yet
a slight shaking is far from an earthquake, and it is surprising to read Pevsner acknowledging the "many additions and alterations" resulting from recent research but stating that "None, however, I am happy to say, [is] of such
a kind as to rock the structure of my argument." Pevsner is unrepentant, and
his own revisions—the "resurrection" of Gaudi and Sant'Elia—were carried
out grudgingly: "This resurrection is symptomatic. When I wrote this book
the architecture of reason and functionalism was in full swing in many countries, while it had just started a hopeful course in others. There was no question that Wright, Garnier, Loos, Behrens, Gropius were the initiators of the
style of the century and that Gaudi and Sant'Elia were freaks and their inventions fantastical rantings."[88]

Although included in the main text because he is "symptomatic," Sant'Elia
is still rejected in 1960, because "from Sant'Elia the way of twentieth-

century architecture leads once more to Expressionism,"[89] and Expressionism is based on "the whims of individual architects, the stroke of genius of others [which] cannot be accepted as an answer to the serious questions which it is the responsibility of the architect to answer."[90] That Expressionist forms signified a certain state of mind, attitude, or even set of values was, as we have seen, something that Banham implicitly, and on occasions even explicitly, rejected.[91] Such apparently impermeable historical and critical absolutes did not lend themselves to the dynamic conditionality of the relationships between forms, attitudes, and values in Banham's version of the Modern Movement. But what Pevsner and Banham shared was an involvement with current as well as First Machine Age architecture, and this led to an intermingling of history, theory, and polemics in their writing that prevented both *Pioneers* and *Theory and Design* from being wholly disinterested historical accounts.

Reprinted more than ten times and translated into Italian, German, Japanese, Polish, Spanish, Hebrew, and French, *Theory and Design* rapidly became a canonical text and has had enormous influence on generations of academics, students, and architects. Kenneth Frampton, for example, recently described it as "brilliant" and acknowledged that his own *Modern Architecture: A Critical History* (1980) was "deeply indebted" to it.[92] At the time of its publication, it was hailed as a "landmark";[93] however, its reviews were mixed, which is not surprising, given the major recasting of conventional wisdom that the book offered.[94] There were some comments that were perceptive and, indeed, prescient of later criticisms of Banham's writing. Paul Goodman was fulsome in his praise for its scholarship, but complained that it detached architecture and its theories from the society that was producing them: "It is astonishingly blank of even a rough sketch of the political, economic, moral and religious background." It also failed to mention "Marx, Veblen or Pragmatism . . . the Weimar Republic and hardly any progressive education or psychoanalysis."[95] Sibyl Moholy-Nagy granted that the book was "highly erudite and industriously constructed" but accused Banham—ironically, given his own attacks on the condition—of being too academic: "[he] suffers from a gross over-estimation of the effect of books and theories on the actual creation of art and architecture."[96] Goodman also noted bias and naiveté in Banham's enthusiasm for technology and the technological attitude: "he devotes not one sentence to examining the 'technology' itself, but treats it as simple datum to be accepted en bloc and not subject to selection."

Alan Colquhoun drew attention to the ways in which Banham's own prejudices were apparent: "That he evidently does not look upon the facts that he has uncovered with detachment shows itself in his constantly perjorative use of the term 'academic.'"[97] Banham, Colquhoun continued, allowed his own position on technology to intrude into what was otherwise a major piece of scholarship and insight. *Theory and Design* might be a scholarly work, but it was also polemical, and revealed Banham as a technological optimist. But, as we will see in subsequent chapters, he seldom wrote as a disinterested historian: *Theory and Design,* like his other books, has an agenda. History, for Banham, was never an end in itself, but a means to being polemical in and about the present. This is one of the ways in which he can be described as the "historian of the immediate future."

Revisionism Continued

With the publication of *Theory and Design in the First Machine Age,* Banham's interest in the architecture of the First Machine Age did not come to an end, but the book does represent the broad conclusion of one particular project. Banham, as we will see in chapters 3 and 4, returned to the First Machine Age in works such as *The Architecture of the Well-Tempered Environment* (1969), but he had a significantly different intention than the historical *revisionist* project of *Theory and Design.* However, some research which accords with the broad thesis of *Theory and Design* continued in the 1960s, and carried on up to near the end of Banham's life.

Among those who were reassessed were Mies van der Rohe[98] and Le Corbusier[99]—both of whose reassessments included obituaries—Frank Lloyd Wright,[100] Hugo Haring and Hannes Meyer,[101] Hermann Muthesius,[102] and, to the extent that he could be claimed as a genuine "pioneer" of the Modern Movement (in the Pevsnerian sense), William Morris.[103] The Bauhaus also came in for further scrutiny.[104] Sometimes it was individual buildings that were analyzed or reassessed.[105] Assessed for the first time was Pierre

Chareau's Maison de Verre—Banham admits he had not known the build-ing in the 1950s—which he acclaimed as exemplifying "how Modern might have been quite different;"[106] and the furniture designs of Eileen Gray,[107] whom Banham does not consider a major talent. Indeed, in his article on Gray, written in 1973, Banham credits the discovery of Gray to

. . . the growing nostalgia among architectural academics for the nice neat certainties, the tidy moral categories, of the Heroic Age of Modern Architecture in the twenties. This tends to concentrate all the proliferating historical talent on the finite number of undis-covered pioneers still available. The resultant battle for crumbs of reputation, and nit-picking over minutiae of priority, gets down to [an] almost theological level . . . It begins to be difficult not to feel that even if Eileen Gray had been much less competent as a de-signer, and had produced even less, she would still have been ripe for the treatment by now.

Banham's criticism was of the academicization of art history that had moved away from what he saw as the big issues, to the "nit-picking over minutiae." By the 1970s, it had become an "industry" which had "expanded far faster than its raw material . . . Art historians in some fields are compelled to sieve through material that has already been worked, more than once, in search of original topics for research." Banham recounted that "In the early fifties I, personally, was reckoned to be the only art-history student in London who intended to specialise in 20th century architecture."

However, there were some historians and publications that were deemed to have contributed to genuine revisionism. For example, what Donald Bush's "important and pioneering" *The Streamlined Decade* (1976) revealed was that, according to Banham,

. . . streamlining was not the opposite of European modern design but its logical con-tinuation . . . For, where the European modernists began to abandon those old Futurist mechanical analogies and engineering exegetics as soon as machinery ceased to re-semble their own preferred abstract style . . . the Big Streamliners of American design tried to stay with machinery into the new age when it had ceased to look like architec-ture on casters, and had begun to turn low, organic and curvaceous.[108]

This recalls the conclusion to *Theory and Design*, in which Banham had written about the shift in vehicle design and technology away from simple to streamlined forms. Banham also compared the American designer Walter Dorwin Teague with his European Modernist counterparts: "Teague, while not very struck with the Bauhaus, was more than just well-informed about Le Corbusier; he matches him [in his *Design This Day*] almost idea for idea and image for image (particularly about the Parthenon) as far as Le Corbusier goes. And then he goes on when Le Corbusier's nerve fails him as an *homme de l'ère machiniste.*" Yet it seems that Banham is not taking into account the difference in publication dates between *Vers une Architecture* and *Design This Day.* The seventeen-year gap—more, if one remembers that Le Corbusier's book comprises articles from *L'Esprit Nouveau*, which commenced in 1920—surely enables Teague's retrospection to move well beyond Le Corbusier's position. Banham is being more of a polemicist than a historian.

Banham celebrates the arrival of the "streamlined ships, the tear-drop cars, those classic trains like the Burlington Zephyr—and finally a whole streamlined future expounded in a series of exhibitions culminating in a *locus classicus* of Futurism if ever there was one, the New York World's Fair of 1939 with its 'Highways and Horizons,' 'Futurama,' 'Democracity,' 'Road of the Future,' its 'Rocketport.'" But the criticism arises that such manifestations are superficial—no more than theatrical effects to conjure up an updated image of "traditional" modernity. This was, of course, similar to the accusation leveled at Sant'Elia by Pevsner—Sant'Elia's "passion for the Great City was no more realistic than Gautier's for the metallic architecture or Turner's for steam and speed."[109] But Sant'Elia's imagery has the context of the "Manifesto" and the varied values of Modernism with the myriad relationships to other positions around the same time. To claim New York World's Fair as a locus classicus of Futurism, a quarter of a century after the "Manifesto of Futurist architecturè," is reducing an attitude of vitality and acceptance of change to a seductive sideshow image of futurology which lacks the depth and authenticity of the original vision.

Banham is presumably in favor of streamlining because it characterizes the "mechanical sensibility" and expresses a wholly positive attitude to

Ford Motor Company exhibit, New York World's Fair, 1939 (courtesy *The Architectural Review*)

technology. However, it would be hard to argue convincingly that it signifies a "profound reorientation towards a changed world." He admits
that "it might seem paradoxical that a style of ornament and sculptural
form claiming to derive from the further extremes of powered flight should
find its most satisfactory expression as the last livery of that most ponderous
of earthbound transports, the steam engine."[110] The paradox becomes a
contradiction if one returns to Banham's "Machine Aesthetic" article of
1955, in which he rails against "feeble intellects [who] 'adopt a modern
style.' . . . Such men are academics, since their . . . skin-deep modernism is
soon seen through."[111]

Even if one accepts that streamlining was originally justified functionally,
Banham admits that it became little more than a "whimsy for all of the second half of the decade, since it was in 1935 that Wunnibald Kamm demonstrated that pointed tails and long tear-drop forms are not significantly
better, aerodynamically, than forms with the flat back of a bread-van or

London bus." "Whimsy" was not a word Banham had used in connection with Modernists and their unwillingness to give up Classicism in the late 1920s. He goes so far as to claim that streamlining in the second half of the decade was "sustained less by aerodynamic science than by the spirit of the age"—another contradiction in his writing in which he readily dismissed the concept of the zeitgeist as nothing more than "a record of our ignorance of the communications that took place in any particular epoch."[112]

Nor, paradoxically, was streamlining a significant influence on architecture: Frank Lloyd Wright's offices for the Johnson Wax Company, "difficult to place in modern architecture as commonly understood precisely because they look so much like industrial design, find a natural place [in *The Streamlined Decade*] as the first (last?) masterpiece of the streamlined architecture." Buildings looking like items of industrial design seem a long way from those "masterpieces" discussed in *Theory and Design,* such as the Barcelona Pavilion and the Villa Savoye, which are "of the order of the Sainte Chapelle or the Villa Rotunda."[113]

In the end one suspects that Banham's review of *The Streamlined Decade,* even though its publication in the *Times Literary Supplement* should have meant otherwise, reveals Banham the polemicist and controversialist rather than Banham the historian or even Banham the historically informed theoretician. The praise of streamlining is too glib, the criticism too superficial in the light of his profound revisionism of the 1950s. One suspects, too, an element of Banham's wanting to *épater la bourgeoisie* (to coin one of his occasional phrases)—the bourgeoisie in this instance comprising the orthodox Modernist historians and critics who had dismissed streamlining as "bogus"[114] or "a source of danger and bondage,"[115] or eminent Modernist designers who had lambasted American designers such as Teague as "imitators who prostituted our fundamental precepts into modish trivialities."[116] Streamlining epitomized commercialism, and Banham's sympathy for it underlined his impatience with the earnestness and the moral high ground of European Modernism, as we will see in chapter 2.

The American Connection

A related issue which we will be discussing in due course is the impact of American values on theory (chapter 2), architecture (chapters 3, 4, and 5), and design (chapter 6). Within the context of the present chapter, the discussion of streamlining brings in an American perspective to Banham's revisionism of the Modern Movement. That perspective changed fundamentally after Banham began to visit the West Coast of the United States in the mid-1960s. For example, in 1967 he discovered the work of Rudolph Schindler, declaring that his architecture "has been an unsettling revelation, undermining . . . long-held preconceptions about the nature and history of the Modern Movement."[117] Praise is accorded the Lovell beach house of 1925–1926 because "it is so good; it is so early; and it is such a long way from the places where modern architecture is thought to have been happening at the time." It may have exemplified International Style principles, but "it is not European Modern in exile, it was the next step in California domestic."

But Schindler's key work for Banham is the Schindler/Clyde Chase house of 1921: "persistently ignored by the standard literature it remains one of the most original, and ingenious domestic designs of the present century."[118] Its spatial flow and relationship to regional climate and culture give the house an ease which, in Banham's opinion, could not be farther from the angst of European Modernism—Schindler's "pioneering without tears" shows that Modernism need not have been so anxious and so "Heroic."[119] Indeed, the "well-temperedness" of American Modernist architects (such as the Greene brothers, Charles and Henry, Irving Gill, and, of course Wright) and European "exiles" working in the United States (including Schindler and Richard Neutra) is praised in two texts which continue the revaluation of the American contribution: *The Architecture of the Well-tempered Environment* (1969) and *Los Angeles: The Architecture of Four Ecologies* (1971), both of which will be discussed in chapter 4.

A Concrete Atlantis

In his last major book, *A Concrete Atlantis: U.S. Industrial Building and European Modern Architecture,*[120] Banham returns to reassessing the influence on Europe of American industrial buildings such as the daylight factory and

Rudolf Schindler, Schindler/Chase house, Los Angeles, 1921

the grain silo. He moved to the United States in 1976 to take up a post at the State University of New York at Buffalo. The location enabled him to study at first hand many early twentieth-century industrial structures, not as an end "in their own right," as industrial archaeology, but—typically for Banham—so as to "argue that there is a causal, cultural, and conscious connection between such masterworks of explicit architectural modernism as the Cité de Refuge or the Villa Savoye and the utilitarian structures of a certain period and type of North American industry."[121] His argument (based on scrupulous research which was, in contrast to *Theory and Design,* comprehensively footnoted) was a fascinating one which posited that the influence of the American utilitarian structures operated on the level neither primarily of techniques of construction, nor of formal preference, nor even of functional appropriateness, but

. . . as a form of allegory. The appearance of industrial resemblances in nonindustrial buildings was construed . . . as a *promise* that these buildings would be as functionally honest, structurally economical and, above all, as up-to-the-minute as any of the American factories that Le Corbusier hailed as "the first fruits of the New Age." The forms of factories and grain elevators were an available iconography, a language of forms, whereby promises could be made, adherence to the modernist credo could be asserted, and the way pointed to some kind of technological utopia.[122]

The fact that these buildings existed—as actuality rather than as idea—made them, to Modernists, part of an Atlantis[123] rather than a Utopia. The Atlantis could, of course, have been considerably closer to home—Modernists could have chosen industrial buildings from Europe as their source—but the mythical associations of America for the pioneering generation—one thinks of the mythologizing by Loos and Le Corbusier in particular—conjured up a spellbinding concoction comprising the primitivism of noble savagery and the universalism of aesthetic essentialism. Banham rehearses the view that had Modernists studied the industrial buildings at first hand, they might have realized that they were solutions to functional problems whose form, furthermore, changed in relation not only to "new" materials but also to changing practices, both industrial and economic. An example he gives is the replacement of multistory factories by single-story structures at the Ford plant in Detroit.

Change brought about by increasing efficiency was so rapid that by the time the first Modernists elevated the elevators, they were "a doomed building type which . . . had already ceased to be modern enough to satisfy the needs of innovative American industry."[124] As it was, Modernist architects, ever influenced by form, mistook the appearance of structures determined by functional requirements and conditioned by economic considerations at a particular historical juncture, for a glimpse of the absolute which accorded with their aesthetic preferences for the Phileban solids—this was essentially the enduring argument Banham had offered in "Machine Aesthetic" thirty years earlier.

That firsthand knowledge would have changed their minds is probably unlikely, but the significance of the distant and remote sources "brings up a matter of extraordinary historical importance . . . insofar as the International Style was copied from American industrial prototypes and models, it must be the first architectural movement in the history of the art based almost exclusively on photographic evidence rather than on the ancient and previously unavoidable techniques of personal inspection and measured drawing."[125] The Modernists—often literally, sometimes metaphorically—rewrote the captions to the photographs, thereby changing the meaning of the structures. Their actual designers "had no ideological axes to grind, no revolutionary postures to maintain, even if they knew . . . that revolutions in industrial architecture had been wrought. Piecemeal, the dynamics of building in a market economy at a time of rapid technological advance would produce every aspect of an architectural revolution except the revolutionary intent."[126] That intent—the captions that appeared literally in publications such as *Vers une Architecture* as well as those which existed symbolically—was provided by the European Modernists. And the captions became ever more eulogistic: whereas for Gropius the industrial buildings "had been simply exemplars for a better modern industrial architecture, for Le Corbusier they had become—like the Tempietto of Bramante—exemplar. for all architecture, forever, much as the book is entitled simply 'Towards an Architecture.'"[127]

A Concrete Atlantis is Banham's final contribution to the reassessment of the Modern Movement. It was critically well received, and recommended by one reviewer "to anyone who enjoys good architectural writing in the tradition of Pevsner, Summerson, Ackerman and, of course, Banham himself"![128] The book's detailed research contributes to our knowledge of Modernism, not just at the scale of footnotes but also, as Banham would have it, at the scale of the canon: writing of the United Shoe Machinery plant in Beverly, Massachusetts—a building designed by Ernest Ransome and constructed between 1903 and 1906—he claims that "Its absence from the general literature on the history of modern architecture is a permanent reproach to scholarship, for even on the score of stylistic 'modernity,' let alone technical proficiency and inventiveness, it is the match for anything built anywhere in the world at that time"[129] by architects including Peter Behrens and Hans Poelzig. *A Concrete Atlantis* also makes the important contribution to our conceptual understanding of the Modern Movement in terms of the meaning for European architects of those elevators and silos, and the role they played in advancing and defining values and aesthetics. In the final chapter, "Modernism and Americanism," Banham discusses two major European buildings in order to assess the impact of American industrial building.

The first of these is the canonical Fagus factory by Gropius. The second makes for a fitting end to this chapter. The Fiat factory in Turin was begun in 1916 and construction continued for about ten years, although the main body of the building was effectively in place by 1920.[130] Banham is clear that it is "a factory in the American style. Its resemblances to the kind of regular Daylight factory discussed earlier in this book are as striking in small details as they are in its general structure or its large-scale composition; indeed, the very magnitude by which it exceeds in size any of the Fiat company's previous installations is part of its consciously American intentions—to rationalise production and to achieve 'the economies of scale.'"[131] But its plan is unlike Ford's factories, where, by 1920, single-story steel-framed facilities resulted in "a totally different conception of industrial building and organisation." Indeed, Banham considers that it most resembles Ransome's United Shoe Machinery plant (1903–1906) and "it would have looked equally antiquated to American eyes."[132] Just whose American eyes is one matter—perhaps Banham is making too much of a general awareness of a developmental progression in industrial architecture.

But, more important, Banham does not conjecture on reasons why the particular plan was adopted. There may have been good local reasons—economic, organizational, functional, technical—to adopt an "antiquated" plan, and Banham's assumption otherwise may be a further example of his progressivist tendencies. Surely the choice of plan—if not justified by specific local factors which militated against a more up-to-date option—resulted from the predictable time lag between innovative solutions in one place and their worldwide dissemination. Banham seems to entertain this explanation with some reluctance:

If one sees it simply as a derivative and provincial version of a manner of building whose metropolitan heartland was elsewhere, however, one must yet recognise that the vision

Albert Kahn and Edward Grey, Ford Old Shop, Highland Park, Detroit, 1908 (courtesy Mary Banham)

Ernest L. Ransome, United Shoe Machinery plant, Beverly, Mass., 1903–1906 (courtesy Mary Banham)

Giacomo Matté-Trucco et al., Fiat factory, Turin, 1914–1926 (courtesy Mary Banham)

of that distant heartland was still optimistic, futuristic, and utopian; and the choice of an American model for that envisioned future is a mark of what had changed, and how profoundly, not only in industrial architecture, but in the modernist view of architecture at large. Because it is the most literal-minded realisation of the European dream of the Concrete Atlantis, it is also the most poignant.[133]

Banham quotes at length from the reminiscences of Edoardo Persico, a young and highly regarded Italian designer who was persecuted by the Fascists and died in the 1930s. Persico sings the praises of the Fiat factory but also writes in more general terms about "how large a part an obsession with American culture must have played" in the Futurist manifesto of 1914 and how Sant'Elia "dreamed of New York."[134] For Banham, the Fiat factory is nothing less than "Europe's own talismanic American building and a very touchstone of modernity,"[135] and *A Concrete Atlantis* succeeds in helping us understand that the relationship between Americanism and Modernism was not primarily one of direct architectural influence—whether industrial buildings or Frank Lloyd Wright—but a more general and diffused association with modernity and progress. In being such, it is similar to the general association of American streamlining with modernity and progress in the 1930s.

It is hardly surprising that Marinetti praised the Fiat factory, not only as a symbol of the modernization of Italy but also as the "prime invention of Futurist construction."[136] The Futurist element is what, ultimately, makes the Fiat factory "a very touchstone of modernity": it is an element, Banham is assuredly right in suggesting, that "(perhaps all) American factory builders would have regarded as a piece of economic folly"[137]—the supposedly high-speed test track on the building's roof. The organization concept of the building is the reverse of the American "gravity-flow" sequence in which materials and components are delivered to the top of the building, and leave as finished products at the bottom. At the Fiat factory, the parts enter at the ground floor and the completed car emerges from the factory on to the test track for testing, before returning to the ground-level parking and storage yards. In practice the test track was seldom used: the plan of the building resulted in a long, thin, rectangular track with unrealistically sharp and steep bends at the ends that reduced speeds to suburban norms.

It may have been a failure at the functional level, but Banham proves the test track was an undoubted success in other ways. Emerging from the concrete spiral ramp onto the roof, and seeing it

. . . for the first time, as I did, through the windscreen of a moving car is a nerve-tingling experience. One is entering one of the sacred places of European modernism, sanctified and certified by the photographically documented presence of practically every European Futurist, modernist, or other progressive spirit of note throughout the twenties and early thirties. And the shock of recognition is reinforced by the fact that it still looks exactly as it did in those historic photographs.[138]

Here, Americanism, modernity, progressivism, and speed combine to make the Fiat factory a compelling symbol of the First Machine Age and the "mechanical sensibility," even if the "profound reorientation towards a changed world" occurs more at a symbolic and experiential, rather than a functional, level.

It is significant to the present study, and in particular this chapter, that Banham records his personal response to visiting the factory: "It was a strangely disturbing and moving experience for me, a kind of historian's homecoming for one partially Americanised European whose prime subject of study has been the International Style."[139] For it reminds us that Banham's emotional home in the Modern Movement was Futurism, and that his last major contribution to the revaluation and revision of the Modern Movement ends with a discussion—even a celebration—of a symbolically Futurist building which he had originally discussed nearly thirty years earlier without changing his mind about it.[140] Nor did he discover any reason to lose faith in his judgment, made in "Machine Aesthetic" in 1955, that the First Machine Age created some "magnificent architecture." However, in the same article, he declares the need to "salute its grave" and not be "sentimental over its passing." For what concerned him increasingly during his research into the Modern Movement was the implications for architecture and design in his own times—the Second Machine Age.

ROUGH POETRY

-rutalism, and Architecture Autre

2
POPULAR DESIRES AND ROUGH POETRY
The Independent Group, New Brutalism, and *Architecture Autre*

Banham's revision of the Modern Movement fulfilled two functions. First—as we saw in chapter 1—it was historically necessary to redress "selective and classicising" biases and, second, it was a means to an end of providing an intellectual framework for living in contemporary society—for living life to the full in the Second Machine Age. However, the intellectual framework that Banham sought did not derive exclusively from an examination of the Modern Movement: it also derived from the conditions and experience of contemporary culture, both popular and esoteric. His own enthusiasm for popular culture and technology, as well as his enthusiasm for some aspects of avant garde culture, principally *art autre,* were shared by others associated with the Independent Group, a small, occasional, and informal gathering of individuals—the number at any one meeting seldom exceeded twenty—who strove to establish a basis for understanding the conditions and values of the changing culture in which they were not only existing, but happily immersed.

This chapter is not going to trace the history of the Independent Group in great detail—that has been done more than adequately in other recently published books[1]—but will start by examining the Group's activities, including their interest in contemporary American popular culture, and the implications of their ideas for cultural theory in the Second Machine Age. It then goes on to discuss one of the key cultural values that emerged and was taken up by Banham: the characteristics and role of obsolescence and an "aesthetic of expendability." He was fully aware that expendability had major cultural ramifications and might even form an alternative theory and vision of design. Banham also identified a second radical alternative in the writings and architecture of Peter and Alison Smithson, whose work included both New Brutalist architecture and Pop-influenced design. This chapter will examine those alternatives, the relationships between them, and Banham's debt to the Independent Group.

The Independent Group

In recent years the Independent Group (IG) has been critically reassessed. From the early 1960s it had been cast as the beginning of Pop art: indeed, some of the members had cast themselves—in the title of a 1979 film about the Group—as the "Fathers of Pop."[2] In addition to giving the Group's activities a fine art emphasis and significance which is not historically accurate—fine art was merely one of their interests—it reduces the Group's sphere of influence to Pop and pop culture, whereas it was, as we shall see, far more inclusive. The Group comprised different tendencies which sometimes coalesced but, at other times, contradicted or just coexisted. Its inclusiveness also militated against a common IG position, and one must be wary retrospectively of attributing a consistent or coherent IG viewpoint to any activity. Indeed, to use the term "Independent Group" can be to imply not only a coherent position but also a sense of identity and group dynamic and awareness that were not necessarily felt at the time by those directly involved in its activities, but which certain individuals, including Banham, may have attributed with hindsight, which may have emerged through selective memory, or which may have been invented to serve historical mythmaking and a jockeying for position.[3]

The Group did not commence with a manifesto and clear position, but emerged slowly and informally from its host institution, the Institute of Contemporary Art (ICA). The choice of name was relatively fortuitous, having been selected practically and pragmatically rather than self-consciously and ideologically,[4] but it was entirely appropriate because it signified an independence from the ICA's view of art, which, at that time, was enmeshed in prewar Modernist formal values of aesthetic universality, timelessness, and transcendence. The ICA neither welcomed nor valued the radical experimentation and innovation of Abstract Expressionist action painting or *Tachisme,* and other forms of *art autre.* The refined and uncompromising position was personified by the Modernist theorist and writer Herbert Read, then president of the Institute. Richard Hamilton remarked that "if there was one binding spirit amongst the people at the Independent Group, it was a distaste for Herbert Read's attitudes."[5] Lawrence Alloway, during the IG era a visiting lecturer at the Tate Gallery and the Courtauld Institute, and from 1955 assistant director of the ICA, added that Read was disliked less for his actual theory of art than for the terms in which he discussed it. Read subscribed to conventional Modernist beliefs about the artist as a leader in society, the "antennae of the race," seeking higher-order eternal truths and transcendent forms, and dismissing mundane daily existence.

Hamilton and Alloway both admitted to a certain embarrassment on a personal level about attacking Read, who remained encouraging to members of the Group, but, as Alloway explained, there was no one else to attack at the time—no one else in Britain so thoroughly represented entrenched Modernist values and attitudes. As Banham himself remarked retrospectively, his generation had "grown up under the marble shadow of Sir Herbert Read's Abstract-Left-Freudian aesthetics and suddenly, about 1952, [were] on strike against it."[6] This meant that "We were against direct carving, pure form, truth, beauty and all that . . . what we favoured was motion studies. We also favoured rough surfaces, human images, space, machinery, ignoble materials and what we termed non-art (there was a project to bury Sir Herbert under a book entitled *Non-Art Not Now*)"—an anti-art antidote to Read's *Art Now* (1933), which had been revised in 1948.

The IG's strike against established values commenced in the spring of 1952 with three sessions, with admission by invitation to about a dozen people only, at the ICA, then in Dover Street in London. The first talk of the season was by the sculptor Eduardo Paolozzi, who used an epidiascope to project a large collection of photographs and advertisements culled from American popular magazines. No single image was important: what mattered was the rapid turnover and random juxtaposition of images of science fact and fiction, car advertisements, robots, food—consumer goods which created the impression of a time-based collage. The significance for Banham was the "imageability"—a word to which we shall return—and the non- or even anti-high art sources that derived from European avant garde *art autre*—a concept to which we also shall return. It was followed in the series by a talk by the philosopher A. J. Ayer on logical positivism, and the third session was a discussion of the work of the American kinetic artist Edward Hoppe.

The IG recommenced in the autumn of 1952, still with admission by invitation. Banham became the convenor and gave the sessions a science and technology focus up to the end of the series in June 1953. Some members of the Group, notably Banham himself, shared considerable technological experience through their previous work or wartime experiences, but various experts were invited to lecture on more specialized topics, such as "The Helicopter as an Example of Technical Development" and "Are Proteins Unique?" The philosophical anti-idealism introduced by Ayer was continued with a discussion titled "Were the Dadaists non-Aristotelian?" It was argued that the Dadaists subverted normal hierarchical forms of categorization by recontextualizing or reordering objects in new relationships, an idea influenced by A. E. van Vogt's 1948 *The World of Null-A*—"Null-A" meaning non-Aristotelian—which had recently been serialized in *Astonishing Science Fiction.* Banham contributed a talk that was part of his ongoing revision of the Modern Movement—a version of it was published in 1955 as his "Machine Aesthetic."

In 1953 there was no series of IG talks but some members worked on the "Parallel of Life and Art" exhibition at the ICA. The principal impetus for the exhibition came from the architects Alison and Peter Smithson, Paolozzi, and the photographer Nigel Henderson. Together, in 1952, they had realized they shared an enthusiasm for *art autre* and its sources, such as graffiti. "Parallel of Life and Art" contained 122 large, grainy-textured photographs of machines, slow-motion studies, X-rays, materials under stress, primitive architecture, children's art, plant anatomy, and other miscellaneous images which flouted conventional standards of formal order, beauty, and meaning—the only "high art" image permitted was a photograph of Jackson Pollock working on a painting. The criterion of selection was, again, "image-ability" and emotional impact. The photographs—extremely varied in size and scale—were hung environmentally from walls, ceiling, and floor. Organization was assiduously nonhierarchic and anti-formal, something which offended the sensibilities of many visitors. Two years after the exhibition, Banham recalled how critics had "complained of the deliberate flouting of the traditional concepts of photographic beauty, of a cult of ugliness . . . 'denying the spiritual in Man.'"[7] "Parallel of Life and Art" marked the public surfacing of the anti-art aesthetic associated with a strand of the IG.

Also in 1953 and continuing into 1954, to counter accusations of exclusiveness, the ICA organized a series of seminars, open to subscribers, entitled "Aesthetic Problems of Contemporary Art," chaired by the art critic Robert Melville.[8] Banham was convenor and presented the first topic, "the impact of technology." It drew on his Modernist revisionism[9] and explored the "technological approach . . . as a characteristic mental attitude of the mid-century; its effect on the subject matter of art through the mechanisation of the environment, and on the status of the work of art itself, through the growth of techniques of mass reproduction."[10] In addition to Banham's Walter Benjamin-like topic, radical and avant-garde subjects were covered, including "new sources of form," "new concepts of space," "mythology and psychology," and "non-formal painting," in which Toni del Renzio welcomed the "abolition of classical ideas of a closed pictorial composition."[11] The seminars served to emphasize the theoretical and attitudinal differences between the ICA's mainstream, formally oriented Modernism and the younger generation's interests and concerns with an art which was often anti-classical and, in conventional ways, anti-aesthetic.

The seminars also served to draw into IG circles people such as the artist and futurologist John McHale, Lawrence Alloway, and the Cordells, musical

"Parallel of Life and Art," ICA, London, 1953 (courtesy Peter Smithson)

producer Frank and artist Magda. These new recruits became stalwarts of the second and final series of IG meetings which took place from February to July 1955. Alison and Peter Smithson also attended the second series regularly, introduced to the meetings by Paolozzi and Henderson with whom they had collaborated on "Parallel of Life and Art." Banham's commitments to his doctorate caused him to turn over the convening to McHale and Alloway, both of whom had attended the end of the first series of IG lectures. McHale recalls that he was enthusiastic about the Group's attitude to what he then called "demolishing history," but which would now be more accurately termed "deconstruction."[12]

There were two significant changes in the second series. First, the emphasis shifted from technology to communications, art, and American popular culture. Second, the meetings—which averaged seventeen attenders—relied less on external speakers and more on internal speakers or group discussion. The two lectures by external speakers were on probability and

"Man, Machine and Motion," Newcastle, 1955 (courtesy Richard Hamilton)

information theory, and aesthetics and Italian product design. The "internal" sessions included Richard Hamilton's new paintings, which made use of the sort of serial imagery normally associated with popular culture (main speakers included Hamilton, McHale, Banham, and Alloway); American advertisements "with reference to the interplay of technology and social symbolism" (Peter Smithson, Paolozzi, McHale, and Alloway); "intensive, multi-layered analysis of one advertisement as exemplar of descriptive method with 'performance as referent'" (Alloway, McHale, Paolozzi, and del Renzio); fashion and fashion magazines (del Renzio); and "commercial music in its producer-consumer relationships" (Frank Cordell). Banham lectured on the symbolism of Detroit car styling, titling it "Borax, or the Thousand Horsepower Mink." The remaining session returned to a theme from the first series: "Dadaists as non-Aristotelians," analyzing postwar "anti-absolutist and multi-valued" tendencies which "connect Dada with the non-Aristotelian logic of provisional possibilities."[13]

The IG ceased to exist at the end of the lecture series in July 1955, but the ideas it gave rise to were already having a practical, as well as a theoretical, effect. Two exhibitions reveal particularly strong IG influences. Richard Hamilton devised and designed "Man, Machine and Motion," which overlapped with part of the second Group lecture series. Hamilton has described the exhibition as "a survey of appliances invented by man to overcome the limits imposed on them by the physical attributes provided by nature,"[14] and the two hundred large photographs, hung environmentally, also had something of the "Parallel of Life and Art's" direct emotional impact and evocative appeal. Banham contributed the catalogue notes.[15]

The second exhibition—to which we will return—is the celebrated "This Is Tomorrow," held at the Whitechapel Art Gallery in 1956. Twelve groups, each of three members—notionally a painter, a sculptor, and an architect— were formed, and each presented an environmental exhibit relating to the title and theme of the exhibition. Some of the exhibits were unambiguously Modernist in their integration of architecture, sculpture, and painting as abstract environmental form, but with a third of the participants IG regulars— including Hamilton, McHale, Alloway, Paolozzi, the Smithsons, Henderson, and del Renzio—and with Alloway and Banham on the organizing committee and contributing catalog essays, alternative visions and ideas were on offer, and reflected a range of IG interests.

Thus the character of the IG's topics and activities was diverse and varied, and cannot be simplified to a common focus—such as popular culture— without a loss of historical accuracy. There were some discernible tendencies in the Group, based around individuals. The Smithsons, Henderson, and Paolozzi were especially sympathetic to any *art brut* and "outsider" tendencies; and McHale, del Renzio, Hamilton, and Alloway, augmented by the Cordells, favored communication studies. However, the movement between groupings was fluid, and another grouping around popular culture and advertisements included Peter Smithson, Alloway, Hamilton, McHale, del Renzio, and Banham. A further grouping was those interested in cultural theory—Alloway, Banham, McHale, and Hamilton—whom Alison Smithson termed the "grey men," implying the groupings were not without an element of suspicion and even friction.[16] However, the friction may have been a form of what Alloway described as "antagonistic cooperation"[17] that, alongside the genuine co-operation, resulted in the variety which was one of the most significant achievements of the Group. The diversity and inclusiveness of interests not only undermined conventional high/low culture hierarchies, but also opened up interconnections and relationships which might not have arisen had the focus been more clearly defined or the scope delimited.

Taking into account Banham's contemporaneous Modern Movement revisionism, it becomes clear that the IG discussions and activities provided both stimulation and an opening out of topics, and a set of radical or lateral viewpoints which Banham could absorb into his thinking and, when appropriate, apply to his architectural subjects. For example, in 1958 Banham wrote about science fiction and architecture, describing the changing character of recent science fiction toward the "sociological and anthropological," and the ways in which architects would benefit from coming to terms with—and enjoying—science fiction as a spur to "imaginative technology."[18]

Other IG topics and approaches reappear in Banham's writings. In a 1955 article, science fiction is related to industrial design through an investigation of concepts of "space," which, in the case of science and science fiction, "is a product of the break in the scientific tradition at the beginning of this century, and is thus new, as well as essentially curved, polydimensional and limitless," as opposed to the space associated with Cubism and the fine arts, which is "essentially rectangular, three-dimensional and limited—it is the space between flat planes."[19]

Popular Culture—"Pop"

Members of the IG thought popular culture ought to be studied because of its impact on people's lives. As Banham put it, "When something is so largely consumed with such enthusiasm and such passion as many aspects of pop culture are, then I don't think any social critic in his right mind should simply reject it as being a load of rubbish or even the opium of the people."[20] But more important than the fact of studying popular culture was the ways in which the Group presented and discussed it. Rather than appearing in a dry, dispassionate, academic format, topics were debated enthusiastically and with passion, revealing them to be live interests and pet subjects. Popular culture—which was referred to in IG circles in the 1950s as "Pop" or "pop"[21]—was not discussed just as a social phenomenon but as pleasure. Alloway recalls, probably accurately, albeit from the "mythmaking" stage, that members

. . . had in common a vernacular culture that persisted beyond any special interest or skills in art, architecture, design, or art criticism that any of us might possess. The area of contact was mass-produced urban culture: movies, advertising, science-fiction, Pop music. We felt none of the dislike of commercial culture standards amongst most intellectuals, but accepted it as fact, discussed it in detail, and consumed it enthusiastically. One result of our discussion was to take Pop culture out of the realm of "escapism," "sheer entertainment," "relaxation" and to treat it with the seriousness of art.[22]

One of the most convincing examples of Alloway's claim is Banham's lecture on Detroit car styling, which was reworked as an article and published in 1955. "Vehicles of Desire" typifies the IG tone of enthusiasm and provocation. As a polemic and argument it is undoubtedly serious, but it is far from earnest in its style, as the opening paragraph demonstrates:

Cadillac, early 1950s (courtesy Mary Banham)

The New Brutalists, pace-makers and phrase-makers of the Anti-Academic line-up, having delivered a smart KO to the Land-Rover some months back, have now followed it with a pop-eyed OK for the Cadillac convertible, and automobile aesthetics are back on the table for the first time since the 'Twenties. The next time an open Caddy wambles past you, its front chrome-hung like a pearl-roped dowager, its long top level with the ground at a steady thirty inches save where the two tail-fins cock up to carry the rear lights, reflect what a change has been wrought since the last time any architect expressed himself forcibly on the subject of the automobile.[23]

That "Vehicles of Desire" closely followed "Machine Aesthetic" into print comes as no surprise because some of the former's "seriousness" derives from the substantive intellectual points of the latter. But Banham shifts the argument to deal with the car as an object *of* and *in* popular culture:

Far from being *uomini universali* architects are by training, aesthetics and psychological predisposition narrowly committed to the design of big permanent single structures, and their efforts are directed merely to focusing big, permanent human values on unrepeatable works of unique art. The automobile is not big—few are even mantelpiece high—it is not permanent—the average world scrapping period has lately risen, repeat risen, to fifteen years—and they certainly are not unique.

This relocates the car away from the architectural paradigm with its traditional values and hierarchies, to the consumerist, private-affluence paradigm of popular culture, in which impact and sales appeal are key values. The car ceases to be seen as an offshoot of architectural "good form" and becomes

. . . an expendable, replaceable vehicle of popular desires [which] clearly belongs with the other dreams that money can buy, with *Galaxy, The Seven Year Itch, Rock Rattle 'n' Roll* and *Midweek Reville,* the world of expendable art. . . . The motor car is not as expendable as they are, but it clearly belongs nearer to them than to the Parthenon, and it exhibits the same creative thumb-prints—finish, fantasy, punch, professionalism, swagger. A good job of body styling should come across like a good musical—no fussing after big, timeless abstract virtues, but maximum glitter and maximum impact.

Banham then goes on to discuss the role of body stylists, presenting their work as significant and serious (but certainly not earnest), and as something very far from the "escapism," "sheer entertainment," and "relaxation" that Alloway complained was popular culture's given status:

The top body stylists . . . aim to give their creations qualities of apparent speed, power, brutalism, luxury, snob-appeal, exoticism and plain common-or-garden sex. The means at their disposal are symbolic iconographies, whose ultimate power lies in their firm grounding in popular taste and the innate traditions of the product, while the actual symbols are drawn from Science Fiction, movies, earth-moving equipment, supersonic aircraft, racing cars, heraldry and certain deep-seated mental dispositions about the great outdoors and the kinship between technology and sex. Arbiter and interpreter between the industry and the consumer, the body stylist deploys, not a farrago of meaningless ornament, as fine art critics insist, but a means of saying something of breathless, but unverbalisable, consequence to the live culture of the Technological Century.

Terms such as "symbolic iconographies," and "innate traditions," and the discussion in terms of sources, expression, symbolism, iconography and iconology, make Banham's text, once one disregards the content, seem like an academic art historical discourse which undoubtedly treats its subject with—in Alloway's words—"the seriousness of art."

The seriousness of treatment had come about for intellectual reasons; the enthusiasm for the subject matter was part of some of the Group members' backgrounds. Banham explained that they were

. . . all brought up in the Pop belt somewhere. American films and magazines were the only live culture we knew as kids—I have a crystal clear memory of myself, aged sixteen [1938] reading a copy of *Fantastic Stories* while waiting to go on in the school play, which was Fielding's *Tom Thumb the Great,* and deriving equal pleasure from the *recherché* literature I should shortly be performing, and the equally far out pulp in my mind. We returned to Pop in the early 'fifties like Behans going to Dublin or Thomases to Llaregub, back to our native literature, our native arts.[24]

Alloway expressed much the same sentiments, pointing out that "the mass media were established as a natural environment by the time we could see them."[25] The immersion in popular culture was, up to a point, genuine—many of the IG members had backgrounds that were not typical of academics or professionals. Banham had left school early to go into engineering; Richard Hamilton trained as an engineering draftsman and worked as a jig and tool draftsman; and Eduardo Paolozzi, Edinburgh-born, came from an Italian family who sold ice cream. However, a comment by Banham in *Fathers of Pop* that they were "a rough lot" is not wholly accurate, and mythologizes the social makeup of the Group. Nigel Henderson came from a privileged, Bloomsbury background with many European artistic connections; Del Renzio, born in Russia and educated in England and Switzerland, studied mathematics and philosophy at Columbia University and the University of Bologna; the backgrounds of the Smithsons could in no way be described as working-class, let alone "rough."

This did not mean that their enthusiasm for popular culture was contrived or condescending, although conventional "high culture" critics found this hard to comprehend. The art critic Basil Taylor's jibe that those associated with the IG were destined to "inevitable failure" because they were "trying to deal in a sophisticated way with material that is either, like folk art, unsophisticated or like the products of the mass media of a different order of sophistication,"[26] was passionately rejected as symptomatic of those who become, in Banham's memorable phrase, "isolated from humanity by the Humanities."[27] It was the "different level of sophistication" that more than worried many cultural commentators. Richard Hoggart, in *The Uses of Literacy* (1957), expressed the feelings of many British intellectuals about the Americanized mass media fare that seemed to be sweeping the country: "Most mass-entertainments . . . are full of a corrupt brightness, of improper appeals and moral evasions . . . they tend towards a view of the world in which progress is conceived as a seeking of material possessions . . . and freedom as the ground for endless irresponsible pleasure."[28] He argued that the new mass entertainments made no demands on their audience, provided nothing which taxed the brain or heart. In so doing, they replaced "the more positive, the fuller, the more co-operative kinds of enjoyment, in which one gains much by giving much."

Hoggart's thesis was that universal literacy had been sold short—his book was intended to be titled *The Abuses of Literacy*—with commercially oriented media appealing to the lowest common denominator replacing the supposedly wholesome fare that guaranteed civilized cultural norms and standards. He also viewed the mass media as eroding traditional working-class culture, with healthy diversity being replaced by bland uniformity: "The old forms of class culture are in danger of being replaced by a poorer kind of classless, or by what I was led earlier to describe as a "faceless" culture, and this is to be regretted."[29] As far as Hoggart was concerned, not to take a resolute stand against the new culture was to allow "cultural developments as dangerous in their own way as those we are shocked at in totalitarian societies."[30]

There were two substantive claims here about American popular culture: that it is exploitative, and that it lessens—indeed, undermines—democracy. Banham's defense of these attacks came primarily in the early 1960s rather than the later 1950s, when his main thrust was developing a theory of pop design. In a 1963 public lecture, he looked at his background and growing interest in popular culture, acknowledged that exploitation existed in popular culture, but denied this invalidated it: "That there is commercial exploitation in pop culture nobody in his right mind would deny, but there has to be something else underneath, some sub-stratum of genuine feeling, a genuine desire for the thing, which has to be touched off before the market will really move."[31] He went so far as to claim that, far from it all being a case of crass commercialism and exploitation, "There is a great deal of evidence available to suggest that whatever the intentions of the entertainment industry, the public is not being, and apparently *cannot* be, manipulated to that extent."[32]

The "great deal" of evidence was not cited, but an anecdote about the success of the Twist and the failure of the Madison dances was used as "evidence to show that the Twist stands for something real which might have happened even without commercial exploitation."[33] Just what it was that was "real" or not "real" was not discussed, and so Banham's case remained a belief and assertion rather than a demonstration. How he would have explained the success of a manufactured group such as the Monkees is not apparent. Banham suspected that part of the motivation for the attacks on popular culture were to do with taste and class, and had political connotations. In a 1963 piece, "A Flourish of Symbols," he analyzes some current transistor radios, acknowledging that they are both

. . . flashy and vulgar without being coarsely detailed—a radically new situation this, which raises the question whether *flashy* and *vulgar* are quite the terms of abuse they used to be when deprived of coarseness. Flashy a lot of this stuff has to be because its economic life depends in its impact on the public eye at a very competitive point of sale; vulgar it has to be because it is designed for the *vulgus,* the common crowd (including you and me) who are the final arbiters of everything in the pure theory of democracy.[34]

Hoggart would have agreed with Banham on the reasons for a product's flashiness—determined by the economic system—but would doubtless have thought this grounds for changing the economic system. As regards vulgarity, Banham slides from pejorative "vulgar" to the more neutral "vulgus" in order to make a point about taste and democracy. It was an attack on those who set themselves up as "guardians of culture" and who professed to "know better" than the common crowd. He deplored the paternalism of these guardians whose "concept of good design as a form of aesthetic charity done on the labouring poor from a great height is incompatible with democracy as I see it."[35] However, his argument has the weaknesses of any populist position, and certainly would not accord with his professed left-wing political affiliations on a range of matters from the Cold War to capital punishment.

Banham concluded that "If you want Pop design to be tasteful and beautiful instead of flashy and vulgar, you must envisage a drastic and illiberal reconstruction of society."[36] He is here equating consumer capitalism with democracy and implicitly rejecting not only the command economy of the Eastern bloc and the utopianism of the Arts and Crafts idealists, but even what he denigrates as the "sort of Hoggart-ish 'spontaneity'" associated with the supposed "authenticity" of folk art.[37] Alloway had made much the same point about diversity and choice: "It is not the hand-crafted culture which offers a wide range of choice of goods and services to everybody . . . but the industrialised one . . . As the market gets bigger consumer choice increases: shopping in London is more diverse than in Rome; shopping in New York more diverse than in London. General Motors mass-produce cars according to individual selections of extras and colours."[38]

This argument ignored criticisms about the illusory freedom of capitalist choice and the market, and disregarded the danger of monopolistic power. Diversity and choice were positive symptoms of the new popular culture, as far as Group members were concerned. One of the points of conflict arose from the use of emotive words such as "mass" and "depersonalisation," which are associated with an undifferentiated and bland fare. Hoggart had argued that the mass media make people uniform, and offer an inauthentic "kind of palliness" which involves a high degree of "passive acceptance" on the part of the audience.[39] But IG members retorted that once the mass media were scrutinized carefully, the "mass" fragmented into innumerable specialized interests that facilitate individuality and choice. "The audience today," Alloway stated, "is numerically dense but highly specialised . . . by age, sex, hobby, occupation, mobility, contacts etc."[40] Within a genre there were different emphases: for example, McHale differentiated between *Astounding Science Fiction,* which was aimed at scientifically and technically minded readers, and *Galaxy Science Fiction,* which tended toward a dramatic storyline.[41]

Diversity and choice were also positive symptoms, in that they represented a more active and critical audience. Alloway admitted that whereas once it may have been true that popular culture was passively consumed for escapism and relaxation, "Now leisure occupations, reading, music, movie-going, dressing are brought up into the same dimensions of skills as work which once stood alone as a serious activity."[42] Banham believed that there was now no such thing as an "unsophisticated consumer," because "All consumers are experts, have back-stage knowledge of something or other, be it the record charts or the correct valve timing for doing the ton."[43] The new audience was characterized by what both Alloway and Banham described as "knowing consumers"[44]—sophisticated consumers who were not blindly manipulated but were able to "read" and understand the symbols of their culture. The popular culture generated by consumer capitalism was, IG members claimed, enhancing democracy, not undermining it. At the turn of the 1960s, Banham was confidently claiming that "One of the things we learned in the 'fifties was that it was possible to construct a morally and democratically justifiable philosophy of design on a consumer oriented basis."[45] Others were less convinced, and interpreted the IG's ideas as a naive enthusiasm for things American.

The Fear of Americanization

Lurking behind the fear of the collapse of high culture was an antagonism to the United States, which represented, to many critics in Britain (and Europe), extreme cultural degeneracy and the decay of civilized values. When recalling the realization of how IG members had taken popular culture out of the realm of escapism and sheer entertainment, Alloway went on to conclude that "These interests put us in opposition . . . to the anti-American opinion in Britain."[46] The opposition was not exaggerated. The overwhelming majority of British intellectuals in the 1950s—whether on the Left or the Right—were hostile to what they interpreted as the Americanization of society. The new popular culture *was* American culture. Hollywood movies, Tin Pan Alley tunes and rock 'n' roll, commercial television, glossy magazines, and consumer goods were dismissed as symptoms of moral decay, material greed, or cultural degeneration.

The issue of the culture's Americanness was taken up by IG members. Alloway and Banham both asserted that it was not its being American that gave it its appeal. As Alloway put it, "It is not a nostalgia for the US. It is simply that American pop art is a maximum development of a form of communication that is common to all urban people. British pop art is the product of less money, less research, less talent, and it shows."[47] As the wealthiest and technically most advanced country, the United States produced the most sophisticated and professional popular culture. For Banham, the contrast with British indigenous culture was not only quantitative but qualitative: he was full of appreciation for the "gusto and professionalism of wide-screen movies or Detroit car styling [which] was a constant reproach to the Moore-ish yokelry of British sculpture or the affected Piperish gloom of British painting."[48]

Nevertheless, the IG were to some extent romanticizing the United States and its popular culture because of its distance and exoticness—by 1958 only John McHale of the Alloway/Banham tendency of the Group had actually been there. The United States, as it had been during and since the Second World War, was the land of opulence and glamour to those suffering the nutritional deprivations of rationing and the sensory deprivations of British cultural austerity. It was seen not only by the IG but also by the British public at large as the hyperreality of the imagery of Hollywood and Madison Avenue. The accusations of romanticization must have rankled, because Alloway unconvincingly wondered why it should be that he (as representative of the IG) had "lost more by my taste for the American mass media (which are better than anyone else's) than have those older writers who look to the Mediterranean as the 'cradle of civilisation.'"[49]

The cultural embeddedness of values and the role of tradition did not seem to feature significantly in IG thinking at times. More convincing was Alloway's judgment that "We are (a) far enough away from Madison Avenue and Hollywood not to feel threatened (as American intellectuals often do), and (b) near enough (owing to language similarity and consumption rates) to have no ideological block against the content of US popular culture."[50] Apart from being something of an admission of romanticization, it is also a declaration of ideological sympathy which is at the core of the clash between cultural critics such as Hoggart and Raymond Williams (and even Read), and the IG.

For Banham there was a real political dilemma. In the late 1960s he recalled the problem that members of the Group had experienced in reconciling their "admiration for the immense competence, resourcefulness and creative power of American commercial design with the equally unavoidable disgust at the system that was producing it."[51] This was because "we had this American leaning and yet most of us are in some way Left-orientated, even protest-orientated."[52] It seemed to the IG that if one was going to try to understand popular culture as a serious (and even positive) phenomenon, it followed that it was necessary to suspend disbelief about (and distaste for) the underlying political, social, and economic system in order to evaluate the cultural manifestations critically. Others would have found that suspension impossible, either because the two were so representative of the same values, or because the political was seen as the direct cause of the cultural.

The criticism that, to some extent, can be leveled fairly at both the Group and commentators such as Hoggart is that their judgments were determined by, at best, special pleading and, at worst, prejudice. In 1963 Banham admitted that when he and sympathetic colleagues referred to the mass media, "we are not talking about the whole spread of mass communications but a very restricted section of a spectrum."[53] The IG focused on "progressive" popular culture—car styling, science fiction, fashion, graphics, and movies—which reflected technological and cultural change and prepared its consumers for the "technological and fast-moving culture" by affecting "attitude-forming channels" in a constructive and critical way.[54] Such popular culture was not necessarily typical, however, and the IG would have found it difficult, if not impossible, to make the same claims for conservative or reactionary popular culture, such as television soap operas, cottage-style furniture, and romantic novels. Scrutinize American popular culture, the IG claimed, and it reveals critical sophistication and healthy diversity. Scrutinise American popular culture, Hoggart claimed, and all you find is a "uniform international type" of fare.[55] Of course it partly depends on the particular popular culture that is scrutinized, and also on the value assumptions—aesthetic, cultural, and political—that are brought to it by an individual.

The popular culture studied by the IG was certainly not typical of popular culture in Britain in the early to mid 1950s, but nor would they be likely to make that claim. It is more likely they would argue that the culture they were studying was symptomatic of the new, sophisticated, and knowing American popular culture which was *replacing* the old, passive version. History has not proved this to be the case, and such a belief reveals more about the IG's progressivist attitude than it does about any change in the nature and characteristics of popular culture. Hoggart and other conservative cultural critics may have mythologized and romanticized working-class values and lifestyles, but the IG mythologized and romanticized American popular culture. However, the significance of the IG is not diminished, for historically, theirs was an intervention which was necessary in order to counter the prejudice and complacency of British cultural orthodoxy with its rigid distinctions between high and low and unchallenged assumptions about value.

Cultural Hierarchies and Continuums

The implications of the IG's concerns with popular culture went beyond a shift of attitude, and raised major questions about cultural value. It followed that "high culture" critics "no longer possess the power to dominate all aspects of art," wrote Alloway. "It is impossible to see [the mass media] clearly within a code of aesthetics associated with pastoral and upper class ideas because mass art is urban and democratic."[56] It was no use judging Elvis Presley by the standards of conventional classical music. Nor, the IG implied, should one judge a pastoral symphony by the standards of rock 'n' roll. With a commitment to absolute, transhistorical, and timeless standards and pure form, a Modernist such as Herbert Read would reject popular culture as unworthy even of consideration. Indeed, in the revised edition of *Art and Industry,* published in 1956, Read bemoaned the new interest in popular culture and asked whether it was

. . . really necessary to make a virtue out of this vulgar necessity? Such, however, is the affirmation of certain critics, who decry the Purists and traditionalists, and would have the artist and the industrial designer accept the taste of the masses as the expression of a new aesthetic, an art of the people. The supermarket and the bargain basement replace the museums and art galleries as repositories of taste, and any ideals of beauty or truth, refinement or restraint, are dismissed, in the language of the tribe, as "square."[57]

A cultural critic like Hoggart was more sympathetic to popular culture so long as it was "authentic" and grew out of working-class customs and mores. However, he not only rejected American popular culture but, of more significance here, believed that "authentic" popular culture could be relatively good only "of its type," and that even the best was never the equal of high culture. In other words, Hoggart, in the orthodox manner be-fore the IG deliberations, envisioned a rigid hierarchical distinction between high and popular culture. Popular culture might have values which were germane to it, but they were intrinsically lesser than the values of high cul-ture. In orthodox discourses, "high" and "popular" equated with "supe-rior" and "inferior" even if there were distinctions of "better" and "worse" within each self-contained and mutually exclusive category.

Not surprisingly, neither of these models was acceptable to the IG. Both Read's and Hoggart's models conformed to the pyramidal structure of "high culture" at the top and "popular" at the bottom: "high" was serious, durable, and worthwhile; "popular" was escapist, expendable, and there-fore of little or no value. As John McHale put it, "Historically, in the West, the fine arts have been those channels of communication, painting, sculp-ture, literature, music and drama, which served, and were maintained, by an elite topping a vertical hierarchy. Cultural belief and dogma supplied the absolutes, 'eternal beauty,' 'universal truth,' etc., which accreted into the classical canons by which the arts were judged."[58]

The radical implication of IG thinking was a rejection of the pyramidal structure and rigid hierarchy, to be replaced by a new definition of, and ap-proach to, culture. Alloway argued in 1959 that "acceptance of the mass me-dia entails a shift in our notion of what culture is. Instead of reserving the word for the highest artefacts and the noblest thoughts of history's top ten, it needs to be used more widely as the description of 'what a society does.'"[59] This in itself was not new. Even as conservative a social commentator as T. S. Eliot had suggested over ten years earlier that the word culture "includes all the characteristic activities and interests of a people," from Gothic churches, the music of Elgar, and the Henley Regatta to Wensleydale cheese, a Cup fi-nal, and the pin table.[60] But what mattered was the ordering of the con-stituent parts and the way they shaped the new model.

Models varied from member to member of the Group, and even changed over a relatively short time. For example, in 1957 Alloway wrote that his "first strategy was the surrealist one of looking for hidden meanings to unify John Wayne and Bronzino, Joan Crawford and René Magritte. . . . A trap for the consumer looking for a unifying but tolerant aesthetic is the alignment of the top and bottom without the middle. On this scale Picasso is fine and so are comic books, but in between is the unspeakable middlebrow."[61] The "unifying but tolerant aesthetic" Alloway had in mind was, as he acknowledged, little different from the one which found magical and artistic qualities in the ordinary and everyday. On another level it was also not dissimilar to finding vitality and spontaneity in the folk or popular arts, which, under certain conditions, could enter the realm of the transcendent.[62]

Alloway's next strategy was to assume that high and popular culture were brought together less by a "unifying but tolerant aesthetic," but could be seen as

. . . part of a general field of communication. All kinds of messages are transmitted to every kind of audience along a multitude of channels. Art is one part of the field; advertising is another. We begin to see the work of art in a changed context, freed from the iron curtain of traditional aesthetics which separated absolutely art from non art. In the general field of visual communications the unique function of each form of communication and the new range of similarities between them is just beginning to be charted. It is part of an effort to see art in terms of human use rather than in terms of philosophical problems.[63]

The absorption of the high/popular hierarchy into the "general field of visual communications," based on an analysis of varied discourses, is a radical shift which prefigures fully fledged postmodern theory and ideas. Traditional concerns about definition, quality, and value—"philosophical problems"—were replaced by an interest in the social role and function of different visual discourses—"human use."

By 1959 Alloway was equating this move toward "the general field of visual communications" to "modern arrangements of knowledge in non-hierarchic forms. This is shown by the influence of anthropology and sociology on the humanities."[64] It led him to propose that the inclusiveness meant that "unique oil paintings and highly personal poems as well as mass-distributed films and group-aimed magazines can be placed within a continuum rather than frozen in layers in a pyramid." He rightly contrasted this "permissive approach to culture" with that of Eliot (et alia), who goes on, like Hoggart, to discriminate between the value of different types of cultural manifestations, thus conforming to the pyramid model. The continuum model—we would now refer to it as a "visual culture" model—accepts diversity and sees all the components or discourses as of equal value-in Alloway's case, all as manifestations of communication. Dada was claimed as a precursor of the model. In 1956 Alloway had praised its inclusiveness, through which a Dada work "may be made of bus tickets or it may look like an advertisement. It may be an ad." This was part of its "acceptance of the multiple value of life," which means that "it does not insist upon the abstraction of fixed aspects of life for aesthetic treatment. It effectually consigns art to the tangled channels of everyday communications."[65]

The continuum visual culture model was, indeed, a radical shift from the conventional pyramidal model, and equates with what the IG interpreted as the shift from universalist, Aristotelian values to non-Aristotelian ones. The adoption of the model also marks a key moment of a change from traditional or Modernist values to postmodern concerns. But there are two features of the continuum model which differentiate it from later postmodern versions. The first is that its linearity has implications. At the "edges" of each discourse, there may be an interconnectedness or overlap, but each discourse is still thought of as retaining a distinct identity. As Alloway expressed it, "the unique function of each form of communication" is respected. In writing about "art (published) and movies (unpublished)," Alloway may have assumed both to be "part of a general field of communication," but "art is one part of the field, another is advertising."[66]

Now, to use McHale's distinction, "the situation was characteristically 'both/and' rather than 'either/or,'"[67] but both dualities implied identifiable differences which might then permit recourse to different systems of value. In other words, the horizontal continuum may maintain not only distinctive discourses but also a "vertical" element that permits relative "good" and "bad" judgments. McHale in 1959 used the phrase a "plurality of elites" to describe the new cultural situation.[68] These elites may "relate, and overlap, horizontally," but they do not merge into one de-differentiated system. Furthermore, their dimension of verticality makes each "value system" a separate elite.

A year later, Richard Hamilton was making use of a similar model in which "Each of [society's] members accepts the convenience of different values for different groups and different occasions."[69] Looking back from the time of the making of the *Fathers of Pop* film (1979), Alloway described a model which comprised "multiple elites, multiple aesthetics," which is some way from his earlier idea of the single "unifying but tolerant aesthetic." With the emotive connotations of the word "elite," the model perhaps can best be summarized as a "plurality of hierarchies."[70]

The plurality of hierarchies model perfectly suited Banham's needs and beliefs. It enabled him to write about a range of types of visual culture from Le Corbusier to potato chip bags, but to discuss them separately and address each in terms appropriate to it. In 1961 he wrote that, in the mid-1950s, the "protagonists of 'pop' art at an intellectual level . . . maintained that there was no such thing as good and bad taste, but that each individual group or stratum of Society had its own characteristic taste and style of design"[71]— good and bad, that is, in any universal, absolute sense. Furthermore, in the *Fathers of Pop,* Banham responds to Alloway's coining of "multiple elites, multiple aesthetics" by adding that "All the elites were equally good." For Alloway, all discourses could be seen in terms of communication; for Banham, all were responses to living in the "Technological Century"[72]—each having the potential for more or less "profound reorientations towards a changed world"—and, in that sense, potentially equally good or valid.

As we saw in chapter 1, Banham identified in Modern Movement architecture a continuum between "Futurist dynamism and Academic caution" (or the "engineering" and "mechanical" sensibilities), and (theoretically) opposed an a priori status for any particular architectural discourse. However, as important, the model allowed Banham the "verticality" to make qualitative judgments within each discourse, so he was perfectly comfortable pronouncing the Villa Savoye and the Barcelona Pavilion "masterpieces" while, at the same time, extolling the virtues of the latest Cadillac or Buick—a perfect example of "both/and." Thus, although Banham seldom deals directly or abstractly with cultural models, the IG thinking developed principally by Alloway and McHale underpins his values and writings.

One clear influence is the emphasis on content and meaning in his writing on design and popular culture. We will see the manifestations of this in chapter 6, but the general point is an appropriate one to make in the current context. In an article published originally in Italian in 1955, and translated into English in 1960, he describes how, "Unlike criticism of the fine arts, the criticism of popular arts depends on an analysis of content, an appreciation of superficial rather than abstract qualities, and an outward orientation that sees the history of the product as an interaction between the sources of the symbols and the consumer's understanding of them." The emphasis on content may address form, but not as an end in itself. He offers an example:

To quote Bruno Alfieri about the 1947 Studebaker, "The power of the motor seems to correspond to an aerial hood, an irresistible sensation of speed." He sees a symbolic link between the power of the motor and the appearance of its housing, and this is made explicit by the use of an iconography based on the forms of jet aircraft. Thus we are dealing with a *content* (idea of power), a source of symbols (aircraft), and a popular culture (whose members recognise the symbols and their meaning).

Not only did this describe the role of the critic; it also defined the role of the designer in popular culture: "The connecting element between them is the industrial designer, with his ability to deploy the elements of his iconography—his command and understanding of popular symbolism."[73]

Banham shared the IG emphasis on content and meaning, but his individual contribution was the analysis both of some of the salient characteristics of popular culture and of the design manifestations. We now turn to the discussion of the characteristics of popular culture which, for Banham, were crucial to understanding and judgment.

Expendability as Theory

In "Vehicles of Desire," Banham had distinguished between the universalism and permanency of conventional architecture and the "symbolic iconographies" and consumerist impermanency of the contemporary Detroit car, positioning the latter—that "expendable, replaceable vehicle of popular desires"—in the same league as "the other dreams that money can buy," the "world of expendable art."[74] In a 1962 article, he uses the phrase "massive initial impact and small sustaining power" to describe the Pop aesthetic, pointing out that "physical and symbolic consumability are equal in Pop culture, equal in status and meaning." However, he continued, the distinction was yet to inform cultural evaluation and criticism, which still upheld the traditional, hierarchical cultural model with its assumption of the priority of permanency and Platonic ideals. The problem was that

. . . we are still making do with Plato because in aesthetics, as in most other things, we still have no formulated intellectual attitudes for living in a throwaway economy. We eagerly consume noisy ephemeridae, here with a bang today, gone without a whimper tomorrow—movies, beach-wear, pulp magazines, this morning's headlines and tomorrow's TV programmes—yet we insist on aesthetic and moral standards hitched to permanency, durability and perennity.[75]

This pinpointed a major issue confronting cultural value and criticism—the issue of expendability. As Banham put it, "The addition of the word *expendable* to the vocabulary of criticism was essential before . . . [popular culture] could be faced honestly, since this is the first quality of an object to be consumed."[76] And the object to be consumed could galvanize the public through its "emotional-engineering-by-public-consent" and create, in the case of Detroit autos, "vehicles of palpably fulfilled desire. Can architecture or any other Twentieth Century art claim to have done so much? and, if not, have they any real right to carp?"[77] Expendability was being linked to the emotional and expressive quality of daily life; the positive embracing of expendability is, as he concludes in "Vehicles of Desire," "a means of saying something of breathless, but unverbalisable, consequence to the live culture of the Technological Century."

Detroit cars provided what Banham, in "Space for Decoration: A Rejoinder" (1955), termed the "aesthetic of expendability."[78] "This cannot," he explained, "be an aesthetic which depends upon the discovery and contemplation of subtle abstract relationships—there isn't time—but must deal with a language of signs which are as immediately recognisable and legible as a dropped neckline or a raised eyebrow. The aesthetics of serial production must be the aesthetics of the popular arts, not of fine arts."[79] The IG model of the "plurality of hierarchies" is to the fore of Banham's thinking at this time, and he declares that "From now on, as long as serial production lasts, there will be two aesthetics, one for the fine arts, one for consumer goods." He may here have been describing a duality rather than a plurality of hierarchies, but the principle remained that it was not a question of one *or* the other—either/or—but of both/and: "this is not cynicism or 'letting-go-of-standards,' the survival of either aesthetic depends upon their differentiation."

Banham's 1955 "rejoinder" had been a response to an article by a member of the Design Council, Peter Blake. Blake was offered the chance to reply to Banham and concluded his comments by regretting that, to the discriminating designer, "Banham's thesis must appear to be a depressing acceptance of the more vulgar manifestations of machine art, the sops offered by commercialism to greater sales."[80] Blake's comment highlights one of the battles taking place in design theory and criticism in the mid-1950s between those, like Blake, who were suspicious of commercialism because, in the Bauhaus tradition, they saw design in terms of social and moral improvement, and those, like Banham, who were excited by the possibilities of commercialism and popular culture. The battle lines were not, of course, determined just by different views of design, but also by the relationship of design to society and the sort of vision and values represented by different systems of design. To praise American commercial design was to run the risk of being identified with a system that was hostile to European notions of restraint and good taste: one in which—to put it as crudely as the detractors—commercialism was more important than civilization.

Commercialism, expendability, and Americanness were thus bound up with each another. This was historically correct. In their influential book of 1932, *Consumer Engineering: A New Technique for Prosperity,* Roy Sheldon and Egmont Arens had presented the case for a positive acceptance of style obsolescence by manufacturers. Rather than fearing it as the "creeping death to his business," the manufacturer was beginning to understand that obsolescence "has also a positive value; that it opens up as many fields as ever it closed; that for every superseded article there must be a new one which is eagerly accepted. He sees all of us throwing razors away every day instead of using the same one for years. He turns in his motor car for a new one when there is no mechanical reason for so doing. He realises that many things become decrepit in appearance before the works wear out."[81]

This notion of style obsolescence was the basis of Banham's "aesthetic of expendability," the difference being that Sheldon and Arens were writing from the producer's point of view, and Banham (arguably) from the consumer's. The producer had to come to terms with the way consumers behave in order to plan and promote obsolescence—or, as the authors somewhat euphemistically described it, "progressive waste" or "creative waste."[82] The consumer was, for Banham, the happy and willing recipient of this progressive or creative waste. In *Theory and Design in the First Machine Age* (1960), he wrote that "Even a man who does not possess an electric razor is likely—in the Westernised world at least—to dispense some previously inconceivable product, such as an aerosol shaving cream, from an equally unprecedented pressurised container, and accept with equanimity the fact that he can afford to throw away, regularly, cutting edges that previous generations would have nursed for years."[83]

The similarity of this quotation to the one by Sheldon and Arens goes beyond the subject matter of cutting edges and razors, and reveals the similarity of value with, in both cases, obsolescence being seen as a wholly positive phenomenon. Only the emphasis in the two quotations is different: for the earlier writers, the significance of obsolescence is economic—the business opportunity it provides; for Banham its significance is sociocultural insofar as obsolescence is symptomatic of the "transformations" which have "powerfully affected human life, and opened up new paths of choice in the ordering of our collective destiny."[84]

That obsolescence involved wastefulness was readily admitted by Sheldon and Arens: "We are perhaps unwise and enormously wasteful, as our conservation experts tell us." But they concluded, in a rationalized way which actually avoided the ecological issue, "we are concerned with our psychological attitude as an actuality."[85] The bottom line was financial, and so, "In America today we believe that our progress and our chances of better living are in positive earning rather than in negative saving."[86] They described the whole system as "the American Way." Banham was directly responding less to 1930s American design theory than, like other members of the IG, to the postwar affluence of the United States and its dreams that money could buy. However, the underlying value system of American design remained intact and expanded in the era of high mass consumption and market saturation.

The keynote of the system was high consumption, and so the major problem, in the words of J. Gordon Lippincott in his forthright book *Design for Business,* published in 1947, was continually "stimulating the urge to buy"[87] once the market was saturated. Lippincott, a proselytizer for the "free enterprise," "capitalist" system, justified high consumption in a way which became standard in the 1950s: "Any method that can motivate the flow of merchandise to new buyers will create jobs and work for industry, and hence national prosperity . . . Our custom of trading in our automobiles every year, of having a new refrigerator, vacuum cleaner or electric iron every three or four years is economically sound." Tied to this economic justification for obsolescence was a social one: "Surely in no other country in the world can a worker earning $45 a week drive to his job in his own automobile. He enjoys this privilege only because of the aggressive selling methods of the American automobile industry."[88] High consumption and obsolescence were, therefore, *democratic* because the prosperous middle-class consumer trades in last year's model for the new dream , thus passing down the line his "style-obsolete"[89] model, which continues a useful life "until it finally hits the graveyard and becomes scrap metal for re-use in industry."[90] Commercialism, expendability, and Americanness thus had "democratic" added to them as part of the established value system of design that Banham embraced, albeit with his political reservations.

By the time of the IG activities, expendability was accepted as a major part of the American system of design, accounting for much of its financial success and contributing significantly to the country's prosperity. In 1955 Harley Earl, chief stylist at General Motors, unashamedly announced that "our job is to hasten obsolescence. In 1934 the average car ownership span was five years; now it is two years. When it is one year, we will have a perfect score."[91] According to Banham, the phrase "Detroit-Macchiavellismus" was coined in

Germany to describe "everything that was felt to be hateful about US design"[92] with its commitment to expendability. The justification offered by Earl for continual change was that "the public demands it, [so] there must be born new ideas, new designs, new methods of making the automobiles of a coming year more beautiful than those of yesterday and today."[93] Accepting expendability was supposedly part of being a "knowing consumer" in a visually sophisticated, democratic society.

Manufacturers had a vested interest in obsolescence, but even astute critics upheld the system. For example, in *Industrial Design,* also in 1955, Eric Larrabee wrote approvingly that the American car had "taught its owners to consume, and its makers to produce, for an economy in which the strictures of historical scarcity no longer apply. It has made waste through overconsumption one of the indispensable gears of that economy, and has made it socially acceptable as well."[94] A year later the internationally respected designer George Nelson was putting forward the view that "What we need is more obsolescence, not less."[95] Nelson, too, saw obsolescence as part of the "American Way" of design, but "only in a relatively temporary and accidental sense. As other societies reach a comparable level [of consumerism], similar attitudes will emerge."[96]

With the growth of private affluence in British (and European) society, Banham's championing of expendability and its concomitant values can be seen as little more than the fulfillment of Nelson's prediction about the spread of American attitudes. But such an interpretation would not do justice to Banham's cultural understanding of the relationship of expendability to popular culture and technology, and, most important, its implications for values and standards which the Alloway/McHale strand of the IG had so clearly articulated. Banham was analyzing expendability culturally and drawing historically significant conclusions, yet the enthusiastic tone and partisan nature of his writing likened him to those free market Americans, from Sheldon and Arens to Lippincott and Larrabee, who welcomed expendability as part of a high consumption, capitalist economy.[97]

Banham was, as one would expect, aware of the relationship between expendability, affluence, and capitalism, and wrote in 1961 that the "*problem* of Industrial Design . . . is still a problem of affluent democracy . . . [in which] the whole manner of squaring up to the subject matter of Industrial Design has changed."[98] [italics added]. But he chose to examine the manifestations rather than the system, dismissing those who engaged with the latter—an example was Vance Packard, whose books included *The Hidden Persuaders* (1957), *The Status Seekers* (1959), and *The Waste Makers* (1960)—as "professional Jeremiahs." Banham did not engage with the substantive criticisms of the system developed by Packard but, as ever, concentrated on what he saw as the positive gains on a personal level, in the way that Marinetti had thought of machines in the First Machine Age as "a source of personal fulfilment and gratification."

Banham's analyses of expendability and its implications for cultural theory had a lasting and profound effect on his own writing about design and some aspects of architecture from the time of the IG's activities throughout the 1960s and beyond, as we shall see in chapters 3 and 6. Other members of the Group also acknowledged a debt to Banham. For example, in 1958, writing about his *Hommage à Chrysler Corp.* painting, Richard Hamilton declared that he had been influenced by the "pop-art pre-occupation of the Independent Group at the ICA and using directly some material investigated by Reyner Banham in his auto styling research, I had been working on a group of paintings and drawings which portray the American automobile as expressed in the mag-ads."[99]

"This Is Tomorrow"

The influence of the IG in general on Hamilton's thinking at that time was also spelled out in a letter of January 1957 he wrote to the Smithsons in which he listed "a number of manifestations in the post-war years in London which I would select as important."[100] These included the exhibitions "Parallel of Life and Art" and "Man, Machine and Motion"; "the Independent Group discussion on Pop Art-Fine Art relationship"; Paolozzi's, McHale's, and the Smithsons' "Ad image research," and "Reyner Banham's research on automobile styling." The letter also contained Hamilton's oft-cited definition of American popular culture as "Popular (designed for a mass audience); Transient (short-term solution); Expendable (easily forgotten); Low cost; Mass produced; Young (aimed at youth); Witty; Sexy; Gim-

micky; Glamorous; Big Business." The letter was outlining the scope of a possible exhibition which would follow on from "This Is Tomorrow." Hamilton's
view was that "the disadvantage (as well as the great virtue)" of "This Is Tomorrow" was its "incoherence" and that it was relatively "chaotic."

To see incoherence and chaos as virtues is to reinterpret them as diversity
and openness, which is akin to the IG mentality and ethos. "This Is Tomorrow" may have been seen by some as incoherent and chaotic, but its diversity and openness of ideas reflects a range not only of IG attitudes and
values, but also some of the elements in Banham's own thinking which
formed an alternative to the orthodoxies of the time. There were, in fact,
three collaborations in the exhibition which represented strands of the
Group's thinking.

The first is the one which tends to be written about in art history books as
if it were the sole exhibit: the collaboration between Richard Hamilton,
John McHale, and the architect John Voelcker (who designed the structure
but who then left for the CIAM conference). Their environment combined
perceptual ambiguity—black and white undulating patterns and Duchamp-
influenced "rotorelief" disks—with imagery from contemporary mass media and popular culture which included a life-size photograph of Marilyn
Monroe; a cardboard cut-out of Robby, the robot from the science fiction
film *The Forbidden Planet* (1956); and a jukebox which pounded out the top
twenty hits of the day. "Tomorrow" was expressed in terms of sensory bom-
bardment, appealing domestic technology, and the "expendable ikon."[101]
Hamilton's poster for his group's display, *"Just What Is It That Makes Today's
Homes So Different, So Appealing?,"* illustrated what he felt were the essential ingredients of contemporary American popular culture, and it became the first icon of the nascent Pop art.

The second IG-influenced collaboration was the Alloway, del Renzio, and
Geoffrey Holroyd environment which demonstrated Alloway's interest in
what he was later to describe as the "general field of visual communications," in which art, advertising, film and other discourses are viewed as sign
systems rather than more or less distinct expressions of human creativity or
aesthetic form. The environment that served the idea comprised various systems with struts, pegs, and panels with the intention that the spectator

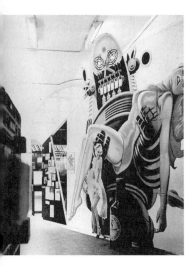

"This Is Tomorrow," Hamilton/McHale/Voelcker exhibit, 1956 (courtesy Mary Banham)

Richard Hamilton, *"Just What Is It That Makes Today's Homes So Different, So Appealing?,"* 1956

(courtesy Richard Hamilton)

"This Is Tomorrow," Alloway/del Renzio/Holroyd exhibit, 1956 (courtesy Peter Smithson)

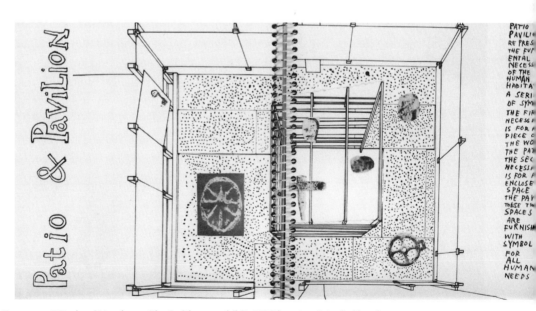

"This Is Tomorrow," Paolozzi/Henderson/the Smithsons exhibit, 1956 (courtesy Peter Smithson)

would "learn how to read a tackboard, a tackboard being a convenient method of organising the modern visual continuum according to each individual's decision." The cultural model of the visual continuum was here presented in visual form.

The third collaboration was *Patio & Pavilion* which the Smithsons, Eduardo Paolozzi, and Nigel Henderson worked on together. *Patio & Pavilion* was a symbolic semi-recreation of Henderson's own backyard in Bethnal Green and represented (according to the statement in the catalog) "the fundamental necessities of the human habitat in a series of symbols. The first necessity is for a piece of the world—the patio. The second necessity is for an enclosed space—the pavilion. These two spaces are furnished with symbols for all human needs."[102] The debris of daily life scattered around the exhibit—a bicycle tire, rocks, tools, a pin-up—symbolized desires and aspirations that were supposedly basic and humble. *Patio & Pavilion* recalled the anti-formalism of "Parallel of Life and Art"—it featured the same team—and, together, the two exhibits revealed the anti-classical, *art brut* aesthetic of coarseness and physicality that was one of the tendencies in the IG (and which we will be discussing more fully in due course).

Banham reviewed "This Is Tomorrow" for *Architects' Journal* and *Architectural Review.* In the *Journal* he claimed that he found the Hamilton et al. exhibit "the most exciting thing I have seen in an exhibition in years."[103] In the *Review* he adjudged that the diversity, openness, or "ambiguity was part of a general feeling of broken barriers and questioned categories that constituted the most stimulating aspect of the whole exhibition."[104] The Alloway et al. exhibit was acknowledged as "an invitation to smash all boundaries between the arts, to treat them all as modes of communicating experience from person to person . . . modes that could embrace all the available channels of human perception."[105] Particular praise was accorded the Hamilton et al. exhibit, which, with its "optical illusions, scale reversions, oblique structures and fragmented images," succeeded in disrupting "stock responses, and put the viewer back on a *tabula rasa* of individual responsibility for his own atomised sensory awareness of images of only local and contemporary significance."[106] This contrasted with images of art historical or supposedly transcendent significance—the cultural baggage that was greater than any one individual and which was likely to result in a "stock response."

Such thinking may have evolved from IG discussions, but the following comment makes connections that reveal Banham's own attitudes and perspective. Referring again to the Hamilton et al. exhibit, he remarked that "curiously, their section seemed to have more in common with that of the New Brutalists [the Smithsons, etc.] than any other, and the clue to this kinship would appear to lie in the fact that neither relied on abstract concepts, but on concrete images—images that can carry the mass of tradition and association, or the energy of novelty and technology, but resist classification by the geometrical disciplines by which most other exhibits were dominated."[107] The three exhibits associated with the IG thus comprised Pop, technology, visual information and communications, and *art brut*—a seemingly diverse collection of tendencies, but ones which featured prominently in IG activities, and which were far from mutually exclusive or even contradictory in Banham's thinking at this time.

Art Brut and *Architecture Autre*

In his review of "This Is Tomorrow," Banham had linked the Hamilton and Smithson groups' exhibits through a rejection of abstract concepts and an involvement with concrete images—"images that can carry the mass of tradition and association, or the energy of novelty and technology." *Patio & Pavilion* actually carried rather too much tradition for Banham's liking, showing the work of the Smithsons, Paolozzi, and Henderson at "its most *submissive* to traditional values"[italics added].[108] But this was not a rejection of Brutalist ideas in general, only of a particular manifestation. Not only did Banham and the Smithsons share many values associated with the IG, but Banham was one of the keenest supporters of the Smithsons' work. In 1957 the Smithsons explained that "Brutalism tries to face up to a mass production society, and drag a rough poetry out of the confused and powerful forces which are at work."[109] Banham recognized this and saw the Brutalists' "rough poetry" as an alternative to the sophisticated stylization associated with pop culture—both were authentic and valid responses to the contemporary conditions of "mass production society."

In typical IG style, it was not an "either/or" choice between tradition and novelty, for the Smithsons, like Banham, were inclusive in their sources and enthusiasms. In a 1955 statement they reflected on the fact that "1954 has been a key year. It has seen American advertising rival Dada in its impact of overlaid imagery; that automobile masterpiece the Cadillac convertible, parallel-with-the-ground (four elevations) classic box-on-wheels; the start of a new way of thinking by CIAM; the revaluation of the work of Gropius; the repainting of the villa at Garches."[110] Indeed, the Smithsons' own work, as we shall see, drew on the sophisticated stylization of pop culture as well as the rough poetry of *art brut.* For Banham, both options promised the possibility of *une architecture autre*—an architecture that rejected abstract, formally derived concepts and forms in favor of human presence, signs of life and symbols of living in the "mass production society" that was the Second Machine Age.

Banham first used the term *une architecture autre* in an article titled "The New Brutalism," which appeared in *Architectural Review* in December 1955.[111] It was used as analogous to the concept of *un art autre,* the subject and title of a book written by the French art critic Michel Tapié and published at Paris in 1952.[112] What Tapié had in mind in employing the term were the postwar anti-formal and anti-classical tendencies that could be observed in both American and European art. There were three main tributaries that made up *art autre.* The first—the one prewar legacy—was the process-oriented Surrealism that made use of automatic and semiautomatic techniques which, its proponents believed, extracted the uninhibited and primordial subconscious.

The second was found most convincingly in the work of Jackson Pollock. Pollock was greatly influenced by the process orientation of "absolute" Surrealism and the notion of unfinishedness and flux, and was attracted to the notion that "there is no beginning and no end."[113] Banham admitted that he and other IG members "were grappling with the Jackson Pollock phenomenon. Action painting was important to us because of its anti-formality and its quality as a record of the artist's gesture."[114] Yet what made Pollock a radical painter was not his action technique but his rejection of figure/ground relationship in favor of an allover, nonhierarchic composition—

it could be interpreted as non-Aristotelian—without value contrasts or contrived points of focus.

To a modern art public weaned on European canons of formal order, balance, and qualitative judgment, Pollock's work seemed bewildering and even subversive. Indeed, even for a would-be radical like Banham (aged twenty-eight in 1950), Pollock's work was, he recalled in 1966, "almost incomprehensible to European eyes. Yet it left an indelible 'image' on many minds and when it seemed to be time to try and overthrow the classical tradition (and with it, the dominance of France in European intellectual life) then Pollock was immediately remembered, and became a sort of patron saint of anti-art even before his sensational and much published death [in 1956]."[115] The avoidance of conventional hierarchies struck a chord with most IG members, and Pollock's anti-formalism had a major influence on Banham's understanding of an *architecture autre.*

The third was the *art brut* championed by Jean Dubuffet: a "raw art" untainted by polite conventions of civilized refinement. Art for Dubuffet was nothing to do with taste, classical harmony, or skill, but an innermost and primordial impulse that existed in everyone and that should be communicated directly and spontaneously. His work exemplified the *art brut* anti-aesthetic. Surfaces of various materials, including mud, sand, glue,

Jackson Pollock, *Yellow Islands,* 1952 (courtesy The Tate Gallery)

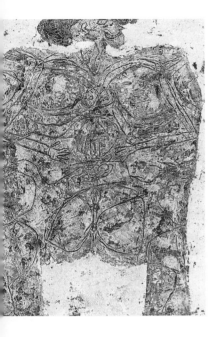

Jean Dubuffet, *Le Metafisyx,* 1950 (courtesy The Tate Gallery)

and asphalt, revealed apparently haphazard scratches and blemishes, and his attitude to materials, which was inclusive and nonhierarchical. No material was rejected out of hand because of a lowly status. Each and every material was as good as any other; each had its own characteristics, however conventionally unappealing, and must be used "as found."

Art autre, at its most dynamic and radical, brought together flux and unfinishedness as a state of being; nonhierarchic and nonrelational anti-formalism; a primordial universality; and a direct, anti-elegant, even ugly use of forms, materials, and colors. It was not a new formalism, and certainly not a new style, but a new and uncompromising attitude to creating that eschewed high-minded notions of art and the characteristics and associations of classical aesthetics.

Banham's understanding of *art autre* and its implications was sound. Any misinterpretations that may have arisen were dispelled by direct contact with the British artist whose work during the 1950s could most convincingly

Eduardo Paolozzi, *Bunk,* 1952 (courtesy The Tate Gallery)

be described as *art autre:* Eduardo Paolozzi. On graduating from the Slade in 1947, Paolozzi had moved to Paris for more than two years. During his stay there he met many artists, including Brancusi, Giacometti, Arp, Tristan Tzara, and Dubuffet. Access to Mary Reynolds's large collection of Dada and Surrealist documents, and visits to the Musée de l'Homme and Dubuffet's collection of *art brut* helped immerse Paolozzi in modes of anti-art and *art brut.* Banham met Paolozzi when the latter gave his celebrated "Bunk" epidiascope show at the first meeting of the newly formed IG in 1952. Although the subject matter of the show was proto-Pop, the somewhat relentless manner in which the images were projected had a marked anti-art character—Paolozzi showed no regard for logic, development, continuity, scale, or meaning. The anti-art/*art brut* character was certainly consistent with Paolozzi's sculpture of the 1950s, which had changed from the Giacometti- and Picasso-influenced work of the late 1940s, to the rough-hewn and primitive Dubuffet-inspired heads and figures.

The 1953 exhibition "Parallel of Life and Art" revealed that the Smithsons shared Paolozzi's *art autre* sympathies. They were well versed in *art autre* tendencies—and had even seen Pollock's work at Venice in 1949. "Parallel of Life and Art" has come to assume major historical significance in the development of an *architecture autre.* Looking back from the vantage point of 1966, Banham wrote how the exhibition had undermined "humanistic conventions of beauty in order to emphasise violence, distortion, obscurity and a certain amount of 'humeur noir' . . . [it] was a subversive innovation whose importance was not missed."[116] However, Banham's contemporary review was somewhat different and, while stressing the anti-monumentalizing "imageability" of photographs as "the common visual currency of our time," also warned of the danger of seeing "photographic evidence as the equivalent of personal participation." If, in 1953, Banham had not fully appreciated the *autre* potential of the "Parallel of Life and Art" aesthetic, he was soon to realize the significance of the aesthetic when manifested in architecture as the New Brutalism.

The New Brutalism

There were strong parallels between the New Brutalism and *art autre,* including the rejection of a transcendent classical aesthetic; there were differences, too, defined by Banham in terms of *art autre* representing a rejection of "both the forms and the theory of the Thirties; the Brutalists have rejected the forms, on the ground that they are false to the theory."[117] Forms needed to grow out of the conditions of life as lived: "It is necessary to create an architecture of reality," wrote the Smithsons,

an architecture which takes as its starting point the period 1910—of de Stijl, Dada and Cubism . . . An art *concerned with the natural order,* the poetic relationship between living things and environment. We wish to see towns and buildings which do not make us feel ashamed, ashamed that we cannot realise the potential of the twentieth century, ashamed that philosophers and physicists must think us fools, and painters think us irrelevant. We live in moron-made cities. Our generation must try and produce evidence that men are at work.[118]

The tone of the passage recalls Dubuffet and, although the New Brutalists and *art autre* artists were scrutinizing different sources, they were both seeking a rekindling of the "primitive," raw, and direct *attitudes to* creation in their disciplines, which, for all their differences of chronological location, both parties believed to be essentially ahistorical.

Hostility was felt by the New Brutalists (who, to all intents and purposes in the early 1950s, *were* Alison and Peter Smithson) toward the "New Empiricism" or "New Humanist" architecture, characterized by pitched roofs, brick or plaster/cement walls, window boxes and balconies, paintwork, and picturesque grouping. The "New Humanism" was hated for its reasonableness and lack of conviction by the Brutalists, who, in their impatience with what they saw as the Establishment's complacency, paralleled the "Angry Young Men," their literary counterparts.[119] The origins of the term "New Brutalism"—both the straightforward and the esoteric—have been examined elsewhere,[120] and here we need only note that it combined, as the Smithsons pointed out, a "response to the growing literary style of the *Architectural Review* which, at the start of the 'fifties, was running articles on . . . the New

Alison and Peter Smithson, Hunstanton School, 1950–1954 (courtesy Peter Smithson)

Empiricism, the New Sentimentality, and so on";[121] reference to *beton brut* (raw concrete), which had been one of the most controversial features of Le Corbusier's recently finished Unité block in Marseilles; and, not least, the *art brut* of Dubuffet.

The term was first used in public by Alison Smithson to describe a small house project of 1952 for a site in the Soho district of London. The statement which accompanied the design indicates an *art brut* aesthetic of materials "as found": "It was decided to have no finishes at all internally, the building being a combination of shelter and environment. Bare bricks, concrete and wood . . . It is our intention in this building to have the structure exposed entirely."[122] The belief in "truth to materials" is part of the legacy of the aesthetico-moral tradition of the nineteenth century that continued into the twentieth century. Its manifestations percolated through Modernist art and architecture, whether Henry Moore or Mies van der Rohe, but where the New Brutalists parted company with the Modernists was in the end to which the means were put. Modernists ultimately believed that each material had intrinsic *qualities* that could be brought out by the artist so as to create beauty. The New Brutalist attitude to materials was to present them *as fact,* the effect of which might be inelegance and even ugliness.

The unconventional aesthetic ends to which the materials were put was the cause of much confusion and controversy in the Smithsons' early buildings and projects. Nowhere was this more apparent than in their best-known early work—the school at Hunstanton in Norfolk. Although the design of the building (1950) predates the movement's name, the school is accepted as one of the key buildings of the New Brutalism. In its use of undisguised steel and glass it appeared to resemble the work of Mies, but in an assessment of the school written on its completion in 1954, Banham argued that it was free of the "*formalism* of Mies van der Rohe. This may seem a hard saying, since Mies is the obvious comparison, but at Hunstanton every element is truly what it appears to be."[123] [italics added]. He developed the point to discuss the resultant

new aesthetic of materials, which must be valued for the surfaces they have on delivery to the site—since paint is only used where structurally or functionally unavoidable—a valuation like that of the Dadaists, who accepted their materials "as found," a valuation built into the Modern Movement by Moholy-Nagy at the Bauhaus. It is this valuation of materials which has led to the appellation "New Brutalist," but it should now be clear that this is not merely a surface aesthetic of untrimmed edges and exposed services, but a radical philosophy reaching back to the first conception of the building. In this sense this is probably the most truly modern building in England, fully accepting the moral load which the Modern Movement lays upon the architect's shoulders. It does not ingratiate itself with cosmetic detailing, but, like it or dislike it, demands that we should make up our minds about it, and examine our consciences in the light of that decision. [124]

Banham is emphasizing both an *art autre* and an early Modernist attitude, not only to materials but also to the building's total conception and execution. This shifts the term of reference away from an aesthetic to a moral frame. It is not, however, to be confused with the *aesthetico-moral* approach beloved by nineteenth- and twentieth-century rationalists who were convinced that their *true* style or aesthetic had moral authority. The Smithsons and Banham both adopted James Gowan's dictum of "a style for the job," which implied a pragmatic and inclusive attitude to visual matters, not a preconceived or ideal one. [125]

The same was true for the plan of the building. Hunstanton's plan was essentially symmetrical, and some critics presumed this showed the influence of Rudolf Wittkower's recently published *Architectural Principles of the Age of Humanism* (1947), and of Colin Rowe's researches into mathematics and proportion in architecture. [126] Certainly the Smithsons were aware of this recent scholarship and, equally certainly, they were influenced by it. But the influence they absorbed and applied was filtered through an anti-idealist outlook. Classical planning—or even classical proportions—could be used in a New Brutalist building because New Brutalism was inclusive. The quintessential change, however, was that the transcendent and idealist associations of classicism—the metaphysical dimension in which the particular always referred to the general—were dropped so that any classical aspect was merely another option, another tool at the architect's disposal, and on the par with all others. These distinctions between classical aesthetics and pragmatics— crucial if one is to understand the influence of *art autre* on architecture in this period—seem to have eluded most commentators, whose judgments were based on superficial visual characteristics.

Banham, as we saw in chapter 1, accepted the classical, once stripped of its transcendent and idealist connotations, as a legitimate option, whereas Philip Johnson in 1954 applauded the "*inherent* elegance" (italics added) of the Smithsons' Mies-influenced design. Johnson regretted that, in their succeeding work, the Smithsons had "turned against such formalistic and 'composed' designs towards an Adolf Loos type of Anti-Design which they call the New Brutalism (a phrase which is already being picked up by the Smithsons' contemporaries to defend atrocities)."[127] By then, the New Brutalism was synonymous in most critics' minds with raw concrete and was being discussed in primarily stylistic terms. The Smithsons themselves tried to make the point that "Brutalism has been discussed stylistically, whereas its essence is ethical."[128] The aesthetics of *art brut* and the concept of *art autre* were passed over by all but a tiny number of informed commentators.

Whether such an uncompromising ethico-aesthetic high ground should be foisted on the sensitive minds and delicate bodies of the children (let alone teachers) who daily populated the school was a moot point. Whereas the purchasers of one of the Smithsons' private houses probably knew what they were taking on—at least they had the alternative to buy somewhere else—this was obviously not so for the users or inhabitants of an *architecture brute* public building. The Smithsons' attitude was redolent of the-architect-as-moral-crusader and artistic trailblazer that had characterized early and arrogant Modernism: the public was expected to come to terms with what could be a stark and unforgiving architecture.

The anti-formalism of the Smithsons in the 1950s can best be observed in their unsuccessful entry for the City of London's Golden Lane public housing competition of 1952. The New Brutalists' link with advertising surfaced, as we have seen in their 1957 quote about their commitment to being "objective about 'reality'—the cultural objectives of society, its urges, its techniques, and so on. Brutalism tries to face up to a mass production society, and drag a rough poetry out of the confused and powerful forces which are at work."[129]

"Reality" was related to the way that the Smithsons believed working-class people actually lived in contemporary society, rather than the way that middle-class architects (or cultural critics) thought they *should* live, and it formed the basis of their Golden Lane project. It incorporated the idea of the street deck (subsequently taken up by Jack Lynn and Ivor Smith at Sheffield), which the Smithsons hoped would facilitate an updated community-oriented life based on the traditional terraced street. The deck was also a means of pedestrian circulation, and it linked clusters of buildings. The anti-formalism of the project was most clearly in evidence in the layout of the blocks, which were not arranged in any aesthetically ordered or systematic way but were placed according to the topography of the site. Rather than deriving from the Picturesque tradition of "consulting the genius of the place" and enhancing it, the Smithsons' attitude to layout was, like their attitude to materials, "as found."

The Smithsons developed their topographical approach in their Sheffield University extension (1953) and "Cluster City" (1957) projects. The latter, with an emphasis on the "realities of the situation, with all their contradictions and confusions,"[130] brings to mind Robert Venturi's influential *Complexity and Contradiction in Architecture,* which it predates by nine years. The similarity between the two serves to remind one just how much the anti-formalism of the 1950s was taken up in the next decade.

Banham and the New Brutalism

Banham's first major article on the New Brutalism appeared in the *Architectural Review* in December 1955. In it he discusses the Smithsons' Soho house, Hunstanton school, Sheffield University extension, and several other projects, including their competition entry for Coventry Cathedral (1951). Banham is unambiguously partisan, not only praising the Smithsons' work but also attempting to locate it in the contexts of postwar architectural history and IG-derived anti-classical aesthetics and ideas—there is even advice to consult *Astounding Science Fiction!*[131] Nonarchitectural illustrations accompanying the article include an "all-over" painting by Pollock (*Number Seventeen,* 1949; a work also illustrated in *Un Art Autre,* but misdated by Banham as 1953); an *art brut* burlap piece (undated) by Alberto Burri,

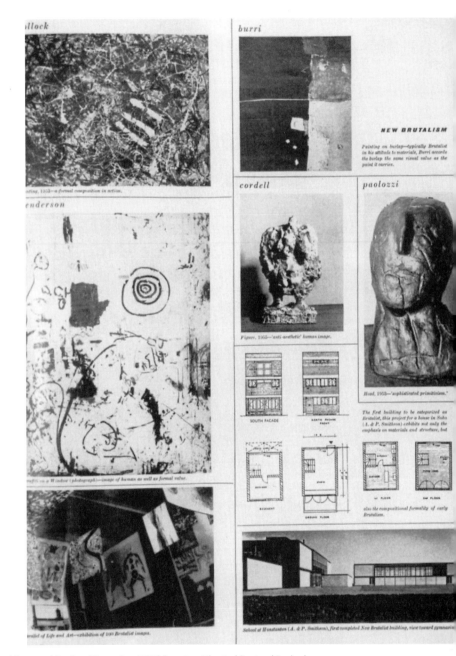

"The New Brutalism," *Architectural Review* (December 1955) (courtesy *The Architectural Review*)

described as "typically Brutalist in his attitude to materials;"[132] a Paolozzi head (1953) evincing "sophisticated primitivism"; a Magda Cordell "anti-aesthetic human image figure"; a photograph of window sgraffiti by Nigel Henderson; and an installation shot of "Parallel of Life and Art."

The chief characteristics of the New Brutalism were summarized by Banham as "1. Formal legibility of plan; 2. clear exhibition of structure, and 3. valuation of materials for their inherent qualities 'as found.'"[133] However, he acknowledged that this description could also apply to non-Brutalist buildings, and therefore suggests there was a further key ingredient: "In the last resort what characterises the New Brutalism in architecture as in painting is precisely its brutality, its *je-'en-foutisme,* its bloody-mindedness."[134] This led him to revise the first characteristic as "memorability as an image."[135] Banham appreciated the stark imageability of the *art brut* aesthetic of the Hunstanton school, where "Water and electricity do not come out of unexplained holes in the wall, but are delivered to the point of use by visible pipes and manifest conduits." Such a comment anticipates his enthusiasm for "High Tech" architecture in the 1980s (see chapter 5). It is clear that what Banham liked about the New Brutalism was its *art brut* character. Of the Sheffield University project, he wrote that its "aformalism becomes as positive a force in its composition as it does in a painting by Burri or Pollock,"[136] and he applauded the aformal siting of the blocks, which "stand about the site with the same graceless memorability as martello towers or pit-head gear."

It is at this juncture that Banham introduced the idea of *une architecture autre:* "Sheffield remains the most consistent and extreme point reached by any Brutalists in their search for *Une Architecture Autre.* It is not likely to displace Hunstanton in architectural discussions as the prime exemplar of The New Brutalism, but it is the only building-design which fully matches up to the threat and promise of *Parallel of Life and Art.*"[137] He regarded "Parallel of Life and Art" as the *"Locus classicus"*[138] of the New Brutalism: a visual and conceptual manifesto of the *art autre* aesthetic.

So, by late 1955, Banham had nailed his colors to the mast of the New Brutalism. In 1966 he published a history of the movement in which he detailed its characteristics and qualities more systematically:

. . . an architecture whose vehemence transcended the norms of architectural expression as violently as the paintings of Dubuffet transcended the norms of pictorial art; an architecture whose concepts of order were as far removed from those of "architectural composition" as those of Pollock were removed from the routines of painterly composition (i.e. balance, congruence or contrast of forms within a dominant rectangular format . . .); an architecture as uninhibited in its response to the nature of materials "as found," as were the composers of "musique concrète" in their response to natural sounds "as recorded."[139]

The abandonment by *musique concrète* of the traditional structures of Western music "gave a measure of the extent to which 'une architecture autre' could be expected to abandon the concepts of composition, symmetry, order, module, proportion, 'literacy in plan, construction and appearance'" as it had been understood from classical times to the Modern Movement. Primarily for Banham, *architecture autre* was an ethico-aesthetic matter, and questions about function and the daily demands of the occupants were secondary.

The Smithsons' New Brutalist work may have satisfied Banham's definition up to the time of his December 1955 article, and there were occasions when their Brutalist-derived projects of the later 1950s—"Cluster City," for example—continued to conform to his definition, but in 1956, Banham began to doubt the *architecture autre* integrity of the Smithsons' New Brutalist work, and turned toward a new source of *architecture autre*. Ironically, this new source also directly involved the Smithsons.

The project which Banham had doubts about was the *Patio & Pavilion* environment at "This Is Tomorrow," which he had criticized for being too "submissive to traditional values." There was a point at which rawness and primitivism could become part of an appeal to traditionalism and thus, for Banham, conservative rather than radical. The Smithsons' attempt to depict the "fundamental necessities of the human habitat in a series of symbols" was deficient in this way. Reflecting on the exhibit ten years later, Banham wrote:

Such an appeal to fundamentals in architecture nearly always contains an appeal to tradition and the past—and in this case the historicising tendency was underlined by the way in which the innumerable symbolic objects . . . were laid out in beds of sand in a manner reminiscent of photographs of archaeological sites with the finds laid out for display. One or two discerning critics . . . described the exhibit as "the garden-shed aesthetic" but one could not help feeling that this particular garden shed . . . had been excavated after the atomic holocaust, and discovered to be part of European tradition of site planning that went back to archaic Greece and beyond.[140]

What for Banham was a criticism—and redolent of his attacks on traditionalism in *Theory and Design*—was not necessarily so for the Smithsons, who had frequently emphasized their desire for continuity with the earlier periods of architecture, from the heroic period of the Modern Movement[141] back to, indeed, ancient Greece.[142] *Art brut* may have eschewed classical notions of transcendent form, but it embraced transcendence as manifested in the timelessness of the "rough poetry" of the human mark. Banham was mistrustful of the *art brut* tendency at the point where the primitivism became a contrived aesthetic rather than an open-minded attitude. By 1956 the suspicion was growing that the Smithsons were becoming seduced by aesthetics rather than ethics: inelegance as a manifestation of an attitude of bloody-mindedness was giving way to sophistication.

However, Banham did not completely change his mind about the Smithsons' New Brutalist-influenced work. Their Sugden House at Watford (completed in 1957), a mixture of suburbia and *architecture brute,* was described by one offended commentator as a "shocking piece of architectural illiteracy in plan, construction and appearance."[143] To Banham it was the Smithsons' last "subtly subversive" building. Later work, such as their next important building, the Economist Cluster in St. James's, London (1959–1964), demonstrated more conventional architectural solutions in which the Smithsons turned their backs on the notion of *une architecture autre.*[144] The same was true of the New Brutalism as a movement. Where once for Banham it had promised to be an alternative to conventional architecture, it rapidly became just another stylistic option characterized by rough-cast concrete: "In the last resort they [the Smithsons and other Brutalists] are dedi-

Alison and Peter Smithson, the Economist Building, 1959–1964 (courtesy Peter Smithson)

cated to the traditions of architecture as the world has come to know them: their aim is not *une architecture autre* but, as ever, *vers une architecture.*"[145] Few Brutalists would have disagreed; nor, by the 1960s, would they have believed it should be otherwise. The problem, they thought, was Banham's: as Alison Smithson once remarked, "Poor Peter [Banham], he's forever condemned to be disappointed, don't you know."[146]

The *House of the Future*

If 1956 marked the moment of decline of New Brutalism in its potential as an *architecture autre,* it also marked the rise of a new alternative—the Smithsons' *House of the Future,* commissioned for the Ideal Home exhibition. At "This Is Tomorrow," *Patio & Pavilion* had presented "rough poetry," whereas the Hamilton et al. exhibit offered sophisticated stylization. With the *House of the Future,* the Smithsons showed that they, too, could offer sophisticated stylization which grew out of the "reality" of "mass production society." In the second IG season, the Smithsons had spoken about the gulf between consumer expectations and conventional architectural solutions. They warned the architect that "Mass production advertising is establishing our whole pattern of life—principles, morals, aims, aspirations and standard of living. We must somehow get the measure of this intervention if we are to match its powerful and exciting impulses with our own."[147] Here we can see the Smithsons purporting to accept the "reality of the situation," namely, "the cultural objectives of society, its urges, its techniques and so on"[148]—a reality in which "mass production advertising" is dominant. Advertising represented dense, direct, and effective communication, and was strong in imageability:

To understand the advertisements which appear in the *New Yorker* or *Gentry* one must have taken a course in Dublin literature, read a *Time* popularising article on Cybernetics and to have majored in Higher Chinese Philosophy and Cosmetics. Such ads are packed with information—data of a way of life and a standard of living which they are simultaneously inventing and documenting. . . . They are good "images" and their technical virtuosity is almost magical. Many have involved as much effort for one page as goes into the building of a coffee-bar. And this transient thing is making a bigger contribution to our visual climate than any of the traditional fine arts.[149]

An interest in information and communication is combined with popular culture in true IG fashion. What were the implications of this thinking for architecture?

Brutalism usually implied single, unique buildings. An architecture which came to terms with popular culture would have to be mass producible. This, the Smithsons pointed out, was already under way: "the mass production industries had already revolutionised half the house—kitchen, bathroom, laundry, garage—without the intervention of the architect, and the curtain wall and the modular pre-fabricated building were causing us to revise our attitude to the relationship between architect and industrial production."[150] The *House of the Future* took this development to a further stage. It was an ingenious mixture of building industrialization and Detroit-influenced car styling. The components that comprised it were to be mass-produced but, as with car production, each component was used only once in each unit/house. This solved the problem of industrialization leading to standardization and repetition. Obsolescence was an integral part of the design concept which facilitated the idea of an annual model change. This meant that the styling was designed with the consumer in mind, and features were included—for example, a chrome strip on the exterior which recalled car styling—to make the "product" fashionable and desirable. The interior boasted a range of up-to-date services and technical equipment, such as a dishwasher, and a service trolley which housed television and radio. "Space-age" consumerist gadgets, including an "electro-static dust collector," meant that items of personal daily use could be permanent, and recognized, as Banham wrote in a review, "that the prime domestic virtue—house-pride—resides in permanent possessions."[151]

In the late 1950s the Smithsons continued their research into the house as a consumer product of expendable design with two "Appliance Houses." Both would be mass-produced, capable of dense grouping, and "contain a glamour factor"[152] to ensure their appeal to consumers. By 1959 the Smithsons thought it a real possibility that "a future architecture will be expendable,"[153] but demanding commissions like the Economist Building greatly reduced their interest in experimental projects and conceptual conjecturings.

The key building of IG-influenced architecture remained the *House of the Future.* The fundamental differences between it and other experimental all-plastic houses of the 1950s—such as Coulon and Schein's Maison Plastique, also of 1956—were its conceptual basis in product design, its sophisticated styling with the acceptance of the need for consumer appeal, and the premise of obsolescence. Other plastic houses were essentially in the tradition of mass-produced prefabricated housing which stretched back to heroic Modernism but did not challenge any of the fundamental assumptions of the house or housing. The Smithsons' design looked not toward architecture for guidance, but toward the apogee of consumer-oriented product design in the 1950s, and one of the cultural icons of the IG—the American automobile. The result was, Banham thought, a "necessarily powerful and memorable visual image."[154]

Alison and Peter Smithson, *House of the Future,* 1956 (courtesy Mary Banham)

The *House of the Future* has a strong claim to be accepted as an example of *architecture autre* because it signifies a radical break with conventional architectural concepts and practices. The Smithsons were proposing an architecture that took its lead from industrial design, thus offering the public, as Banham wrote in a review in 1956, "new aesthetic and planning trends and new equipment, as inextricably tangled together as the styling and engineering novelties on a new car."[155] Furthermore, just as those novelties tended to achieve "massive initial impact and small sustaining power," so, as with the car, they would contribute to the rate of obsolescence. Could this be an even more authentic *architecture autre* than the New Brutalism? Indeed, was this the fulfilment of the Futurists' promise that "the fundamental characteristics of Futurist architecture will be obsolescence and transience"? The Futurists had squared up to technology and had expressed the "mechanical sensibility" of the First Machine Age—obsolescence and transience had never before been elevated to the position of inherent characteristics. The Smithsons' *House of the Future* and associated projects were taking similar concepts and applying them to the changed conditions of the Second Machine Age with its consumer culture and private affluence. The combination of these changed conditions and the industrial design premise of the *House of the Future* amounted to nothing less than a potential paradigm shift in architecture.

Traditionally, there was a "sovereign hierarchy of the arts under the dominance of architecture,"[156] with product design following in its wake, but the *House of the Future* might be a pointer to paradigm shift in which, according to Banham, "the foundation stone of the previous intellectual structure of Design Theory has crumbled—there is no longer universal acceptance of Architecture as the universal analogy of design."[157] It may have been reasonable, he continued, for architecture to hold this position in the First Machine Age: "Architects alone of arts men had any technical training even remotely applicable to product design; alone of tech-men they had a sufficiently liberal education to be able to relate their designs to the general environment of human life," but, in the Second Machine Age, "no single viewpoint is sufficiently widely held to make effective communication possible, arguments tend to be conducted in an eclectic framework of postulates gathered from a variety of disciplines."[158] One of those disciplines was legitimately "pop-art polemics at the ICA," with the implication that architecture could derive from styles and trends in consumer product design.

This appeared to be a perfect *architecture autre,* but Banham expressed a fundamental reservation. In 1962 he declared that "there is no Pop architecture to speak of, and never will be in any ultimate sense, because buildings are too damn permanent."[159] His point was that to adopt product design as the architectural paradigm was flawed because of a fundamental misconception. He explained: "Appliances are made in one place, shipped to another to be sold, and then consumed somewhere else. The bulk of housing . . . is made, sold, and consumed in one and the same place, and that place is a crucial aspect of the product."[160] Houses are, therefore, not like consumer products because they are not portable: the Smithsons' *House of the Future* seems to have been a false promise of an *architecture autre.*[161] However, an influence of industrial design was to be welcomed if it made architects rethink their attitudes to housing, including recasting the occupant as a discriminating and style-conscious consumer rather than an undifferentiated member of the visually illiterate proletariat.

Image and Imageability

The belief that people were becoming more style-conscious and visually sophisticated was a major assumption in Banham's thinking in the later 1950s and early 1960s. The need for "massive initial impact" in the case of expendable design in a consumer society meant that a product's image became crucial to consumer appeal and financial viability. But "image" becomes far more than just keen styling and, as we have seen, has implications for Banham's idea of an *architecture autre*. The closest he came to defining it comes in his 1955 "New Brutalism" article:

A great many things have been called "an image"—S. M. della Consolazione at Todi, a painting by Jackson Pollock, the Lever Building, the 1954 Cadillac convertible, the roofscape of the *Unité* at Marseilles, any of the hundred photographs in *Parallel of Life and Art* . . . Where Thomas Aquinas supposed beauty to be *quod visum placet* (that which seen, pleases), image may be defined as *quod visum perturbat*—that which seen, affects the emotions, a situation which could subsume the pleasure caused by beauty, but it is not normally taken to do so, for the New Brutalists' interests in image are commonly regarded . . . as being anti-art, or at any rate anti-beauty in the classical aesthetic sense of the word. But what is equally as important as the specific kind of response, is the nature of its cause. What pleased St Thomas was an abstract quality, beauty—what moves a New Brutalist is the thing itself, in its totality, with all its overtones of human association. These ideas of course lie close to the general body of anti-Academic aesthetics currently in circulation.[162]

If the New Brutalist was moved by "the thing itself . . . with all its overtones of human association," so, too, was the aficionado of popular culture, whether IG "knowing consumer" and "Pop-art connoisseur"[163] or, as Alloway described it in 1958, the "absorbed spectator" and even those—perhaps former elementary school children—who "like to talk, neck, parade."[164] Such was the emphasis on the evocative strength of the image that canonical Modernist texts, including Moholy-Nagy's *The New Vision* (reprinted in 1946), Sigfried Giedion's *Mechanisation Takes Command* (1948), and Amédée Ozenfant's *Foundations of Modern Art* (reprinted in 1952), although being read or reread by Modernists, were valued by IG members for their illustrations only. Alloway recalled that what he liked about these books was their "illustrations that ranged freely across sources in art and science," presenting "fact condensed in vivid imagery."[165] For Banham, Sant'Elia's images of the Futurist city had had a similar direct and emotional appeal that was the reverse of dispassionate or disinterested.

Imageability is an underlying factor that links Banham's championing of the New Brutalism, popular culture, and the Futurists. The year 1954 may have been a key one for the Smithsons, but Banham's 1955 was its match with "Machine Aesthetic" (April), "Sant'Elia" (May), "Space for Decoration: A Rejoinder" (July), "Vehicles of Desire" (September), the original, Italian version of "Industrial Design and Popular Art" (November), and "The New Brutalism" (December). To the casual reader their subject matter may appear diverse to the point of being irreconcilable, but to the knowing consumer of Banham, there were key linking themes, such as the importance of "image." We will see in chapter 3 that "imageability" becomes even more important in the 1960s with the blossoming of Pop, and becomes a central ingredient in Banham's search for an architecture appropriate to the Second Machine Age.

3

SCIENCE FOR KICKS

An Architecture of Technology for the Second Machine Age

Theory and Design in the First Machine Age (1960) may have revised the issues surrounding the "selective and classicising" tendencies of the Modern Movement around the 1920s, but it also declared that similar issues were still live and, indeed, urgently in need of resolution. In the book's introduction, Banham pointed out that

> . . . while we yet lack a body of theory proper to our own Machine Age, we are still free-wheeling along with the ideas and aesthetics left over from the First. The reader may therefore, at any turn, find among these relics of a past as economically, socially and technologically dead as the city-states of Greece, ideas that he is using every day of his life. Should he do so, may he ask himself two things: firstly, are any of his ideas as up-to-date as he thinks them to be, this is the Second Machine Age not the First; and secondly, how out-moded in truth are the ideas he dismisses as mere fashions of the Jazz decades, for one Machine Age is more like another Machine Age than any other epoch the world

has ever known. The cultural revolution that took place around 1912 has been superseded, but it has not been reversed.[1]

This evokes the comments made by Banham—discussed in chapter 2—about the need to come to terms with the "throwaway economy" and its intrinsic expendability, and the problem of "making do with Plato" when nothing less than new criteria were required. The twentieth century may have the continuity of being a "technological century" but, within it, different Machine Ages threw up different demands and issues.

This chapter examines what Banham considered to be a "body of theory proper to our own Machine Age"—the Second Machine Age—and its implications for an architecture integrally related to technology. His thinking about architecture in the first half of the 1960s grows out of many of the ideas and approaches of the Independent Group (IG), including their sympathy for *art autre* and Banham's own search for an *architecture autre,* and the importance of a technologically sophisticated popular culture. In developing different approaches to technology—which in this chapter are defined as "pragmatic," "radical," and "Pop"—Banham sought three versions of an architecture of technology which, to a greater or lesser extent, responded not only to the technological, but also to the cultural, conditions of the day with its increasingly youthful, Pop sensibility.

The Second Machine Age

Just as the First Machine Age was characterized by the impact of technology, so, in the Second, "any label that identifies anything worth identifying . . . will draw attention to some aspect of the transformation of science and technology, for these transformations have powerfully affected human life."[2] It is the domestic scale of the effect in the Second Machine Age that marks it out from the First:

Many technologies have contributed to this domestic revolution, but most of them make their point of impact on us in the form of small machines—shavers, clippers and hairdryers; radio, telephone, gramophone, tape recorder and television; mixers, grinders, automatic cookers, washing machines, refrigerators, vacuum cleaners, polishers. . . . A housewife alone, often disposes of more horsepower today than an industrial worker did at the beginning of the century. This is the sense in which we live in a Machine Age.[3]

The level and scale of technological sophistication led Banham to define the Second Machine Age as "the age of domestic electronics and synthetic chemistry," in opposition to the First, which was "the age of power from the mains and the reduction of machines to human scale." The difference between the two Ages was, however, "more than quantitative," and affected society and culture qualitatively: "In the Second, highly developed mass production methods have distributed electronic devices and synthetic chemicals broadcast over a large part of society—television, the symbolic machine of the Second Machine Age, has become a means of mass-communication dispensing popular entertainment." By contrast, in the First Machine Age, only cinema directly touched the lives of a broad public whose domestic circumstances were little altered by the new technology. It was only upper-middle-class homes that experienced the modernity of innovative technology and developed an appetite for the mechanical sensibility in the First Machine Age. Marinetti may have epitomized that class, and the automobile the new, powerful technology at human scale of that era; but while Banham declared television the new symbolic machine, it was still the car which gave the measure of the qualitative difference between the Ages: "the average automobile of today, running on such roads as have been especially contrived for it, provides transport more sumptuous in vehicles more gorgeous than palanquin-borne emperors knew how to desire."[4]

This brings to mind Banham's IG musings on the Detroit automobile with its "means of saying something of breathless, but unverbalisable, consequence to the live culture of the Technological Century."[5] It also points up the qualitative difference between the two Machine Ages: a characteristic of the Second is that technology had become "naturalised"—it had become not only domestic but domesticated, widely available and expendable. Marinetti may have tentatively approached technology as if it were an untamed and unfriendly "snorting beast," but Second Machine Age technology was faithful and dependable:

Even a man who does not possess an electric razor is likely—in the Westernised world at least—to dispense some previously inconceivable product, such as an aerosol shaving cream, from an equally unprecedented pressurised container, and accept with equanimity the fact that he can afford to throw away, regularly, cutting edges that previous generations would have nursed for years. Even a housewife who does not possess a washing machine dispenses synthetic detergent from synthetic plastic packs on to synthetic fabrics whose quality and performance makes the jealously-guarded secrets of silk seem trivial. A teen-ager, curled up with a transistorised, printed-circuit radio, or boudoir gramophone, may hear a music that literally did not exist before it was committed to tape, reproduced at a level of quality that riches could not have brought a decade or so ago.[6]

IG members, including Lawrence Alloway and John McHale, had written about the postwar years—Banham's Second Machine Age—being the age of the common man and woman, rather than the age of rulers and the wealthy; and this, indeed, seemed to be borne out by the increasingly widespread availability of a standard of technology that would have been the envy of previous generations. Furthermore, as Banham indicated, technology impinged on the lives of both genders and all ages. Its frequent obsolescence and replacement may have made some aspects of technology relatively commonplace and, consequently, produced "equanimity" in its recipients and users. In this sense technology had become ordinary and, in effect, *invisible*—part of the routine of everyday life and unremarkable existence.

On the other hand, some technology had glamour and was highly visible. Consumers in the Second Machine Age may have increasingly expected technology to be readily available and to deliver a high level of performance, but the Modernist-derived passion for technology also endured, especially with the more consumer-oriented and stylized manifestations of the Second Machine Age, such as hi-fi, sophisticated advertising and, of course, cars. In another text of 1960—"Futurism for Keeps"—Banham describes how in the 1950s his generation had suddenly discovered that they were living amidst a new mechanical sensibility:

As Richard [Hamilton] and I and the rest of us came down the stairs from the Institute of Contemporary Arts those combative evenings in the early fifties, we stepped into a London that Boccioni had described, clairvoyantly. We were at home in the promised land that the Futurists had been denied, condemned instead to wander in the wilderness for the statutory forty years. . . . No wonder we found in the Futurists long lost ancestors, even if we were soon conscious of having overpassed them. Overpassed or not, they seemed to speak to us on occasions in precisely the detail that the ghost spoke to Hamlet.[7]

Banham draws a number of parallels between Futurism and contemporary experimentation and innovation, including Luigi Russolo's "Art of Noises" and *musique concrète,* and Marinetti's "Words in Liberty" and Beat poetry. First Machine Age manifestations listed by Boccioni in one of the manifestos—"gramophone, cinema, electric advertising, mechanistic architecture, skyscrapers . . . nightlife . . . speed, automobiles, aeroplanes"—parallel contemporary culture: "hi-fi, stereo, cinemascope and (in Richard Hamilton's succinct phrase) 'Polaroid Land and all that jazz.'"[8] If the Futurists were the First Machine Age's "primitives of the new sensibility," then the IG and fellow travelers were the sophisticates of the Second. Banham argued that

Marinetti's tag-line about "the man multiplied by the motor" is a fair indication of the characteristic inhabitant of contemporary culture. If you make "motor" stand for mechanisation in general—which is what Marinetti intended—then the phrase nicely brackets Charles Eames with his power tools, Cousteau with his aqualung, Malraux and his imaginary museum of photographs, and the anonymous man with his transistor radio belting out Beethoven in his beach-shirt pocket.[9]

The Futurists, Banham wrote, "saw, as nobody else outside the realms of science and technology seems to have seen, what a mechanised culture could do for its denizens." In this, they were "the true voice of twentieth century feeling" and, therefore, a guide to technological attitudes in the Second Machine Age. The new Machine Age had taken to heart Marinetti's discovery that, in Banham's words, "machines could be a source of personal fulfilment and gratification."[10] Similarly, Banham proposed that Sant'Elia had contemporary relevance to urban planning, in that he based "his whole design on a recognition of the fact that in the mechanised city one must circulate or perish." The Futurist architect seemed to "have foreseen the technological cities of the Fifties."[11] Banham's conclusion was that "the Futurist spirit, it appears, is with us for keeps, while we remain a technological civilisation."[12]

Second Machine Age Architecture

The relationship of architecture to the "technological civilisation" was, as we saw in chapter 1, a live issue, but was seldom debated in a way which, in Banham's opinion, broke out of the confines of First Machine Age terms. For example, the International Union of Architects' 1961 congress, with its theme of "Architecture and Technology," provided Banham with the opportunity to castigate the architectural profession for its "heroically naive" statements about technology.[13] He spelled out in the concluding paragraph of *Theory and Design* what he felt was at stake in the relationship:

It may well be that what we have hitherto understood as architecture, and what we are beginning to understand of technology are incompatible disciplines. The architect who proposes to run with technology knows now that he will be in fast company, and that, in order to keep up, he may have to emulate the Futurists and discard his whole cultural load, including the professional garments by which he is recognised as an architect. If, on the other hand, he decides not to do this, he may find that a technological culture has decided to go on without him.[14]

Banham did not seem to be entertaining any possibility of a synthesis, but was more interested at this point in the possibility of a technological *architecture autre.* The question which most vexed him was whether the new architecture would be largely self-effacing and—like the disposable razor—accepted with equanimity, or comprise the dreams that money could buy—like the Detroit car, whose sophisticated styling would be celebrated and cherished. As we will see in this chapter and the next, Banham kept both options open and worked through their implications and values.

The Futurist spirit that Banham thought vital had, to some extent, lived on in New Brutalism. The Brutalists may have rejected the forms of the architecture of the First Machine Age but, wrote Banham in 1958, "the theory they accept in its full, moralistic, functional and rationalistic rigour"[15]—and this included a commitment to an architecture of technology. He thought a misunderstanding about Brutalism had arisen because the Smithsons had rejected the machine aesthetic associated with the 1920s: this led "certain established modern dead-heads to suppose they have rejected technological culture, and the fact that they have expressed an interest in certain movements, such as Futurism and Expressionism . . . has caused other dead-heads to call the younger architects 'old-fashioned.'" In fact, their sensibility, in keeping with the culture and technology of the Second Machine Age, was plural and inclusive:

To find the junior avant-garde admiring with equal fervour peasant houses on Santorin, and the chrome-work on Detroit cars; the *Cutty Sark,* Chiswick House, *Camel* cigarette packs, and Le Corbusier's chapel at Ronchamp; Pollock, Paolozzi and Volkswagens—all this sounds like the complete abandonment of standards. In fact it is nothing of the sort—it is the abandonment of stylistic prejudice, and its replacement by the concept of the "style for the job." This abandonment opens the way for a more viable integration of design with practicalities of machine age existence.[16]

This IG inclusiveness may have promised much but, as we saw in chapter 2, its radical "otherness" crumbled faster than the surfaces of the facades on its buildings as its ethic became just an aesthetic. By the late 1950s, Banham lost any faith that Brutalism might provide a technologically based architecture for the Second Machine Age.

What was also beyond question was that the conventional architecture of the First Machine Age was irrelevant to the Second. Le Corbusier may have still been practicing in the 1950s and 1960s and offering a new *art brut* aesthetic based on the "rhetoric of the big, swinging, personal, primitive gesture"[17] but, according to Banham, "the order which Le Corbusier had to offer proved finally, and in spite of all the carryings-on about the motor car, etcetera, to be the pre-technological order of a peasant economy."[18] This was not to say that Banham was not moved by Le Corbusier's postwar work: "It still grabs me. About where Stonehenge, the terraces of Praeneste or the facade of San Miniato grab me. There are pictures of pieces of the parliament building at Chandigarh in the last volume of the *Oeuvre* that pin me, stunned, to the chair. But they are monuments from the past, not the architecture of here and now."[19] Such monumental, heroic architecture could not be the *architecture autre* that seemed to Banham ready to emerge from the middle years of the Technological Century.

Nor did it seem that Mies van der Rohe's postwar architecture was any more relevant. At the time of his death in 1969, Banham was lauding Mies as "the last master" of the tradition of architecture because "the painstaking devotion to the craft of construction was Mies's greatness and his limitation. Scrupulous attention to detail, within the limits of available technology; constantly refined skill, focused within a narrow cone of vision; unstinted concentration on the job in hand: this is a pure demonstration of the traditional virtues of the architect."[20] The strength of this approach is that it could lead to "great architecture"—his Berlin Museum was "the deftest and most effective celebration" of that city's neoclassical tradition. The weakness was that his approach conjured up "always the predictable answer" and, in the age of dynamic change that was the Second Machine

Ludwig Mies van der Rohe, Berlin Museum, 1962–1968

Age, his buildings' "neatly assembled certitudes may never stand up to human scrutiny again."

Mies's postwar work did not come to terms with technology's characteristics or possibilities. Yet, in the early 1960s, Banham took another view of Mies's work that presented it as a valid and viable architecture of technology for the Second Machine Age. His argument was that to categorize Mies as a classicist *methodologically* was to misunderstand his work. Each Mies building should not be read as the "attempted progress towards an ideal"—the "common ambition of classicists"—but as the "development from one *ad hoc* compromise solution to another without an ultimate goal." Such an approach "has only come in consciously with the rise of mass-production technology and research" and is, thus, part and parcel of the Second Machine Age. It may even appear subversive: "Its lack of any acknowledged ultimate destination appears dangerous to some social critics, but there is, in fact, a goal in view—a goal that is constantly under revision." That goal is similar to the one defined by the development engineer who "defines his goal in the light of what he has learned to do better since the last time he designed a comparable product."[21] This pragmatic, anti-idealist approach to technological problem-solving was likened by Banham to "US speed-buffs" who find authority in

. . . hot-rods, built up from catalogued parts and adapters, but not in all-out racing specials which are purpose made and purpose designed right through. Mies's detailing of this really authoritative quality adumbrates an almost unique attitude to technology—he accepts it. To be more precise; his very relaxed attitude towards it depends largely on his ability to select an array of techniques that lie readily to hand and exploit them within their accepted working limits.[22]

More colorfully, Banham describes how Mies "has walked along the shores of technology and made architecture from what he picked up along the way." This beachcombing image of Mies responding to technology *as found* and bricolaging it together to form architecture is not wholly convincing, given the evidence of the buildings; and by the time of Mies's death, Banham had readopted his previous, more conventional reading. But, in

1962, he seemed genuinely to believe that Mies espoused a hot-rodding, beachcombing approach or, slightly more plausibly, that his work indicated this approach as a possibility which represented a Second Machine Age architecture of technology.

Banham's 1962 article was one of a six-part series titled "On Trial" which appeared in *Architectural Review* that year. Together with his five-part "stocktaking" series of 1960, also in *Architectural Review,* these essays—which grew out of the conclusion to *Theory and Design*—form the core of his theory of a technologically derived architecture for the Second Machine Age. While the emphasis on architecture's relationship to technology underlies all the essays, three possibilities for an *architecture autre* emerge based on approaches to technology which might be classified as "pragmatic," "radical," and "Pop."

Architecture and . . . Pragmatic Technology

The pragmatic, "as found" approach to technology, supposedly in evidence in Mies's architecture, existed in its purist form in the early 1960s in the British CLASP (Consortium of Local Authorities Special Programme) prefabrication system, which, Banham judged, was a "text-book example of this kind of non-idealistic development."[23] Its success was internationally acknowledged, and it won the top award at the 1960 Milan Triennale.[24] The inclusive kit-of-parts was described by Banham in one of the 1962 essays as "permissive," in that it was neither underpinned by a "compact and closed system of components" in which choice was, consequently, strictly controlled, nor was it predicated on "some universal modular discipline" in order to enforce a predetermined aesthetic. The permissiveness did not appear radical—"indeed, CLASP's penchant for the tried and available material to do any particular job has done much to disguise its truly revolutionary content." This seemed to indicate that CLASP's permissive attitude to technology might be the authentic architecture of the Second Machine Age:

Is it, then, an *architecture autre,* an *other* architecture? If this concept is defined on radical grounds, not the purely formalistic ones . . . the proposition has some force. This is

CLASP school, Milan Triennale, 1960 (courtesy Mary Banham)

not, in any visible sense, architecture considered as one of the accepted fine arts; not architecture as the expressed will of a highly developed personality. And yet it carries its own visual conviction, the air of being the expressed will of something or some body of things, the product of some highly developed creative force.[25]

The proposition may have "some force" in that it related to Banham's intellectual criteria for a technological architecture, but its self-effacing modesty and aesthetic conservatism did not suit his preference for demonstrable conviction.[26]

With undoubtedly greater appeal to his aesthetic preferences, while still sharing CLASP's flexible, pragmatic "hot rod" approach to technology, were the "off-the-peg" approaches of both Charles Eames and Bruce Goff.[27] Eames drew from manufacturers' catalogs of standard units, and Goff made use of a variety of technologies, including reclaimed Nissan hut frames! This led Banham to describe them (elsewhere) as *"agents-provocateurs"* for their "habit of radical enquiry."[28] "Both," he claimed, "have a sort of hot-rodder attitude to the elements of building, ingeniously mating off-the-peg components, specials, and off-cuts from other technologies."[29] However, in 1962, Banham's "On Trial" verdict favored CLASP because "the great virtue of the hot-rod method—and this cannot be said too often or too loud—is that it demonstrates how to make architecture out of what is available, not just once, as with the Charles Eames house, nor through shock tactics, as with Bruce Goff's army-surplus architecture, but by taking thought."[30] Eames's and Goff's architecture may have been largely "off-the-peg," but the results were far from self-effacing.

The other major "pragmatic" technological tendency Banham was championing in the early 1960s was the very model of self-effacement, almost to the point of invisibility. In the opening "On Trial" essay, titled "What Architecture of Technology?," Banham discussed "one of the most sophisticated elements in the technology of architecture"[31]—the suspended ceiling. Because they were part of the interior, and therefore less a part of the reproduced image of monumental architecture, and because they appeared to the eye as a mere anonymous surface, and therefore not an individualistic tour de force, suspended ceilings were unsung as part of a Second Machine Age technological architecture. Yet they "represent probably the greatest

Charles Eames, Case Study House, Los Angeles, 1949

achievement to date in accommodating technology to architecture."[32] Furthermore, they achieved this "without once ever stepping outside what have passed . . . for architectural usages." In spite of its unself-consciousness, the suspended ceiling "sets a standard, a very hot standard, by which other attempts to tame technology can be assayed."

The integration of services into architecture, whether unself-consciously and "invisibly" like the suspended ceiling, or consciously and even monumentally like the Richards Medical Research Building by Louis Kahn,[33] was a theme that Banham was pursuing at this time, and it culminated in his *Architecture of the Well-tempered Environment* (1969). We will be returning to the theme in chapter 4, in relation to the creation of "fit environments for human activities." In the present context, however, the integration of services into architecture represents a largely pragmatic attitude which offers "some scope for a more flexible approach to the technology of architecture." But, as Banham continued in "What Architecture of Technology?," the flexible approach could pay dividends with architecture transformed, if two changes occur: "One is a general mental accommodation towards technology and its mental disciplines (one of the main themes of the 1960 series). The other is . . . the incorporation of the products and usages of technology into architecture, making architecture out of them."[34] The next two sections of this chapter deal with those more assertive and overtly technological approaches.

Architecture and . . . Radical Technology

He may have described CLASP as "the first wild outsider of the 'sixties";[35] Eames as "like a hot-rodder born"; and Goff as a "hundred-per cent-pure, good-to-the-last-drop, rolled-from-better-leaf" all-American architect,[36] but the greatest technological radicalism that Banham identified at the time of his two series was provided by Buckminster Fuller, "a technologist by nature and methods, who has blazed through architecture leaving behind a trail of barely exploited possibilities for other people to develop."[37] Fuller's approach was the antithesis of Mies's—Fuller thought technologically from start to finish. It was not, Banham argued, the resulting forms that would revolutionize architecture, but the attitude underlying them.

The architectural profession misunderstood Fuller, Banham wrote in the introductory essay of his 1960 "Stocktaking" series, who was "admired for his structures and accepted as a form-giver, while his elaborate body of theory and fundamental research into the shelter-needs of mankind is mostly dismissed unread."[38] In *Theory and Design,* Banham allots a considerable part of the conclusion to a discussion of Fuller's work. The purpose of this is to illustrate how a genuine architecture of technology may differ from the machine aesthetic of the 1920s. Banham quotes at length Fuller's vitriol about European designers. In part it reads:

The "International Style" brought to America by the Bauhaus innovators . . . used standard plumbing fixtures and only ventured so far as to persuade manufacturers to modify the surface of the valve handles and spigots, and the colour, size, and arrangements of the tiles. The International Bauhaus never went back of the wall-surface to look at the plumbing . . . they never enquired into the overall problem of sanitary fittings themselves . . . In short they only looked at problems of modifications of the surface of end-products, which end-products were inherently sub-functions of a technically obsolete world.[39]

Here, Banham is using Fuller to place the Modern Movement in conceptual and cultural perspective. By featuring Fuller's criticisms of International Style architecture, he further exposes the artistic bias of Modernism and the fact that it was in search of, first and foremost, a machine *aesthetic* rather than a profound or radical application of technology to what had been perceived as architectural problems. Fuller was offering a radical, *autre* approach, and not a conventional or even traditional "architectural" one.

The role Fuller plays in Banham's argument is clear enough but, historically, there is a flaw. Fuller's quotations in *Theory and Design* are undated (as well as unfootnoted), and the impression is given that they are contemporaneous with the pronouncements by the First Machine Age masters in the 1920s. In fact, they come from an at-the-time unpublished letter of 1955 from Fuller to John McHale, a Fuller enthusiast.[40] At one level this is interesting because it confirms a formal link between Fuller and IG members. At another level it is even more interesting because it raises questions about Banham's historical methodology and reveals the extent to which polemics can override disinterestedness. It could be argued that by effectively juxtaposing two quotes from different eras, Banham is misleading just as much as Le Corbusier did when he infamously juxtaposed classical architecture and supposedly standardized cars. In both cases, it is the force of the polemical point, rather than the historical precision or conceptual equality, that convinces.

This does not invalidate the substance of Banham's thesis, which would have been better served had he drawn on Fuller's "Universal Requirements of a Dwelling Advantage," which, although regularly revised and amended, dates back to 1927 and so was contemporaneous with the key European texts. Banham seems to have realized the significance of Fuller only late in the 1950s; he does not feature in his Ph.D. dissertation, but appears in the conclusion to *Theory and Design,* which was added after the doctorate.[41] Banham first wrote at length on Fuller in 1959,[42] and it tends to be his contemporary ideas, mediated by McHale, that he draws upon.

For Fuller, the chief characteristic of technology was the "unhaltable trend to constantly accelerating change."[43] An "architectural" solution was, therefore, only one possible solution to a functional and technological problem, and even then it was not "architecture" as it was generally recognized—as form. Fuller's Dymaxion House of 1927 was not the equivalent of a Modernist object-type "machine for living in," with its connotations of aesthetic formalism, but part of his "concept of air-deliverable, mass-producable, world-around, human life protecting and nurturing scientific dwelling service industry."[44] Other (or perhaps *autre*) inventions by Fuller—such as the Wichita House of 1946 (an updating of the Dymaxion House) and his famous geodesic domes, highly unconventional in architectural terms—became well known at the turn of the decade but, as Banham pointed out, led to a misunderstanding about his intentions and ideas.

Fuller described himself not as an architect (or engineer) but as an inventor—a distinction that, for Banham, was significant: "the architectural profession started by mistaking him for a man preoccupied with creating structures to envelop spaces. The fact is that, though his domes may enclose some very seductive-seeming spaces, the structure is simply a means towards, the space merely a by-product of, the creation of an environment, and that given other technical means, Fuller might have satisfied his quest for ever-higher environmental performance in some more 'other' way."[45] In spite of the fact that Fuller was made a member of the Association of International Architects—largely on the grounds, Banham suggested, that the profession "tolerates a few peripheral radicals"[46]—architects frequently were extremely hostile to Fuller's work, arguing that it ignored one of the most vital ingredients of architecture in the traditional sense: the aesthetico-symbolic. Philip Johnson spoke for many at the time: "Let Bucky Fuller put together the Dymaxion dwellings of the people so long as we architects can design their tombs and monuments."[47]

However, for Banham, Fuller's attitude to technology as "unhaltable change" and his uninterest in form in a closed, aesthetic way, seemed to point to a radical technological *architecture autre* for the Second Machine Age that was the heir to Futurism. Indeed, Futurism was a living presence rather than a dead relative in the Second Machine Age. As Banham wrote in 1960: "While life remains as Futurist as it has been, indeed becomes increasingly so, concepts of art and aesthetics based on eternal values will probably continue to prove perishable, like Roger Fry's, while Futurism, founded on change and '. . . the constant renewal of our environment,' looks to be the one constant and permanent line of inspiration in twentieth-century art."[48]

Banham makes Fuller's relationship with Futurism explicit in *Theory and Design*'s conclusion. Having praised Futurism's positive attitude to technology and chastised First Machine Age architects for cutting themselves off from the "philosophical aspects of Futurism," he presents Fuller as Futurism's heir:

There is something strikingly, but coincidentally, Futurist about the Dymaxion House. It was to be light, expendable, made of those substitutes for wood, stone and brick of which Sant'Elia had spoken, just as Fuller also shared his aim of harmonising environment with man, and of exploiting every benefit of science and technology. Furthermore, in the idea of a central core distributing services through surrounding space there is a

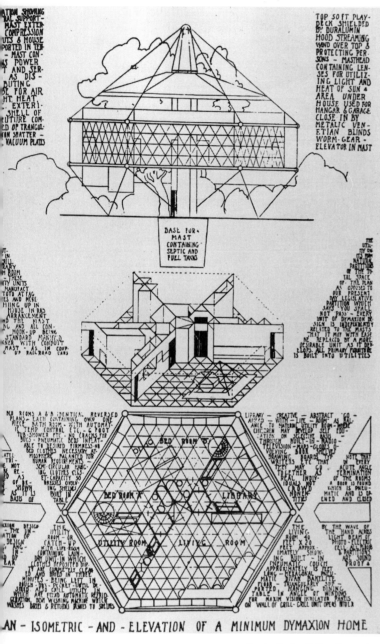

Buckminster Fuller, *Dymaxion House,* 1927–1929 (courtesy Mary Banham)

concept that strikingly echoes Boccioni's field-theory of space, with objects distributing lines of force through their surroundings.

Many more of Fuller's ideas, derived from a first-hand knowledge of building techniques and the investigation of other technologies, reveal a similarly quasi-Futurist bent.[49]

Banham may have been fanciful to parallel the Dymaxion House's central core with Boccioni's field theory, and it is highly improbable that Fuller would have been happy to have been likened to the Futurists, for he thought of all European Modernists as primarily engaged with aesthetics rather than seriously immersed in technology. Indeed, had Banham himself applied to Sant'Elia (as well as other favored *autre* architects, including the Smithsons) the criteria he believed were practiced by Fuller, he would have had to class his favored First Machine Age architects as machine aesthetes rather than radical technologists.

The theme of architecture arising from a radical approach to technology dominated the series of five "Stocktaking" articles, for which Banham was editor. Two of the articles were written solely by him; the others were multiauthored, including the concluding article, which featured responses to the series as a whole by the members of the *Architectural Review* editorial board, and a transcript of a discussion involving Banham, two architects, an academic, and erstwhile IG member Lawrence Alloway. An IG format was used for the remaining article in the series, which comprised short essays, each introduced by Banham, by three experts from "cutting edge" disciplines, on weapons systems, computers, and human sciences. These disciplines may have been outside the conventional frame of architectural reference, but Banham included them to make a point about architects needing to keep abreast of, and respond to, current technological and sociological developments. The IG ethos of inclusiveness, lateral thought, and radical perspectives was, significantly, alive in the "Stocktaking" series.

The first article set the agenda for the series by contrasting "tradition" and "technology" or the differences between conventional architectural habits of thought and technological ones. Banham defined the main premise of the series in terms reminiscent of Fuller: "technology will impinge increasingly on architecture in the next ten years, and . . . technological habits of thought are hostile to architectural habits of thought."[50] He questioned what was meant by "radical," and attacked First Machine Age architects for adopting the (only) apparently radical "Functionalist slogan that 'a house is a machine for living in' . . . because it begins by presupposing a house. Far more seditious to the established attitude of architects is the proposition that, far from caravans being sub-standard housing, housing is, for many functions, sub-standard caravans. Outside the context of architectural discussion this would be a pretty radical criticism of current architectural concepts."[51]

With an attitude that prioritized "measurable performance rather than some cultural sanction," Banham continued that "it becomes possible to define 'home' without reference to hearth or roof, but simply as the integration of a complex of intrapersonal relationships and mains-services." Not only the "operational lore" of architecture but also the cultural symbolism of "home" was being radically rethought in terms of some form of sociotechnological behaviorism. Here was Banham at his most Fulleresque, convinced, as he later expressed it, that it was an "either/or" situation between the "engineer-technologist" and the architect[52]—an assumption which appears to be at odds with his "both/and" approach of IG times.

But committed radicalism necessitated certainty and even a degree of intolerance. A genuinely radical scientific and technological attitude, Banham argued in the second article, "The Science Side," "could sweep away architecture as we know it now and leave in its place, precisely, that *other architecture* produced by the team-work of specialists in colour, heating, lighting, acoustics, market-research, group psychology—an architecture comparable to other aspects of creative technology—such as aircraft design or television—that are neither encumbered nor ennobled by a great tradition such as architects carry with them everywhere they go."[53] The idea of architecture becoming transformed and radicalized by embracing new thinking in adjacent disciplines—and becoming a genuine *architecture autre*—greatly appealed to Banham at this time.

With Fuller to the fore of his mind, Banham concluded in the third article of the "Stocktaking" series, "The Future of Universal Man," that "the architect must either become a member of an integrated team—contributing, perhaps, organisational skills, or talents akin to the product design stylist— or receive a comprehensive, scientific education."[54] The latter was very close to Fuller's stated belief that an architect's education should comprise "chemistry, physics, maths, bio-chemistry, psychology, economics, and in- dustrial technology."[55] It seemed, too, equally close to Hannes Meyer's pro- nouncement of 1928 that a house "is an industrial product and the work of a variety of specialists: economists, statisticians, hygienists, climatologists, industrial engineers, standardisation experts . . . and the architect? . . . he was an artist and now becomes a specialist in organisation!"[56]

The radical attitude to architecture expounded by *Bauhausler* Meyer would seem tailor-made to fit with Banham's theory of a Machine Age *ar- chitecture autre,* but Banham paid little attention to Meyer either in his Modernist revisionist articles in *Architecture Review* or, even more surpris- ingly, in *Theory and Design.*[57] It might seem that had Banham wished to do so, he could have cited Meyer's 1928 essay "Building," which was published in one of the Bauhaus books,[58] as a major source of *architecture autre,* for it contains many sentiments with which Banham sympathized. An "anti- architectural" spirit pervaded the essay with sentiments being expressed such as "Architecture as 'a continuation of the traditions of building' means being carried along by the history of architecture."[59] Meyer seems to pre- figure Fuller both in the content and in the tone of his writing, but Banham's uninterest in Meyer is hinted at in his description of the *Bauhausler* as being part of the "neo-Rationalist movement."[60]

The neo-Rationalist movement also, in Banham's view, went on to include the Hochschule für Gestaltung (HfG) at Ulm, about which he wrote: "While it asks some searching questions and produces some truly radical answers, [it] does so within a mental concept that substantially accepts the limits that the architectural profession has set itself."[61] Banham saw Meyer as tarred with the brush of Rationalism: his solutions may appear radical, but they are so within a context that does not challenge, let alone demolish, the funda- mental premises of architecture as conventionally or traditionally practiced.

There may be another reason for the relative statuses of Fuller, Meyer, and the HfG. Meyer's and the HfG's belief systems were fundamentally different

---

from the individualistic and idiosyncratic content and tone of Fuller's apolitical, technophilic pronouncements. Banham was suspicious of abstract and ordered intellectual and political systems, and once admitted his preference for "English pragmatism" over "continental systematics."[62] Temperamentally, too, he identified with the anti-establishment "lone voice" (a point we will return to in the conclusion). The generally unsympathetic or hostile response of the other *Architectural Review* editors to the "Stocktaking" series was predictable, and helped to underline Banham's reputation—akin to Fuller's—as a freethinking radical.[63]

Architecture and . . . Pop Technology

If the "radical technology" approach elicited some hostility from the architectural Establishment, Banham's third option regarding a technological architecture for the Second Machine Age caused an even greater outcry because it seemed to be shedding not only the cultural baggage of the "operational lore" but also architecture's seriousness of purpose. And even Bucky Fuller could never be accused of forsaking seriousness.

In one way, Pop technology overlapped with radical technology in that it could draw on the expertise of specialists, combine the data by employing a rational methodology, and produce a radical solution. The difference in Pop technology is that the solution would have to keep consumer taste in mind and not risk alienation by producing something as extreme or culturally unrecognizable as a Dymaxion structure. Recalling his IG enthusiasm for Detroit automobiles, Banham returned in "Stocktaking" to the argument that architects had much to learn from car design: "automobiles as the manifestation of a complex and agitated culture-within-a-culture producing discrete objects which are themselves environments for human activities, provide a standard of comparison for the activities of the architectural profession."[64] The profession may, for example, "draw from the work of stylists some sobering conclusions about the possibility of tailoring aesthetics to fit the aspirations or social status of the clients" by making use, among other things, "of scientifically accurate market research." The result of this would not be to design buildings which resembled cars—"there is no ambition to imitate automobile form"—but to change architects' attitudes so as to provide a relevant "standard of comparison."

The *House of the Future* is the example which readily comes to mind: in its design, Banham had written in 1956, "architect and technician find themselves as closely embroiled as marriage partners"[65] and, in "Stocktaking," he even cites the *House of the Future* as the "exception to the rule" of architecture imitating the car's form, based on the Smithsons' assumption that "mass-produced houses would need as high a rate of obsolescence as any other class of mass-produced goods." But, he remarked, "such a sentiment is rare . . . because the operational lore of architecture seems not to include the idea of expendability."

However, the idea of expendability in architecture was not fully dismissed, and even led Banham to contradict himself in the same series. In the "Propositions" collection of statements in the "Stocktaking" series, the other *Architectural Review* editors summarily dismissed of the idea of a team of specialists taking a lesson from automobile design: for Hugh Casson, "The product that in industry results from this sort of exercise is the Corn-Flake Packet";[66] and for Pevsner, "The prospect is not only not pleasing, the whole thing is out of the question."[67] Banham retorted in his commentary notes that "One of the great worries at the margins of the architectural profession is that building design just does not match the design of expendabilia in functional and aesthetic performance. Admittedly those functions and those aesthetics are not those of buildings, but the comparison remains damaging."

The admission would, for many, be the crux of the matter, but Banham took it as a lesson about an architecture *for* the Second Machine Age. Furthermore, the comparison with expendabilia may be more than a rhetorical device: "if it is admitted that buildings are only 'more permanent,' then it seems unfair to discriminate between them and 'expendables.' They are simply long-term expendables."[68] Banham did not elaborate on what the design implications were for "long-term expendables" in terms of their aesthetics. Did seeing all buildings as relatively expendable mean that architects should take their aesthetic lead from pop culture? If so, this seemed to contradict his 1955 declaration that there are two aesthetics: "one for the fine arts [including architecture], one for consumer goods." And "The survival of either aesthetic depends upon their differentiation."[69]

The reintroduction of expendability into the argument about architecture for the Second Machine Age seemed to other commentators like going one concept too far; but even farther out was the notion of playing "science for kicks," the title of a short essay which appeared at the end of the "Propositions" article. The phrase conjures up a situation of pleasure and almost indulgence that seems very different from the seriousness and rationalism associated with the "radical technology," or the reasonableness and moderation of the "pragmatic technology" approaches. Banham had no doubt about the reception of the phrase, which "will shock and repel a large number of persons inside the sciences, and quite a number of persons outside the sciences whose theoretical position is based on the idea of science as a tough and noble discipline."[70] What he meant by the phrase, he then qualified:

The scientist cannot play science for kicks, any more than an architect can play architecture for kicks—in either case it is a man's calling, and the sort of calling that is going to absorb most of his capacity for solid thinking. What one does for kicks is strictly outside office hours, for compensation, stimulation, relaxation or whatever. To treat science in this way may be one very proper attitude, in the present condition of architecture in a technological society.

So, while the responsibilities and rigors of professionalism prevent the scientist from playing science for kicks, the architect might not only legitimately play it in this way, but might gainfully do so. Banham then goes on to explain what it actually entails: it is a way "of using the mind for pleasure, or just the hell of it, in such a way that it flourishes, not vegetates."

This attitude was reminiscent of the activities of the IG, typified by the sentiment "the more rock 'n' roll you consume, the better it gets. In addition, the company of fellow-addicts also brings its rewards . . . sharpening one another's appreciation of the art." Some forms of culture obviously had their limitations: in the case of most "finite, simple kick-seeking," a point could be reached where first expertise, and then comprehensive knowledge and understanding, could produce boredom with the activity being studied. But science

. . . is neither finite, nor simple. Its primary fascination will always be that no man can embrace the whole of it, and even in one particular field, the limit of research is apt to be advancing faster than even the talented amateur can pursue. In Science-fiction, which is science-for-kicks in almost its purest form, not only do new fields of subject-matter constantly open up for exploitation, but old ones are equally constantly being revived because they have been extended by new research or theoretical revision.

If the connoisseur of science fiction got to know "a lot about ballistics, rocket dynamics, gravity, radiation, planetary atmospheres, galactic structures and cosmic dust," then the connoisseur of science, it followed, would gain similar knowledge and understanding through playing for kicks and would become a full and enthusiastic member of the Second Machine Age: "The man who doesn't get any kick out of science will, by definition, get no kick either from the Twentieth Century which . . . knows no other God . . . The man who plays science for kicks is, in our present situation, a life-enhancer, and if he functions in the visual field he will be the better able to produce the kind of symbols by which we identify ourselves as members of the scientific adventure to which we are all committed in our smallest acts."[71] The architect, therefore, has a *responsibility* to play science for kicks; otherwise he "is clearly unfitted to put up monuments symbolising or otherwise expressing its values."

"Kicks" posits the model of a thoroughly professional architect who is open-minded toward and enthusiastic about technology. As Banham stated in the essay, the advanced state of knowledge in science means that for architects "to pretend to take science 'seriously' is an act of monstrous arrogance." Banham would also distinguish between "seriously" and "earnestly": there is no reason to take science "owlishly, solemnly, reverently"—playfulness is perfectly acceptable and, indeed, in keeping with the "way that scientists take it" in the Second Machine Age. Architects had played it this way before: "modern architecture, in its most dizzily productive phase, from about 1910 to 1927, was doing just this, playing science for kicks, surf-boarding the crest of a wave of invention, discovery and application that finally broke about 1930."[72]

Therefore, the Second Machine Age architect with a fully Pop attitude to technology would be a combination of the Futurists, Fuller (whom Banham mentions in the essay), and an industrial designer such as a car stylist. And it is a total commitment: "He is in it for life—unless his nerve fails." The last sentence of "Science for Kicks" is pure Banham: "The lesson . . . seems to be clear—to go on with our scientific surf-ride on which we are newly launched, to play it for all the kicks it can produce, and stay with it till it is exhausted, instead of trying to jump off while we think the going is good and finding ourselves at the mercy of the next breaker behind." Nothing could better illustrate not only Banham's Pop- or IG-influenced way of thinking, but also his style of writing, which was liable to seduce or infuriate!

A more radical version of a technological Pop architecture appeared in "Towards a Pop Architecture," the penultimate article in the "On Trial" series, and it was to be prophetic. The word "Pop" holds the key. In the early 1960s its 1950s meaning of "popular culture" was being superseded by a more specific connotation of "Pop art" as an art historical movement. Referring to the emergence of Pop artists and the associated "breakthrough for a kind of sensibility that takes fine and Pop equally in its stride"—a sensibility first appreciated, of course, by the IG—Banham remarked that "it is believed in some circles that any revolution or upheaval in the pure arts must, of some historical necessity, be followed by an equivalent upset in architecture, [and so] it is anticipated that the *cordon-sanitaire* between Pop-Art and architecture is about to be breached like a metropolitan green belt, and a Pop-architecture emerge about 1966."[73] With his IG background and sensibility, understanding of the cultural significance of expendability, and knowledge of the *House of the Future,* one might have expected Banham to commit himself to this option and predict a Pop architecture as some sort of equivalent to Pop art, but in 1962 he was skeptical, arguing that "this 'necessity' will not stand up to historical examination." Moreover, "it is not clear how it might benefit architecture."[74] Nothing could better illustrate Banham's dictum that "the only way to prove you've got a mind is to change it occasionally," for he was soon to become very clear in his mind about the benefit of such a constituted Pop architecture.

Some might argue that such a change of mind is symptomatic of superficial or shallow thinking, or that it represents opportunism and a willingness to jump on the most fashionable bandwagon. Some might also argue that Banham's varied approaches to a technological architecture—the pragmatic, radical, and Pop—typify inconsistency and "trying to have it all ways" rather than the development of a clear and consistent theory. I would argue that the "inconsistency" is actually not significant, but is explained by each approach representing a version of the same theory of technology-based architecture for the Second Machine Age. Banham, as we will see in chapter 5, was attracted to the idea of the "style for the job," which was a combination of British pragmatism and IG non-Aristotelian thinking which rejected binary absolutes by accepting "both/and." In the case of the pragmatic/radical/Pop options, all three were valid responses to particular situations and could be utilized accordingly. Again based on IG thinking, they existed on a continuum, not hierarchically; the continuum ensured that they overlapped and were not self-contained. Banham was more attracted to the radical/Pop section of the continuum, and spent relatively little time expounding the virtues of the pragmatic approach—principally because, temperamentally, he was attracted to assuming a more extreme and polemical critical position.

In chapter 4 we will trace the development of Banham's "radical" approach to technology, and the ways in which it could result in the complete rejection of the conventional and even traditional "operational lores" of architecture. The remainder of this chapter concentrates on the development of Banham's Pop technology option, in which "science for kicks" epitomizes the spirit of the architectural projects.

Archigram: "Science for Kicks"

Between 1960 and 1962, Banham was exploring ideas that were to coalesce into Pop architecture in 1963. These included the idea of playfulness and "science for kicks"; expendability as an intrinsic condition of technology; styling and consumer taste as a determining factor of form; and the sort of *art autre* aesthetic of ruggedness that contravened orderliness and "good taste." This last had been most clearly evident in the Smithsons' Brutalism, and it could be identified in the first issue of *Archigram,* published in May 1961—initially a cheaply produced, simple, and direct broadsheet aimed at young architects disenchanted with contemporary architecture and the complacency of the architectural profession. Part of the text that constituted the front page of the first issue declared: "A new generation of architecture must arise with forms and spaces which seem to reject the precepts of 'Modern' yet in fact retains these principles. WE HAVE CHOSEN TO BY-PASS THE DECAYING BAUHAUS IMAGE WHICH IS AN INSULT TO FUNCTIONALISM."[75] The statement recalls not only Banham's revisionism but also the Smithsons' call to return to the pioneering spirit and principles of the Modern Movement of the 1910s and 1920s. Moreover, one of the other claims, that "We want to drag into building some of the poetry of countdown [and] orbital helmets,"[76] fixes the intention within a context of the Second Machine Age. *Archigram* was the vehicle for an architecture that was as emotionally and technologically connected to the 1960s "space age" as the Smithsons' consumerist projects belonged to the 1950s "jet age" of Detroit car styling.

Archigram's contributors included Peter Cook, Warren Chalk, Dennis Crompton, David Greene, Ron Herron and Mike Webb. With the exception of Chalk (aged thirty-four) and Herron (thirty-one), all were in their middle twenties in 1961. Banham's *Theory and Design in the First Machine Age* was a book which gave academic credibility to their dissatisfaction with the architectural status quo, and his "Stocktaking" series provided the sort of *architecture autre* based on technology that appealed to this new generation who would have been Angry Young Men had they not been so excited by the opportunities of consumer culture.

The second issue of *Archigram* was published in 1962 and, like the first, included a disparate collection of projects by members of the nascent group, friends, and students. However, it was the third issue of the magazine, published in 1963, which attracted the greatest attention to date. With this manifesto-like issue, the title began to refer to a group as well as to a publication. The manifesto/theme was emblazoned across the cover: "Expendability: towards throwaway architecture." All the material in the issue was relevant to this theme, ranging from consumer products to old and new architecture, including projects by Buckminster Fuller. Archigram's own work comprised projects for complex buildings which had long-term frameworks and short-term and expendable shop or living units. In the editorial, group member Peter Cook listed the increasing number of expendabilia that were now socially acceptable—paper tissues, polyethylene wrappers, ballpoint pens, and others—and commented that at "every level of society and with every level of commodity, the unchanging scene is being replaced by an increase in change of our user-habits and thereby, eventually, our user-habitats."[77]

Cook was favourably disposed to this change, interpreting it as the "product of a sophisticated consumer society, rather than a stagnant (and, in the end, declining) society." Cultural critics and Modernists would doubtless have taken issue and read "sophisticated" as a euphemism for "exploitative." Cook, however, believed that expendability should be enthusiastically embraced, and was disappointed by what he saw as the public's inconsistency: "Why is there an indefinable resistance to planned obsolescence for a kitchen, which in twelve years will be highly inefficient (by the standards of the day) and in twenty years will be intolerable, yet there are no qualms about four years obsolescence for cars." The fashion industry provided the model for expendability: "After all," Cook continued, "my wife wears clothes which will be an embarrassment in two years." Cook, like members of the IG, futurologists, and American industrial design pundits, implored consumers to think again:

Our collective mental blockage occurs between the land of the small-scale consumer product, and the objects which make up our environment. Perhaps it will not be until such things as housing, amenity-place and workplace become recognised as consumer products that can be bought "off the peg"—with all that this implies in terms of expendability (foremost), industrialisation, up-to-dateness, consumer choice, and basic product-design—that we can begin to make an environment that is really part of a developing human culture.[78]

This signified a position different from Banham's. Banham had largely discounted the contribution of the *House of the Future,* arguing that buildings and products were fundamentally different because the former were tied to specific locations. Expendability might be an appropriate condition of a product, but it was not an intrinsic part of a building. Archigram, however, emphasized the "significant sameness." A collage in *Archigram 3* showed some nonpermanent buildings such as garden sheds and huts, but pointed out that they did not express their expendability; rather, they visually referred to permanency—and as such, "all have failed." Another collage showed designs which were "serious attempts at direct design for obviously limited life-span objects" and "succeeded in being produced as such": these included Abstracta System domes, Fuller's Dymaxion car and Wichita House, a London County Council temporary house, and a plastic telephone exchange. The same collage also showed packages of cereal, disposable tissues, frozen food, and matches. The visual and conceptual point was that "The connection is much greater between the truly designed expendable building and the package, than between it and the 20 year life-span house with the 80 year life-span look."[79]

Archigram's message was clear: expendable technology should be a joyous fact of contemporary life, and everything should be regarded as a consumer product: "the home, the whole city, and the frozen pea pack are all the same . . ."[80] Though Banham may have celebrated expendable technology with equal joy, he had resolutely refused to dedifferentiate between architecture and consumer products, and this raised questions about how he would respond to Archigram's basic premise about expendability.

Several projects by Archigram developed their conceptual premises, none more so than their notorious Plug-in City of 1964, an enormous megastructure the size of a city. A long-term (forty-year) framework contained essential services into which were "plugged" shorter-term units catering for a variety of needs and "planned for obsolescence."[81] Archigram portrayed Plug-in City as a "visually wild, rich mess"[82]: visual sources included oil refineries, space and underwater hardware, launching towers, Second World War sea forts and, linking the group even more directly with the IG, science fiction imagery. Peter Cook was aware of the historical precursors of Archigram's attitudes and admitted that Plug-in City could not have existed without, inter alia, the Futurists and the Smithsons. He emphasized both continuity and development: Archigram's ideas expressed "a maturity stemming out of the '50s."[83]

In 1964 the fourth issue of *Archigram* was published. Its full title was *Amazing Archigram 4 Zoom issue,* and it was laid out like a comic with pages of collaged science fiction imagery. The consistent theme—directly recalling the IG's activities—was the relationship of science fiction to architectural fact and contemporary practice. As we saw in chapter 2, in 1956 Alloway had written about the role of science fiction in orienting its readers "in a technological and fast-moving culture," and in 1958 Banham had similarly written of its value to architects as a "spur to imaginative technology." Archigram seemed to have heeded their comments, announcing that science fiction imagery was part of a "search for ways out from the stagnation of the architectural scene"[84] which put architecture in touch with live technology. In the First Machine Age the Futurists had praised cars, railway and electricity stations, and dams. In the Second Machine Age, the group looked toward "the capsule, the rocket, the bathyscope, the Zidpark [and] the handy-pak" for an up-to-date image of technology. The significance of the imagery was not lost on Banham—in the American journal *Design Quarterly* in 1965, he was moved to praise Archigram for providing "the first effective images of the architecture of technology since Buckminster Fuller's geodesic domes first captivated the world fifteen years ago."[85]

Banham and Archigram

Banham's first significant comments about Archigram appeared in the 1965 *Design Quarterly* article and were reprinted later the same year in *Architectural Design.*[86] The discussion of Archigram was part of a wider essay by Banham titled "A Clip-on Architecture," which comprised the whole issue of *Design Quarterly* on the general theme of "endlessness and indeterminacy" in architecture. Banham discussed concepts of endlessness in the work of Richard Llewelyn Davies and his "scientific and systematic approach to both architectural design and constructional methods."[87] But, whereas the "clip-on" aspect of Llewelyn Davies's concept operated at the level of "structural

Archigram, expendability collage from *Archigram 3,* 1963

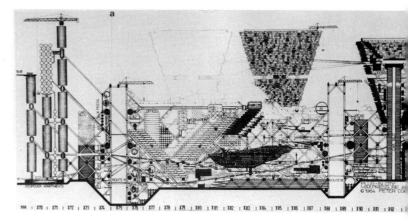

Archigram, **Plug-in City,** 1964 (courtesy Archigram Archive)

Archigram, *Amazing Archigram 4,* 1964

units that could be added up into a usable volume,"[88] the Smithsons, in projects including their *House of the Future,* "were offering usable volumes that could be added up into something more complex. The concept was less intellectually pellucid, but more emotionally appealing—it is difficult to identify oneself with a pair of vertical mullions, an underwindow air-conditioner and an area of tinted glass, but easy to identify with a room you can stand up and walk about in." The problems he raises about identification do, again, seem to show an inconsistency in his thinking around this time. Why should Llewelyn Davies's architecture pose a problem if Fuller's definition of home in terms of "the integration of a complex of intrapersonal relationships and mains-services" did not? Perhaps, again, it was a case of Fuller meeting Banham's criterion of a radicalness that went beyond architectural lore, whereas Llewelyn Davies's concepts were radical only within that lore.

Banham was more sympathetic to the clip-on development which he traced from the Smithsons, through projects by Ionel Schein and Jacques Coulon, to a 1959 study by Jaques Baudon.[89] What these projects shared was the idea not only of the repetitive cell, "producing a series of projects for habitable units that came to look more and more like industrial designer's products, and less and less like architecture," but also a development, prefiguring Archigram, that moved toward "independent living-capsules" which were fully serviced, mobile, and transportable. Their significance was that they "made the psychological and aesthetic break necessary to free themselves from architecture's time-honoured roots in the ground."[90] Those time-honored roots had, previously, led Banham to distinguish clearly between architecture and product design, with implications for expendability, in terms of the former's fixed relationship to particular locations. Was Banham now rethinking and even rejecting that premise?

In retrospect, it is more likely that Banham was suspending his disbelief and that what was really changing was his assessment of the value of a Pop architecture. He had seen little value in a Pop architecture in 1962, but now, with Archigram, he saw it as a major boon to architectural attitudes, radical thinking, and imageability. Archigram may not have been the first to replace the "clip-on" with the "plug-in" approach, but they were to develop the idea most evocatively and with the greatest visual impact. The "clip-on" approach was epitomized by the outboard motor with which "you can convert practically any floating object into a navigable vessel. A small concentrating package of machinery converts an undifferentiated structure into something having function and purpose."[91] Whereas, with the "plug-in" idea, "you reverse the proposition. The generalised structure becomes the source of power, service and support, and the specialised clip-ons become the habitable units. The outboard motor analogy has to be replaced by something more like the connection of domestic appliances to the house's electrical supply." Banham saw these as variations of the same basic concept: both were employed by Archigram—Capsule Homes and Plug-in City, for example—and sometimes in the same project. However, what was important was neither one nor the other, but the fact that the aesthetic was "multiplied by a wild, swinging, pop-art vision that is a long way from the intellectual austerities of the speculations of . . . Llewelyn Davies."[92] He might have added that the austerities were not only intellectual but also visual.

Banham argued that Archigram's appeal was that "it offers an image-starved world a new vision of the city of the future, a city of components on racks, components in stacks, components plugged into networks and grids, a city of components being swung into place by cranes." This seemed to be an appeal which was an updating of Sant'Elia's—a "new vision of the city" for the Second Machine Age, not the First. But it was more than just an updating: part of its significance was that it demonstrated a major change in sensibility that was occurring at the time of Plug-in City. Whereas a First Machine Age architect would more than likely have taken it as an insult, Archigram

. . . make no bones about being in the image business—like the rest of us they urgently need to know what the city of the future is going to *look* like, because one of the most frustrating things to the arty old Adam in most of us is that the wonders of technology have a habit of going invisible on us. It is no use cyberneticists and O and R men telling us that a computerised city might look like anything or nothing: most of us want it to look like *something,* we don't want form to follow function into oblivion.[93]

This appeared to be a shift from Banham's early 1960s approaches of CLASP pragmatism and Fulleresque radicalism to the fully blown "science for kicks" option. Both CLASP and Fuller are referred to critically: the former, far from being hailed as an authentic *architecture autre,* as it had been in 1962—is linked with conservatism and orthodoxy—Banham now condescendingly dismissed "the architecture of the establishment [which] rusticates in the picturesque prefabrication techniques of the tile-hung schools of the CLASP system."[94] And Fuller may have "captivated the world 15 years ago" with "the first effective image of the architecture of technology," but Archigram's difference from Fuller "hardly needs to be rubbed in, except to hope that the opposite mistake will not be made. Fuller offered (offers) a manner of thinking radically about the control of the environment and soon got bored with playing with it. A lot of po-faced technicians are going to pooh-pooh Plug-in City's technological improbabilities and brush it off as a Kookie teenage Pop-art frivol, and in the process the formal lessons of the Plug-in City might be missed."[95]

The real lesson to be drawn from Archigram was that the earlier notion that radical or even pragmatic technology could usurp aesthetics might be completely overturned. Banham drew attention to the way his argument "started with . . . cautious propositions about what technology might do to aesthetics; we finish with aesthetics offering to give technology its marching orders." But it also reflected his own changing priorities about the nature of technology, the relationship of technology to aesthetics at a particular historical juncture, and, in particular, the importance of "image-ability" with—as we saw in chapter 2—its resounding emotional appeal. "Science for kicks" was now becoming the most appropriate expression of technology in the increasingly visually oriented, visually sophisticated culture of the "high Pop" years.[96]

Banham, in effect, returns to the distinction between seriousness and earnestness, and their relationship to "science for kicks" in a short essay about Archigram, published in 1972:

Archigram is short on theory, long on draughtsmanship and craftsmanship. They're in the image business and they have been blessed with the power to create some of the most compelling images of our time . . . [Their work is] all done for the giggle. Like designing for pleasure, doing your own thing with the conviction that comes from the uninhibited exercise of creative talent braced by ruthless self-criticism. It's rare in any group—having the guts to do what you want, and the guts to say what you think—and because it's so rare it's beyond quibble. You accept Archigram at its own valuation or not at all, and there's been nothing much like that since Frank Lloyd Wright, Mies and Corb.[97]

This placed Archigram amongst the highest company and spelled out that "the giggle" might be the opposite of earnestness but was, in Banham's thinking, evidently related to seriousness when allied to conviction, creativity, and the "ruthless self-criticism" supposedly employed by Archigram. So it was not Plug-in City's feasibility and functionality that are the lessons— "even Archigram can't tell you for certain whether Plug-in City can be made to work"—but its image and imageability: "if people are to enjoy manipulating this kind of adaptable mechanical environment . . . then they will have to be able to recognise its parts and functions, so that they can understand what it is doing to them, and they can understand what they are doing to it." Archigram, like other young architects in the mid-1960s, were creating "up-to-the-minute" architecture that, Banham remarked at the time, frequently exhibited "rounded corners, the hip, gay, synthetic colours, pop-culture props" which combine to suggest "an architecture of plastic, steel and aluminium, the jukebox and the neon-lit street"—an architecture of technology for the affluent, urban young that resembled the beloved boutiques and nightclubs that formed the "scene."[98]

Archigram's graphics reinforced the uncompromising youthfulness of their vision. The space comic format of *Amazing Archigram 4* featured superhero characters depicted in the acknowledged style of Roy Lichtenstein, but most later projects included photographs of young, fashionable, affluent, and leisured people clipped from color supplements. Analyzing their presentation style, Banham reflected in 1976 that Archigram were "voracious consumers of collageable material with which [they] . . . populate and animate their drawings. They raided the illustrations and advertisements in colour magazines and came up, inevitably, with 'leisure people,' because colour magazines in those affluent years contained little else [than] . . . the leisured post-industrial world of the New Utopians."[99]

Banham denied that this was intentional or even programmatic, and refuted the criticism that Archigram's buildings and cities were just for the young and beautiful, claiming "nothing could more neatly illustrate the dangers of mistaking a piece of British graphic opportunism for an ideological programme. The presence of all these leisure people in Archigram's permissive cities is as much an empirical solution to the problem of finding someone—anyone!—to populate them as it is a theoretical proposal for who *should* populate them."[100]

This, however, is Banham at his least convincing. Recourse to the color magazines of the day shows that far more than "leisure people" were featured, and Archigram could have found a wider range with little difficulty. Moreover, as aficionados of the "image business," members of Archigram would have had more visual material to hand than color supplements. With them taking so much pride in the quality and professionalism of their graphic work, it is highly improbable that the group would have used images with which they were not fully satisfied. The incorporation of a specific type of person did undoubtedly indicate the particular type of environment Archigram wished to create: Archigram were designing a Pop environment for the urban young. Members of the group were quite aware of this, and Warren Chalk, for example, admitted that "You don't have to live in Plug-in City." Somewhat understatedly he continued, "Retired people probably won't."[101]

Expendability and the Pop Sensibility

Archigram, ever the technological optimists, created the perfect architecture for—Banham's phrase—"the leisured post-industrial world of the New Utopians." The "dreams that money can buy" of the 1950s had become the daily lifestyle products of the 1960s that the young increasingly thought of as their birthright. In the early to mid-1960s, Britain entered its own "high mass-consumption stage." The manifestations may not have been as excessive or flamboyant as those in the United States a decade earlier, but a major *relative* increase in consumerism was there for all to admire. The Second

Machine Age was entering a new phase characterized by widespread affluence and consumerist attitudes, and an architecture for the Second Machine
Age would need to reflect the zeitgeist of that new phase. The dramatic social and aesthetic changes that Britain was undergoing shaped Banham's response to Archigram, and affected his architectural sensibility as a whole.
Banham was a man of, and the man for, his time.

The mood among the progressive and socially mobile was for change. In
1963, Harold Wilson, who had recently become the Labour party's leader,
outlined his vision of a progressive and classless Britain that would be
"forged in the white heat of the scientific revolution,"[102] and in 1964 Labour
was elected to office where they remained for the rest of the decade. Until
the political mood became *plus ça change* after 1966, the decade was a time
of optimism when the country seemed to be turning its back on decades of
inequality and class warfare, and embarking on a new age of classlessness
and modernization, with progress through technology.

Design responded to the new mood, especially at the more consumerist
end of the activity, and the newly founded "coloursupps" promoted a view
of design that oozed excitement and change. For example, writing about
contemporary furniture in the *Sunday Times Colour Supplement* in 1964,
Priscilla Chapman popularized the Second Machine Age, progressivist idea
that "technological change is going to move so fast that people won't tol-
erate machines or furniture or even rooms which are more than a few years
old . . . Responsible design will be throwaway design . . . [People] throw
away their paper bags, their television sets and their cars. The public just
don't realise how close they are to throwing away their furniture too."[103] In
other words, change—and hence obsolescence—was no longer under the
control of scheming manufacturers, but was an inevitable symptom of an
advanced technological society.

This technological determinist view not only echoed Archigram, but also
recalled the Banham/Alloway/McHale "progressivist" faction of the IG. Between about 1963 and 1967, the relationship between optimism, technology and design was particularly strong among the affluent urban young
for whom "genuine obsolescence" did seem to become one of the main
criteria in design, the corollary of massive initial impact. Youth became an

important consumer market group in the 1960s, primarily for economic reasons: full employment and the increased affluence of their parents meant that young people had disposable income in enticing quantities and so became a much sought-after consumer target group. The "children of the Age of Mass Communication"[104] were the first generation who were born *after* the war and who had little memory of postwar austerity. They had no difficulties with conspicuous consumption and pleasure, and often conflated the two.

Banham's IG-derived ideas about culture, and Pop as it was being lived, were undoubtedly close. By 1966 Britain was being hailed as the world leader in Pop culture. *Time* famously proclaimed, "In a decade dominated by youth, London has burst into bloom. It swings: it is the scene." Expendability, that cultural condition identified by Banham as central to contemporary values, was at the core of fashion design. The young were urged by one fashion journalist to "make the break—throw out the old—discard the dreary. There's so much fun around fashion and you'll miss out if you don't."

The continuity between the 1950s and 1960s phases of the Second Machine Age was readily apparent. For example, Mary Quant argued that the designer's role was to provide constant novelty, so as to ensure continual change: "All a designer can do is to anticipate a mood before people realise that they are bored with what they have already got. It is simply a question of who gets bored first. Fortunately I am apt to get bored pretty quickly. Perhaps this is the essence of designing."[105] These were sentiments remarkably similar to those expressed by automobile stylist Harley J. Earl in 1955: "Discontent, dissatisfaction, and restlessness . . . seem to be absolutely necessary . . . for any person engaged in the field of automobile design. A car stylist must be discontent with past achievements, dissatisfied with present accomplishments, and continuously in search of new ideas."[106]

Massive impact and small sustaining power—Pop culture in the mid-1960s offered endless change and constant stimulation. Excitement, action, fun, constant change, and disposability were presented as the hallmarks of the Pop lifestyle. As the Futurists had rhetorically called for the burning down of the "old" culture, so youth rejected the values, attitudes, and cultural modes of their parents. The "generation gap" seemed unbridgeable in the

Pop fashions, mid-1960s

Disposable paper furniture, mid-1960s

early to mid-1960s, and Banham's sympathies were increasingly with the younger, rebellious generation.

The Countercultural Critic

That Banham felt he was a part of the Archigram generation of young architects is encapsulated in his 1966 "Zoom Wave Hits Architecture," an article in which he writes about the new wave of underground architecture magazines in Britain. These magazines were as far from the "plush glossies and cool scientific journals" as could be imagined. Reflecting Pop culture, magazines like *Archigram, Megascope,* and *Clip-Kit* were "rhetorical, with-it, moralistic, mis-spelled, improvisatory, anti-smooth, funny-format, cliquey, art-oriented but stoned out of their minds with science-fiction images of an alternative architecture that would be perfectly possible tomorrow if only the Universe (and especially the Law of Gravity) were differently organised."[107] He held *Clip-Kit* in especially high regard, partly because of its title:

> . . . two more charisma-laden words just don't exist in this context. "Kit" is the emotive collective noun for Goodies (which are usually ideas, images, forms, documents, concepts raided from other disciplines) and "clip" is how you put them together to make intellectual or physical structures. Alternatively, you can plug them in to existing structures or networks. But plug-in or clip-on, it's the same magpie world of keen artefacts, knockout visuals and dazzling brainwaves assembled into structures whose primary aim seems to be to defy gravity, in any sense of the word.

The clip-on concept had been absorbed by the Archigram generation and made fully Pop. In this way, it became part of the "war of the generations" in the architectural world. Banham, as one would expect, identified foursquare with the rebels:

> The anti-gravity aspect, which delights students, makes the teaching establishment dead nervous. Even architects I would normally regard as far from square make worried noises, and the January issue of the Architectural Association's *Journal* devoted two pages to an attempt to put *Archigram* in the doghouse. Any prospective student reading this partic-

ular performance would probably decide to go somewhere else and study: paragraph by wooden paragraph it plods along, occasionally laying a genuine cardboard egg.

Banham rebukes the *Journal*'s authors for accusing Archigram of "illiteracy and a lack of humour," and sympathizes with *Megascope* "when it complained of 'the failures who teach in our schools' and of 'the mass of mediocrity seen in almost every field of architectural endeavour in this country.' When faced with dreary projects and obsolete problems, it is no wonder that students are unable to produce anything but dreary solutions, balsa models and grey, grey drawings." Here is Banham confirming his position as the anti-Establishment, radical critic on the side of the young, rebellious outsiders, opposing conventional lores and the status quo. The 1966 version of 1960's "science for kicks" is the work of Archigram and other young groups of architects.

Banham, importantly, also makes the point that the 1966 version of "science for kicks" is not the 1914 one. He chastises the editors of *Clip-Kit* for devoting "two giant fold-outs" to Futurism: "Being an Edwardian futurist doesn't make a man relevant to *our* future." The chastisement seems rather two-faced, given the amount of praise (and prose) Banham had heaped on Futurism, and not just because it proposed a valid architecture of technology in the First Machine Age—he frequently cited it, of course, as a movement that showed the way to architects of the Second Machine Age.[108] The point he is making is that a live and up-to-date approach and attitude are all-important, not the approach and attitude—let alone the appearances and forms—of a bygone movement.[109] If the dismissal of *Clip-Kit*'s inclusion of Futurism seems somewhat harsh, it may be explained by Banham's desire, more than half a decade after the publication of *Theory and Design,* to rid himself of what he thought might have become a reputation as the "rediscoverer of Futurism" and, thus, too close an association with architecture's history rather than its present. It is a tension between Banham's dual role as a historian of the First Machine Age and a polemicist of "science for kicks" in the Second Macine Age.

Like the 1960 version of "science for kicks," the architecture of Archigram and the other radical groups was certainly not earnest; but it was serious and, according to Banham, relevant to the society of the day, in which architecture was no longer elevated into "a higher order discipline of abstractly ordering the masses about for their own good," but was formed by "what this week's dolly-girls are wearing, ergonomics, inflatable air-houses, the voice of God as revealed by his one true prophet Bob Dylan, what's going on in Bradford and Hammersmith, the side elevation of the Ford GT-40, napalm down the neck, the Royal College of Art, caravan homes, Sealab, and like that." This notion of relevance is IG-derived (in form and "pinboard" style) and accepts popular culture and its values as the basis of daily living in the Second Machine Age. At worst, Banham's notion of "relevance" is mere fashionableness. Furthermore, references to "dolly-birds" and (quite unbelievably) "napalm down the neck" reveal a sensibility, however fashionable, that can be offensive and is, in the latter case, obnoxious. The sensibility was, however, one which further endeared him to the young generation of architects.

Banham's rejection of the architectural Establishment reached its peak in a short, two-sentence statement he contributed to the Bristol architectural students' magazine *Megascope* in 1965. The statement, presented as a speech bubble emanating from a photo of Banham on his Moulton bicycle, read: "I take it as a good sign that an increasing number of students are flunking out of architectural schools in disgust of what they are being taught there. I take it as a hopeful sign that the next generation recognise that architecture is too important to be left to the architectural profession."[110] The second sentence was one that Banham uttered on more than one occasion, and it was calculated to infuriate the profession. The statement puts one in mind of the title of the final chapter in Le Corbusier's *Towards a New Architecture:* "Architecture or Revolution." Le Corbusier's final words on the matter were "Revolution can be avoided."[111] His faith rested on what he believed to be the transcendent powers of architecture. For Banham, on the other hand, architecture was a poor alternative to revolution—at least, revolution within architectural thought and practice.

At the beginning of the 1960s, in "Stocktaking," Banham had demanded a choice between "tradition" and "technology"; in *Theory and Design* he had warned that "what we have hitherto understood as architecture, and what we are beginning to understand of technology are incompatible disciplines." CLASP, with its "pragmatic technology," had seemed to offer an architecture of technology, but in spite of its relative radicalness, it remained too much within architectural lore to satisfy Banham's requirements. "Pop technology" had reintroduced the vital ingredient of expendability into the reckoning, and spiced it with Day-Glo graphics, the popular culture "glamour factor," and an attitude of "science for kicks." And Fulleresque "radical technology" had questioned the very basis of architecture, preparing the ground for an *architecture autre* which comprehensively embraced technology and technological thinking. In the student or alternative magazines of the mid-1960s, "radical technology" and "Pop technology" merged one into the other to form an *autre*.

For example, in the issue of *Megascope* in which Banham's statement was published, there were features on Archigram and Arthur Quarmby's work on inflatable structures, and experimental aluminum domes. Furthermore, there was an extract from a lecture by Buckminster Fuller which contained the assertion that "With the ever increasing scientific development, the environment will be completely controlled and the concept of the house will be eliminated—we are working towards the invisible house—what will you do with architecture then?"[112] This seemed to promise not an architecture of technology, but technology which went beyond architecture: the concept of architecture, with all its cultural baggage, practices, and lores could be replaced by the promise of controllable or responsive environments.

As we will see in chapter 4, this development greatly appealed to Banham, in spite of its lack of imageability, let alone Pop iconography. To Fuller's question, "What will you do with architecture then?," Banham's likely response, to use one of his favorite phrases, would be that we should replace it with the concept of "fit environments for human activities."[113]

4
THE EXPANDED FIELD
Fit Environments for Human Activities

In chapter 3 we saw how Banham's analysis and understanding of the conditions of the Second Machine Age led him to different versions of an architecture of technology: the pragmatic, the radical, and Pop. All three were versions of an *architecture autre.* The radical approach—epitomized by Bucky Fuller—and the Pop approach—exemplified by Archigram—were overlapping by the mid-1960s: a continuum existed, especially in the minds and projects of students. A Pop sensibility might be used to flavor or even determine the radicalism of the architectural vision, with a fashionable and expendable Pop aesthetic providing strong imageability. On the other hand, image-ability could be completely ignored if Fuller's equally radical idea of the "invisible house" with its replacement of architecture by the responsive environment was pursued.

This chapter follows Banham's development of a radical approach to a technological architecture which would go well beyond architectural lore and conventions, toward a rethinking of architecture in terms of "fit environments for human activities," a phrase he had employed since the beginning of the 1960s,[1] but which came into its own once he began to think of architecture "in the expanded field." The latter phrase is not Banham's, but was coined by the art historian and theorist Rosalind Krauss in 1979, in relation to sculpture. Krauss was interested in the way that the category "sculpture" had been "kneaded and stretched and twisted" during the 1960s and 1970s, to the extent that it might "include just about anything"[2] from video installations, through earthworks, to minimally material concepts. The effect was that "sculpture" had become just one term within "a field in which there are other, differently structured possibilities. And one has thereby gained the 'permission' to think these other forms."[3]

There is a strong parallel in Banham's thinking about architecture in the same period, as we will see in this chapter. "Architecture," as it was conventionally understood, became just one option within a range of possibilities of "fit environments for human activities." The advantage of the Krauss parallel is twofold: it reminds us, first, that all creative disciplines were undergoing radical questioning in the second half of the 1960s; and, second, that the questioning was part of a "historical rupture" that, according to Krauss, ushered in "postmodernism."[4] In chapter 5, we will be assessing the extent to which Banham can be described as a Post-Modernist, but in this chapter, three developments require analysis: an architecture which is understood and assessed in terms of mechanical services rather than more conventional formal or structural concerns; an architecture in which the "hardware" of form becomes subservient to the "software" of activity; and a larger-scale understanding of "fit environments for human activities" which operates at the level of urban form and undermines conventions of "the city."

An appropriate place to begin the discussion is Banham's 1965 "A Home Is Not a House," because it deals directly with the issues which led to two of this chapter's destinations: an architecture which expresses or even dramatizes mechanical services, and an architecture which—in Banham's concept of the "unhouse"—becomes "invisible" and subservient to the software.

A Home Is Not a House

At the same time that Buckminster Fuller was declaring that "the environment will be completely controlled and the concept of the house will be eliminated,"[5] Banham was publishing his "unhouse" idea as part of his argument that "A Home Is Not a House." The unhouse was based on the Fulleresque notion that

When your house contains such a complex of piping, flues, ducts, wires, lights, inlets, outlets, ovens, sinks, refuse disposers, hi-fi reverberators, antennae, conduits, freezers, heaters—when it contains so many services that the hardware could stand up by itself without any assistance from the house, why have a house to hold it up? When the cost of all this tackle is half of the total outlay (or more, as it often is) what is the house doing except concealing your mechanical pudenda from the stares of folks on the sidewalks.[6]

The half-cost balance of expenditure on the mechanical services of the house was significant in symbolic and actual terms: symbolically, it underlined how relatively ignored were mechanical services, compared to form and style, by both architects and architectural writers; and, in actual terms, it revealed that a historical stage had been reached in which mechanical services could determine form.[7]

There had so far been two main responses to the perceived problem: to make an architectural "drama of mechanical services," or to downplay them. One "solution" to the first option was to elevate the service to the status of architectural form. Le Corbusier had done this, for example, with the foul air extract on the roof of the Marseilles Unité Building—the stack is presented as abstract sculptural form rather than a mere utilitarian service. Though this approach made use of the service part of the building, it did so by aestheticizing service.

A parallel approach in the early 1960s was Louis Kahn's Richards Medical Research Center in Philadelphia, which similarly elevated the services to the status of form, with the regrettable result, according to Banham, that "the pressing problem of services [was] capable of being discussed in the traditional terminology of massing and plan."[8] As a gesture toward accepting

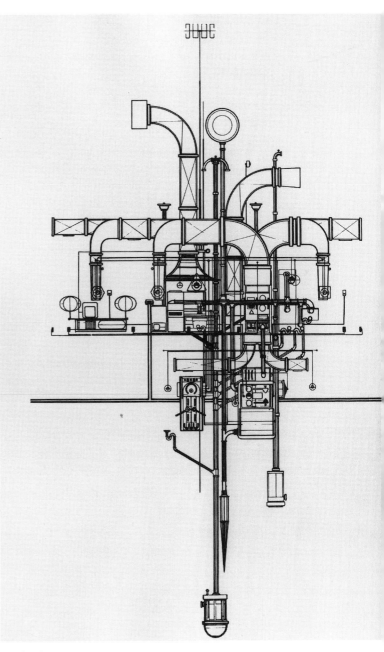

Banham's "unhouse," 1965 (courtesy Mary Banham)

the presence of services, he continued, Kahn's solution might have some validity, but as a form of technological architecture, it was not convincing, especially because Kahn himself, as quoted by Banham, was grudging in his attitude to the potential of mechanical services: "I do not like ducts, I do not like pipes. I hate them really thoroughly, but because I hate them so thoroughly, I feel that they have to be given their place. If I hated them and took no care, I think that they would invade the building and completely destroy it."[9] This was a sentiment in the tradition of Le Corbusier and the Modernists of the First Machine Age, and the hierarchical distinction between "architecture" and "services" did not augur well for an architecture of services, let alone a more radical architecture of technology. The problem of services would remain so long as architects worked with a traditional "architectural" mind-set that resulted in the designer being "thoroughly out of sympathy with more than half the capital investment in a building of this kind."[10]

At the other extreme of an architecture of mechanical services was their downplaying. In "A Home Is Not a House," Banham deploys Philip Johnson's glass cube house at New Canaan as an example of a radical, even subversive, playingdown of mechanical services. We will be discussing his ideas about this building in the second section of this chapter. At this stage, however,

Louis Kahn, Richards Medical Research Center, Philadelphia, 1957–1961 (courtesy Mary Banham)

it is the link between "A Home Is Not a House" and one of Banham's most celebrated books that we need to explore. A note in the article describes how the book was a direct product of the research Banham was carrying out in the United States, made possible by a fellowship from the Graham Foundation of Chicago, into the role of mechanical services in the rise of modern architecture. The culmination of that research was Banham's most architecturally radical book: *The Architecture of the Well-tempered Environment* (1969).

The Architecture of the Well-tempered Environment

The Architecture of the Well-tempered Environment attempted two tasks: to trace the historical development of key mechanical services in buildings and to assess the implications of those services and their architectural values. In terms of architectural writing, this was innovative.[11] The book merits attention at this point in the chapter because it is Banham's major work on an architecture of mechanical services and its relationship to "fit environments for human activities." His stated assumption was that the history of architecture, in an expanded field, "should cover the whole of the technological art of creating habitable environments . . . [but] the fact remains that the history of architecture found in the books currently available still deals almost exclusively with the external forms of habitable volumes as revealed by the structures that enclose them."[12]

Banham intended *The Architecture of the Well-tempered Environment* as an antidote to the conventional history of architecture, which "by default and academic inertia . . . [has] become narrowed to the point where almost its only interest outside the derivation of styles is haggling over the primacy of inventions in the field of structures."[13] Most debates focused on the building's external form: "no matter how profound the alterations wrought in architecture by the electric lamp, or the suspended ceiling (to cite two major instances of revolutionary inventions), the fact that these alterations were not visible in outward form has denied them, so far, a place in the history of architecture."[14] The "revolutionary inventions" had to be studied as a part of architectural history if that history was going to fulfill Banham's assumption that it should "cover the whole of the technological art of creating habitable environments."

Moving away from the architect or architectural groupings structure of the revisionist *Theory and Design in the First Machine Age,* the radical *Architecture of the Well-tempered Environment* includes chapters which follow the history of mechanical ventilation; heating and lighting in the nineteenth century and their impact on large and on domestic buildings; and the ways in which Frank Lloyd Wright integrated environmental and architectural qualities compared to the "environmental and human inadequacies" of European Modernist architecture (which becomes the subject of two chapters).

The chapter titled "Towards Full Control" illustrates well the dual task of the book. Banham traces the development of air-conditioning, which he describes as almost "the classic example of a technology applied first in units of large capacity to industrial needs and to correct grossly deleterious atmospheric conditions, and then slowly sophisticated towards a condition where it could be subdivided and rendered subtle enough to handle domestic requirements."[15] The contributions of pioneers around the turn of the century, such as William Havilland Carrier—the "father of air-conditioning"[16]—who referred not to "air-conditioning" but to "man-made weather," and Stuart W. Cramer, who coined the term we now use, are historically exhumed and assessed. This involved a sound knowledge of the scientific practices and processes themselves—Banham's technical background obviously served him well in this regard—and an economic and social understanding of why air-conditioning was utilized, and by whom: economic profit, rather than human well-being, was the normal determining factor for the adoption of air-conditioning, but there were exceptions "where simple human comfort offered a profit margin proportionately large enough to make investment worth while."[17] Hotel dining rooms and ballrooms came within this class, "as did Pullman cars and—above all—theatres," followed by cinemas, where "comfort jobs," as they became known within the profession, "introduced the general public to the improved atmospheric environment."[18]

With it beginning to work at the level of small room-units, rather than just large auditoriums, air-conditioning was moving toward domestication. Economic recessions and the war slowed its development, and it was not until 1951 and "the cumulative effect of miniaturisation and other improvements" precipitated by wartime technology, that a compact and self-contained unit became widely available. Developing alongside systems which have outlets connected to some form of mains supply, 1950s air-conditioning became the commodity we now recognize almost as a genre: a "self-contained unit that can be installed in a hole in the wall or an opened window, plugged in to the electrical main, and can deliver genuine air-conditioning."[19] The air-conditioning unit has become a domestic commodity on a par with "the cooker, the refrigerator and the television set—a neat box with control knobs and a mains connection." However, as important, "it is a portent in the history of architecture."

This is the point at which the history and development of the service turn into the second role of the book—an examination of its architectural implications. Both functions contribute to Banham's examination of an architecture of mechanical services, but it is the latter which raises issues about architectural theory in a technological age.

Add-on air-conditioning unit

The installation of air-conditioning units in suburbia may have had little visual impact because "the evergreens have already grown up in front of the units," but in apartment blocks in cities, "such installations can bring the environmental improvements of the householder into direct conflict with the visual intentions of the architect." Although Banham accepted that a number of architects had begun to "make their peace with the seemingly inevitable eruption of room-conditioners on their facades, few have set out to exploit the neat visual detailing of their intake grilles, nor the convenience for interchangeability of their easy installation and removal."[20] Architects were berated for their "general failure" to make provision for this increasingly standard fixture.

An exception was the Olivetti factory in Argentina, designed by Marco Zanuso in 1964. Here, the air-conditioning was provided by exposed units hung from a steel chassis cantilevering above girders supporting the main structure. The girders' hollow interiors were used as ducts for air distribution. Outlet slots were designed at intervals in the lower faces of the girders, under which most of the piping and conduitry were hung as well. Banham describes this as a "classic 'clip-on' solution," similar to the way in which propulsive power is applied to a boat by an outboard motor. This not only makes sense, because the units are easily accessible for servicing, "but also seems to satisfy a deep intellectual and moral need: the need to be able to see the difference between the structure, which is supposed to be permanent, and the services, which are hoped to be transient, and to see that difference made expressive. The building is serviced, and manifestly seen to be serviced."[21] Banham also describes the "frank and gratifying clarity" that Zanuso's solution provides and, with his reference to the "deep intellectual and moral need," the reader is quite clear about Banham's own values, which are grounded within a Modernist rationalism, however much expanded, revised, or even redefined.

Both the radicalism of *The Architecture of the Well-tempered Environment* and the Modernist rationalism underlying his judgments come to the fore when Banham is writing about the innovatory nature of mechanical services in relation to the conservatism of external form. The key building in this regard is the Royal Victoria Hospital in Belfast (1903), by the Birmingham architectural firm of Henman and Cooper, which "represents a level of mechanical innovation and originality of plan that would have been hard to equal anywhere at the time."[22] The innovation of the Royal Victoria "lies in its total adaptation in section and plan to the environmental system employed. What makes it even more interesting historically is that more than one environmental system is employed, the architecture changing to suit."[23] Accommodation not served by the air-conditioning system—areas which had conventional heating by gas fires and natural ventilation—reverted to conventional tall and thin architectural forms with pavilion-style plans: "the external massing of the various parts of the hospital thus give direct 'expression' to two different kinds of environmental management, a low, top-lit format corresponding to mechanical systems, and a tall, side-lit format to natural systems."[24]

Thus, the Royal Victoria Hospital merits inclusion as an important building in the history of architecture recast, in the expanded field, as "the technological art of creating habitable environments."[25] What, for Banham, prevented it being hailed a "masterpiece" was the historicism of its styling, which "demonstrates with painful clarity the total irrelevance of detailed architectural 'style' to the modernity of the functional and environmental parts."[26] Its conceptual and technical modernity was considerable: in the relationship of environmental control to functional disposition, it anticipates "the advanced practices of some thirty years later, and in the implied extensibility of its plan along the line of the corridor, it is still of interest to proponents of 'indeterminate' architecture some sixty years later." But this monument of the architecture of mechanical services was fatally flawed for Banham by its "art architecture" decoration, which "belongs dismally and irrevocably" to "a style already thoroughly discounted and out of fashion among consciously progressive architects of 1900."[27]

The resonances of First Machine Age Modernism in Banham's judgement are tangible, whether it recalls Adolf Loos's praise for "bath tubs and American basins" in opposition to decorative architecture,[28] or Le Corbusier imploring his readers to "listen to the counsels of American engineers. But let us beware of American architects."[29] *The Architecture of the Well-tempered Environment* may have been radical in seeking to expand the field of architecture so that it became "the technological art of creating habitable environments," but "old" criteria such as the right commitment to modernity still mattered to Banham.

The Wright Fit for Human Activities

Indeed, supposedly radical new criteria produced a recurring hero: Frank Lloyd Wright, who "by any standards, must be accounted the first master of the architecture of the well-tempered environment."[30] Wright's Larkin building of 1906 is, Banham suggests, the only building on a par with the "radicalism and ingenuity" of the contemporary Royal Victoria Hospital. Its exterior form recommended itself to the Modernist aesthetic of the stripped classical aesthetic, and thus finds "a natural place in the history books, unlike the Royal Victoria Hospital."[31] However, its inclusion is based "exclusively on the felicity of its interior spaces and their relationship to the great monumental volumes of the exterior, without observing that the system of environmental management mediates crucially between interior and exterior form."[32] But it was the relationship between mechanical services and architectural form that made the Larkin "something of a watershed."[33]

Like the Royal Victoria Hospital, the Larkin "must be judged a design whose final form was imposed by the method of environmental manage-

Frank Lloyd Wright, Larkin Building, Buffalo, 1906 (courtesy Mary Banham)

ment employed, rather than one whose form derived from the exploitation of an environmental method. This is in no way to denigrate the masterly manner in which Wright managed to turn those impositions to his architectural purposes." The Royal Victoria had only presented "the image of new functional needs and mechanical possibilities bursting through a crust of conventionally conceived architectural forms," whereas with the Larkin building, the form of the exterior "appears to be keeping pace with transformation of the interior economy of the building-type."[34]

There are two problems with Banham's approach in *The Architecture of the Well-tempered Environment*. First, it tends to deal with buildings as models of environmental management rather than buildings as used in reality. However ingenious Wright's design, the reality was often more mundane. A more radical book might have examined the actual performance of a building in the way that Stewart Brand examines *How Buildings Learn* (1994). The implication of Brand's approach is to move away from great architects and canonical buildings to look closely at particular buildings, and generalize from them. The case studies would inevitably, if one was seeking to study environmental performance, draw on diverse types and styles, including vernacular buildings. Banham does not entertain any serious analysis of vernacular buildings because he has little sympathy for them in principle:

[the] good-enough for general purposes vernacular procedures may not only fail under extreme conditions, but they may also stretch the limits of physiological tolerance to the point where only a deeply entrenched culture can prevent the resultant human and social inconveniences becoming intolerable. . . . Anthropology abounds in examples where cultural rigidity and fixed repertoire of architectural forms are welded into a seemingly permanent deadlock with results that may perhaps preserve a body of ancient wisdom—or an embalmed corpus of ancestral folly.[35]

He is equally dismissive of low-tech buildings (as we will see in chapter 5) and pays scant attention to energy-conscious building design.

The second problem of Banham's approach is implicit in his statement that the Larkin "serves as a bridge between the history of modern architecture as commonly written—the progress of structure and external form—and a history of modern architecture understood as the progress of creating human environments."[36] This is a telling statement because it reveals that, however supposedly radical *The Architecture of the Well-tempered Environment* may be, Banham is still operating within concepts of "modern architecture." This not only explains the exclusion of vernacular and traditional buildings, but also shows why, to some extent, the book is a reshuffling of the architects and buildings in *Theory and Design.* The environments he writes about have to be well-tempered *Modernist* ones, not just to delimit the scope of his thesis also but because of his own preferences and commitments. *The Architecture of the Well-tempered Environment* only *potentially* broke the mold of architectural value. Once again, polemics and implicit values play as important a part as historical research. Wright remains a "towering genius" and "one of the most fluently inventive architects that ever lived."[37]

Technology as a Cultural Problem: Europe Versus the United States

Wright's status was based on his "resourcefulness in the deployment of power technology and structure together in the elaboration of domestic environments."[38] The judgment is symptomatic not only of an individual architect but also of different cultures, a point which becomes one of the major conclusions in *The Architecture of the Well-tempered Environment.* In two of the chapters, Banham takes to task, first, the Europeans in general and, second, Le Corbusier in particular for their uncompromising pursuit of a machine aesthetic at the expense of "fit environments." The epitome of the Modernists' "retreat from comfort"[39] was the use of the naked electric lightbulb, without shade or diffusion. Banham argues that, for the Modernist masters,

. . . lamps and heaters alike seem to have been simply sculptural objects, to be composed according to their aesthetic rules, along with the solids and voids of the structure, into abstract compositions. As for their environmental performance, this seems to have been honoured only by the observance of certain simplified rules (or, possibly, eroded habits of mind) by which the radiators were placed flat against the outside walls, and the lamps hung from the centre, or the centre-line, of the ceiling. Where there is any conspicuous departure from such a rule, it usually emerges as a purely aesthetic "improvement" without regard to its environmental consequence, or a desperate attempt to remedy an environmental mistake already made.[40]

In the case of Le Corbusier, Banham concludes that "the nudism of the light-source must also have been programmatic."[41]

Such unfit environments for human activities were tolerated only "by the notorious willingness of intellectuals to suffer in the cause of art,"[42] and they signified a "bleak interlude." It is indeed surprising to find Banham describing the design of First Machine Age environments in this way. Not only does it resemble the pronouncements made by the sort of Modernist establishment figures Banham had rebelled against—Herbert Read referred to the "justifiable dissatisfaction with the bleakness of a pioneering functionalism"[43]—but the tone of his writing evokes the *anti*-Modernism of a British traditionalist:

. . . pure white light was to survive only as the weapon of the Secret Police interrogator, the brain-washer and the terrorist. But before that relegation to the underworld of Western culture, it had almost a two-decade career in the visible and progressive overworld, as architects of the International Style—with the noblest aspirations, and clear consciences which the clarity of the light was supposed to symbolise, no doubt—subjected doctors, art-collectors, publishers, teachers and the other law-abiding bourgeois who were their clients, to a Gestapo-style luminous environment, with light streaming from bare, or occasionally opalescent, bulbs and tubes and glaring back from white walls.[44]

This does not sound like the Banham of *Theory and Design in the First Machine Age,* the champion of Futurism, or enthusiast for "science for kicks."[45] The explanation may lie partly in the reason he attributed to the European Modernists for their disregard of environmental performance: he accused them of viewing "the Machine" as a "portentous cultural problem, rather than something that the architect could use to make houses 'perfectly sanitary, labour-saving . . . where the maximum of comfort may be had with the minimum of drudgery.'"[46] It was typical of the way that "questions which are susceptible of straightforward physical investigation are nudged up to the 'higher' plane of cultural problems" by the European intelligentsia.[47] The Europeans were continuing "the old-fashioned prejudice" of Banham's bête noire, John Ruskin, but standing it on its head. Whereas Ruskin had made "technology a problem, not an opportunity,"[48] the Modernists saw technology as part of a moral crusade for social and cultural advancement.

What is particularly surprising about Banham's reassessment was that he had previously praised the "masterpieces" of Le Corbusier and Mies van der Rohe in *Theory and Design,* and had not dealt with the environmental performance of their buildings in any serious way, let alone analyzed the degree to which they achieved "comfort" in their buildings. By the late 1960s, after direct experience of the United States, Banham was seeing the architecture versus technology opposition in European versus American terms. In the Second Machine Age, technology no longer had to be symbolized (as it had been by the masters of the First Machine Age), but utilized in order to create fit environments for human activities.

The contrast in attitude became sharp when one studied technologically progressive buildings in the United States. Banham quotes Le Corbusier relishing the interior of Radio City in New York: "A solemn temple, hung with sombre marbles, gleaming with clear mirrors framed in stainless steel. Silence, vast corridors and landings. Doors open, revealing silent lifts discharging clients. No windows anywhere, muted walls. Conditioned air everywhere, pure, dust-free, tempered."[49] Le Corbusier's phraseology is described by Banham as being as "deft and efficient as the mechanical services of the building," but he could have made a more telling comment by noting Le Corbusier's tendency to liken the interior environment to a "solemn temple" rather than a fit environment for human activities, for this is the substance of the argument Banham goes on to make:

. . . while European modern architects had been trying to devise a style that would "civilise technology," US engineers had devised a technology that would make the modern style of architecture habitable by civilised human beings. In the process they had come within an ace of producing a workable alternative to buildings as the unique means of managing the environment, and had thus come within an ace of making architecture culturally obsolete, at least in the senses in which the word "architecture" had been traditionally understood, the sense in which Le Corbusier had written *Vers une Architecture.*[50]

The Americans had developed an attitude which rejected the "ideal of the machine-aesthetic as preached by Le Corbusier, [in favor of] the facts of machine technology as they existed on what had become . . . their home ground, the USA."[51]

Banham's argument was a restating of his "Stocktaking" series of almost a decade earlier, in which he argued for technological habits of thought over architectural ones. In 1960 he had predicted that technology makes it possible to "define 'home' without reference to hearth or roof, but simply as the integration of a complex of intrapersonal relationships and mains services."[52] His researches into mechanical services, culminating in *The Architecture of the Well-tempered Environment,* had enabled him to gauge the different possibilities that thinking in terms of creating "fit environments for human activities" offered. It was, potentially, no longer necessary to think about "architecture"; there was no need, even, to commit oneself to an architecture of mechanical services; the expanded field offered far more radical options that were "other." We now turn to the second major development of a radical approach to creating habitable environments—environments in which the hardware of form becomes subservient to the software of activity.

The Controlled Environment

At this point we need to return to the important "A Home Is Not a House." In it, Banham proposes that there are two basic ways of controlling environment: "one by avoiding the issue and hiding under a rock, tree, tent or roof (this led ultimately to architecture as we know it) and the other by actually interfering with the local meteorology, usually by means of a campfire. . . . Unlike the living space trapped with our forebears under a rock or roof, the space around a campfire has many unique qualities which architecture cannot hope to equal, above all, its freedom and variability."[53] The pursuit of "freedom and variability" ultimately takes Banham beyond architecture: conventional buildings are perceived as a problem, not a solution. However, some of the buildings that form part of the established architectural canon do point the way toward this more radical end. One such building, discussed at some length in both "A Home Is Not a House" and *The Architecture of the Well-tempered Environment,* is Philip Johnson's glass cube house at New Canaan, Connecticut (1950).

Johnson's house was usually thought of as the ultimate statement of Miesian *Wenig ist Mehr,* and so "at first sight nothing but monumental form,"[54] and linking with a tradition deriving from—as Johnson describes it—High Modernism, Karl Schinkel, C.-N. Ledoux, Baroque spatial organization, Renaissance fenestration patterns, and Greek planning.[55] Nonetheless, Banham argued that it could be reinterpreted as comprising two "permanent" elements: a heated brick floor slab, and a standing unit which is a chimney/fireplace on one side and a bathroom on the other, comprising a service core which determines the structure onto which other elements or enclosures—in the New Canaan case, glass—could be attached or hung. This made it, in Banham's mind (and in spite of Johnson's pronouncements), tantamount to being an "unhouse," and thus the exact opposite of monumental form.

The precedents for this approach were American, and included Fuller's Dymaxion and Wichita houses with their service cores, and even the country's "pioneer house builders" who supplied a brick chimney on a brick floor slab to which was anchored a balloon frame. But the important argument, based not only on inspection but also on habitation, was that this lightweight building with its "undifferentiated enclosure of glass" is habitable in winter, not because of the fireplace which provides an essentially "psychologically satisfying display of combustion," but because the floor is entirely heated *invisibly* by electrical elements in both the floor and roof slabs. In the summer it remains equally habitable, which is "baffling at first sight because of the lack of any visible sun-controls beyond some internal curtaining." The cooling and sunshading provisions are, however, "concealed" in the surrounding landscape—a bank of well grown trees rooted at a lower level to the bluff on which the house stands "give adequate shade, when in leaf, to the thermally critical south and west walls. Furthermore, the slope and

Philip Johnson, house at New Canaan, Conn., 1950 (courtesy Mary Banham)

its trees seem to encourage a mildly breezy local micro-climate even when there is no general wind, so that the opening of two or more of the doors will provide any necessary cross-draught."[56] The result was a "masterly remixture of mechanical and architectural environmental controls."[57]

Johnson and Banham disagreed as to whether the house could be described as a "controlled environment." Johnson denies it could be characterized in this way because, as Banham paraphrases him, "when it gets cold I have to move toward the fire, and when it gets too hot I just move away." But, Banham responds, Johnson "is simply exploiting the campfire phenomenon (he is also pretending that the floorheating does not make the whole area habitable, which it does) and in any case, what does he mean by a controlled environment? It is not the same thing as a uniform environment, it is simply an environment suited to what you are going to do next, and whether you build a stone monument, move away from the fire or turn on the air-conditioning, it is the same basic human gesture you are making."[58]

The distinction between a controlled and a uniform environment was significant in more ways than one. The uniform environment had reached its (theoretical) apotheosis in Le Corbusier's quest for a *"respiration exacte"* of 18° centigrade: "one single building for all nations and climates."[59] The master announced that this would mean that "we control things so that the surface of the interior membrane holds 18°C. And there you are!" Banham's riposte was "And there you are indeed, all over the world, pegged to a standard temperature of eighteen centigrade whether you liked it or not. . . . Rarely had his passion for 'the standard, *l'invariant'* been pushed to such pointless and impractical extremes."[60] This was a uniform environment motivated not by human well-being, comfort, or diversity, so much as by the desire to "control things" and decide for people how they should live. On one level the uniform environment represented homogeneity; the controlled environment, heterogeneity. In Banham's opinion, they represented the difference between European and American cultural attitudes.

If Johnson's New Canaan house, albeit transitional in the shift from monument to controlled environment, was still a member of the architectural canon, another building from the 1950s which Banham praised represents a farther point away from architecture as it was generally recognized. In *The Architecture of the Well-tempered Environment,* one of the last projects Banham discusses is the demountable, 230-foot-long, inflatable pavilion designed for the U.S. Atomic Energy Commission (AEC) in the late 1950s by Victor Lundy, architect, and Walter Bird of the Bird-air Corporation. Its significance, Banham suggested, was that it

. . . presents us with a total reversal of traditional roles in architecture and environmental management. Instead of a rigid built volume to which power must be applied to correct its environmental deficiencies, we have here either a volume which is not built and rigid until environmental power is applied to it, or a manufactured environment (conditioned air) and a bag to put it in. Either way, this might be claimed as a more subversive proposition than simply doing without built enclosure altogether . . . and by any stan-

Victor Lundy, U.S. Atomic Energy Commission building, late 1950s (courtesy Mary Banham)

dards it is a development alongside which most of the purely architectural revolutions of recent years must appear rather trifling.[61]

Described in this way, architecture as "built enclosure" or "rigid volume" was being superseded by some form—or formlessness—of "environmental management," which was a manifestation of "the technological art of creating habitable environments," in order to produce "fit environments for human activities." Allied to the reference to the "subversive proposition," we are reminded where Banham's commitment to an *architecture autre* was located at the end of the 1960s.

The AEC pavilion was not primarily interesting or significant as "architecture" but as a "controlled environment." A few years after the pavilion had burst onto the scene, Banham, in the significantly titled "A Home Is Not a House," was arguing that an inflatable dome could be an integral ingredient in a domestic architecture so radical that the two words "domestic" and "architecture" would have to be rethought. His premise was that the controlled environment in a North American context could relate to the "campfire" or "interference" solution, rather than to the "rock" or "hiding" one: "the monument is such a ponderous solution that it astounds me that Americans are still prepared to employ it, except out of some profound sense of insecurity, a persistent inability to rid themselves of those habits of mind they left Europe to escape."[62] If the Futurists, with their "mechanical sensibility," represented the "profound reorientation towards a changed world" in the First Machine Age, it was progressive Americans who represented the same attitude and ideal in the Second.

For Americans, "left to their own devices . . . do not monumentalise or make architecture. From the Cape Cod cottage, through the balloon frame to the perfection of permanently pleated aluminum siding with embossed wood-graining, they have tended to build a brick chimney and lean a collection of shacks against it."[63] Commercially produced motor homes and trailers moved the tradition forward, but the really radical, progressive, Second Machine Age manifestation was a "standard-of-living package (the phrase and the concept are both Bucky Fuller's)." Banham described his vision of a "properly set-up standard-of-living package, breathing out warm air along the ground (instead of sucking in cold along the ground like a campfire), radiating soft light and Dionne Warwick in heart-warming stereo, with well-aged protein turning in an infra-red glow in the rotisserie, and the ice-maker discreetly coughing cubes into glasses on the swing-out bar."[64]

The significance of the vision is that it is described in terms of environmental performance and effects rather than architectural form. The form was merely a means to an end: what really mattered was the anti-architectural "campfire" attitude to environment in counterdistinction to the almost canonically inclined "rock" tendency. The shift is from form and hardware to service and software, a shift whose credibility "hinges on the observation that it is the American Way to spend money on services and upkeep rather than on permanent structure as do the peasant cultures of the Old World."[65]

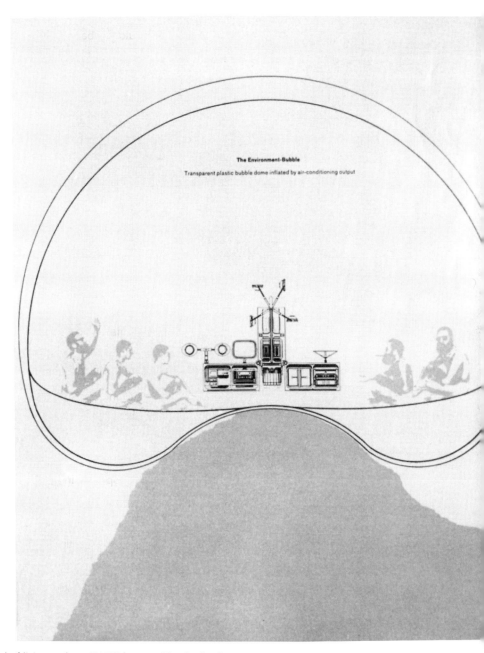

The Environment-Bubble

Transparent plastic bubble dome inflated by air-conditioning output

Banham's "standard-of-living package," 1965 (courtesy Mary Banham)

The fact that "Americans have always been prepared to pump more heat, light and power into their shelters than have other peoples"[66] reveals a cultural attitude that, Banham believed, partly explains Americans' attitude to their cars. And it is the car that he sees as a model for replacing architecture in the traditional (European) sense or, at least, expanding the field of architecture: it can play the role of a traveling power plant: "Beefed-up car batteries and a self-reeling cable drum could probably get this package breathing warm bourbon fumes o'er Eden long before microwave power transmission or miniaturised atomic power plants come in."[67]

The car may be playing its part in the standard-of-living package, but other items were equally necessary. Some of those items would necessarily be gadgets, or "gizmos." Realizing their importance for the controlled environment and architecture in the expanded field, Banham wrote directly about them in 1965.

Gadgets and Gizmos

"The Great Gizmo" appeared less than six months after "A Home Is Not a House." Appropriately, both appeared in American publications: *Industrial Design* and *Art in America,* respectively. Banham's argument was that the gizmo, an important element of the standard-of-living package, was rooted in the American psyche if not in its soil: "The man who changed the face of America had a gizmo, a gadget, a gimmick—in his hand, in his back pocket, across the saddle, on his hip, in the trailer, round his neck, on his head, deep in a hardened silo."[68] From the Franklin stove and the Stetson hat, through the Evinrude outboard motor to the walkie-talkie, the spray can and the cordless shaver, "the most typical American way of improving the human situation has been by means of crafty and usually compact little packages." The "great American gizmo" was designed to operate independently of an infrastructure. Had it needed one,

. . . it would never have won the West or opened up the transcontinental trails. The quintessential gadgetry of the pioneering frontiersman had to be carried across trackless country, set down in a wild place, and left to transform that hostile environment without skilled attention. Its function was to bring instant order or human comfort into a sit-

uation which had previously been an undifferentiated mess, and for this reason it is . . .
deeply involved with the American mythology of the wilderness.[69]

This further develops Banham's argument away from architecture in any
conventional usage, and toward the idea of a standard-of-living package
which transforms an environment as did the proverbial campfire, albeit in a
technologically sophisticated way appropriate to the demands and desires
of the Second Machine Age.

Banham generalized that the archetypal American gizmo "is a small self-
contained unit of high performance in relation to its size and cost, whose
function is to transform some undifferentiated set of circumstances to a
condition nearer human desires. The minimum of skill is required in its installation and use, and it is independent of any physical or social infrastructure beyond that by which it may be ordered from catalogue and delivered
to prospective user."[70] An example was Ole Evinrude's outboard motor. To fit
an inboard motor to an existing boat required craft skills and "mathematical aptitudes of a sort normally found only in places with a long tradition of
boat-craft," including the equipment to bore a shaft hole through a keel or
transom, fit a tube and shaft, make it watertight, and calculate and fabri-
cate the pitch and diameter of the propeller. But Evinrude's outboard motor, in line with the ethos of the gizmo, which demands that you are able to
"peel off the packaging, fix four bolts and press the Go button," means that
"you can order a stock outboard from the catalogue with the right propeller
for its own power and your size of boat, fix it with two clamps, add fuel and
pull the starter."[71] Gizmos—whether an outboard motor or a portable air-
conditioning unit—were transformative vehicles which helped to create
"fit environments for human activities."

The Responsive Environment

When contrasting a controlled environment with a uniform environment,
Banham had defined the former in terms of its potential for change so that
it was "suited to what you are going to do next."[72] Around the mid-1960s
there was a subtle but significant shift in Banham's thinking about architecture in the expanded field. It can be summed up in the distinction between

the *controlled* and the *controllable* or *responsive* environment. In the first, one might have a limited range of environmental management choices that could be utilized to facilitate the right background conditions for what one wanted to do. In the second, the environment was more fully and directly responsive to a range of personal needs and desires that were culturally innovative, and could facilitate what Banham once described as an "interdeterminate participatory open ended situation."[73] As a phrase, this perfectly suited Cedric Price's Fun Palace project, one of the canonical works of the 1960s avant-garde, and one which exemplified much of his thinking about the responsive environment as being one more fully "suited to what you are going to do next."

The Fun Palace was Price's first major project, and it commenced in 1961 at the level of a pilot study. The client was Joan Littlewood, a founder of the Theatre Workshop at the Theatre Royal in Stratford, London. By 1964 the pilot had developed into a main project with a proposed location of London's East End, and Littlewood's progressivist tendencies led her to talk of the complex as a "university of the streets" or "laboratory of fun." Fun was not seen as passive relaxation or even "mere entertainment," but active participation and involvement, stimulation, knowledge, and personal growth. There would be music improvisation, dance, science playgrounds, film studies, drama therapy, modeling and making areas—a general atmosphere of experimentation and ethos of playfulness in keeping with the libertarian, progressivist times.

Price's response was to propose an unenclosed steel frame structure, fully serviced by a traveling gantry crane and containing hanging auditoriums and movable walls, ceilings, walkways, and even floors. There would be a technologically sophisticated environmental system which included vapor barriers, warm-air curtains, fog dispersal plants, and horizontal and vertical lightweight blinds. Here was a project that would fulfill the promise of the standard-of-living package. It could be described less as a building, more accurately as a facility, a responsive environment, fully in accord to what the user was "going to do next."

Banham's views on the role of the architect were profoundly influenced by Price: both believed the radical model of the architect was that of en-

"Clip-on" outboard motor (courtesy Mary Banham)

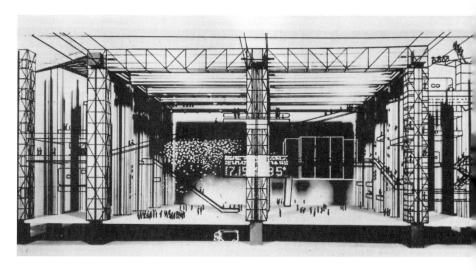

Cedric Price, Fun Palace, 1961–1967 (courtesy Mary Banham)

abler, in opposition to the Modernist notion of the form giver. The architect, pronounced Price, "takes his place in the ongoing process as a provider of opportunities for experience and change not as a master builder of immutable (and rapidly outdated, in terms of use) monumental structures."[74] Price made a similar point when he wrote about the Fun Palace in 1965: "The whole complex, in both the activity it enables and the resultant structure it provides, is in effect a short-term toy to enable people, for once, to use a building with the same degree of meaningful personal immediacy that they are forced normally to reserve for a limited range of traditional pleasures."[75] In the same article, Price argued that the "self-participatory element of the activities must extend to a degree of control by the users of their physical environment." He also wrote about the users' "freedom of choice," which would help create "new activities, at present without name"; and he even championed the "positive delight in changing one's mind." Banham at this time was probably more influenced by Price than any other architect or thinker.

Banham first wrote about Price's Fun Palace in 1964. As one might anticipate, he was fulsome in his praise of this "wild, mod dream,"[76] this "entertainment kit that the non-institutionalised aspects of leisure can improvise upon, a gigantic junk-playground for sophisticated grown-up people to whom the handling of mechanical tackle is nowadays as natural as breathing."[77] There was sympathy for Price's steadfast refusal to release any pictures of what the Fun Palace "will actually *look* like. He may well not know, but that doesn't matter because it is not the point. Seven nights of the week it will probably look like nothing on earth from the outside: the kit of service towers, lifting gantries and building components exists solely to produce the kind of interior environments that are necessary and fitting to whatever is going on."[78] What did, of course, matter was that the complex responded to what users were going to do next and thus became a fit environment for human activity. It would be, Banham declared, "the first building in Britain with full (not token) mechanical services and environment controls [and] it is quite possible that many activities will need no more enclosure than a roof over their heads."

Except that this is not building as it is normally understood: "sorry, the word 'building' got in there by mistake (old cultural habits die hard). There probably isn't going to be any building in the normal scope of the concept at all." The Fun Palace was architecture in the expanded field; a standard-of-living package regarding which, to quote Price, it is "essential to eliminate [the] unreal division between leisure time and work time."[79] Perhaps the Fun Palace is better described as a standard-of-playing package for *Homo ludens.* Eschewing Archigram's Pop imagery, Price sought "well-serviced anonymity."[80]

The assumptions underlying *Homo ludens* are, I would argue, central to Banham's thinking in relation not only to the Fun Palace, but also to his wider cultural thought.[81] The term was invented by the Dutch historian Johan Huizinga in his book of the same name published in 1938 and translated into English in 1949. Huizinga studied the element of play across cultures and found it to be a necessary and inherent aspect of *Homo sapiens.* For cultural optimists like Banham, playfulness was being facilitated and encouraged by the prosperity and technical advances of the Second Machine Age. Popular culture in the era of the Independent Group, Banham and his colleagues supposed, offered an increasingly sophisticated level of enjoyment and playfulness. In the 1960s, more education, better health, a reduction of the drudgery of manual labor brought about by technological advances, and more free time and disposable income made "the leisure society" one of the central pillars of belief and a stock phrase of the media. Leisure was a serious business in the 1960s, and Lawrence Alloway was prophetic when he noted at the beginning of the decade that "leisure occupations, reading, music, movie-going, dressing, are brought up into the same dimensions of skill as work which once stood alone as serious activity."[82] The Fun Palace was for the serious leisure of active participation and experimentation.

It was also a key—and highly influential—project in the mid-decade shift from hardware to software. One of the most fruitful influences was on Archigram's thinking. Their notion of "architecture as a consumer product" placed an undoubted emphasis on architectural *hardware*—the thing to be consumed, used, or lived in. What began to matter more to Archigram after Price's Fun Palace was the experience facilitated by the environment—

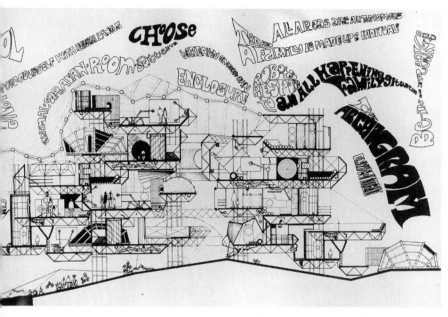

Archigram, "Control and Choice," 1966–1967 (courtesy Archigram Archive)

the *software*. One no longer threw away the hardware, as one would an obsolete product, but changed the environment to suit one's current needs or desires.

Their "Plug 'n' Clip" exhibit, presented in late 1965, typified this trend. Hardware was still in evidence, but its significance lay in what it could do. "We can," claimed Peter Cook, "reproduce the images of yesterday by photograph or film, and the slide show has taken the place of the family album. It is only an extension of all these to conceive of a living room that could simulate by colour, sound, or projected images, any atmosphere one required simply by throwing a switch."[83] A year or so later, in their "Control and Choice" project, Archigram pursued this idea to an even more extreme conclusion: "The determination of your environment need no longer be left in the hands of the designer . . . it can be turned over to you yourself. You turn the switches and choose the conditions to sustain you at that point in time. The 'building' is reduced to the role of carcass—or less."[84] The concern now was with change, but it was change through the participation of the inhabitant and the flexibility and responsiveness of the environment.

"Control and choice" was an appropriate name, not only for a particular project, but also for Archigram's general approach to designing from the mid- to the late 1960s. The group was taking to heart Banham's thinking about architecture needing to be redefined so that a building was not the assumed solution. As Cook phrased it, "For architects the question is: do buildings help towards the emancipation of the people within? Or do they hinder because they solidify the way of life preferred by the architect?"[85] What the group was attempting to achieve, according to Cook in the editorial for *Archigram 8* in 1968, was to produce an "active" solution which "attempts to sharpen to the maximum its powers of response and ability to respond to as many reasonable potentials as possible. If only we could get to an architecture that really responded to human wish as it occurred then we would be getting somewhere."[86]

The Triumph of Software in the Brave Pneu World

Archigram's visualizations around this time invariably featured inflatables, partly because their "short life-span (7–10 years average) implies a genuine throw-away product,"[87] and therefore appealed to the Pop sensibility. However, from the mid-1960s to the early 1970s, the inflatable was more than just an ingredient of the standard-of-Pop-living package; it was a symbol of the responsive environment and a symptom of architecture in the expanded field. Banham had made several references to pneumatic structures, including inflatables, in his writing of the period, but in "Monumental Windbags," a *New Society* piece of 1968, he discussed their significance more fully.

In 1967 and 1968, inflatables were at their most newsworthy. From window displays of blow-up furniture in Habitat, through major exhibitions such as the one of inflatable structures at the Musée d'Art Moderne in Paris, to pneumatic structures at Expo 67 in Montreal, and artworks including Andy Warhol's free-floating inflatable silver clouds, inflatables epitomized the Pop avant-garde sensibility. In "Monumental Windbags," Banham sketched the history of air-supported buildings back to 1917, and mentioned the Lundy and Bird inflatable structure for the AEC, but argued that

What is new is a confluence between changing taste and advances in plastic technology. The taste that has been turned off by the regular rectangular format of official modern architecture and Bauhaus-revival modern-antique furniture, is turned right on by the apparent do-it-yourself potentialities of low-pressure inflatable technology. Transparent Mylar and related materials are temptingly easy to work with, and the inflating mechanism need be no more complex than a domestic vacuum cleaner.[88]

Low-pressure inflatables—which relied on the volume rather than the pressure of air—thus not only were part of a new sensibility, but also represented a participatory approach to design.

Banham identified the low-tech characteristics of inflatables which made them "do-it-yourself" and, therefore, potentially responsive. Furthermore, a low-pressure inflatable environment is responsive in that it is directly affected by losses and gains of air as people come and go, appearing to carry on "like a neurotic bull-frog, puffing itself up, straining, creaking, wrinkling along the seams, trying to lift itself off the floor."[89] The symbiotic type of responsiveness was one Banham felt was significant, but little commented

Late 1960s inflatables (courtesy Mary Banham)

upon: "This tendency to behave like a living organism when roused is what I find missing in most accounts of the inflatable experience. Unlike conventional architecture which stands rigidly to attention and deteriorates . . . inflatables (and tents, to a lesser extent) move and are so nearly living and breathing that it is no surprise that they have to be fed (with amps, if not oats)." This made the inflatable's membrane more like the skin of a living creature than the metaphorical "skin" of the glass curtain wall of conventional architecture.

Not only did inflatables provide a more "organic" architecture than had previously been achieved, but they were in the spirit of an *other* architecture. They brought out a Utopianism in some commentators. Arthur Quarmby, a designer at the forefront of inflatable and pneumatic experimentation, believed that "pneumatics are the most important discovery ever made in architecture, that they can free the constraints which have bounded it since history began and that they can in consequence play an immeasurable part in the development of our society."[90] The claim may have been overinflated, but it is indicative of the cultural symbolism attached to inflatables. Its optimism and belief in the transformative powers of architecture recalls Paul Scheerbart's opening paragraph of *Glass Architecture* in 1914: "We live for the most part in closed rooms. These form the environment from which our culture grows. Our culture is to a certain extent the product of our architecture. If we want our architecture to rise to a higher level, we are obliged, for better or for worse, to change our architecture. And this only becomes possible if we take away the closed character from the rooms in which we live. We can only do that by introducing glass architecture."[91] Change "glass" to "inflatable" architecture, and the organic, *other,* alternative architecture of 1914 becomes the organic, *other,* alternative architecture of 1968.

When discussing the physical responsiveness of inflatables, Banham related them to the radically new cultural conditions: "In the established critical tradition . . . such a physically responsive structure of course doesn't stand a chance of a fair evaluation. But the influence of that bad old school of platonic abstraction is on the wane; the kind of direct-participation, real-space, real-time involvement-aesthetic that is replacing it—epitomised in events like light-sound happenings (which often feature inflatables)—favours this sensitive kind of environment."[92] Banham was echoing the widespread belief within progressive circles about inflatables' wider cultural, rather than mere architectural, significance. Inflatables, a form of architecture in the expanded field, took their place among a culture in an expanded field.[93]

Fit Cities: Pragmatic, Pop, and Radical

If architecture could be redefined and rethought as "fit environments for human activities," there was no conceptual problem in so rethinking the city or, at least, the larger-scale environment. The problem existed at the level of interpretation and judgment as to what made the environment "fit"; what made it an environment "suited to what you are going to do next"? In chapter 3, we saw that in the early 1960s Banham entertained three approaches toward a technological architecture: the pragmatic, the Pop, and the radical. He recognized the potential of two—the Pop and the radical. But when it came to the scale of the city in the later 1960s, it was only one approach—the radical—that he felt was the appropriate solution to the cultural and technological conditions of the age.

The problem he saw with the pragmatic approach to large-scale design was that it did not address any fundamental problems. That decisions and modifications were justified in pragmatic terms meant that society was likely to end up with "the high-density architect-preferred city" which was not taking into account the fundamental changes in technology and culture that made it "possible and necessary to construct alternatives." Pragmatism without an underlying context of radical rethinking—the sort of radical rethinking underlying CLASP's form of pragmatism earlier in the decade—had little appeal for Banham, who attacked the assumptions that the *type* of solution being proposed took no account of the "fundamental changes in technology and culture."

The Pop City

Archigram's Plug-in City of 1964 had provided a fully Pop vision of the future city, but Banham had placed it in a tradition of urban design which, because of its singularity and coherence, was no longer tenable. As we have seen, Archigram themselves, following their shift of interest from hardware to software, were by 1968 seeing the limitations of their earlier work. Peter Cook, in retrospect, even acknowledged the conventionality of Plug-in City: it was, he admitted, "very much of its period: the classic A-frame with community space in the centre,"[94] and hence a part, however apparently avant-garde, of a long tradition. Archigram's development of responsiveness and participation in Control and Choice was extended into their urban design projects, most notably Instant City, which was, in Cook's words, "an assembly of instantly mounted enclosures, together with electronic sound, and display equipment that could be used to tour major provincial towns, and thereby inject into them a high intensity boost that would be sustained by the slow development of a national communications and information network that would advertise and further relay events and entertainments."[95] Hardware comprised audiovisual display systems, projection television, trailered units, pneumatic and lightweight structures and entertainment facilities, gantries, and lighting—the kit of parts would be tailored to the particular location. But, in keeping with late-1960s avant-garde values, Archigram's expressed desire was for "a replacement to architecture that (for once) responds environmentally to the individual."

Archigram, Instant City, 1969 (courtesy Archigram Archive)

Following studies of particular locations, Archigram illustrated an Instant City visit to a typical English town.

As well as providing a further vehicle for Archigram's ideas about flexibility, software, and the responsive environment, Instant City acknowledged the significance of the counterculture of the Underground,[96] urban activism, and technological innovation. Cook acknowledged the events that "have been going on under our nose: Hyde Park, Woodstock, EVR, street theatre, control by tenants, rehabilitation rather than rebuilding, the Airship as an opportunity lost, simpler scaffolding, boredom with light shows, people sitting under flags, telex, Emerson making Bach and Dylan part of the same counterpoint."[97] Instant City, illustrated in its Pop graphic style, was about the temporary transformation of an ordinary and mundane place into an extraordinary and special one, with the hope that a legacy of the transformation would remain when the hardware moved on. But, just as the instantaneous Pop festival city invariably became little more than a muddy, litter-strewn mire once the festivities were over, so, too, Instant City would be unlikely to transform provincial culture into a "metropolis of the national network."[98] With its spontaneity, energy, dynamism, transitory events, and ephemerality, Instant City may have been a true Pop environment; it may have shared a sensibility with the "million-volt light and sound" events that Banham praised as a healthy symptom of a culture of "free-form self-fulfilment"; but, in spite of its conceptual resemblance to an earlier project by Bucky Fuller,[99] Banham did not feel it was a significant contribution to the city in the expanded field.

Archigram identified a Pop *cité trouvé* that, for the group, had some of the major ingredients of the Instant City. That place was Las Vegas, a city which "suggests that a really powerful environment can be created simply by passing an electric current—in daytime the hardware is nothing. Lights combined with cinema projection can make the whole place a city where there is no city. It is suggested that the visitor himself could play with large areas of this lighting so that he makes it happen rather than gawp at it."[100]

Archigram's characterization of Las Vegas as a potentially responsive Instant City was different from the two standard characterisations of that city in the 1960s. Tom Wolfe, in his 1965 essay "Las Vegas (What?) Las Vegas

(Can't Hear You! Too Noisy) Las Vegas!!!," had brought the city to the attention of an initially incredulous architectural profession. His writing represents the first characterization. Wolfe's argument was that Las Vegas shared only with Versailles, in the Western world, the distinction of being an architecturally unified city: "Las Vegas is the only town in the world whose skyline is made up neither of buildings, like New York, nor of trees, like Wilbraham, Massachusetts, but signs. One can look at Las Vegas from a mile away on Route 91 and see no buildings, no trees, only signs. But such signs!"[101] For Wolfe, the achievement, virtue, and appeal of Las Vegas was its *quality* as a Pop city, manifested through its electric signs.

The second characterization of Las Vegas was the more influential one—at least in terms of the developing architectural theory of Post-Modernism—that interpreted it as a precursor, and even model, of architectural semiotics: Las Vegas, in the words of Denise Scott Brown and Robert Venturi, as a "phenomenon of architectural communication."[102] Their initial response to Las Vegas resulted in the article "A Significance for A&P Parking Lots, or Learning from Las Vegas," which appeared in 1968.[103] This formed the basis of the seminal Post-Modern text *Learning from Las Vegas* (1972), which presented the concept of the "decorated shed," in which "systems of space and structure are directly at the service of program, and ornament is applied

Las Vegas signs

independently of them."[104] The decorated shed was the characteristic building type of Las Vegas, and was used by the authors to shift the emphasis
away from abstract form to applied decoration and symbolism as agents of
direct and unambiguous communication.

Wolfe pointed out that "signs have become the architecture of Las Vegas," and Venturi and Scott Brown acknowledged the sheer exuberance of
the signs: the two standard architectural characterizations of Las Vegas
were not mutually exclusive,[105] but they did, perhaps, reveal a difference between a Pop and a fully Post-Modern outlook. Banham, as we have seen,
was sympathetic to the Pop city model and, as we shall see, unsympathetic
to the Post-Modern one. However, the significance of Las Vegas was, for
him, less the stylistics of the signs than the notion of a transformed, or controlled, environment. Archigram had commented on this aspect of Las
Vegas in 1969, and in the same year, in *The Architecture of the Well-
tempered Environment,* Banham wrote:

What defines the symbolic spaces and places of Las Vegas—the superhotels of The Strip,
the casino-belt of Fremont Street—is pure environmental power, manifested as coloured
light. . . . [T]he fact remains that the effectiveness with which space is defined is overwhelming, the creation of virtual volumes without apparent structure is endemic, the
variety and ingenuity of the lighting techniques is encyclopaedic. . . . And in a view
of architectural education that embraced the complete art of environmental management, a visit to Las Vegas would be as mandatory as a visit to the Baths of Caracalla or
La Sainte Chapelle.[106]

The reference to the "coloured light" of Las Vegas is meant to recall, as
was the case with inflatables, a link with the *other* architecture of Paul
Scheerbart and his First Machine Age call for "more coloured light!"[107] It is
an *other* architecture which is also radical: Banham succinctly defines Las Vegas as representing a "change from forms assembled in light to light assembled in forms."[108] Thus, as far as Banham was concerned, the "point of
studying Las Vegas, ultimately, would be to see an example of how far environmental technology can be driven beyond the confines of architectural
practice by designers who (for better or worse) are not inhibited by the tra-

ditions of architectonic culture, training and taste." This shifts the significance of Las Vegas away from its "monument to Pop" status, to one more akin to representing a "controlled"—rather than "responsive"—environment, albeit on a large scale.

Although he did not use the terms, Banham made a distinction between "controlled" and "responsive" at the level of the city in the expanded field. Las Vegas may be worth studying, but, for Banham, it "has been as much a marginal gloss on Los Angeles as was Brighton Pavilion on Regency London."[109] This introduces Los Angeles into the reckoning, the place that came closest to being a posturban, radical city for the Second Machine Age.

The Radical City: Los Angeles

One of Banham's most widely read books is *Los Angeles: The Architecture of Four Ecologies* (1971). He first visited Los Angeles in 1965 to participate in a symposium hosted by the Urban Design Department at the University of California, and visited thereafter on several occasions before taking up a full-time post in 1976. *Los Angeles* was published at the end of a period when the city was receiving serious attention as a city from the younger and/or progressive members of the professions of architecture and town planning. The book generally reflects some of the values of the 1960s, but it can be fully understood and appreciated only if one understands the themes and issues in Banham's writing at this time and, in particular, his interest in radical alternatives to orthodoxies, whether within architecture or at the level of urban form. As we will see, *Los Angeles* provides a qualitative analysis of the experience of Los Angeles as an example of a *radical* city.

The subtitle of the book is somewhat misleading, in that it does not necessarily imply that this is architecture in the expanded field, which is one of the book's distinguishing characteristics. In the opening chapter/introduction, Banham discusses his aim for the book, pointing out that it is not a standard architectural history text. Partly this is because David Gebherd and Robert Winter's *Architecture in Southern California* (1965) exists as "a model version of the classical type of architectural gazetteer—erudite, accurate, clear, well-mapped, pocket-sized."[110] Furthermore, Esther McCoy's edited book *Five California Architects* (1960), with essays on Bernard

Los Angeles, 1960s postcard

Maybeck, Irving Gill, Rudolph Schindler, and the brothers Charles and Henry Greene, had established the credibility and detailed the achievements of Southern California architecture. Banham saw no need to cover this architectural ground again.

But the more compelling reason was that Los Angeles meant to Banham something far more than the sum of the architectural parts. This ruled out a conventional historical monograph: "Can such an old-world, academic, and precedent-laden concept claim to embrace so unprecedented a human phenomenon as this city . . . ?"[111] What the phenomenon required was a different approach—one might describe it as "other" or "radical"—in which the form was sympathetic to the content: "It's a poor historian who finds any human artefact alien to his professional capacities, a poorer one who cannot find new bottles for new wine." The new bottle would have to take a more inclusive view of architecture than conventional histories had. The Gebherd and Winter book, for example, did not refer to "hamburger bars and other pop ephemeridae at one extreme, nor freeway structures and other civil engineering at the other,"[112] both of which were important parts of the Los Angeles environment and experience. This expanded notion of architecture would be presented "within the topographical and historical context of the total artefact that constitutes Greater Los Angeles, because it is this greater context that binds the polymorphous architectures into a comprehensible unity that cannot often be discerned by comparing monument with monument out of context."[113] One might argue, therefore, that the book's subtitle would better be expressed "the *architectures* of four ecologies." The architectures could be fairly easily explained; by "ecology," it becomes clear that Banham means the interrelationship of "geography, climate, economics, demography, mechanics and culture."[114]

The four ecologies of the subtitle comprise "Surfurbia" (the beaches and beach culture); "Foothills" ("foothill ecology [is all about] narrow, tortuous residential roads serving precipitous house-plots that often back up directly on unimproved wilderness"[115]); "The Plains of Id" (the "great service feeding and supplying the foothills and beaches"[116]); and "Autopia" (the freeways). There are also four architectures: "Exotic Pioneers" (a revisionist Modernist account of the work of Irving Gill, the Greene brothers, and Wright); "Fantastic" (the nonconventional, "expanded" Pop architecture of hamburger bars and fast food restaurants, signs, Disneyland, and Simon Rodia's Watts Towers); "The Exiles" (principally Schindler and Richard Neutra); and "The Style That Nearly . . ." (Charles Eames, and the Case Study house style). Five other chapters include an introduction ("In the Rearview Mirror") and conclusion ("An Ecology for Architecture"); "The Transportation Palimpsest" (the growth of the rail and road networks); "The Art of the Enclave" (communities and areas, planned and unplanned); and "A Note on Downtown . . ." ("because that is all downtown deserves."[117]).

Apart from the introduction and conclusion, the book is not particularly sequential: it is not a major problem in terms of the overall coherence and argument if the chapters "are visited at the reader's choice or fancy."[118] This was an expression of the form/content relationship, and part of the "new bottle" design for the new, California wine. It was a statement about a rejection of conventions (of textual sequence, to an extent; of orthodox urban hierarchies, undoubtedly) in favor of possibilities, options, and the "responsive" city in which the citizens had the chance to "do-their-things." That "Reyner Banham Loves Los Angeles"[119] was not in doubt—although, surprisingly, it was not always so.

Indeed, Banham initially found the city "incomprehensible," a response shared by many critics. It is important to be aware of predominant professional—and popular—opinion about Los Angeles. Banham quotes novelist and writer Adam Raphael, whose judgment, aired in the liberal *Guardian* newspaper, was that Los Angeles was "the noisiest, the smelliest, the most uncomfortable, and most uncivilised major city in the United States. In short a stinking sewer."[120] Add to the list of sins the city's ability to induce fear and panic in its visitor, and it is hard to believe that Banham was over his "culture-shock and topographical dismay within 24 hours and feeling perfectly at home in Los Angeles."[121] What had enabled him so completely to "change his mind" about Los Angeles? I would suggest three things. First, familiarity—once Banham got to know his way around, literally and metaphorically, the culture shock dissolved. Second, his disposition to like Los Angeles—he wanted to like it, and thus looked forward it as "an experience to be anticipated and relished." And third, it conceptually represented, as we shall see, a city in the expanded field, a (more or less) fit environment for human activities in the Second Machine Age.

Los Angeles: Hardware and Software

Los Angeles is full of buildings that provide "the ill-defined city of the Angels [with] a well-defined place of honour."[122] It is significant that these range from "high cultural," even canonical, Modernist works, through buildings which typify aspects of architecture in and for the Second Machine Age, to Pop ephemera and, finally, monuments to "doing your thing." The significance is threefold: first, that buildings—"hardware"—still matter to Banham, and constitute a major ingredient of the Los Angeles experience; second, that, in keeping with the Independent Group sensibility of inclusiveness—the "both/and" approach—he celebrates a range of aesthetics and architectural values; and third, the buildings are seldom discussed as isolated monuments, but are seen in the contexts of their particular "ecology" and the wider milieu of Los Angeles.

Examples of the inclusiveness reveal Banham's values, and help to explain the relationship of the architectural content to his interpretation of the city. A Modernist, high cultural example is Rudolph Schindler's house for himself and Clyde Chase, described by Banham as the "the most remarkable design" Schindler was ever to produce. As well as being an example of Banham's "revisionist" Modernism (as we saw in chapter 1), the house was an example of a Modernism related to "social milieu and climate,"[123] and avoided the uniformity and standardization of the European mainstream. It was a good example of an architecture of a particular ecology. A second architectural example, the Water and Power Building of 1964, by Albert C. Martin and Associates, was included not because it is canonical, but because it is

. . . the only public building in the whole city that genuinely graces the scene and lifts the spirit (and sits in firm control of the whole basis of human existence in Los Angeles). . . . In daylight it is a conventional rectangular office block . . . but at night it is transformed [when] . . . from the flanking curves of the freeways one sees only this brilliant cube of diamond-cool light riding above the lesser lights of downtown. It is the only gesture of public architecture that matches the style and scale of the city.[124]

Here is a building that, merely competent during the day, becomes at night a symbol of the city's vital ingredients and transformative capacities of water and electricity. Both this and Schindler's house constitute a form of "critical regionalism"[125] in which style and design are directly related to regional circumstances, whether natural (climate) or cultural (technologies).

The third example is of a type excluded from conventional architectural books—commercial structures, including buildings and signs. Some historians would reject this sort of architecture as trivial; others would go further and write of the "visual pollution by commercial advertising." Banham's response to such a criticism is that "anyone who cares for the unique character of individual cities must see that the proliferation of advertising signs is an essential part of the character of Los Angeles; to deprive the city of them would be like depriving San Gimignano of its towers or the City of London

Albert C. Martin and Associates, Water and Power Building, Los Angeles, 1963–1964 (courtesy Mary Banham)

of its Wren steeples." They should be not just tolerated, but celebrated for their "flamboyance, and the constant novelty induced by their obsolescence and replacement"[126]—commercial architecture continued Banham's Independent Group-derived Pop sensibility.

An example included in *Los Angeles* is the popular culture style of the "so-called Polynesian restaurants" typified by the Aztec Hotel, Monrovia (1925): buildings as "strikingly and lovingly ridiculous as this represent well enough the way Los Angeles sums up a general phenomenon of US life; the convulsions of building style that follow when traditional cultural and social restraints have been overthrown and replaced by the preferences of a mobile, affluent, consumer-oriented society, in which 'cultural values' and ancient symbols are handled primarily as methods of claiming or establishing value."[127] Banham accepts the commercial architecture amorally, and sees it as typical—indeed, a perfectly valid expression—of one of Los Angeles's important ecologies. The Aztec Hotel thus takes its place in *Los Angeles* alongside Schindler's house and the Water and Power Building as representing alternatives within the permissive diversity of the "polymorphus architectures" of the city. That these buildings are all valid, and are discussed critically, reminds one that the Independent Group "plurality of hierarchies" model was still upheld by Banham.

A final architectural example is the Watts Towers, because they, too, represent a significant aspect of the city's culture:

Their actual presence is testimony to a genuinely original creative spirit. And in the thirty-three years of absorbed labour he devoted to their construction, and in his uninhibited ingenuity in exploiting the by-products of an affluent technology, and in his determination to "do something big," and in his ability to walk away when they were finished in 1954, Rodia was very much at one with the surfers, hot-rodders, sky-divers, and scuba-divers who personify the tradition of private, mechanistic *satori*-seeking in California.[128]

Banham interprets the Watts Towers as the "most triumphant monument, ever, to the art of doing your thing."[129] In the text of one of his 1968 radio broadcasts, he wrote that the phrase "doing your thing" had only recently gained international currency, "but it perfectly expresses what Los Angeles believes itself to be about. The promise of this affluent, permissive, and free-

Robert Stacy-Judd, Aztec Hotel, Monrovia, Los Angeles, 1925 (courtesy Mary Banham)

Simon Rodia, Watts Towers, Los Angeles, 1921–1954

swinging culture is that every man [*sic*], in his own lifetime and to his own complete satisfaction, shall do exactly what he wants to."[130]

There were significant forms of nonarchitectural hardware. Because "Angelenos are . . . the privileged class of pop culture today . . . ," they are responsible for having "invented and decorated artefacts that are the envy of the world and go so far beyond mere physical need as to be perfectly useless."[131] Among other things in *Los Angeles,* Banham writes about the surfboard, the "prime symbolic and functional artefact" of the culture and cult of California surfing. Another form of "doing your thing" was car customization: "in the uninhibited inventiveness of master customisers like George Barris and Ed Roth, normal straight Los Angeles found something that sprang from the dusty roots of its native culture . . . tamed it, institutionalised it, and applied it in some form to almost every vehicle awheel in the City of Angels. . . . The customised automobile is the natural crowning artefact of the way of life, the human ecology, it adorns."[132] Both surfboards and cars are items of hardware that facilitate movement and, Banham would argue, personal expression and potential fulfillment.

Unrelated to personal expression but undeniably related to movement is the final example of hardware from *Los Angeles:* freeway structures, which are "as crucial to the human ecologies and built environments of Los Angeles as are dated works in classified styles by named architects."[133] For most of its miles, the freeway is important for providing "well-serviced anonymity," but there are particular places which demand the highest praise, including the

. . . wide-swinging curved ramps of the intersection of the Santa Monica and the San Diego freeways, which immediately persuaded me that the Los Angeles freeway system is indeed one of the greater works of Man. . . . It is more customary to praise the famous four-level intersection which now looks down on the old Figueroa Street grade separation, but its virtues seem to me little more than statistical whereas the Santa Monica/San Diego intersection is a work of art, both as a pattern on the map, as a monument against the sky, and as a kinetic experience as one sweeps through it.[134]

Banham had described that kinetic experience in one of his radio broadcasts, declaring that "to drive over those ramps in a high sweeping 60-mile-an-hour trajectory and plunge down to ground level again is a spatial experience of a sort one does not normally associate with monuments of engineering—the nearest thing to flight on four wheels I know."[135] This is, of course, Futurist in tone and sensibility, and recalls Sant'Elia and Marinetti's passion for the "immense, tumultuous, lively . . . dynamic" city in which "the street will descend into the earth on several levels."[136] For Banham, the promise of the Futurist City of the First Machine Age with its "mechanical sensibility" had come to fruition in the Los Angeles of the Second.

His sympathy for Futurism had been based, in part, on its embrace of experience and sensation rather than its dispassionate detachment toward the contemplation of Platonic form. The way Banham describes the experience of driving in Los Angeles is also Futurist in its sensibility:

> . . . the actual experience of driving on the freeways prints itself deeply on the conscious mind and unthinking reflexes. As you acquire the special skills involved, the Los Angeles freeways become a special way of being alive, which can be duplicated, in part, on other systems . . . but not with this totality and extremity. If motorway driving anywhere calls for a high level of attentiveness, the extreme concentration required in Los Angeles seems to bring on a state of heightened awareness that some locals find mystical.[137]

Banham plays down the mundane realities of driving and the traffic jams in order to summon up a Romantic image of those carefree, car-loving "Angeleno freeway-pilots . . . [whose] white-wall tyres are singing over the diamond-cut anti-skid grooves in the concrete road surface, the selector-levers of their automatic gearboxes are firmly in *Drive,* and the radio is on."[138] To an extent he is overstating his case in order to counter the usual criticisms, often repeated without direct evidence, that the freeway system was a polluting, frustrating, extended traffic jam which brought out aggression and fueled alienation.[139] But, however polemical he was attempting to be, Banham can justifiably be criticized for writing about driving on the freeways from the restricted point of view of relatively affluent, mobile, independent, solo, white-collar-professional, alert, fulfilled, (usually white) males, and thus generalizes that Angeleno drivers "are relaxed and well-adjusted characters without an identity problem in the world, for whom the freeway

Surfboards, mid-1960s (courtesy Mary Banham)

Intersection of Santa Monica and San Diego freeways (courtesy Mary Banham)

is not a limbo of existential *angst,* but the place where they spend the two calmest and most rewarding hours of their daily lives."[140] Driving also signified a commitment to a progressive way of life. If downtown's mediocre buildings were "memorials to a certain insecurity of spirit among timid souls who cannot bear to go with the flow of Angeleno life," then "rolling at night along the four freeways that box in the central downtown cavity" was the expression of "those who do go with the flow."[141] To be a "motorised citizen" in Los Angeles was to be a full citizen of the Second Machine Age.

Las Vegas's "coloured light" had put Banham in mind of the Scheerbartian, Expressionist version of *architecture autre;* the experience of driving on the Los Angeles freeways now had unambiguous associations with Futurism and its Machine Age credentials. Banham was not being nostalgic; he was identifying a contemporary manifestation of the "mechanistic sensibility." Was it this that made Los Angeles an alternative city, a contemporary radical city in the expanded field?

A Field of Possibilities

Only in part. What makes Los Angeles a radical city is its form in relation to its content. Los Angeles has an international scale "in terms of size, cosmopolitan style, creative energy, international influence, distinctive way of life and corporate personality";[142] its content makes it possible for creative individuals "to do their thing with the support of like-minded characters and the resources of a highly diversified body of skills and technologies"; and the optimism with the "sense of possibilities still ahead is part of the basic lifestyle of Los Angeles."[143] The form matches the creative ethos: "the point about this giant city, which has grown almost simultaneously all over, is that all its parts are equal and equally accessible from all other parts at once. Everyday commuting tends less and less to move by the classic systole and diastole in and out of downtown, more and more to move by an almost random or Brownian motion over the whole area."[144] Banham may have adjudged that "freedom of movement . . . is the prime symbolic attribute of the Angel City,"[145] but it is important to realize that the "form" of freedom is matched by the "content" of activity. Los Angeles offers its inhabitants choice at an urban scale.

The form and content of the city became for Banham, whether consciously, or not, a realization of Independent Group ideals. The "sense of possibilities" echoes the "non-Aristotelian logic of provisional possibilities" that the Independent Group discussed in 1955.[146] (And how typical of Banham's Independent Group-influenced writing to refer—without elucidation or reference—to "Brownian motion"![147]) Los Angeles paralleled those "modern arrangements of knowledge in non-hierarchic forms"[148] explored by Banham, McHale, Alloway, and others in the 1950s. It was a continuum— and thus inclusive and permissive—rather than a "pyramid" with its exclusive sets of values "frozen in layers," as Alloway had put it—in urban form terms, a pyramid equated to a traditional, hierarchical, differentiated, clustered layout.

The Independent Group's continuum model of culture accepted diversity and saw all the components or discourses as of equal value—a field of possibilities, a network with links actively made by the participant. For Banham, Los Angeles was the continuum model in urban form in which "all its parts are equal and equally accessible from all other parts at once." The possibilities it provided also made it the urban version of a responsive environment, in tune with what the user was "going to do next." It could be seen as the urban equivalent of Cedric Price's *other* architecture with its well-serviced anonymity, "self-participatory elements" and "freedom of choice" which would help create "new activities, at present without name." Banham observed that "from the ornamentation of sports gear to the environmental planning of new suburbs, Los Angeles celebrates the culture of 'fun.'"[149] The significance of fun as part of the changing, Post-Modern culture also links Banham's view of Los Angeles with Price's architecture, and, in passing, it is worth noting that *Los Angeles: The Architecture of Four Ecologies* is dedicated to Cedric Price.

The field of possibilities may have *theoretically* meant that "all parts are equal," but it is an equality as a potentiality rather than an actuality. There were at least three factors that militated against the possibility being fulfilled. Banham admits that what sometimes happened was that the open-ended, fluid situation would become "functional monocultures":

. . . in Los Angeles you tend to go to a particular place to do a particular thing, to another to do another thing, and finally a long way back to your home, and you've done a hundred miles in a day. The distances and reliance on mechanical transportation leave no room for accident, even for happy accidents. You plan the day in advance, programme your activities, and forego those random encounters with friends and strangers that are traditionally one of the rewards of city life.[150]

This acknowledged a reality which was some way from the image of relaxed, freewheeling Angelenos spending the most "rewarding hours of their daily lives."

A related, second, danger was the tendency of Los Angeles "to fragment into self-contained, specialised areas—social monocultures."[151] In the field of possibilities, not everyone will be in a position to translate the possibilities into actualities. This was profoundly true of the economically disadvantaged. In the text of one of his radio broadcasts,[152] Banham muses on the poverty trap that characterizes many Watts residents: without a car, they cannot travel to more lucrative jobs; without those jobs, they cannot afford a car. Banham even criticizes the author of a March 1965 article on Los Angeles for claiming that in Los Angeles, "freedom of movement has long given life a special flavour . . . , liberated the individual to enjoy the sun and space that his environment so abundantly offered, put the manifold advantages of a great metropolitan area within his grasp."[153] The criticism relates to the article's "slightly quaint air from having been written in the last months of untainted optimism before the Watts riots."[154] Yet Banham's optimism is hardly less tainted, and his response to the Watts situation is to seek an economic solution which upholds the urban form, rather than to see a problem resulting from urban form—the somewhat simplistic solution is to improve economic conditions so that Watts residents can become stakeholders in their society, thereby seeing themselves, no doubt, as "Angeleno freeway pilots . . . going with the flow."

The third factor militating against the field of possibilities was that the "equality" might operate at the lowest common denominator and be manifested as a homogeneity of suburban sprawl—there might be mere anonymity without being well-serviced. Banham countered that "to speak of 'sprawl' in the sense that, say, Boston, Mass., sprawled centrifugally in its street-railway years, is to ignore the observable facts."[155] Los Angeles may represent the "most potent current version of the great bourgeois vision of the good life in a tamed countryside," and inevitably, therefore, sprawl it does; but this does not result in the chaos predicted by Le Corbusier when the "dream" bourgeois villa is multiplied one million times. Rather, "the chaos was in his mind, and not in Los Angeles, where seven million adepts at California Dreaming can find their way around without confusion."[156] Nor has the "culture of rampant automobilism"[157] turned the form into an extended parking lot: "The fact that . . . parking-lots, freeways, drive-ins, and other facilities have not wrecked the city-form is due chiefly to the fact that Los Angeles has no urban form at all in the commonly accepted sense."[158]

Banham's point is that the car is not the cause of this situation, as it often was assumed to be, because the freeway system echoed the five main communication network lines established by the railway companies in the second half of the nineteenth century. Therefore, "the uniquely even, thin and homogeneous spread of development . . . has been able to absorb the monuments of the freeway system without serious strain." Ultimately for Banham, Los Angeles merits international status because of its unique form/content relationship: "when most observers report monotony, not unity, and within that monotony, confusion rather than variety, this is usually because the context has escaped them; and it has escaped them because it is unique (like all the best unities) and without any handy terms of comparison."[159]

As he expressed it in 1968: "The unique value of Los Angeles—what excites, intrigues and sometimes repels me—is that it offers radical alternatives to almost every urban concept in unquestioned currency."[160] The use of the word "radical" is significant: there were lessons to be learned from the city about an urban design for living in the Second Machine Age, but this did not mean that Banham was presenting it as "the prototype of all future cities," as a generalizable model. Indeed, the particular ecologies of Los Angeles—"the splendours and miseries of [the city], . . . the graces and grotesqueries, appear to me as unrepeatable as they are unprecedented." It is its specificity that gives Los Angeles its unique character and makes it unlikely "that an even remotely similar mixture will ever occur again."[161]

The chief lesson was that "there are as many possible cities as there are possible forms of human society." The success of Los Angeles "emphatically suggests that there is no simple correlation between urban form and social form."[162] As architects like Bucky Fuller and Cedric Price challenged architectural lore, so Los Angeles challenged urban lore and expanded the field of possibilities. Just as architects ought to reject outworn conventions and radically rethink the premise of their activity in terms of providing "fit environments for human activity" rather than assuming a building would always be the solution, so town planners ought similarly to rethink their assumptions about urban form. The failure rate of buildings was high but, Banham continued, "The failure rate of town planning is so high throughout the world that one can only marvel that the profession has not long since given up trying."[163]

Banham's invective was aimed at the profession not only for producing unsuccessful solutions but also for holding on to anachronistic values and habits of thought: "Where it threatens the 'human values'—oriented tradition of town planning inherited from Renaissance humanism . . . is in revealing how simple-mindedly mechanistic that supposedly humane tradition can be, how deeply attached to the mechanical fallacy that there is a necessary causal connexion between built form and human life, between the mechanisms of the city and the styles of architecture practised there."[164] The attack recalls Banham's jibe about those who are "isolated from humanity by the Humanities"[165]—the new group to be included in that infamous gang are obviously town planners—and the basis of the isolation, the reader might recall from chapter 2, was class-determined. Los Angeles represented a more democratic, permissive, populist society, and so "the common reflexes of hostility are not a defence of architectural values, but a negation of them, at least in so far as architecture has any part in the thoughts and aspirations of the human race beyond the little private world of the profession."[166] And beyond architectural value, they were, as far as Banham was concerned, an attack on democracy.

Not all reviewers agreed. One of the main contemporary criticisms of the book was that it "glosses too lightly over the social consequences of mandatory mobility, of pollution, poverty, race, and politics."[167] Reviewers acknowledged that most books on Los Angeles "have suffered from excessive negativism; but this one begins to fall apart because of its unbridled positivism."[168] If Banham had to experience the freeway jams and air pollution "on a daily basis as a matter of social and economic necessity, then his optimism would fade. As it is, the Angeleno becomes aware of 'the author as voyeur.'"[169] Another Angeleno reviewer put it succinctly: "the trouble with Reyner Banham is that the fashionable sonofabitch doesn't have to live here."[170] He never did.

Non-Plan and Milton Keynes

After his radio broadcasts, and while he was writing his book on Los Angeles, Banham joined with Cedric Price, Peter Hall, and Paul Barker to produce the manifesto-like "Non-Plan: An Experiment in Freedom" essay in *New Society* in 1969.[171] All four were enthusiasts of Los Angeles, and the manifesto, as the title implies, essentially took Banham's "lessons" of Los Angeles and applied them to three areas of Britain and asked "what would happen if there were no plan? What would people prefer to do, if their choice were untrammelled? Would matters be any better, or any worse, or much the same?"[172]

Banham's contribution can be detected at many points, including his attack on the very word "planning" because it is "misused": it is currently used "for the imposition of certain physical arrangements, based on value judgements or prejudices; and . . . should be scrapped. . . . Worst of all: they are judgements about how they think *other* people—not of their acquaintance or class—should live."[173] The attack on "planning" was aimed at British conservatism and the complacency of the profession. Planning needed to change and reflect three of the most "compelling" developments of the last ten years, categorized by the authors as "the cybernetic revolution; the mass affluence revolution; and the pop/youth culture revolution." The pop revolution was considered especially influential because it had been at the forefront of wider social and cultural changes and had had "the remarkable effect in breaking down class barriers." The Pop sensibility had profound implications for planning:

Most importantly for Non-Plan, it is frenetic and immediate culture, based on the rapid obsolescence cycle. Radio One's "revived 45" is probably three months old, and on the New York art scene fashions change almost as quickly as on the King's Road. Pop culture is anti high bourgeois culture. . . . Pop culture in Britain has produced the biggest visual explosion for decades—or even, in the case of fashion, for centuries. Yet its effect on the British landscape has been nil, for the simple reason that the planners have suppressed it.[174]

The "spontaneity and vitality" of Pop should be reflected in urban form and design.[175] This was happening in California, where "the living architecture of our age" was the outcome of Non-Plan. Planning should be an expression of vital culture, but in Britain, "we [still] seem so afraid of freedom."[176]

However objectionable to the mainstream, there were signs that some of the ideas represented by Non-Plan were having a tangible effect on British planning. The concept underlying the new city of Milton Keynes, designated in 1967, was described by its chief planner, Lord Llewelyn Davies—Banham's old head of department—as "a modified Los Angeles system."[177] The car was seen as an important ingredient in the design, and as the provider of "freedom of choice and opportunity." The six goals of the plan were the following:

1. Opportunity and freedom of choice
2. Easy movement and access, and good communications
3. Balance and variety
4. An attractive city
5. Public awareness and participation
6. Efficient and imaginative use of resources.[178]

The first two come close to characterizing Banham's description of Los Angeles, and he would have been unlikely to disagree with any of the others. The nature and priority of these goals depart significantly from previous "top-down," highly controlled planning concepts, and traditionalists, Banham recalled, were "implacably hostile to both Los Angeles and its putative offspring up the A5 beyond Bletchley."[179] Banham was particularly sympathetic to the loose grid system "with its infrastructure of roads and services" in which all the enclosed squares were "equal in importance and potential," and to the unwillingness to impose a grand design, "rather to create the conditions in which it could design itself, changing organically according to need."

The "promise of . . . open, non-directed, well-serviced anonymity" at Milton Keynes was not fulfilled because, in the end, the appetite for and culture of permissiveness did not exist in the way it did in Los Angeles. It did indeed seem that Britain, even after the "swinging sixties," was still "so afraid of freedom," as the authors of Non-Plan had put it.

Thus, by the early 1970s Banham's commitment to a redefinition of architecture and urban form in terms of "fit environments for human activities . . . suited to what you are going to do next" had taken him into the expanded field where there was an emphasis on well-serviced anonymity, the responsive environment, and software. The respective lessons of Los Angeles and Milton Keynes taught him that the European approaches to architecture and planning did not facilitate the permissiveness, inclusiveness, and pragmatism that he sought, whereas the United States, at least the less European-influenced West Coast, offered a real "sense of possibilities."

Banham's apparent rejection of the cultural baggage of Europe—indeed, in effect, he expressed it in both *The Architecture of the Well-tempered Environment* and *Los Angeles: The Architecture of Four Ecologies* as Europe's baggage of culture—seemed also to be a rejection of Modernism, even the revisionist Modernism of *Theory and Design in the First Machine Age*. Did this mean that the field was expanded to the point at which Modernist values melted into the air? Paralleling Rosalind Krauss, did the "sense of possibilities" lead Banham to identify with Post-Modern values and priorities? In chapter 5 we will be analyzing Banham's response to the growing movement of architectural Post-Modernism.

5

LATE OR POST?

Banham's Modernist Values

During the 1960s, the development of a radical approach to architecture led Banham, as we saw in chapter 4, beyond architectural lores and conventions—beyond, indeed, architecture—to the idea of "fit environments for human activities" "suited to what you are going to do next." There was a great deal of radicalism in progressive circles in the 1960s, and some of it was intentionally subverting architectural norms. Peter Cook recalled in 1975 how, at the end of the 1960s, "it was fashionable to introduce a project as an 'anti-building,' or a 'conglomeration of environmental elements.'"[1] The first brings to mind Banham's "un-house"; the second, *The Architecture of the Well-tempered Environment,* and hints at Banham's status and influence—his radicalism was indeed symptomatic of the libertarian, permissive, anti-conventional era in which he was writing. However, changes of sensibilities, attitudes, and even values in the years after 1968 meant that he could be cast as reactionary rather than radical.

Banham had always been used to being on the *attack,* usually against the mainstream. His previous radicalism had guaranteed there would be attacks on him—we saw some of these in chapter 3—but these were from "lore and conventions" mainstreamers, against what they saw as his championing of an extremist movement or group, New Brutalism or Archigram, for example. What was new in the 1970s was the unaccustomed situation of being on the *defense* against those who were claiming either a reborn traditionalism or a different radicalism which repositioned Banham as a leading prophet of an old but discredited religion, and even as someone whose values were part of the problem rather than a solution.

This chapter will examine Banham's architectural writing and ideas at a time of change, when not only were Modern Movement architectural values under attack, but the assumptions about technology and progress that underlay them were being called to account. There are two broad sections to the chapter: the first studies Banham's writings about James Stirling in the middle years of the 1960s, in order both to differentiate Banham's and Pevsner's values, and to relate their shared values to the wider changes of attitude and value that were taking place in society. The second section discusses Banham's writing of the 1970s and 1980s to gauge his changed position in architectural criticism and discourse. We start by discussing two important articles by Nikolaus Pevsner in 1966/1967 which attack what their author saw as the contemporary "neo-Expressionist" tendency typified by architects such as James Stirling. By then dealing with Banham's response to neo-Expressionism and Stirling's architecture, we can identify some of the explicit or implicit assumptions and attitudes which became contentious around 1968, when a sea change was occurring in wider architectural values.

Architecture in Our Time

At the end of 1966 and beginning of 1967, Pevsner presented two radio talks, subsequently published in *The Listener,* which purported to discuss "architecture in our time." Pevsner's revised, 1960 edition of *Pioneers of Modern Design,* the reader will recall from chapter 1, had somewhat grudgingly included Gaudi and Sant'Elia, but its author was still of the opinion that his fundamental thesis about the validity of International Style architecture as "the style of the century" did not need significant revision or accommodation. Pevsner was not a person transformed by the attitudes and values of the "swinging sixties." His 1966/1967 pronouncements could have come out of the conclusion to the revised *Pioneers,* and the underlying assumptions out of the original, 1936 edition—the Pop revolution had no influence on his thinking, and neither did Banham's differentiation along qualitative lines of the First and Second Machine Ages. The growing evidence of the characteristics of the Second Machine Age during the 1960s did not shake Pevsner's certainty about the timelessness of his Modern principles. In his talks he repeated the necessity for impersonality, anonymity, mass production, and aesthetic lightness, strongly objecting to what he thought of as the contemporary tendency of "one, self-expression of the artist-architect; two, a fervent avoidance of lightness, of anything that could be called elegant, and also of anything that could be accounted for purely rationally; and, three, forms of overpowering—what shall I say?— yes: brutality."[2]

Banham's reaction to this argument was mostly, but not quite wholly, predictable.[3] While acknowledging that *Theory and Design* was "definitely revisionist," he was at pains to stress that it was not "anti-Pevsnerian"[4] and that, by and large, in agreement with his mentor about the irrelevancy of neo-Expressionist buildings like Le Corbusier's Ronchamp referring, as we have seen in chapter 3, to the "big, swinging, personal, primitive gesture" as a monument "from the past, not the architecture of here and now."[5] This was not a rejection of Ronchamp (et alia) because it was neo-Expressionist, but because *both* neo-Expressionism *and* contemporary International Style architecture were aesthetically driven;[6] both were architectural formalism "within the limits of a professional tradition, albeit that tradition is now wide enough to span from . . . Mies van der Rohe to Bruce Goff."[7] This line of argument logically led him, as we have seen in chapters 3 and 4, toward a radical architecture that was based on technology—Bucky Fuller, Cedric Price, Archigram etc.—or to the concept of "fit environments for human activities."

James Stirling and "Bloody-mindedness"

However, the tradition was acceptable if it contained real radicalism. In the second of his two talks, Pevsner uses Stirling and James Gowan's Engineering Faculty at Leicester University as a "test case" of neo-Expressionism. Pevsner accepted that it seemed to function in a more or less satisfactory manner, but criticized elements such as the ramp, the angle of which would seem to have been determined more by the consistent use of diagonals than by utilitarian considerations such as manageable access to the building, and the "curious prisms of glass which end each bay of the (incidentally, diagonally disposed) skylighting of the low workshop range. I have tried in every way, and yet I cannot see that they have any functional justification. . . . They are purely expression." Furthermore, they appear aggressive rather than calm or elegant: "this aggressive angularity repeats all over the building. So to me the Leicester Engineering Faculty is Expressionism, as much as Poelzig's *Grosse Schauspielhaus* and Taut's fantastic *Stadtkrone.* It is architecture heightened in its emotional effects by sharp stabbing angles, an expression not of the character of the building but of the architect."[8] This was not a position held by Banham, who wrote two articles about the building in 1964, soon after it had opened.

Banham contributed an article to a lengthy analysis of the Engineering Faculty in *Architectural Forum* in the summer of 1964, having published a critically similar piece in *New Statesman* in February.[9] The lengthier article, with references in the first paragraph to a workshop looking like a "good building," the university getting such "good architecture," and the surprise that results when laboratories turn out to be "good buildings,"[10] leaves the reader in no doubt that Banham judges the building to be "a pretty extraordinary piece of contemporary architecture." In fact, he concludes that it is nothing short of being "the first world-class building to be put up in England for a great many years."[11] Where Pevsner sees willful Expressionist idiosyncrasy, Banham sees "spectacular aspects" in the design such as the "crystalline sea flooding across the top of the heavy lab area and erupting in diamond breakers over the solid walls on every side of the podium."[12] He accepts that this is not simple functional or utilitarian design, and that the architect could even be described as acting expressionistically, but if the re-

James Stirling and James Gowan, Engineering Faculty, Leicester University, 1964

(courtesy Michael Wilford and Partners, Ltd.)

sult is "one of the most extraordinary spectacles contemporary architecture has to offer," then that exposes the danger of the Pevsnerian approach with its rigid assumptions.

Banham liked far more than the Expressionist elements. The use of off-the-peg, industrial patent glazing designed for factories and greenhouses gave the building an "as found" aspect which was "unaffectedly crude," albeit functionally compromised—"flashings that flash right out of the frame, panes that have gaps at the edge, nuts and bolts put in back to front."[13] He acknowledges these functional shortcomings, but argues that the "only real functional query" is the "unforeseeable consequences of dropping water nearly 100 feet through straight, large-bore pipes. Somewhere in the system was a construction or bend that triggered an organ-pipe effect, and as the hydraulics lab came up to full flow, a note of pure and unearthly beauty would be heard in the stair tower, building up through a perfect scale, but—unfortunately—getting louder as well, so that when it hit the octave it was more than the human ear could bear."[14] This potentially disruptive fault is turned into an affectionate anecdote: "talk about architecture as frozen music—I was with Jim Stirling the first time he heard it and his face was a study in baffled delight; Muzak was never like this!" The reference to the familiar "Jim" reminds us that Stirling was a friend.[15] Perhaps Banham's judgment was colored by subjective factors.

Formalism, crude detailing, windows with gaps and ear-piercing pipe-work noises are not only forgiven but downplayed to the extent that Banham claims "no serious functional objections have emerged." He continues, with more than a hint of condescension, that "It may be true, as some small, frightened men insist, that Stirling & Gowan have bent some of the functions for the sake of the architecture,"[16] but these are then summarily dismissed. If Banham's criticism seems bloody-minded, it is at least in keeping with Stirling and Gowan's building:

History and style don't bother men like these any more; both are disenchanted with the "white architecture of the '30s," which they regard as little more than a styling gimmick. Yet, as everybody notices, the Leicester labs are the first design for decades that has anything of the zip, clarity, and freshness, the *nonchalance*, of the pioneer machine-aesthetic buildings of the 1920s. It's as though they had invented modern architecture all over again, and one can only wish that other architects would have the wit, sophistication, sense, taste, bloody-mindedness—and in a word, *character*—to do it, too.[17]

There is a sense of *déjà lu* in this. Its spirit and sentiments resonantly recall Banham's response to New Brutalism. He had written in his major article on the New Brutalism in 1955 that the defining ingredient of the movement "is precisely its brutality, its *j'en-foutisme,* its bloody-mindedness"[18]—a description which now almost perfectly matched his response to Stirling and Gowan's Leicester building.

His disillusionment with the Smithsons had risen rapidly from the late 1950s, and in his *Architectural Forum* article Banham makes an aside about how Brutalism has been "screwed up" and now seeks "elegance":[19] it was an interesting coincidence that the Smithsons' Economist Building in London, begun in 1959, was being completed at about the same time the Engineering Faculty opened, thus providing a direct comparison between what he judged to be the ethic that Brutalism had promised, and the aesthetic which it had become; between its potential for *une architecture autre* and its decline into *vers une architecture.* He directly contrasted the two buildings in *The New Brutalism* of 1966. Indeed, they are the last two illustrations in the book, to make a point that (with the Smithsons' building), "the biggest and most important fact about the British contribution to Brutalism is that it is over"; the Stirling building—the final illustration in the book— is a claim that the *spirit* of Brutalism lives on. As Banham writes in the text, the Economist Building "is a work of studied restraint. It may offer a vision of a new community structure, but it does so upon the basis of an ancient Greek acropolis plan, and in maintaining the scale and governing lines of tradition-bound St James's Street . . . it handles the 'street idea' very tenderly indeed. Far from being an example of the 'other' architecture, this is a craftsmanly exercise within the great tradition."[20] Given Banham's *autre* values, belonging to the "great tradition" is not something to which the progressive architect should aspire.

On the other hand, the Leicester University building "comes nearer to Brutalism in the emotional sense of a rough, tough building, and in the dramatic space-play of its sectional organisation it carries still something of the aggressive informality of the mood of the middle fifties."[21] Ultimately, whether or not the Engineering Faculty could be labeled "Brutalist" was not a significant point; what mattered was the building's spirit of bloody-mindedness. A linking of Stirling and Brutalism had been made in an article of 1958, which discussed Stirling and Gowan's Le Corbusier-influenced flats at Ham Common. Banham describes them as "the most accessible example there is of the New Brutalism," and sees the impact of the flats as "like an encounter with some Kline paintings . . .—a smart blow on the head with a carefully shaped blunt instrument" by architects who showed "real guts."[22] This was high praise indeed in *architecture autre* terms.

So, for Pevsner, while 1960s Modernism was still a question of form in relation to aesthetico-moral principles, for Banham it was a matter of form as a manifestation of an attitude, a spirit of conviction, and an unwillingness to compromise. It may not be as radical as an *architecture autre,* but Kenneth Frampton's notion of an "architecture of resistance" is a term—although Banham, as we will see, did not like it—which could be used to describe his belief in the value of buildings like the Leicester Engineering Faculty.[23] The legacy of his First Machine Age heroes, like the Futurists, is apparent here: it is their spirit, manifested in different ways, that appealed to him about Fuller, Price, and Archigram. In "Architecture in Our time," Pevsner may have admitted to being "puzzled" by "my pupil" Reyner Banham and his questioning of the validity of the architecture of the Pioneers,[24] interpreting his pupil's work as an overturning of all that is good, true, and valid in favor of "ineffectual deviationists," but this does not recognize the underlying commonality of their Modernist values, values which were to be challenged in the period following 1968.

Stirling's "Dumb Insolence"

Banham wrote an extended piece about Stirling's controversial History Faculty building at Cambridge University in *Architectural Review* in November 1968. In it, he gleefully comments that the "Stirling-baiters who have been poised to savage him" for reusing the style of the Leicester building are "out of luck" because the new building is "entirely different [in] style." The design concept was different—"unassertive," and contained rather than "rhetorical" and differentiated—but criticism about functional deficiencies was rife, this time about the notorious "glazed pyramid":

For months now, stories of the monstrous solar heat gain through all that glass have been assiduously circulated by that persistent group who, still smarting from their defeat when Leicester was shown to be as functional as it was spectacular, . . . assumed that this time they really had Big Jim hooked on a charge of indictable formalism. This time it would stick, because the stories of sweltering temperatures in the reading room that were going round the lunch-tables of the Architectural Association were all perfectly true and based on personal observation . . . except that the observers had apparently failed to note (or to mention) that the heating throughout the building was being run full blast at the time to help dry out the structure.[25]

Banham may be defending the building on its functional performance, and so upholding the notion of it being a "fit environment," but it is worth noting the tone of the writing—polemical is a generous way of describing it; confrontational, certainly; condescending (about "Stirling-baiters") arguably. The tone is something to which we will be returning.

Banham acknowledged some of the discomforts of the thermal characteristics of the building, but concluded that the combination of normal temperatures and the effect of the ventilating system is that "the glass pyramid must be accounted a reasonable, responsible environmental device, not a formalist extravagance." A second functional controversy concerned the lighting. Under opaque ceilings, Stirling had used "naked fluorescent tubes, without shades or diffusers, mounted on surfaces painted hard gloss white."[26] Banham acknowledges that "as described, it sounds awful; as experienced [in the main reading room] it is never troublesome. . . ." But, in the seminar rooms, "there are bound to be complaints about the lighting because that is a fashionable thing to complain about, but even when allowance for human cussedness and academic conservatism has been made, it seems possible that detail modifications will have to be made in some of the rooms because of localised patches of glare or shadow."[27] Even as seemingly justifiable a complaint as the use of naked, harsh lighting—which Banham himself went on to condemn in no uncertain terms in *The Architecture of the Well-tempered Environment*—is toned down by swipes at fashion-ableness and conservatism.

There was a third subject of complaint. It comprised environmental controls including hot-water convectors in the upstand beam on the edge of the floor slab, ventilating louvres in the patent glazing, and venetian blinds hung in the space between the glazing and the upstand: "Now, with the laudable intention of preventing direct draughts, the louvres are placed so that they are masked by the upstand, and their control handles are therefore a little difficult to reach. But they are also masked by the ventilation blinds when these are in the down position (which they normally will be on days hot enough to require adjustments to the louvres) and it is quite easy to get the control handles fouled up in the slats of the blind."[28]

In other circumstances, one can imagine Banham launching into a tirade of abuse for such functional incompetence, being utterly disparaging about such soft-headedness as "laudable intentions" (while eschewing such forgiving qualifications as a "*little* difficult to reach"). But Stirling receives—consistently received—what can only be described as partisan favoritism. Functional inadequacy becomes Sod's Law—or "Murphy's Law (also known as Finagle's Law), which predicts the probability of mechanical disaster by

James Stirling, History Faculty, Cambridge University, 1968 (courtesy Michael Wilford and Partners, Ltd.)

the following formula: If anything *can* happen, it will." This was a law that Banham invoked selectively. Bad luck was compounded

. . . by the fact that most of the occupants of the building will be humanities-oriented, and therefore likely to fall below the national average in mechanical literacy and competence. Controls that get fouled up through mismanagement by the occupants will tend to be left in that condition while the occupants take verbal revenge on the architects. If revenge is to be taken anywhere, it should be on the University Grants Committee as the agents of a policy of allocating building budgets too skimpy to permit decent environmental installations.[29]

Here is a classic case, not only of special pleading but also of turning defense into attack. Functional inefficiency is no longer the fault of the architect—to contradict one of Banham's main themes in *The Architecture of the Well-tempered Environment*—but is now laid at the door of the commissioning agency (which could hardly be cast as a hands-on, interfering client). Surely Banham himself must have had second thoughts about continuing the article with the sentence "as it turns out, the excellent basic environment provided by Stirling and his consultants will require some skill and intelligence for its proper employment throughout the building," because acknowledging the need for "skill and intelligence" contradicts the assumption that a nonhumanities (i.e., mechanically literate) member of the human race would be able to deal with the "minor" problems.

The point is that Banham is not uncritical about the functional problems, but too forgiving—and, in terms of his wider theories and criticism, inconsistently forgiving—because his personal response to the building, and the architect, was so favorable. Setting aside the personal friendship factors, the response is partly aesthetic and partly historical. When describing the roof of the glass pyramid, he writes how "it will present a continuously interesting overhead spectacle . . . only *interesting* is an inadequate word for this spectacular roof. It is absorbing, not only for its inherent visual qualities, but also because those qualities derive from Stirling having followed the precepts laid down by Paul Scheerbart in *Glasarchitektur* over half a century ago."[30] Banham is not claiming a direct influence of Scheerbart—he acknowledges that Stirling had never read him[31]—but contends that both derive from "common-sense, observation and imagination." Nevertheless, "it is fascinating for an historian like myself to see that when Scheerbart's precepts about the use of a diffusing inner layer, the use of an insulating blanket of air between the two skins, the placing of light sources between the skins (but not heaters) and all the rest of it, the result is quite as marvellous as he prophesised it would be in 1914."[32]

These types of comment are instructive, for they remind us that Banham's criteria are not objective (or "tough-minded") ones about function and creating "fit environments," but are to do with an approach which lies in a Modernist tradition stretching back to the First Machine Age. Pevsner may have been even more exclusively aesthetic in his criteria, but both belong to a shared movement. Pevsner, of course, favored elegance, and loathed the History Faculty, which he described as "anti-architecture . . . actively ugly."[33] He actually draws a parallel between the movement of "anti-art" and "anti-architecture" which takes him close to an acknowledgment that Stirling's building is an example of the *architecture autre* sought by Banham—an "architecture of resistance" characterized by bloody-mindedness and manifesting what Banham describes, remarkably, as "dumb insolence":

To get away with this architecture of dumb insolence in Cambridge requires more than just derring-do; it requires the self-confidence that comes from knowing what you are about, and it implies an attitude. Self-confidence first: that patent glazing is not neutral or neat. The temptation to make it so (as proof that you are a gentleman as well as an architect) would have overwhelmed some architects confronted with Cambridge, but Stirling has permitted roughnesses, irregularities, misalignments. This is in no way to disparage him or the glazing system, which is meant to be assembled thus, and has the necessary degrees of tolerance to even out local inaccuracies. To have assembled it more neatly and with greater nicety of alignment would have been, and would have looked, merely affected—like most other modern architecture in Cambridge.[34]

Banham attacks university buildings in Cambridge for being preoccupied "with trying to prove themselves scholarly adepts at the rituals of a cult, like collegiate planning, historical erudition, urbanity, and so forth," whereas

Stirling's attitude is to construct a (supposedly) working building, rather than a "shrine" to an architectural tradition.[35] There is undoubtedly a class-related aspect to this criticism to which we will return in the conclusion, but, again, ill-fitting windows, as at Leicester, are justified in terms not of environmental performance but of an architectural attitude—heartily approved—of "dumb insolence." The visual quality and historical resonances partly explain the appeal of the building; equally appealing to Banham was what it represented—"the self-confidence that comes from knowing what you are about, and . . . an attitude"—which, consciously or not, he may have seen as the equivalent of his own criticism and its role within the architectural mainstream and establishment. One suspects a further—but important—factor in determining in response to the building was his personal friendship, and identification, with "Big Jim,"[36] a man who is "without the slightest doubt the most widely and sincerely admired British architect with an international top-ten standing only a little below such living legends as Mies van der Rohe and Alvar Aalto."[37]

The stark juxtaposition at Cambridge between the "Festival (i.e., Casson) and Brutalist (i.e., Stirling) generation" was a "tragic farce": the "exposure is ruthless and total," with the result that "all preceding modern buildings in Cambridge"—such as Hugh Casson and Neville Conder's Arts Faculty—appear "effete."[38] Yet Banham was worried that the "dumb insolence" and resistance symbolized by Stirling's building would be lost: "The sad thing is that Cambridge opinion will eventually accept it as part of 'the Cambridge tradition' and then no one will have the guts to pull it down when the useful life for which it was designed has come to an end."[39] Given the depth of feeling about wanting to demolish the building a decade later, there is an irony in Banham's remark.

We can look upon the Cambridge History Faculty as a key building, not in the history of architecture, but in the history of attitudes toward architecture: it can be used to represent the battleground of values that were being contested around the time of its completion. The architectural historian and critic Gavin Stamp, who had direct experience of the building from the time it opened, has written extensively on the building and detailed its functional inadequacies: extreme and unsatisfactory temperatures; serious leaks in not infrequent wet weather; a collapsing ceiling; flooding; falling tiles; totally inadequate sound insulation, with the result that "in some lecture rooms three lectures may be heard simultaneously";[40] and, amongst several others, stairs which are too steep and narrow. The shortcomings were such as to lead to protracted legal wrangles about whether the failure resulted from the architect's design or the constructor's workmanship.

Within a year of moving in, the History Faculty Board seriously considered moving out. The university spent substantial sums of money making the building more habitable, but problems continued. Demolishing was mooted in 1984, and in 1990 extensive repairs were carried out which changed the building in several significant ways. Again ironically, it was Banham's opponents who claimed that its "useful life" had come to an end—except that they would claim it had never even started one. In "Machine Aesthetic" (1955), Banham had solemnly quoted Le Corbusier's polemic about the need to treat an aging building as an "outworn piece of mental equipment and, as Le Corbusier also said in the days of *L'Esprit Nouveau:* 'We have no right to waste our strength on worn out tackle, we must scrap, and re-equip.'"[41] The significant difference between Banham and the would-be demolishers of the History Faculty is that the latter were attempting to remove what they judged to be an inappropriate and inadequate individual building from an otherwise healthy and historically rich environment, whereas Banham upheld the high Modernist cultural value (if not always the practice) of unsentimental replacement of the old by the new, justified on grounds of up-to-dateness and modernity. Like his attitudes to historicism, revivalism, and Englishness, Banham's views about preservation and conservation expressed ingrained Modernist values.

Those values were changing rapidly at the end of the 1960s. Stamp had been a first-year student of history a year before the Stirling building was completed, studying in C. R. Cockerell's nineteenth-century neoclassical library. However, he keenly anticipated the new faculty building, seeing it—in ways which recalled Banham's criticism—as "a bold protest, a piece of appropriate Brutalism in a bland and smug university environment."[42] But, once he became a user of the building, "how cruelly was I disillusioned," as he became aware of the building's major functional deficiencies. One

anecdote epitomizes the change of architectural sensibility that was occurring around 1968. A film crew who came to make a program about Stirling "were disappointed in failing to elicit any favourable spontaneous
reactions from students working in the Library. This was during the period
of High Student Revolt and, far from being in natural sympathy with the
progressive outlook manifested by New Architecture, student opinion saw
the History Faculty as a perfect expression of a 'Big Brother' attitude by
Authority."[43]

The pre-1968 response of those who responded favorably was, like Stamp's,
to see Stirling's design as new, exciting, even a bloody-minded intervention in
a complacent and self-regarding environment. The post-1968 response was
more likely to interpret the building as symptomatic of uncaring Authority,
demonstrating, as Stamp put it, "just how coarse and thoughtless, how arrogant and inhumane" a piece of Modern architecture "by a world-famous,
award-winning architect can actually be."[44] Awards are usually given for the
image of a building, before it has been regularly used. As Stewart Brand put
it: "Reputations based on exterior originality miss everything important. They
have nothing to do with what buildings do all day and almost nothing to do
with what architects do all day"[45]—a sentiment with which Banham—at least
in his *Architecture of the Well-tempered Environment* mode—would have
concurred. For Brand, Stirling typifies this wrong-headed reputation: "The
honours [RIBA Gold Medalist, the Pritzker Prize, a knighthood] kept coming
despite widely reported disasters with his buildings."

1968 and a Change of Sensibility

The opening quotation of David Watkin's *Morality and Architecture* (1975)
qutoes James Stirling recounting his student days at the Liverpool School of
Architecture between 1945 and 1950: "There was furious debate as to the
validity of the modern movement, tempers were heated and discussion was
intense. Some staff resigned and a few students went off to other schools;
at any rate I was left with a deep conviction of the moral rightness of the
new architecture."[46] Watkin uses the quote as typical of a Modernist attitude, which is high-minded and certain. Stamp makes a similar point: "This
armour of moral strength has allowed many modern architects to reject

Classical or traditional styles without needing to employ the tests of suit-
ability, efficiency or beauty. It has also given them the authority to try and
mould society with architecture and planning with little references to the
wishes of clients and the public."[47]

Both Watkin and Stamp found unacceptable the Modernist architect's
claim to the moral high ground, with the resulting assumption of rightness,
tone of arrogance, and attitude of disdain for public taste. It was an attitude
which was ingrained in Modernism: the artist as leader, prophet, and creative visionary; the public as reactionary and needing to be led for their own
good. This was the attitude which was being increasingly questioned and rejected from 1968 on.

The period of what Stamp calls "High Student Revolt" saw increased political involvement on campuses across Europe and the United States. At the
most articulate extreme were the revolutionary students in Paris who declared that "The revolution which is beginning will call in question not only
capitalist society but industrial society."[48] It was, in other words, no longer
about differences in manifestation or niceties of style, but about the system
which underlies them, which has to be radically changed or overthrown. The
Atelier Populaire students and Utopie group attacked architecture which
upheld the status quo of the professional—"architect's architecture; hence-
forth, architects should work *with* and *for* the people, not build for one another with an eye on professional awards." The message was taken up in
Britain by the ARSE group (Architectural Radicals, Students and Educators)
who sought to "build for society by building a new society first."[49] The professional system was bypassed: direct action and squatting were approved
tactics. Studio pin-boards no longer carried images of buildings by Le Corbusier or James Stirling, but *barriada* settlements from Peru or hippie self-
build communities in Colorado. At architectural schools, as in the more
radical end of the architectural press, projects for a "fun palace," "capsule
home," or "responsive environment" were replaced by a "portable hospital," "information centre," or "emergency housing."

The collapse of the Ronan Point tower block in London in 1968 became a
defining moment in the change of mood. Architects and planners were now
seen as arrogant in the way they imposed styles of living such as high-rise,

rather than responded to what people actually wanted in terms of urban regeneration and low-rise, for example. Technology was beginning to be seen as a problem, and not necessarily a solution. In 1969 a writer in *Architectural Design* equated the "downward trend of the human spiritual condition with the advancement of technology. . . . System builders, throwaway utopians and plug-in idealisers will continue the trend to a worsening environment until man has to resort to artificial stimulants. . . . Is Archigram's Plug-in City in fact a Drug-in City?"[50]

The assumptions that more is better and that technology is good were being widely questioned by 1969. The mood was summed up effectively by Michael Middleton, writing in *The Designer.* Middleton described "a movement of public opinion, a developing concern, which is one of the genuinely hopeful events of the decade." He explained that "what is hopeful is that the wider public is now beginning to grasp the scale, the complexity, the interlocking nature of such problems" as speculative property developing, traffic congestion, air and water pollution, and an uncritical commitment to technological "progress." "What is at stake is nothing less than the quality of life itself—not in a century's time, but twenty, ten, two year's time."[51]

These concerns were being voiced throughout the industrial world. The theme of the sixth international conference of the International Council of the Society of Industrial Designers in 1969 was, almost inevitably, "Design, Society and the Future." Much of the debate focused on the role and status of technology and, according to Hasan Ozbekhan, director of planning at Santa Monica, "The problem is to redirect our energies and all the technology which is at our service toward renewed human ends—ends which are not given, as was survival amid scarcity, but are now in need of being invented."[52] At the annual International Design Conference in Aspen, Colorado, in 1970, the radical French Group, in the spirit of Atelier Populaire and Utopie, demanded a reorientation of the conference because they believed that "too many matters, and essential ones, have not been voiced here as regards the social and political status of design, as regards the ideological functions and the mythology of environment."[53] They dismissed the Aspen gathering as "the Disneyland of design," and called for a dozen resolutions on topics ranging from the abandonment of design for profit, to motions on abortion and Vietnam.

A cluster of books reflecting these concerns was published in the early 1970s. For architects and designers with a conscience, the most influential was Victor Papaneks's *Design for the Real World* (1971), which set out an agenda for design priorities and responsibilities. E. F. Schumacher's *Small Is Beautiful* (1973) provided an argument for a reorientation of society away from the technological determinist "big/faster is best." Ecological imperatives included Barbara Ward and René Dubos's *Only One Earth* and the *Ecologist's A Blueprint for Survival* (both of 1972). Numbered amongst the emerging "anti"-architecture books—anti in the sense of opposing notions and traditions of professional architecture, however supposedly radical—were *The Whole Earth Catalog* (1971), *Survival Scrapbooks* (1972), and *Domebooks* (1972). Technology was becoming "alternative," "radical," or "soft."

In effect, the attacks were on the very essence of modernity with its belief in progress through technology. In his significantly titled *Crisis in Architecture* (1974), Malcolm MacEwan criticized writers like Banham for their "failure to realise that, far from living in the 'second machine age,' we are in fact entering the first period of human revolt against unrestrained or misdirected science and technology. In the rediscovery of man and nature lies the hope of the rediscovery of architecture."[54]

It is indeed true that Banham's commitment to technology as a manifestation of modernity—from the revisionist *Theory and Design in the Second Machine Age* (1960) to the radical *The Architecture of the Well-tempered Environment* (1969)—had been unwavering throughout the 1950s and 1960s. Equally, his commitment to an *architecture autre* or "architecture of resistance," however much it undermined the conventions and lores of the Establishment, still positioned him as upholding ideas about the professional architect "knowing best" and "leading the public." Architectural bloody-mindedness and "dumb insolence" were virtues of a progressive architecture; reaction to them was belittled as "human cussedness" and "academic conservatism"—deplorable weaknesses of "small frightened men." Stamp was not alone in finding "intolerably patronising" Banham's assumption that, at Cambridge, mere historians might fail to live up to an architect's vision.[55]

In the late 1960s and early 1970s, Banham still enjoyed guru-like status among sections of the avant-garde of architectural students, and his reputation among certain progressive factions of architects and academics was, indeed, enhanced by the publication of *The Architecture of the Well-tempered Environment* and *Los Angeles.* He had been awarded a personal chair at University College, London, in 1969, but as his Establishment credentials grew, his standing within the wider architectural community lessened as the disillusionment with Modernism increased. It also lessened within other sections of the student avant-garde.

A symbolic moment had occurred in 1970 at the Aspen conference. The radical French Group attacked not only the design establishment but also Banham himself, who was chairing the session, for failing to address the social and political implications of architecture. Looking back on the event in 1976, Banham recalled that the conference "was the most bruising experience of my life. And I'm just beginning to recover now."[56] He was not used to being cast as part of the oppressive Establishment, and in *The Aspen Papers* (1974), he also recalled that "as chairman of that stormy last session . . . I could suddenly feel all these changes running together in a spasm of bad vibrations that shook the conference. We got ourselves together again, but an epoch had ended."[57] The metaphorical foul air of Aspen spread elsewhere, and Buckminster Fuller was picketed in London later in the year. Leaflets attacked him as an amoral, apolitical technocrat. Values were indeed changing.

Heritage, Traditionalism, and the "New Architectural Tories"

The symbolic moment of Aspen pointed in one direction—to a more radically politicized critique of Modernism. Movement in another direction—towards a reborn notion of tradition—was to have an even greater effect on architectural values. The reader may recall that Banham, when discussing Stirling's History Faculty building, attacked contemporary and recent Cambridge University buildings for "trying to prove themselves scholarly adepts at the rituals of a cult, like collegiate planning, historical erudition, urban-

ity, and so forth"[58] The point for Banham was that the approach to "historical erudition" or—in Ernesto Rogers's phrase, a "critical and considered review of historical tradition"—is wrong, whether or not it provides "good
architecture": it is a generalization or principle. Banham continued to de-
test traditionalism, historicism, revivalism, preservation, and conservation,
but the balance of power was shifting toward his enemies.

In the 1970s, Britain's heritage was continually presented as being "under
threat," especially after the Labour government proposed a wealth tax in
1974. Exhibitions which made a great impact, showing "with dramatic effect just what we have lost and what still stands in peril,"[59] included "The
Destruction of the English Country House" in 1974, and "Change and Decay—The Future of Our Churches" in 1977. In his collection of essays on the
1970s, Christopher Booker refers to the "collapse" of Modernist confidence:

Within just a few years, the great conservation movement mushroomed into one of the
most powerful forces of the age. For the first time we had seen the future, and it did not
work. Our architectural and cultural self-confidence disintegrated with quite astonishing speed. From . . . believing that anything new is better, we are now [1977] (generally)
convinced of almost exactly the reverse—that anything new is worse, and that almost
any old building should be preserved at all costs.[60]

This quotation places us firmly in the 1970s with its changes of sensibilities,
attitudes, and values—a period when preservationists were on the *attack*
against the Modernists. It also takes us into the second broad section of this
chapter—Banham's writing of the 1970s and 1980s—with its underlying
cultural baggage in the light of changed values.

In spite of the idea that the only way of proving you have a mind is by
changing it occasionally, the vast majority of Banham's earlier positions and
opinions were unchanged in the post-1968 period. In 1972, for example, he
was arguing—with tongue only slightly in cheek—that one of the most important functions that could be performed by an architectural historian
would be to "make fools of expert witnesses called by preservationists at
planning enquiries. If someone doesn't learn to do this soon, building, architecture, and—possibly—architectural history will all come to a stop in

Great Britain."[61] He stated that he hated the assumption that a historian would always be inclined to preservation, and attacked the "preserve-at-all-costs" brigade because they were "*anti*-historians, trying to deny or destroy history, like someone trying to make the good times last by nailing up the hands of the clock. For history is about process; the objects the process creates are incidental. . . . One way to show you care about history is to help along the changes that are its essence."[62] And in 1981, deploring what had become of the preserved Covent Garden buildings, he judged that "they *do* manage these things better in France. They *pulled down* Les Halles!"[63]

Traditionalism, too, continued to be attacked. Sir Edwin Lutyens represents Banham's villain, especially in the post-1968 period, when the change of sensibility caused a reevaluation and sharp elevation of Lutyens's stature. At the time of the major Lutyens exhibition at the Heyward Gallery in London (1981), Banham assessed the architect as having had "a gift for the resoundingly obvious statement, fatly phrased, that puts him in a class with Lloyd George or Edward Elgar."[64] Banham approvingly quoted Pevsner's remark that "architecture for architecture's sake is for good reasons the *bête noire* of 20th century architects of all schools"[65]—he was referring to historicist, "art architecture" in the nineteenth century, which often appealed to the nouveau riche. So, too, Lutyens's architecture, which, Banham continued, seems to have been the architecture of "*arriviste* groups, cultures, coteries; to those uncertain of their place in the world." That made Lutyens "the choice of those who don't know anything about architecture but would love to know what they are supposed to like."

Banham's article engages little with architectural issues, preferring to deal with the social connotations of both Lutyens's architecture and, even more important, those spearheading the Lutyens revival in general and the "coterie event" of the exhibition in particular. The "Gang of Seven" who were the core of the revival were supposedly part of "the National Trust Navy, those roving bands of mansion-fanciers and peerage-buffs who go round invading stately homes . . . for fun and profit in the guise of historical scholarship."[66] At stake here is much more than traditionalism or even supposedly bad architecture. The revival of Lutyens represents not just the "triumph over a philistine-socialist establishment" (as Banham claims the "Lutyens pressure group" sees it), but the reintroduction of nationalism and class politics into architecture. The lobby is "the lunatic core of the New Architectural Tories"[67]—perhaps, Banham thought, inevitably following in the wake of the election of Margaret Thatcher in 1979.

In the reactionary, post-1979 political climate, Lutyens—the "architect of preference to the terminal years of the British Empire"—fitted perfectly into the "*Ind-Imp-algia*"[68] of the patriotic "last night of the proms" Britain of *Chariots of Fire* (1981) and the booming heritage industry. Heritage, incorporating preservation and conservation, was defined by one Conservative minister around this time in terms of

. . . certain sights and sounds. I think of a morning mist on the Tweed at Dryburgh where the magic of Turner and the romance of Scott both come fleetingly to life; of a celebration of the Eucharist in a quiet Norfolk church with the medieval glass filtering the colours, and the early noise of the harvesting coming through the open door; or of standing at any time before the Wilton Diptych. Each scene recalls aspects of an indivisible heritage and is part of the fabric and expression of our civilisation. Never has there been a wider appreciation of this true quality of life, never a more general determination to preserve and enhance it.[69]

It is hard to imagine a description—like this pastoral, traditionalist, romantic, nostalgic one—more different from the "mechanical sensibility" of the First Machine Age, or the *architecture autre* or "sense of possibilities" of the Second. On one level it was the preservationists against the modernizers; on another, English nationalism against left-wing Internationalist. Whichever, it was Banham's values which were now under attack.

Though Banham's opposition may have been predictable, it was not necessarily fair. His approval of Pevsner's phrase "architecture for architecture's sake" could equally have applied to James Stirling's buildings, which, critics would assert, were about architecture (and subsequent professional awards) rather than people. The disparaging use of the word "coterie" could be leveled at Modernists just as much as at traditionalists. The supposed snobbery of the New Right could be matched by the snobbery of the Old Left and their condescension about "layman's architecture" and "*arriviste* groups." It was simplistic to link traditionalism and right-wing politics as snugly and smugly as did Banham. This was a point made in reply by Gavin Stamp, the demolisher of Stirling, one of the organizers of the Lutyens exhibition, and a self-confessed member of the "National Trust Navy": "I am impressed by New Delhi but have no nostalgia for the Raj; I admire Lutyens's country houses but have absolutely no sympathy for the life that goes on or went on in them."[70] Banham himself had seemed able on numerous occasions to detach the architectural innovation of Futurism from the movement's politics, and did not assume that a present-day version of Futurism carried with it fascist overtones. When it comes to Lutyens, there is an inconsistency, rather than a change of mind.

A further point made in his Lutyens article takes us into the next part of this chapter—Banham's response to Post-Modernism. The sensibility for "eclectic and non-doctrinaire architecture," according to Banham, "ushered in not only IndImpalgia, but the whole jokey-hokey post-modern extravaganza as well."[71] Does Banham's phrase here indicate a wholesale rejection of Post-Modern architectural values? His Modernism—however revisionist—of the mechanical sensibility and *architecture autre* may suggest this would be the case but, on the other hand, his enthusiasm for popular culture, the heterogeneity of Los Angeles, and support for the Pop-inspired Archigram would indicate a genuinely *Post*-Modern sensibility. To what extent was Banham a Post-Modernist?

Banham and Post-Modernism

Banham was consistent in his reaction to Post-Modernism—or at least to what he caricatured as Post-Modernism—but inconsistent in his arguments and values. A telling starting point is his review of the second edition of Charles Jencks's *The Language of Post-Modern Architecture.* This edition, which appeared in 1978, was, Banham thought, "much funnier than the first," which had appeared a year earlier.[72] The reason, "clearly, is that it contains more and sillier buildings than ever before." The basis of his judgment is that Post-Modernism "exists chiefly as a series of smart graffiti on the bodies of fairly routine modern buildings. It is all outward show and could be removed, in most cases, without destroying the utility of the rather ordinary buildings behind the jesting facades." Jencks may have agreed with the second sentence of this statement, but as an observation rather than a judgment—if Modernist architecture had become a series of "dumb boxes" which failed to communicate, was it not, therefore, reasonable to "treat architecture as a language," as Jencks defined the essence of Post-Modernism?[73] In so doing, the architect might make use of ornament and decoration—even whole facades—whose function was "to communicate intended meanings." This did not, however, recommend itself to Banham:

Jencks discusses these works with entirely appropriate superficiality. He does not ask "are the rooms convenient, the windows well placed, the services adequate, the plan serviceable?," because this is not the point of his inquiry, and in most cases was not the point of the design in the first place. These are buildings meant to be read as buildings meant to be read . . . period. The content of the readings and the contents of the buildings are rarely at issue, and almost no interiors at all are discussed, as Jencks himself points out. These are "silly" buildings like the "silly" buckets on the Ancient Mariner's deck—empty. (Let me add that I am as tickled by some of these connections as Jencks is; but don't ask me to treat them as architecture.)[74]

Banham's reaction raises a number of issues about his values. The reference to "graffiti" brings to mind Adolf Loos's famous and influential essay "Ornament and Crime" (1908), in which he posited a fundamental opposition between ornament (degenerate or anachronistic) and plainness (culturally advanced and modern). Modernists were widely suspicious of ornament, which they equated with decorativeness and nineteenth-century historicism. "Proper" architecture—as Banham may have been signaling in the last sentence—was about function, structure, space, materials, and their interrelationship. As we have seen, as a Modernist, Banham was anti-historicist, but this was not synonymous with being against all ornament. In the mid-1950s he had described the ways in which car body stylists utilized "symbolic iconographies" which drew on "science fiction, movies, earth-moving equipment, supersonic aircraft, racing cars, heraldry . . . technology and sex."[75]

Twenty years later, writing about the "purified aesthetic" of Shaker and Modernist design, he recalled American car styling and the "consciousness that the ornaments on these products were actually meaningful enough for interpretation"—that they sought "understood communication."[76] It was not, therefore, ornament and decorativeness that were the problem for Banham, but whether they were meaningful or meaningless—there as an aid to communication or there just for the sake of embellishment. He criticized Loos's rejection of nineteenth-century ornament as "useless" by pointing out that the "real problem was that ornament had become meaningless."[77]

Jencksian Post-Modernism offered the potential for "understood communication," which Banahm ought to have welcomed, but as Jencks argues in a reply to the review, Banham "studiously avoids [the] more substantial issues at stake"—principally communication—by his "silly caricature [which] typifies the Modernist's misunderstanding of the current eclecticism."[78] Far from opposing the ideals of Post-Modernism in principle, Banham would have to admit that he not only supported them, but had been involved in similar work in the 1950s. Indeed, in his 1975 article on ornament, he effectively acknowledged the shared aims and concerns of the Independent Group and Post-Modernists.[79]

Logic may indicate one judgment, but a gut response led to another. In his critique of Jencks's book, Banham appears to think of Post-Modernist decoration as a version of facadism, which, in turn, is usually part of historicist architecture. This was not without credibility, especially because Jencks, in a new chapter in the revised edition of *The Language of Post-Modern Architecture,* located the contemporary origins of Post-Modernism as the historicism of the late 1950s/early 1960s, particularly in Neo-Liberty with its attempts to rekindle historical memory as an element of architecture.[80] So Banham's reaction in 1978 to Jencks's Post-Modernism is predictable (but little more) if one thinks of the Banham of anti-revivalism, of *Theory and Design* and *The New Brutalism.* For one with such an embedded a Modernist sense and sensibility, Post-Modernism's emphasis on the facade would seem to guarantee it a lowly stature. However, when one remembers the Banham of the Independent Group with its pop, anti-classical Modernist sensibility, and thinks of his *Los Angeles*—as well as his acceptance of ornament in principle—his seemingly outright and intolerant rejection of Post-Modern fa-cadism is harder to understand and suggests prejudice.

Banham had not registered any interest in the version of facadism offered by Denise Scott Brown and Robert Venturi in their influential 1972 book, *Learning from Las Vegas.*[81] Celebrating Las Vegas as a model of architectural semiotics, they developed the concept of the "decorated shed"—an "ugly and ordinary" structure accompanied by signs, facade, or graphics that were to be deciphered, literally and/or symbolically. Banham, it may be recalled from chapter 4, preferred to discuss Las Vegas not in terms of semiotics, but as the best example of "how far environmental technology can be driven beyond the confines of architectural practice."[82] Even in the 1975 *Age of the Masters*—chronologically post *Learning from Las Vegas*—Banham contin-ues to see the significance of the city in terms of "gross matter transformed into aetherial substance by the power of light."[83]

But, in spite of his silence on Venturi and Scott Brown's ideas, Banham was not entirely uninterested in the lesson of the decorated shed. In 1976, he ac-tually celebrated the "false front"—that "most time-honoured of American commercial pretences"—and its revival in Buffalo, New York, by the Pon-derosa Steakhouse chain. And his argument was, in effect, a standard Post-Modern—even Venturian—one:

. . . the false front operates at so many different levels of semiotic signification at once that it's hard to keep count without losing your structuralist nut. For a start, it is a bill-board, standing up higher than the main structure in order to flourish the words, PON-DEROSA STEAK HOUSE. . . . It thus satisfies the long-term intellectual programme of architectural theorists like Robert Venturi. . . .

But, the false front is also a symbolic form in its own right, signifying I AM A FALSE FRONT, and therefore signifying (at another level of meaning) I AM A SELF CON-SCIOUSLY WITTY REFERENCE TO THAT OLD WEST YOU ALL KNOW NEVER EXISTED BUT IT'S PART OF THE AMERICAN LEGEND, PARDNER, SO WHAT THE HELL![84]

Banham's appreciation of the layering of the levels of meaning accords closely with Venturi's "intellectual programme" (which was more multi-layered than Banham gave him credit for). Given his lack of enthusiasm for that program, and in light of his later comments about Jencksian Post-Modernism, one would have expected Banham to be dismissive or condescending about the Ponderosa sophistry, but he readily admits that "one has to admire the crafty double-takes which are involved here in making the false front refer back to false fronts *as a concept* rather than as representations of architectural styles." So, if Ponderosa is acceptable, why are Venturi and Post-Modernism wrong?

A possible answer—and one that would accord with Banham's Independent Group thinking—is that popular architecture like the Ponderosa is *authentic* by having been derived from hardheaded commercial factors: such design has *integrity*. If Las Vegas demonstrated how far environmental technology could be taken beyond the conventions of architecture "by designers who (for better or worse) are not inhibited by the traditions of architectonic culture, training and taste," commercial, "pop" architecture could show what could be achieved by designers who were not conditioned by architectural lores and customs.

Banham seemed to be at one with Tom Wolfe, who had praised Las Vegas's sign makers as "America's first unconscious avant-garde"[85] because— not in spite—of their lack of art historical awareness. But Banham reveals that the Ponderosa's design team "is full of architecture-school products,"[86]

Ponderosa Steakhouse, Buffalo, New York, mid-1970s (courtesy Mary Banham)

and so they cannot be described as naifs or (commercial) savages. They were closer to the model of the commercial professional that Banham had lauded in the 1950s: the American car stylist, for example, who created designs with "finish, fantasy, punch, professionalism [and] swagger."[87] From the perspective of 1976, this meant that "it's not something that architects can admire from a distance as some kind of pop art that's nothing to do with them. For many, this creates a difficulty. For them, most design skills that are OK and 'exemplary' when practised by subcultural persons for commercial ends, are anything but OK if practised by cultured persons for the same commercial ends. That makes them 'prostitution.'"[88]

Banham may have believed, as he wrote in *Age of the Masters,* that "the supposedly careless architecture of popular pleasure has often showed far greater awareness of . . . [imaginative] possibilities than has the serious architecture of cultural purpose,"[89] but ultimately he was consistent in his respect for the professionalism of designers, whether or not cultured, who produced good popular or even middle-brow culture. The point that mattered for him was not *who* did it, but how successfully the job was done— not whether or not the designer was culturalized into professional lore, but whether the product or building was appropriate for its function and audience. Whether the building was predominantly driven by cultural or commercial factors, his undeclared criteria concerned authenticity and integrity.

Banham detected an absence of authenticity and integrity in Post-Modernism. In his review of Jencks's book, he acknowledges the way in which the "form follows function" approach led to a "dumb building, if its functions were not worth discussing in public." In previous times, widely held conventions of architectural communication existed.

But take away those unquestioned conventions and the result, in Jencks's post-modern world, is less an architecture that "speaks" than one which shouts, sniggers . . . [and] blusters. . . . And most of them deliver their utterances in as erudite and sneering a manner as possible: the overall effect of the book is one of post-graduate weirdos poncing around among the ruins of "that old modern architecture," mini Neros fiddling with a Rome they haven't the courage to burn down.[90]

The association of Post-Modernism and "post-graduate weirdos"—presumably connoting immaturity in mistaking novelty and cleverness for innovation and profundity—was a characterization that stayed with him. In 1981, for example, he refers to the "normal sensation-seeking Post-Modernist" and the "frantic show-offs idolised by Jencks";[91] in 1984 it was the "seemingly unprincipled eclecticism of so much Fancy-Style Post-Modernism"[92] which he found unacceptable. As Post-Modernism was adopted by major architects, Banham was forced to extend his categories beyond "post-graduate weirdos." Another category was "East Coast academics"—he was now a resident of California—which refers to architects including Robert Stern, Peter Eisenman, Michael Graves, and Venturi, who are "liable to make heavy weather and great polemical bother about every historical quote they use."[93] For example, when discussing the work of a "well-read Post-Modern architect like Stern," Banham refers to his architecture being "academically conceived on the Columbia campus. . . . It looks terrific on the page, but often tawdry on the site, as does much American Post-Modernism. . . . But what's it all got to do with 'real architecture'?"[94]

Erudition and Quality

There are two points here which help us further elucidate Banham's values. The first is about Post-Modernism's "erudition"; the second is about architectural quality. Banham is not prejudiced against architectural erudition per se: for example, he recounted the importance of the historical scholarship on Palladian architecture following the publication of Rudolf Wittkower's *Architectural Principles in the Age of Humanism* in 1949 and its effect on the Smithsons, Stirling, and other young architects at the time of the Picturesque polemics. That it produced designs for "Palladian Power-stations"[95] mattered less to Banham than the "toughness of mind" the erudition about mathematical ratios brought to architects' thinking to counter the self-indulgence and anti-intellectualism of the Picturesque sensibility.

What irked him about Post-Modernism was when erudition became a means of showing off. He was dismissive of "photographic" Post-Modernism—the buildings by "those internationally acclaimed Post-Modernists who are featured in the frequent books by Charles Jencks": these are architects who "trumpet their erudition."[96] Erudition becomes mere *cleverness* with esoteric references and insider jokes. Hatred—probably not too strong a word—is what Banham felt for this attitude, and it made him vitriolic about Post-Modernists, even when he could identify with their aims. After describing the way members of the Independent Group had developed an interest in deconstructing imagery, he goes on to write: "Yet here's the next generation after us, poncing about the campus in the borrowed robes of Sassure and Roland Barthes, claiming to be architectural semiologists, and going through substantially the same numbers, though at a higher rate of syllables per word uttered."[97]

In spite of its claims about communication, Post-Modernism—at its worst—could be esoteric and elitist, and this clearly colored Banham's response. Pevsner had termed historicism "art-architecture"; for Banham, Post-Modernism was academic or "scholastic" architecture. In 1984 he had commented on how "While postmodernism was an inside joke it was one of architecture's more effective mind-clearing and bullshit-removing exercises. The moment it began to take itself so seriously . . . its flimsy ironical structure could do nothing but collapse under the weight of its newly acquired pretensions."[98]

The second key point which illuminates Banham's values is the way the parts of the architecture are put together. It is not that heterogeneity and contrast—or even complexity and contradiction—are themselves a guarantee of bad architecture. The point is how the parts are handled: "In by-the-book Post-Modernism, the schizoid mismatches are willed, and valued for their wilfulness; they are artistic gestures, manifestations of cultural autonomy, or what-not."[99] This sort of cleverness and self-indulgence can be contrasted with the handling of the elements in the work of Frank Gehry, whom Banham wrote about in 1986 and 1987. He comments on the way in which "attempts to push him into any known taxonomy—even postmodernist—tend to leave him uncategorised";[100] Jencks has similarly referred to Gehry's "disdain" for Post-Modern classicists such as Michael Graves.[101] Gehry's buildings have been regularly included in the category of "Deconstructionist" architecture—"an informal style appealing to a substantial taste for the discordant and ephemeral, the unpretentious and tough," according to

Jencks,[102] which came to prominence in the mid-to-late 1980s. What Deconstruction shares with Post-Modernism is a preference for complexity and contradiction, and, often, historical/typological reference.

Such references are evident in the Deconstructionist tendencies that Banham notes in relation to Gehry's own eccentric, "inside-out" house in Santa Monica, California, which he compares to the house of Wonko the Sane in Douglas Adams's *Hitch-hiker* trilogy. More Post-Modern is the Loyola Marymount University Law School, which comprises small classical, reused "ruined" temples fronted by columns made of "totally inappropriate materials like sheet steel [which] have been joined by a Wonko version of a chapel and belfry done in plywood and clear plastic sheet." Also featured is "a flying staircase in trick perspective." The mixture of classical temples, green spaces, and baroque churches "clearly recalls (and Gehry himself has confirmed this more than once) . . . the Forum Romanum . . . [an] apt hatchery for Catholic lawyers, given canon law's double heritage from Rome and Christianity." All this sounds thoroughly Post-Modern but, in Banham's judgment,

> . . . the whole conception is free of the pushy, pasted-on, pastiche classicism that makes routine postmodernism so tedious. There is not a single classical detail to be seen anywhere, but Merrifield Hall, which is the centre of the scheme, is a plain brick box, just like the original Curia in the Forum where the ancient Romans did their legislating, and that is the pitch at which the whole design operates. If you know your architectural history it is a subtly erudite pleasure to be there. If you don't know architectural history it is still a pleasure to be there.[103]

The resonance of reference was a significant quality in Gehry's work because it avoided mere cleverness and scholasticism, but equally significant was the *quality* of the architecture: "Gehry is not a scholar like Stern or Venturi, nor a self-annoting solipsist like Eisenman, and the essential supports for his originality, outside his love of art, come from a practical, hammer-and-nails experience of the business of building in Los Angeles. . . . Gehry also has . . . a humane, urbane sense of the ridiculous, rather than the scholarly 'irony' which Post-Modernists are supposed to exhibit." On the one hand, this quote—with its "hammer-and-nails experience" phrase—con-

Frank O. Gehry, Gehry House, Santa Monica, 1977–1979

Frank O. Gehry, Loyola Marymount Law School, Los Angeles, 1978–1984

firms Gehry's Deconstructionist tendencies, which "are all in some way commentaries . . . on the academic disciplines of architecture (history, draughtsmanship and all that) in terms of the brute facts of how things actually get built (wood, concrete, finance and all those) in the world outside the ivory-painted crudboard towers of academe."[104] On the other hand, it touches on the important point for Banham that Gehry is not a Post-Modern "decorator," but someone who is involved with the three-dimensional realities of the experience of architecture as a Modernist would understand it. As Banham put it, Gehry is "a real nutter, who is also 100 per cent certifiably architect."

Equally certifiable as 100 percent architect in Banham's sense was his old friend James Stirling. Stirling reappeared in Banham's writings in 1984 when he visited the Staatsgalerie in Stuttgart, a building (by Stirling and Michael Wilford) that Jencks includes in the third (1981) edition of *The Language of Post-Modern Architecture,* and describes in the fourth (1984) as an example of "Free-Style Classicism" because of its rusticated base, Egyptian cornice, and occasional pediments and Doric columns.[105] In addition to the Classical elements there are signifiers of Constructivism (the canopied entrances), Le Corbusier (some office exteriors), High Tech (air intakes), and Pop culture (the "kandy-kolored" ramp handrails in pink and blue). Banham comments that

. . . such free-form bravura may sound like the post-modernist omnium-gatherum of eclectic historical details, but isn't. Stirling is not only one of the most visually erudite architects of his generation but—like Le Corbusier, his first hero—is also extremely observant of things which are not particularly architectural, and can turn practically any of them into architectural effect. If the visitor to the Staatsgalerie will look around him at the city beyond with only moderate attention, he will see that with barely a couple of major exceptions . . . the details seem to come from the museum's immediate urban surroundings.[106]

Jencks was in agreement, declaring the gallery a "convincing example of urban contextualism."[107] But this was not a characteristic of the gallery which Banham particularly valued, complaining that a response to surrounding buildings used to be thought of more as "cribbing," but "when the post-modernists and other wets of academe moved into the act, it was elevated to the status of *typology* or *contextualism*. What Stirling and Wilford have done at Stuttgart could just about be called typological in the sense that it looks something like yer typical art gallery, and contextual in that it looks something like its context—ie, the neighbourhood."[108]

One of the differences between Banham's response and that of a committed Post-Modernist is the significance attached to such readings of Stirling and Wilford's gallery. Jencks was impressed by the meaning of the scheme: "the mandala, the 'dome of heaven—the sky,' the 'heart of the city' and the circular *res publica* are . . . key ideas of many Post-Modernists. They are as much ideas of content as purely architectural ideas and seek to raise, if not answer, metaphysical questions which Modernists, in their pragmatic phase, overlooked."[109]

When he complained in his response to Banham's review that his erstwhile mentor had failed to address Post-Modernism's major concerns with "historical memory, participation, urban appropriateness, etc.,"[110] Jencks had identified something of the gulf in priorities. For Banham, Jencks's agenda may have been *interesting*—an important word to which we will return—at a certain level, but it was not what really mattered: "The ultimate

James Stirling and Michael Wilford, Staatsgalerie, Stuttgart, 1977–1984

strength of Stirling's design . . . lies not in its classical references, but in its underlying discipline of modernist compositional methods." These methods produced not mere erudition or contextual reference, but a quality architectural experience:

. . . I have to say that I was almost knocked out by a level of sustained inventiveness and poised wit that I haven't seen in a new building for a long time. . . . Where the design takes off into the realm of inspiration is in the management of a circulation problem peculiar to the site. The pedestrian way up from the *Weg* below to the *Strasse* above begins by ramping across the faces of the terraces, then plunges into a deep rotunda in the centre of the gallery courtyard, climbs around half its perimeter, and finally passes through a narrow slot in the highest parts of the building to emerge at the upper street level next to a couple of enormous high-tech air intakes.[111]

This is a revealing response because it underlines the primacy Banham accords architectural quality, based on personally experiencing the building as a three-dimensional entity. Historical memory has little, if any, importance for him; urban appropriateness is supposedly relevant as the somewhat nebulous "urban texture"; and participation, in spite of the appeal of the laissez faire, individualistic approach he celebrates in *Los Angeles,* and his acknowledgment that "a city or a large part of a city designed by one man, or by any group unified enough to produce a comprehensive design, would be a parlously thin, starved and impoverished environment,"[112] does not lead him to focus on the significance of participation in Post-Modern theory.

Ultimately—and in spite of what he had written in *The Architecture of the Well-tempered Environment*—Banham subscribed to rationalist architectural principles derived from the nineteenth century in which spatial composition and structure were prioritized over facade and decoration. A. W. N. Pugin, for one, had distinguished between decorated construction and constructed decoration—a distinction that helps to explain Banham's response to Post-Modernism. Banham saw Post-Modernism as (show-off) "constructed decoration" typified by what he claimed, in 1984, to be its locus classicus, the Strada Novissima, "a double file of smartass false fronts by practically every postmodernist you ever heard of," first shown at the

Venice Biennale of 1980.[113] The *Strada* was also, Banham continued, Post-Modernism's "last gasp, because it revealed the movement for what it was—a paper-thin set of academic diversions on the margins of architecture, an ironic and evasive commentary on the alleged death of 'that old modern architecture.'"[114] In contrast, "real architecture," however "old," could potentially have any kind of facade or decoration so long as the construction—spatial organization and composition and the construction itself in relation to space and materials—was well conceived and executed. This accounts for his response to the Staatsgalerie. It accounts, too, for his response to Gehry's Loyola Marymount Law School.

Where it does not immediately seem fully to explain Banham's response is to Gehry's Santa Monica house. Its Deconstructionist characteristics could have led him to dismiss it as mere "cleverness," but it was the visit to the house at first hand that must have convinced Banham that the eccentricity was based on a deep involvement with space, construction, and materials. It did not, presumably, look "tawdry on the site," like Stern's work, and so could be classified as "real architecture." Directly experiencing a building was of paramount importance to Banham: architecture was not about looking "terrific on the page," but about a quality of experience. In 1986, reviewing a book about contemporary architecture which included Gehry's work, Banham attacked what he saw as the Post-Modern dismissal of Mies for being "boring" in favor of the new emphasis on "being interesting" (by means of reference and symbol), countering: "it may be that 'boring' old Mies van der Rohe exactly identified what separates Gehry's house from the rest of the buildings discussed when, long ago, he said of his own work: 'I don't want to be interesting; I want to be *good*!'"[115] This is a point of great significance, which we will return to in the conclusion.

Finally, in this discussion about Banham and Post-Modernism, we need to return to his response to the Buffalo Ponderosa Steakhouse because it has some unexplored implications for an understanding of his architectural values. Banham's praise for the building, the reader will recall, was implicitly based on the *authenticity* of the commercial professionalism behind the design, rather than on any criterion of *architectural* quality—it certainly did not provide the sort of experience that Gehry's law school or Stirling's

Strada Novissima, Venice Biennale, 1980 (courtesy Mary Banham)

Staatsgalerie did. In spite of some designed symmetries, the structural system of the Ponderosa was, he explained, "dead ordinary—concrete block walls carrying large roof-trusses spanning right across the eating space."[116] The space itself was equally determined by a "commercial economy of means." Banham may not have described it as "ugly and ordinary,"[117] but it was certainly conventional, and he and Venturi would have had no difficulty describing it as a "decorated shed." But where they would not have been able to agree—and this is a point of significance—is on the status of a building such as the Ponderosa *as architecture.*[118] For Venturi, the decorated shed is an acceptable, even necessary, form of Post-Modern architecture. For Banham, however professional as a design solution to a commercial proposition, it does not meet his criteria of architecture in the full sense, and might be differentiated as a "building" or "design."

This takes us back to Independent Group days and John McHale's distinction, taken up by Banham, as we saw in chapter 2, of the virtues of a "both/and" rather than an "either/or" approach because the former acknowledged identifiable differences which might then permit recourse to relatively discrete systems of value: the model allowed Banham the "verticality" to make qualitative judgments within each value system, so he was perfectly comfortable pronouncing the Villa Savoye a "masterpiece" while, at the same time, extolling the virtues of the latest Cadillac. In the 1970s and 1980s, Banham was reconfirming a commitment to a "both/and" approach—both "architectural quality" (now the Staatsgalerie rather than the Villa Savoye) and "commercial professionalism" (the Ponderosa rather than a Cadillac). Post-Modernists, in contrast, broke down the discrete categories and mixed and matched—architecture could be "ugly and ordinary" (so long as it communicated effectively), architectonic, or complex and contradictory. In his reply to Banham, Jencks emphasized the "double-coding" of Post-Modernism:

. . . half modern and half something else—traditional, local, vernacular, or whatever is locally relevant. The reason for this "double-talk" is not that "White-Man speak with fork tongue" or hypocrisy, but that most people, most societies, are partly modern *and* traditional and so their architectural language is hybrid. This does appear as nonsense and silliness to those who still speak in the purified old language of simplified, Modernistic Esperanto, fumigated as it is of all historical memory and richness.[119]

Jencks was not wholly accurate in his accusation: Banham spoke in two languages, Esperanto (to use Jencks's term) and "popular culture," but the point is that they were separate languages—each was employed only when deemed appropriate, and the language, syntax, and grammar of one did not infiltrate the other. This was how Banham dealt with the architecture of Los Angeles, and it profoundly shaped the way he responded to Post-Modernism. It shows that his values were not changed by the lessons of his *Architecture of the Well-tempered Environment* with its potentially unifying criterion of the fitness of the environment for human activity. Indeed, his response to Post-Modernism demonstrates that his "both/and" thinking of the 1950s never fundamentally changed.

Megastructure

Banham may have been out of line with some of the major tendencies in the post-1968 period, but he found hope in more than the work of individual architects such as James Stirling and Frank Gehry. High Tech was the movement, or at least approach, with which he most closely identified in the 1970s and 1980s, and we will be examining his writings on that topic shortly. Before that, we need to take account of the book that Banham was researching while Jencks was developing his ideas about Post-Modernism—*Megastructure: Urban Futures of the Recent Past,* published in 1976.

Banham starts with a definition provided by Ralph Wilcoxon, planning librarian at the College of Environmental Design at Berkeley, in 1968. Megastructure is

. . . not only a structure of great size, but . . . also a structure which is frequently:
1. constructed of modular units;
2. Capable of great or even "unlimited" extension;
3. A structural framework into which smaller structural units (for example, rooms, houses, or small buildings of other sorts) can be built—or even "plugged-in" or "clipped-on" after having been prefabricated elsewhere;
4. A structural framework expected to have a useful life much longer than that of the smaller units which it might support.[120]

It could be argued that, for Banham at this juncture, the third criterion most suited his needs, and so one can see *Megastructure* as a short-term support structure on which could be hung a number of longer-term ideas such as indeterminacy, leisure, and mobility! The book has a couple of chapters which deal with antecedents—some twentieth century (like Le Corbusier's Algiers scheme of 1931); others more ancient (such as the Ponte Vecchio in Florence); yet others, *mégastructures trouvées* (including piers, oil rigs, and grain elevators). Then it traces the movement from the late 1950s, through "Megayear 1964"; the "Fun and Flexibility" brought to bear by Archigram, Cedric Price, and others; "Megacity Montreal" and the 1967 Expo buildings; and the impact of "Megastructure in Academe." Then finally it charts

Megastructures at Expo 67, Montreal (courtesy Mary Banham)

"Megadecadence: Acceptance and Exploitation," followed by "Epilogue: The Meaning of Megastructure."

   The chapters which focus on the 1960s include a number of tendencies, among them, those of Archigram, whose Plug-In City project of 1964 "radically altered the style and tone of megastructuralism for the rest of the decade."[121] In part, Archigram's influence was due to the group's unashamedly positive celebration of technology as a "visually wild rich mess of piping and wiring and struts and cat-walks and bristling radar antennae and supplementary fuel tanks and landing pads all carried in exposed lattice frames"[122] which linked directly with Futurism, also cited in *Megastructure* as a forebear. This enabled Banham to return to a theme we visited in chapter 1, the "engineering" and "mechanical" sensibilities:

The whole revival of a romantic (as opposed to the established neo-classical) vision of modern technology goes in direct parallel with a revival of architectural historical interest in the Expressionism and above all the Futurism of the early twentieth century. As against the International Style's classicising view of technology and machinery as neat smooth regular solids of anonymous aspect, the younger megastructuralists clearly saw technology as a visually wild rich mess.[123]

   Banham also refers to the "Futurist-revival imagery"[124] at Expo 67 without becoming concerned that megastructures might be responsible for dreaded revivalism, albeit after the 1907 "watershed." The revival, he thought, was more in spirit than in form: the megastructures were the Second Machine Age's version of the Futurists' First Machine Age sensibility, but this was not without its own dangers:

Megastructure . . . contains some elements of atavism, a harking back to the "heroic age of Modern architecture," and a constant preoccupation with the original Italian Futurist movement and with the sketches of Sant'Elia. There was undoubtedly a nostalgia for the past (and a hypothesised future) in which Modern architecture had been (and could become once more) a matter of large clear-cut gestures, without the compromises and dilutions and scalings-down that had corrupted the purity and radicalism of the original intentions.[125]

The appeal of megastructures—at least to the profession—was that they provided a way of reengaging with the Modern claim to have responsibility for the design of the whole human environment, but avoided the "homogeneously designed 'total architecture'" which they now acknowledged as "dead, as culturally thin, as any other perfect machine."[126] The conventional professional desire for control and order was answered by the macro aspects of megastructure, whereas the individualistic "non-professional contribution to the visual urban fabric"—Archigram's Living City and its celebration of "disorder, fun, chance, consumerism and entertainment,"[127] or Pop's individualism and brashness—provided variety, diversity, and vitality at the micro level of individual elements or activities. The short-term aspects of megastructure "would yield to individual desires more pliantly than previous forms of cities, and would derive its aesthetic from a demonstration of that compliance."[128] The combination of macro and micro thus seemed like a plausible solution to urban design because it accepted the aspirations of both architects and citizens of the Second Machine Age. As a movement, megastructure "for one hectic decade [became the] the dominant progressive concept of architecture and urbanism."[129]

It was a dominant concept that was also historically located—"true" megastructures, according to Banham, should look like they date from the 1960s: "a megastructure was not only a building which, say, satisfied the four headings of Wilcoxon's definition; a megastructure was also a building which *looked* like a megastructure"![130] Banham offered a further addition to the definition: "5. And designed before Christmas 1964."[131] Apart from being the year when the word "megastructure" was first used in print, 1964 was, according to Banham, the annus mirabilis because "the rising tide of proto-megastructural activity in the early sixties" was approaching its "peak of creativity." The creativity of 1964 produced the buildings of 1967, including Cumbernauld New Town Centre in Scotland, by Geoffrey Copcutt, sometimes cited as "the most complete megastructure to be built," and described by Banham as "the nearest thing yet to a canonical megastructure that one can actually visit or inhabit."[132]

Banham thought the design epitomized four key aspects of megastructural thinking: concentration, monumentality, symbolism, and a compre-

Geoffrey Copcutt, Cumbernauld New Town Centre, 1967 (courtesy Mary Banham)

hensive traffic solution. Concentration was "the heaping up in one place of all the social facilities of a city, and all the commercial ones as well;"[133] its monumentality arose out of the prominent open-space location out of which the center's "bulk is seen to almost crushing advantage, with no other buildings of even remotely comparable size to compete with it for attention. . . . [It] is also of its time in being monumentality for its own sake, a monument to monumentality."[134] The symbolism was based on the possibility—rather than the probability—of "extendability inherent in its air of only provisional determination"—the idea of indeterminacy which was in such good currency in the 1960s. The traffic solution was to provide major road access right to the center, which also strides across the road in one place: "the spanning over is little more than a ceremonial gesture. However, it is still sufficient to persuade the passing motorist that he is enjoying the Futurist experience of plunging through a vast urban structure, even if all he is really doing is driving down the side of a rather dank loading-dock-cum-bus-station."[135]

A megastructure like Cumbernauld shows the influences on mainstream architecture of the ideas we examined in chapter 3. Mainstream it was, and on its completion in late 1966/early 1967, it received several design awards as well as general critical acclaim. It was, of course, the experimental ideas that interested Banham at the time, rather than megastructures themselves, which were of relatively marginal interest. The closest megastructure had been to radical architecture—even *architecture autre*—was at Expo 67, which "provided a fairly high base-level of experience that was relevant to megastructure as a frame of mind: mechanical movement, multiplicity of levels, emphasis on fun or *ludique* experience, stylish Archigram-type colours, people in complex artificial environments, visual information saturation."[136] But Expo was less a dawn than an epitaph: "What was wanted was 'instant city.' . . . At Montreal Expo 67 it probably came as close as it ever would to realising that promise in physical reality . . . but the gaps between vision and reality could be studied at first hand. The gaps were to become so clear that the former megaradicals could only maintain their radical posture by getting out of megastructure as fast as possible."[137] Megastructure, "deserted by the avant-garde, was left to the despised Establishment as a conventional method for maximising the returns from urban redevelopment. . . . [They] had taken so long to build, because of their great size, that the intellectual fashion that had given them birth had passed away before their completion."[138]

If 1967 was the height of megastructure, 1968 witnessed its sharp decline. The shift in sensibility that occurred in the post-1968 years hit megastructure hard. The high-technology connotations meant that

. . . neo-Marxists and neo-Luddites would therefore unite in finding megastructure unacceptable. Megastructure, almost by definition, would mean the destruction or overshadowing of small-scale urban environments; those who had just rediscovered "community" in the slums would fear megastructure as much as any other kind of large-scale renewal programme, and would see to it that the people were never ready. For the flower-children, the dropouts of the desert communes, the urban guerrillas, the com-

munity activists, the politicised squatters, the Black Panthers, the middle-class amenitar-
ians and the historical conservationists, the Marcusians, the art-school radicals and the
participants in the street democracies of the *événements de Mai,* megastructure was an
almost perfect symbol of liberal-capitalist oppression[139]

Banham was obviously well aware of his enemies! Priorities after 1968, as
we have seen, moved away from "architects' architecture" to conservation,
from the exclusiveness of coherent images to the complexity, contradiction,
and diversity of inclusive forms. Megastructure may have been "one of the
inevitable destinations of the Modern movement,"[140] but its demise did not
mean the movement's death. Banham may have welcomed megastructures
in their early years because they "symbolised the libertarian aspirations of a
whole post-Beatles generation,"[141] but they were not central to his thinking
about architecture and he did not identify with them in the way he had
done with the New Brutalism. Hence the tone of *Megastructure* is far less
polemical than that of *The New Brutalism,* although both are books dealing
with "I-was-there" recent history. New Brutalism grew out of a small but urgent debate among Angry Young Men; megastructures reflected some important ideas of the time but, as Banham admits, "the absence of any
explicit ideology was found disturbing,"[142] and this helped its acceptance—
and watering-down—by the mainstream, and acceptance by Big Business
and the Establishment.

The Centre Pompidou, Late Modernism, and High Tech

Megastructure is not, however, a pessimistic book, and ends on a very high
note indeed, celebrating "the most comprehensive standing memorial to
the aspirations and style of the megastructure age"[143]—the Pompidou Center in Paris by Renzo Piano and Richard Rogers. Not surprisingly, the designs
for the scheme, with their "world of bright colours, keen shapes, inflatables,
clip-on gadgetry, giant projection screens and all the rest of the good old imagery of fun and flexibility, stylishly drawn and photocollaged," greatly appealed to his sense of an appropriate architecture for the Second Machine
Age.[144] When constructed, the building, although altered from its original

Renzo Piano and Richard Rogers, Centre Pompidou, Paris, 1971–1976 (courtesy Mary Banham)

design, retained its "Archigrammatic" visual aspect, recalling Instant City and elements of Plug-In City. The brightly colored external structure

> . . . not only gives the elevations a richer structural imagery, but also creates a servicing zone, outside the main floors, running the length and height of both sides of the building. Within and upon this frame and the zone it creates are hung, almost like sacred relics of the dreams of the sixties, such familiar devices as transparent tubular pedestrian walkways and escalators, coloured ducts and service-runs and equally highly-coloured capsules full of servicing machinery. The visual effect of these two image-rich elevations will ensure that [it] will be perceived to be a megastructure: it answers the ultimate acid-test of looking like one.[145]

The Centre Pompidou marked the end of *Megastructure* and megastructures—Banham was declaring "la megastructure è morta" in 1973.[146] It might have been the "terminal monument" of megastructures and even a monument to "the departed aspirations of 'the swinging '60s,'"[147] but it transcended its time and, as a building—or "facility," as Banham preferred to call it, putting it directly in relation to Cedric Price's Fun Palace—the Pompidou represented an approach to architecture in the Second Machine Age that was not just valid, but authentic.

In its authenticity it was the perfect antidote to traditionalism and Post-Modernism—a riposte to the reactionary attitudes or academic developments of the 1970s: "The spirit of the Modern Movement . . . seems to have taken its revenge on two generations of academic doubters, intellectual Luddites and all those energetic breast-beaters'. . . . Centre Pompidou is the only public monument of international quality the '70s have produced."[148] This statement appeared in 1977 in an extended critique in *Architectural Review* shortly after the building had opened; in 1986 Banham was still adjudging it "a whizz to visit" and "a great architectural experience."[149] The experience was special: "the effect is sensational as one sees it from the Rue du Renard, but equally sensational is that it does not destroy the street in any way,"[150] not because of any conscious or contrived "urban contextualism," but because its scale works well optically with the surrounding buildings.

These comments remind us of the importance Banham placed on the first-hand experiencing of a building as part of an overall judgment. Whatever the Pompidou Centre symbolized, or however historically significant it may be, Banham kept returning—in 1977 and 1986—to the experience of it: "Like the Guggenheim Museum in New York, with Frank Lloyd Wright's great spiral gallery around the echoing central well, Pompidou is an experience in its own right, whatever is going on, and whatever is wrong with the details. . . . Both are knock-out *places.*"[151] Banham obviously thought the Pompidou could hold its own with the best, including not only the Guggenheim but some even more elevated company: "Pompidou is as much a total experience as the Eiffel Tower, whose stairs and elevators can be vastly more disturbing than the escalators and suspended walkways of Pompidou, but are an equally essential component in the excitement of being in a place that is unlike anywhere else on the earth's crust."[152] This is praise at the highest level, and puts the Pompidou in an almost ahistorical category.

It undoubtedly became a canonical building for Banham, partly because it expressed the promise of functionality, delivered at a high level of sophistication. He responded very favorably to the quality of the execution of the building, which had required "immense skill and conviction. The massive steel elements have the blunt authority of high-quality civil engineering construction, which is what they are, without pretentious play-acting at machine aesthetics."[153] The Pompidou was neither a superficially styled building nor a piece of engineering (as some critics claimed). The solutions employed by Piano and Rogers were undeniably *architectural* ones. As Banham wrote about Richard Rogers's Lloyds Building in 1986,

. . . confront any single detail—the fixing of the uprights of the handrails of the external stairs, for instance—and one is looking at a design solution that would be virtually inconceivable in normal engineering practice. An engineer might, indeed, have done a handrail upright for half the price, but the result would not have been half as rewarding as architecture. This is not to say that architecture does not still have an enormous amount to learn from even the simplest practices of engineers . . . [but] engineering is one way of designing things, architecture is another.[154]

What this brings to mind is Le Corbusier's 1920s distinction between engineering and architecture. The engineer, "inspired by the law of Economy and governed by mathematical calculation, puts us in accord with universal law. He achieves harmony."[155] But "architecture goes beyond utilitarian needs. . . . The business of architecture is to establish emotional relationships by means of raw materials."[156] Banham's language might be more prosaic, but there is no mistaking that his values derive from high Modernist ideals.

Banham-approved buildings included Rogers's Pompidou and Lloyds, and his compatriot Norman Foster's Willis, Faber and Dumas office building in Ipswich,[157] IBM headquarters in Portsmouth, and Sainsbury Centre for the Visual Arts near Norwich. Banham responded particularly enthusiastically to the "new, monochromatic and monumental version of High-Tech that is on view at the recently-completed Lloyd's building in the City of London (as well as Foster's Hong Kong and Shanghai Bank on the other side of the world).″[158] He initially had some reservations about the term "High Tech," even preferring the term "appropriate tech" in an essay on Foster's architecture written in 1979.[159] In 1982 he warned against a misleading and unthinking use of the term, which was being employed "indiscriminately to cover both buildings that genuinely are highly technological in some substantive sense (such as going beyond normal structural procedures or having a very high proportion of installed mechanical equipment) and those that might be more usefully described by Sutherland Lyall's label 'Industrial Chic.'″[160]

This is an important distinction which Banham felt was absolutely necessary to make in light of the fashion for the "industrial aesthetic" that had become popular in the mid-to-late 1970s, and was chronicled in *High Tech: The Industrial Style and Source Book for the Home,* published in 1978.[161] He objected that what was described as High Tech was often little more than "a smart shed with prettily coloured ducts stuffed through its roof trusses," epitomized by the architecture of Silicon Valley in California.[162]

However, with these qualifications, the term seemed to him meaningful, and almost historically destined. One of the appeals of genuine High Tech was the range of possibilities that went from the flamboyant expression of the Pompidou, to the cool self-effacement of Renzo Piano's Menil Galleries in Houston[163] or the work of Foster Associates, which "often startles [because of its] inevitable pragmatism [and its] lack of stylistic ideology." Yet the result was "stylish within a comparatively narrow range of stylistic possibilities. Narrow, that is by comparison with Eero Saarinen who, once he had given up Mies-and-Water, thundered off with a totally different 'style for the job' with each successive commission."[164] The concept, pragmatism, and phrase the "style for the job" had long appealed to Banham. It had originally been applied to Saarinen's approach, and Banham thought it perfectly suited the work of James Stirling in the 1960s.[165] Now, in the late 1970s and 1980s, it was a characteristic and virtue of High Tech.

Banham could not disguise his enthusiasm for good High Tech buildings. In 1982 he described Rogers's Inmos factory in South Wales as "the first really challenging building of the 1980s," conveying his "excitement, visual and intellectual, generated by the structure."[166] Entering the promenade

along the main service deck above roof level "is the most astonishing encounter with the sheer mechanics of truly modern architecture that one can
experience."[167] Some of the main qualities were those that belonged to the
tradition of Functionalism, for example, the way in which "its structural
logic is perceptibly relentless"[168]; and this caused Banham to return to "the
father of modern Functionalism," Horatio Greenough, who in the 1850s had
decreed that "beauty is the promise of function, made sensuously pleasing." This, Banham considered,

. . . demands the full exercise of the profession's traditional skill and most prized aesthetic talents. And like other monuments of "Post-Functionalist" Functionalism (that is,
delivered from the moribund routines of the International Style) Inmos reveals the exercise of precisely those skills and talents. The promise of Function—almost a *boast* of
Function—is clearly there and it is made sensuously pleasing whenever the architects'
resolution has not wavered, in the care and ingenuity of the details, in the extraordinary
choice of blue as the colour of the main structure, and the equally extraordinary atmosphere of space and light in the central corridor. But is Greenough right? Is Inmos *therefore* beautiful? The last time I saw it, yes. . . . It was a sustained pleasure to look at it.[169]

The belief in this relationship between function and beauty would seem to
contradict some of the arguments in *The Architecture of the Well-tempered
Environment,* except it should be remembered that stylistic pluralism was
not really accepted by Banham, and he always sought form which *expressed*
function. But his response to Inmos is considerably more aesthetic than one
would have anticipated, and concludes:

The ultimate test of Inmos as architectural art may well be: will it look as good as Gropius'
Fagus factory or its 1911 contemporary, Graphic Controls in Buffalo, New York, when it
has stood the same three-score-years-and-several, given the same degrees of appropriate maintenance? To ask this is not to withhold judgement. . . . Rather, it is to ask that it
be judged ultimately in the full depth and rigour that are implicit in Functionalism in the
grandest and noblest sense of the word.

Norman Foster, head office for Willis, Faber and Dumas, Ipswich, 1975

Norman Foster, Hong Kong and Shanghai Bank, Hong Kong, 1979–1986 (courtesy Mary Banham)

Renzo Piano, Menil Galleries, Houston, 1986 (courtesy Mary Banham)

Richard Rogers, Inmos factory, Newport, Wales, 1982 (courtesy Mary Banham)

The "grandest and noblest sense" of Functionalism was a phrase which one would more associate with a writer like Giedion rather than the Futurist-influenced Banham, yet it reveals the respect in which Banham held that tradition—almost a rediscovery for him in the 1980s—and how embedded in it he felt High Tech to be.

What gave High Tech buildings an authority, authenticity, and coherence was "a desire for clarity and frugality in resolving functional problems within the canons of architecture. All seek to 'make architecture' in solving the technical problems of creating fit environments for human activities, but unlike their Post-Modern contemporaries they enjoy their technologies."[170] The radical "fit environments for human activities" is now within the more conservative context of the canon of architecture. In chapter 4, we witnessed Banham's belief, in "A Home if Not a House," that Americans, "left to their own devices . . . do not monumentalise or make architecture." Now, a generation later, Banham was returning to the virtues of "making architecture" and, it seemed, upholding traditional architectural values. Furthermore, it was traditional *European* architectural values—High Tech was essentially a European movement. Perhaps, now that he was a resident of the United States, Banham's enthusiasm for that country and all it represented to him was waning. Perhaps, too, there was a hint of nostalgia in High Tech's appeal: "The reversion to a pin-jointed system seems almost like archaism or primitivism after 30 years of plastic orthodoxy, but for many of us it will be an almost reassuring return to those elegant and self-sufficient structural diagrams on which classical statics were based, and which we all learned to do as students."[171] In the 1980s, Banham rediscovered the qualities and appeal of European Modernism.

In an important late essay, significantly titled "The Quality of Modernism" (1986), Banham locates High Tech as a "further stage in the ongoing epic of late Modernism, the style that was supposed to die. The falsity of that supposition lay, of course, in construing Modernism as *only* a style, rather than as a style supported by a whole complex of attitudes to design and society inherited ultimately from the latter part of the nineteenth century—the period when so much of the present century was first put into working order."[172] The complex included a particular attitude to structure and materials, but its inherited assumptions had supposedly been revised in the light of post-1968 and Post-Modern developments, so that (especially British) architects like Rogers and Foster were

. . . clearly preoccupied with putting buildings together properly. In [High Tech] . . . , Modernism has come back to haunt its critics with a vengeance, but the returned tradition of the Modern has been properly chastened and transformed as befits the post-critical situation. No virtue is now seen as inhering automatically in "being modern"; rather it now seems to reside in the undertaking of the responsibilities, and the execution of the tasks that are understood as being peculiar to a "modern condition" that refuses to go away. High on the register of both tasks and responsibilities is that of inventing an architecture appropriate to the times.[173]

In the mid-1980s Banham was continuing his 1950s' quest for an architecture appropriate for the times, an architecture of and for the Second Machine Age. The Modernist sense of ethical mission—with reference to the "undertaking of responsibilities"—would, by 1986, sound anachronistic to some, and recalled a Brutalist-like sense of ethical approach; equally, the identification of a "modern condition" (even in quotation marks) could be seen to miss the point of the *Post*-Modern condition. Banham's argument would doubtless be that technology is still a central part, constant presence, and major mythology of contemporary Western life. No one could disagree, but it is Banham's continuing commitment to Modernist assumptions about the need to *represent* technology as the primary condition of society that makes him appear anachronistic. Following his own logic, if "no virtue is now seen as inhering automatically in 'being modern,'" and if the architect's responsibility is to invent an architecture "appropriate to the times," then an option like Ricardo Bofill's massive neoclassical palace at the Abraxas housing scheme outside Paris is, arguably, appropriate because it expresses contemporary ideas about a socially and culturally mobile community.[174] But Banham, while acknowledging that Bofill's work was "technically brilliant," dismissed it as "stylistically depraved"[175] because it was revivalist.

He may have seen High Tech as the latest revisionist version of the continuing tradition of Modernism, but it was a Modernism that was radical rather than pragmatic. He located the High Tech architects in an ethical tradition that emphasizes

. . . honesty and integrity in the use of materials and mechanical details. A key building was the Smithsons' school at Hunstanton. . . . It was a hotly discussed building, bitterly disliked in many quarters. But it was disliked in the sort of way that some more recent Rogers and Foster work has been disliked: because it puts its arrogant tropes on show. There is a tradition there of not quite *épater la bourgeoisie* but *épater la profession*, wishing to step beyond the accepted norms of what you do and what you don't do in architecture.[176]

This linked High Tech with James Stirling and New Brutalism. All rejected "selective and classicising" tendencies in favor of both an attitude and a more expressive and inclusive set of possibilities which is "essentially plural-istic, and does not prescribe any particular set of answers."[177] But High Tech was pluralistic and provided answers only within terms of reference deriv-ing from Modernist assumptions. In "The Quality of Modernism," Banham wrote that the "Lessons of the Masters" reveal that "the actual style and technology of using materials is crucial, that there is some necessary (if perennially inscrutable) connection between the usages that shape the in-dividual pieces of material and the architectural quality of the building that results from them."[178] The problem with its being "inscrutable" is that a self-perpetuating prejudice can replace argument—a particular value system is taken as an absolute one. All of this leaves the reader in no doubt about Banham's values. When we put it alongside his 1983 judgment that Norman Foster's architecture is "the toughest and most aggressive style of mod-ernism available at the moment . . . an assertion that the truest tradition of architecture is constructive, not decorative . . . ,"[179] we are also left in no doubt about the almost absolutist moral authority that those values held in Banham's mind.

"Intermediate/Alternative/Appropriate" Tech, and the Vernacular
When one reads that High Tech's "emphatic complexity of engineer-style detailing [was] a manifest attempt to project an imagery appropriate to the

technological times," it is not difficult to predict what Banham's attitude would be to alternative or low technology. Arguing in 1979 that Norman Foster's architecture could legitimately be described as an example of "appropriate technology," Banham wrote: "The lesson of building history is not that one particular type of construction is superior or less wasteful or more natural than others, but that many modes of construction have long been understood to be subtly appropriate to different sorts and conditions of buildings and that you cannot tell which is the more appropriate simply by looking—the proof is in the performance."[180] This *Architecture of the Well-tempered Environment*-like sentiment sounded very reasonable and tolerant but was, ultimately, misleading as a representation of Banham's position. From what he wrote about Foster—as well as what he had written in the *Well-tempered Environment*—it was more a case of the "style for the job," with the assumption that the job was a building for "the technological times" and the style would be some form of "imagery appropriate" to that time. This effectively ruled out the "windmills and pisé walls" of the "simple-mindedly low-tech" brigade with their "ideologically self-righteous 'solar' (etc.) architecture."[181]

Banham had branded the alternative technology (AT) movement "neo-Luddites" in *Megastructure* in 1976,[182] and his feelings about the "Intermediate/Alternative/Appropriate" technology movement came through in a review in Witold Rybezynski's *Paper Heroes: A Review of Appropriate Technology* (1980). His main point was what he saw as AT's condescension in condemning Third World countries to a "responsible" future, doubting that the movement's "good grey men . . . will ever realise how deeply some Africans and Asians resent the apparent determination to sentence their continents to a pedal-driven future." Not only, in Banham's view, did the Third World have the right to aspire to and enjoy the technological extravagances of First World technology—no doubt swapping their pedal-driven cars for an equivalent of the Detroit dreams that money can buy—but the more general implication seemed to be that he still subscribed to the belief that technology was independent of political structures and organizations. As he had claimed in 1962, technology was "morally, socially and politically neutral."[183]

Banham's Independent Group-derived technological optimism and progressivism seemed to survive the AT critique intact.

A more convincing point about the relationship between alternative technology and politics was in a 1983 review of Steve Baer's solar house in New Mexico. What struck Banham was how the politics of American AT had changed in a decade: "Originally, around 1970, the emphasis on supposedly 'low' or 'soft' technologies . . . was part of the general radical-left revolt against conglomerates, multinationals, the military-industrial complex." However, in the 1980s, the North American AT movement, including Baer, "far from being radical . . . was already individualistic, property-oriented, conservative and defensive. . . . Wood-burning Baer, if you had no idea of his earlier radical entanglements, could easily be taken for a paragon of those old Protestant and craggy New England virtues of thrift, self-reliance, seriousness and moral certainty that most of us sneakily admire or envy."[184] Indeed, American AT connected with the frontier mentality, which, in different ways, had appealed to the apolitical, romantic individualist, anti-establishmentarian—the general "tough-mindedness"—a Frank Lloyd Wright or Bucky Fuller (the latter a guru for many AT believers). It was probably these elements of the tradition with which Banham identified while dismissing the "back-to-nature" softheadedness of the "neo-Luddite" reaction to technology.

In 1984 a revised edition of *The Architecture of the Well-tempered Environment* was published, the first revision of any of Banham's major books.[185] Baer's house was now included to illustrate "the conventional procedures—if not the customary forms—of the Solar orthodoxy in its Passive mode, which is no more than the ancient Conservative mode rediscovered."[186] Banham's opponents might have countered that it was no *less* than that mode rediscovered—his phrasing and his vocabulary (in which "passive" and "Conservative" had negative connotations; their opposites, "active" and "radical" were almost supreme virtues) clearly revealed his values. The "ancient Conservative mode" also gave rise to vernacular architecture which, in Banham's view, should not be rejected out of hand and, indeed, might provide clues to contemporary solutions; but his sentiment about architecture being shaped by an "embalmed corpus of ancestral folly"[187] recalled

Steve Baer, solar house, New Mexico, early 1980s (courtesy Mary Banham)

Marinetti's line about the impossibility of modern man living in the same streets that were built for the life of "four, five, six centuries ago."

Banham's judgment puts one in mind of his attitude to preservation and conservation—vernacular architecture may have been a reasonable solution to general needs in the past, but was not likely to be so in the Second Machine Age with its more exacting and embracing expectations. Even Baer, "a one-time disciple of Buckminster Fuller," departs from the Conservative mode in having "distilled technological expertise . . . at his disposal. Although much is made of the (relative) economic deprivation of that part of New Mexico, the great atomic research facility at Los Alamos brings vast intellectual and computational power to the area."[188] The vernacular, the ancient Conservative mode, needed to be counterbalanced by the progressive, radical one. Half a dozen years earlier, Jencks had described Post-Modernism's double coding in an apparently similar way: "half modern and half something else—traditional, local, vernacular." Banham's analysis of

Baer's house reveals a significantly different emphasis: Jencks's double coding is about communicating through "customary forms"; Banham's is about an attitude to technology, and may not be readily visible and "readable." Indeed, the revised edition of the book ends with a contrast between Post-Modernism and technology:

> Our present post-Modernists who strive to restore . . . customary forms can do so only because environmental technology gives them the freedom to separate those forms from desired environmental performance. If this observation sounds somewhat like the comments made in the nineteenth century about those who hung irrelevant historical forms on buildings constructed out of new materials to serve new functions, then it is just that it should so sound; we see the same situation repeating itself but raised to a higher power by higher and more subtle technologies. And if this is the time when history repeats itself as farce, then it is architecture which is offering to become farcical, not the technologies that have replaced it from its ancient role.[189]

There is an echo here, again, of Le Corbusier, but this time the Master's polemical statement "Architecture or Revolution. Revolution can be avoided"[190] is paralleled but reversed by Banham's architecture or technology: architecture can be avoided, evoking his "Stocktaking" series of 1960.

Baer's house was the acceptable face of the alternative technology movement. Indeed, in Banham's mind, Baer was the grandchild of one of his First Machine Age heroes: houses like Baer's "represent an architectural ideal that may seem curiously familiar to readers of the history chronicled in the preceding chapters. . . . *Mehr Farbenlicht!* More coloured light!—the call of ailing, brick-boxed Paul Scheerbart. For the privileged (but not necessarily wealthy) few, his dream of a glass architecture is habitably real."[191] Scheerbart was once again resurrected as a Modernist hero—he had appeared last as a forebear of James Stirling.

But Baer's work was not typical, and the "ideology" of the low-tech movement "stood in the way" of a more pragmatic and inclusive use of technologies. Thus, "the conscious preference for 'Low' technology was one of the strangest episodes in the recent history of architecture. Not only did it involve the repudiation of much of the Western heritage of technology and most of the professional mystique of architecture—indeed, no architect of major repute was involved—but it has failed so far to produce anything that might be called an impressive monument. . . . So detached from the history and traditions of architecture were these fanatics of 'Passive' solar energy that many of them knew nothing even of the immediate pre-history of solar power"[192]—let alone, no doubt, Scheerbart. With its references to "the Western heritage," the "professional mystique of architecture," architects of "major repute," and "impressive monument(s)," this would be a surprising and curious statement for someone as radical as Banham to make, but to make it in the context of *The Architecture of the Well-tempered Environment* seems downright contradictory, for all the phrases he uses ought, in effect, to have been undermined by the thesis of the book as a whole.

It was obviously a difficult task for Banham to revise a radical book written at a radical, tolerant, and progressive time, when now he saw conservatism and the forces of reaction around him. *The Architecture of the Well-tempered Environment* had become not so much a classic as a period piece. Although High Tech may get close to delivering "fit environments for human activities" within "the craft of architecture,"[193] the general climate was largely hostile. In the revised first chapter, Banham remarked on the historical location of the book: "Even before the Arab oil embargo precipitated the fuel crisis of 1973–74, this book got progressively worse and worse reviews—it was a history of the use of environmental energy and proposed no anathema on that use and was therefore made out to be a tract in favour of *wasting* energy."[194]

The Lure of the Sense of Possibilities

In language that reveals his frustration with the new mood, Banham, in a 1985 essay, recounted the sort of issues that were taken to be a crisis: "the *collapse* of confidence in large-scale design in the early seventies, the *revulsion* against planning, the *neurosis* of 'small is beautiful,' and the *panics* that followed the oil crisis of 1973–74" (my italics).[195] The crisis, at least in Britain, was one of the factors that had led Banham to leave for the United States, where, in 1976, he had taken up the post of professor of architectural history and theory at the State University of New York at Buffalo. In an interview published at the time of his departure, he bemoaned the lack of confidence in British architecture, contrasting it to the more progressive and optimistic Unites States, where, according to the interviewer, as Banham "puts it without cynicism, they are already writing the history of the ecology movement. And he is off to join in. While for Britain? 'It's no longer "whither the Modern Movement." Well I mean, nobody *cares* any more—to hell with the Modern Movement nowadays. . . . I find the situation here . . . slightly spooky at the moment, I must say. . . . I think it's the collapse of self-confidence, professionally and otherwise. There is the economic collapse, but the collapse of professional self-confidence, interestingly, preceded it.'"[196]

In his *Los Angeles* (1971), Banham had written about the "naïvely nonchalant reliance on technology" that characterized California culture—a claim that might be said to apply to American culture in general. However, he had continued by stating that "by comparison with the general body of official Western culture at the moment, increasingly given over to facile, evasive and self-regarding pessimism," the American version "can be a very refreshing attitude to encounter."[197] This was the lure for Banham, and he optimistically set out to rediscover the "sense of possibilities" that he had associated with the Unites States. His time in Buffalo brought out less the optimist than the revisionist historian, culminating in *A Concrete Atlantis: U.S. Industrial Building and European Modern Architecture, 1900–1925*, published in 1986 (and discussed in chapter 1).[198] In 1981 he moved to California to become professor of art history at the University of California at Santa Cruz, again with optimism. He criticized the staffs of architecture schools like the one in Buffalo because "they don't ever use their minds"[199]—let alone change them—and looked forward to working with "my own kind . . . historians."

But American architecture was suffering a malaise similar to its European counterpart: "I think the mood of the profession, particularly as reflected in the schools at the moment, is one of intellectual retrenchment, which is a polite phrase for total loss of nerve. . . . [It is] cautious if not actually cowardly" (but no "betrayal" was mentioned). Even in California, "there isn't much zip or excitement. . . . [T]he present mood is slightly running scared with an un-healthy preoccupation with appearing to be energy responsible."[200]

Alternative technology, preservation and conservation, historicism and re-vivalism, the new architectural Right, Post-Modernism . . . all these had taken their toll in a cultural and social milieu that had ceased to be "well-tempered"—that is, radical, progressive, and bloody-minded—and had be-come an unfit environment for Banham's activities. It is perhaps, therefore, not surprising that one of his least known, most underrated—but, in my view, important—books in the 1980s was not about recent architecture but the American deserts. *Scenes in America Deserta,* published in 1982, throws such important light on Banham's late Modernist values that we will hold over discussion of it until the conclusion.

6

EXPENDABLE ICONS AND SOFTER HARDWARE

Banham's Design Criticism

"History is, of course, my academic discipline. Criticism is what I do for money."[1] Uttered in a conference address in 1964, this remark, however tongue-in-cheek, might lead us to suppose that Banham saw a distinct separation between his "serious" duties as a historian and his relatively trivial activities as a critic, even when one accepts the quip about financial remuneration. This supposition might be reinforced by his "history" being published in hardback books and academic or professional journals, whereas his "criticism" sped in and out of sight via the transient vehicles of weekly or monthly magazines and, occasionally, even newspaper supplements. Banham never wrote a book about design. Given his unambiguous enthusiasm for and interest in design, let alone his great influence on design studies and design history, this seems surprising, but would perhaps seem to confirm his distinction between the importance of history and that of criticism.

Banham's underlying ideas and intentions regarding his different modes of writing need to be understood in order for us to appreciate the importance he ascribed to *both* enduring history writing *and* ephemeral criticism. His design criticism, however enjoyable (as it undoubtedly was) and however apparently flippant (as it may appear), had—ultimately—a very serious purpose. This chapter examines his design criticism in terms of its scope and range, the characteristics of the writing, and its relationship to some of the key ideas and values we have discussed in previous chapters.

Modernist Abstraction and Snobbery

The fundamental premises underlying Banham's design criticism can be traced back to 1955 and two of the major articles which arose from, on the one hand, his doctoral research on the Modern Movement and, on the other, his involvement with the Independent Group.

In "Machine Aesthetic," the reader will recall, Banham had attacked High Modernists for mistaking "conditional attributes of engineering . . . as necessary consequences of machine production."[2] The identification of "simplicity of form and smoothness of finish" confused the manifestations of technology at a particular historical juncture with a supposedly timeless aesthetic that underlay great art—the Modernists' approach was "selective and classicising." It was Marinetti and the Futurists who recognized the impermanency of technology, but who greeted the recognition with pleasure rather than regret, partly because they embraced technology, realizing that "machines could be a source of personal fulfilment and gratification"[3]— as, indeed, they were to Banham. In the First Machine Age, Gropius had castigated those designers who lowered their sights, who played to the market and so "prostituted our fundamental precepts into modish trivialities."[4] Design produced by market conditions was debased design. This attitude not only survived the war, it was even reinforced in some quarters where an "ex-officers and gentlemen" or "Montgomery and soda-water" mentality prevailed.[5]

In the same year that Banham was publishing "Machine Aesthetic" and "Vehicles of Desire," the head of the Council of Industrial Design[6] was imploring manufacturers to raise the standard of their design because "the fight against the shoddy design of those goods by which most of our fellowmen are surrounded has become a duty."[7] The sense of duty should not be diminished by what the Institute of Contemporary Art's president, Herbert Read (whose 1934 *Art and Industry* had been republished in a revised edition in 1956), referred to as the "dull and indifferent public [who are] incapable of appreciating design."[8]

Banham's riposte to Modernism's theoretical shortcomings had come, as we saw in chapter 2, in 1955; his (first) searing attack on the movement's patronizing attitude appeared in 1961 in an article which lambasted the Council of Industrial Design because it "approves of rubbish."[9] His argument used as an example a suitcase included in the Council's Design Index—its list of approved products—which, when subjected to tests by the Consumer Advisory Council, working to criteria set by the British Standards Institution, was deemed "poor" in five of seven tests, and was illustrated by a consumer testing magazine as an example of bad design because it leaked badly, the handle broke off, the fittings rusted, and the lining came out. The Council itself did not test products it included in its Index, and seemed to believe—or hope—that there was "some kind of necessary relationship between the appearance of an object and its performance and quality." But, as Banham continued, "Unfortunately not. 'Form Follows Function' is a slogan, not a statement of fact." However elegant the design, "tasteful rubbish is still rubbish." Banham had astutely noted the confusion in design between matters of function and preferences of taste. From the days of the Dessau Bauhaus, Modernists had conflated the two into "good design," with the result that the "selective and classicising" aesthetic was presented as universal and superior, at the expense of the "plurality of hierarchies" and range of aesthetics that the Independent Group had argued for in the early 1950s.

Modernist crusades for improving design were often little more than attempts to inculcate a certain aesthetic or taste. "It may well be that 'improving public taste' is not a fit occupation for grown men anyhow—at any rate, not if 'taste' is interpreted in the narrow middle-class sense that the Council understands." Rather than information and analysis provided by disinterested ergonomicists, the public was presented with "the collective fancies of bands of strolling aesthetes" who, as unreformed Modernists, perpetuated with their pronouncements "automatic assumptions of moral right." As Banham had written three months earlier, "The concept of good design as a form of aesthetic charity done on the labouring poor from a great height is incompatible with democracy as I see it."[10] That popular taste is always bad is an "old, standardised and unquestioned, public-school-pink" proposition, a proposition that was not only patronizing, but also class-based, and symptomatic of "snobbery intolerable in a Liberal, let alone a Socialist."[11]

A Theory of Design for the Second Machine Age

Such snobbery and patronizing attitudes became, as the 1960s unfolded, completely unacceptable. Popular design, like design for the growing teenage market, Banham wrote in 1963, "may not be 'good' by the Establishment standards of the Design Centre and the Duke's awards, but it usually works as well as anything that gets into the Design Index."[12] Tastefulness, he reminded his readers, was not of significance in the design of objects in the Second Machine Age: look at new transistor radio designs in any high street store, and you will see "an orgy of keen professional design that contrives to be both flashy and vulgar without being coarsely detailed—a radically new situation this, which raises the question whether

Aero transistor radio, early 1960s

flashy and *vulgar* are quite the terms of abuse they used to be when deprived of coarseness."

Taste was returned into the realm of politics: "If you want Pop design to be tasteful and beautiful instead of flashy and vulgar, you must envisage a drastic and illiberal reconstruction of society." This countered the snobbery of the Modernists and "International Design Establishment"[13] with their belief in a universal criterion of good design. Banham did—in "The End of Insolence," a 1960 *New Statesman* piece—acknowledge that "fast buck commercialism can never be made to look good from the consumer-victim's end,"[14] but, as we have seen in chapter 2, he remained muted in his criticisms of the political and social limitations of the market economy. This was undoubtedly the weakest point of his theory of design.

In the Second Machine age, taste was becoming considerably more inclusive. The most "flashy and vulgar" design had been the American automobile of the 1950s, which he had immortalized in his other influential article of 1955, "Vehicles of Desire." The "insolent chariots" may have been on the scrap heap by 1960, "not that the product is any less insolent, in spite of the disappearance of tail-fins—but the insolence is no longer the point." In other words, "flashy and vulgar" design is not the condition of popular design, but only one possibility, one manifestation at a historical juncture. In the early years of the decade the technical innovations were what really mattered: it was not the psychologist and sociologist, but the "technical critic who suddenly has a lot to write about—compacts with rear engines (Chevrolet), with independent rear-suspension (Chevrolet, Pontiac), torsion bar rear-springing (Rambler), radically revised transmissions (Pontiac)." The flamboyant styling of the 1950s was being superseded by a (relatively) restrained and understated approach, but people were wrong if they believed this heralded a change of value:

. . . some voices at the Council of Industrial Design hailed the compacts (in the campfire jargon that seems to be a speciality at Haymarket House) as "a sock-pulling-up operation," and believed that Detroit has seen the evil of her ways. They should get stronger rose-tinted spectacles—the US industry has not altered its commercial pitch, or suffered any change of heart. It has simply observed that it is now possible to sell a non-insolent car on a large enough scale to turn a fairly fast buck.[15]

Banham did not draw the parallel, but the situation was not unlike the one that he had highlighted in "Machine Aesthetic": the Modernists of the 1920s had mistaken a particular historical manifestation of technology as its fundamental, timeless aesthetic. What latter-day Modernists thought was a "sock-pulling-up operation" may have been no more than the current appeal of one sock design over another.[16]

The permanent condition of change was, as we have seen, one that Banham welcomed wholeheartedly. In design terms it brought the stylistic and technical innovations that had been in evidence since the beginning of the 1950s. Not to run with technology was to stagnate. This meant that, as well as attacking the vintage car cult because of its "pure nostalgia (a morbid condition in technology),"[17] Banham also attacked the "sterility" of the approach symbolized by the Volkswagen Beetle, that "objectionable vehicle" which he criticized for its "outstanding design faults": poor visibility and accommodation space; and instability caused by a poor balance between suspension, aerodynamics, and weight distribution. "The only way to cure these faults and offer the public better service," he suggested, "would be to build a different car." Pride seemed to have been taken in the fact that there was no change, and so there remained the deadly "combination of Platonic aesthetics with ignorance of the nature of technology, summed up in the slogan 'a good design is for ever.'"[18] A dynamic technological culture was more likely to deliver "an exciting design for now" to the citizens of the industrial West.

Like other erstwhile members of the Independent Group, Banham believed that the Second Machine Age was a democratic one in which ordinary people possessed the consumer goods that had, in the previous age, been the preserve of the few—in *Theory and Design in the First Machine Age,* for example, he describes the "teen-ager, curled up with a transistorised, printed-circuit radio, or boudoir gramophone [who] may hear a music . . . reproduced at a level of quality that riches could not have bought a decade or so ago."[19] Equally, the average car now "provides transport more

Volkswagen Beetle, early 1960s (courtesy National Motor Museum)

sumptuous in vehicles more gorgeous than palanquin-borne emperors knew how to desire."

Design in the Second Machine Age was exciting and gratifying—for cultural optimists like Banham, gratification was being facilitated and encouraged by prosperity and technical advances. Popular culture in the era of the Independent Group had offered an increasingly sophisticated level of enjoyment and playfulness; in the 1960s, a further increase in personal affluence, better health, a reduction of the drudgery of manual labor brought about by technological advances, and more free time made "the leisure society" one of central pillars of belief and the stock phrases of the media. On a day-to-day basis, for most relatively affluent individuals, technology was manifested in and experienced through product design and the media; the new products that became available were symptomatic of a dynamic and changing society in which technology was in accord with its state of continual change. The condition of design was at its most extreme in Pop culture, which, Banham wrote in 1962,

. . . is about things to use and throw away. . . . The aesthetics of Pop depend upon a massive initial impact and small sustaining power, and are therefore at their poppiest in products whose sole object is to be consumed, that *must* be consumed, whether phys-ically, like soft serve ices, or symbolically, like daily papers that can only last twenty-four hours by definition. In fact, physical and symbolic consumability are equal in Pop culture, equal in status and meaning.[20]

As the temperature of consuming increased in Britain in the late 1950s and early 1960s, the visual awareness of consumers, Banham believed, blos-somed. In 1961 he judged that public taste "has become infinitely more so-phisticated in the ten years since the Festival [of Britain]."[21] The credit was due to the mass media, especially television: "For the first time, almost, in the history of man, a great part of the population was introduced to a constant stream of smart visual images, was shown new products and Old Masters, either in their own right or as the backgrounds to drama and discussion."[22] There was a two-way process: consumers became more so-phisticated because of the greater attention paid to design and the media, and the greater interest in design by the media made consumers more design-conscious. There was also a two-way process in terms of innovation. Banham argued that the Detroit "styling binge" of the later 1950s, first, "has precipitated a number of hidden technical changes required to make cars workable in their ever more fantastic shapes; secondly it has completely pulped all preconceptions about what a car should look like, and thus opened the way for yet more violent changes in appearance necessitated by major technical revisions such as rear engines. The aesthetic revolution ap-pears to have been a necessary forerunner of the technical."[23]

Like innovation and novelty, or symbolic and physical expendability, aes-thetic and technical change were part of the fundamental condition of the Second Machine Age. By the early 1960s, Banham had formulated the "intellectual attitudes for living in a throwaway economy" that he had identified as necessary and urgent in "Vehicles of Desire" in 1955. He was now in a position to apply the appropriate criteria in his design criticism.

The Role of the Critic

Banham saw the primary function of the design critic as deconstructing the "noisy ephemeridae"[24] that the new society was producing and consuming. In "Vehicles of Desire," he had described how Detroit car designers of the later 1950s, akin to artists in a tradition-based culture, were using "symbolic iconographies . . . whose ultimate power lies in their firm grounding in popular taste and the innate traditions of the product." This shifted designing away from the Modernist model of abstraction with its "characteristic primary forms and colours," to a post-Modernist one of product semantics with its culturally loaded, meaningful forms and images. Modernist designers may have thought their primary forms were "readily accessible to everyone," but Banham realized that accessibility was more likely to come through the application of specific cultural codes and conventions that, in view of the need for mass sales in the marketplace, would be based on symbols which had widespread public recognizability and appeal—hence popular and fashionable genres like science fiction, up-to-date and romantic areas such as supersonic flight, and the enduring human fascination with sex. The post-Modern designer was also unlike the Modernist designer in that the latter could remain aloof from popular taste and closeted in the academy: the former would need to understand popular culture and the "innate traditions" of the relevant products, and this required immersion.

Both the designer and the critic, Banham wrote in another important 1955 article, "Space for Decoration: A Rejoinder," "must deal with a language of signs."[25] Both, he confirmed in 1960, needed a "command and understanding of [iconography and] popular symbolism."[26] Good criticism depended "on the ability of design critics to master the workings of the popular art vocabulary which constitutes the aesthetics of expendability."[27] Because design was based on serial production and was consumed in the marketplace, design criticism was, it followed, fundamentally *unlike* art criticism: "The aesthetics of serial production must be the aesthetics of the popular arts, not of fine arts. To apply durable and time-bound aesthetic procedures to consumable and non-traditional products can only cheapen those procedures and—as in so much Victorian design—debases the fine arts without benefiting the expendable arts." Art criticism dealt with form and iconography in a relatively inward-looking way, whereas design criticism "depends on an analysis of content, an appreciation of superficial rather than abstract qualities, and an outward orientation that sees the history of the product as an interaction between the sources of the symbols and the consumer's understanding of them." Design criticism would have to deal with audiences and their use of the object as part of the criticism.

Applying this modus operandi to the expendable American car, Banham explained in 1960, the critic would be responding to "a *content* (idea of power), a *source* of symbols (aircraft), and a *popular culture* (whose members recognise these symbols and their meaning)."[28] The first responsibility of the critic is to understand the language, its contemporary usage, and its history. In the case of car styling,

. . . its propriety to automotive design lies in its symbolic content, which is concerned, more than anything else, with penetration. When this symbol language was young it had an architectural connection, for the only available language of penetration was the misplaced dynamism of Erich Mendelsohn and his imitators, but as the public grew more familiar with the appearance of racing cars, jet planes, space-ship projects and the like, a whole new iconography of penetration-symbols became available to the automobile stylist. Its aptness to the automobile cannot be denied. . . . Its theme is germane to the business of transportation, and its symbols are as firmly built into the technical history of the product as were the useless flutings, guttae, triglyphs and so forth of Greek Doric temples.[29]

The critic could then turn his or her attention from the general to the particular. The particular included the new Cadillac Eldorado convertible that Banham had praised in "Vehicles of Desire." He had expertly demonstrated his understanding of the language of the contemporary automobile with its

. . . repertoire of hooded headlamps, bumper-bombs, sporty nave-plates, ventilators, intakes, incipient tail-fins, speed-streaks and chromium spears, protruding exhaust-pipes, cineramic wind-screens—these give tone and social connotation to the body envelope; the profiling of wheel arches, the humping of mudguards, the angling of roof-posts—these control the sense of speed; the grouping of the main masses, the quality of the main curves of the panels—these balance the sense of masculine power and feminine luxury. It is a thick ripe stream of loaded symbols—that are apt to go off in the face of those who don't know how to handle them.[30]

To analyze and evaluate designs within a design language or discourse, the critic would need to be fluent in the language to the extent of recognizing its dialects, inflections, and nuances. To misread the language would, as Banham indicated, harm the critic and expose a lack of credibility.

One of the problems in the 1950s was that there were few critics who had escaped the straitjacket of Modernist criteria in their criticism. However, in Banham's opinion, there was one who "possesses a shame-faced, but invaluable, ability to write automobile-critique of almost Berensonian sensibility."[31] Her name was Deborah Allen, and her criticism appeared in the American publication *Industrial Design.* From 1954 until the end of the decade, Allen annually reviewed the styling of the new Detroit models. Banham found both her critical position and her language a model of expertise. She was a skeptical, "knowing consumer" of the cars, describing the latest

Cadillac Eldorado Biarritz, 1957 (courtesy National Motor Museum)

models as being "as expensive, fuel-hungry, space-consuming, inconvenient, liable to damage, and subject to speedy obsolescence as they ever have been."[32] But, unlike British cultural critics, she was not simply damning or dismissive. What particularly attracted Banham was her feeling for the design language and vocabulary of the automobiles, and her stated belief that the car designer should be "deeply and boldly concerned with form as a means of expression." In 1955 she described how the 1955 Buick

. . . is perpetually floating on currents that are conventionally built into the design. This attempt to achieve buoyancy with masses of metal is bound to have the same awkward effect as the solid wooden clouds of a Baroque baldachino; unless you like to wince the purist's wince at every Buick or baldachino, the best recourse is to accept the romantic notion that materials have no more weight than the designer chooses to give them. . . . The Buick's designers put the greatest weight over the front wheels, where the engine is, which is natural enough. The heavy bumper helps to pull the weight forward; the dip in the body and the chrome spear express how the thrust of the front wheels is dissipated in turbulence toward the rear. Just behind the strong shoulder of the car, a sturdy post lifts up the roof, which trails off like a banner in the air. The driver sits in the dead calm at the centre of all this motion—hers is a lush situation.[33]

This style of design criticism profoundly affected not only Banham but also other members of the Independent Group. In Richard Hamilton's case it led him to make a painting—*Hers Is a Lush Situation* (1957–1958)—based on Allen's Futurist-like, almost poetic writing.

Banham quoted Allen's writing in "Vehicles of Desire," claiming: "This is the stuff of which the aesthetics of expendability will eventually be made. It carries the sense and the dynamism of that extraordinary continuum of emotional-engineering-by-public-consent which enables the automobile industry to create vehicles of palpably fulfilled desire." However, Allen's criticism was not so much an example of "reading" the styling of the car or deconstructing its meaning through a "language of signs," as it was a formal analysis of the expressive qualities of the car styling. She wrote in an objective and detached style, in the way an art historian might describe how the visual vocabulary employed by an artist produces particular emotional or

Buick Century, 1955 (courtesy National Motor Museum)

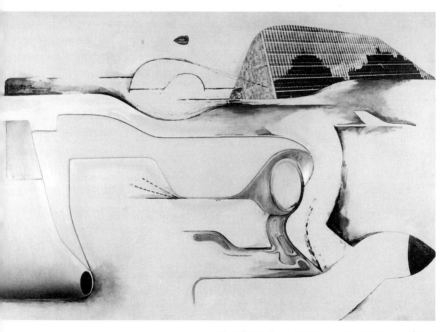

Richard Hamilton, *Hers Is a Lush Situation,* 1957–1958 (courtesy Richard Hamilton)

expressive effects: the appeal to Banham was Allen's aesthetic sensibility for the subject matter rather than any use of "symbolic iconographies."

Closer to "symbolic iconographies" was the writing of Roland Barthes, whose *Mythologies* was first published in 1957. It included essays on popular culture such as wrestling, soap powder, margarine advertising, striptease, film, toys, and cars. Of the Citroen DS, for example, Barthes wrote: "Until now, the ultimate in cars belonged rather to the bestiary of power. . . . [I]t is now more *homely,* more attuned to this sublimation of the utensil, which one also finds in the design of contemporary household equipment. The dashboard looks more like the working surface of a factory. . . . One is obviously turning from an alchemy of speed to a relish in driving."[34] These are the sorts of comments that might have been made by Banham in his contemporaneous writings about the Detroit automobile. Barthes's role, like Banham's, seems to be the interpreter or iconologist who deconstructs meaning from popular culture or the artifacts of design.

The difference between the two is in the end to which the means is employed. Barthes is ultimately interested in the mythologies that help define the bourgeoisie; Banham is interested more in the design itself, its "innate traditions," and its social role for a particular group. The tones of their writing are also different. Barthes writes in a detached, conventional academic way, and the reader gets little sense of personal excitement from the author about his subject matter; Banham usually wrote with wit, and always with verve and enthusiasm—he was immersed in his subject matter. By temperament, Banham was optimistic about his subject matter; he was a believer that the design and popular culture of the period were making society better.

Intellectually, the two men belonged to different traditions. In the mid-1960s Banham revealingly wrote of his preference for "English pragmatism" over "continental systematics":[35] the latter represented to him "scholasticism" and resulted in "selective and classicising" Modernism, for example, or dry theory, which led the writer to be "isolated from humanity by the Humanities."[36] The immersion in and enjoyment of the subject matter, as well as the strong human presence that was to become a feature of Banham's articles, was largely absent in the criticism of both Barthes and Allen.

Barthes was not an important figure in British Pop culture in the 1960s, largely because his work was little known outside very small esoteric circles until the translation of *Mythologies* in 1972. Considerably better known and—as far as Banham was concerned—considerably more relevant, was the Canadian academic Marshall McLuhan. *The Mechanical Bride,* an analysis of the layered readings of American advertisements, had been published as early as 1951, but widespread availability was limited by indignant and litigious manufacturers. However, the concern with imagery and meaning, which paralleled the Independent Group's own interest, guaranteed the book a "semi-legendary"[37] status among erstwhile members when they discovered it in 1956.

In the 1960s, McLuhan became the doyen of technological optimism, but in the 1950s his position was more guarded. In the preface to *The Mechanical Bride* he wrote that the aim of the contemporary mass media seemed to be "to get inside [the collective public mind] in order to manipulate, exploit [and] control. . . . And to generate heat not light is the intention. To keep everybody in the helpless state engendered by prolonged mental rutting is the effect of many ads and much entertainment alike."[38] At this stage, McLuhan sounded like Vance Packard, one of the "professional Jeremiahs," as Banham termed them. However, McLuhan did acknowledge that the mass media were "full . . . also of promises of rich new developments," and it is those which became the focus of his *The Gutenberg Galaxy* (1962) and *Understanding Media* (1964). McLuhan's influence was not at its greatest until 1966 and 1967, when his diagnosis of the technico-cultural condition seemed a plausible and convincing explanation of High and Late Pop culture.[39]

Where McLuhan and Banham differed most is in the importance they attached to subject matter and content. McLuhan's famous phrase "the medium is the message" conveys the minor importance he ascribed to content. Banham concurred with the significance of the medium—especially the potential of the electronic technologies to democratize, demolish class boundaries, and challenge conventional hierarchical distinctions—but he remained committed to his Courtauld art historical approach with its emphasis on content and iconographical meaning. As he wrote in 1967, "in general, the message is the sole reason why the medium exists, even if it is a new medium that facilitates the transmission of unprecedented messages."[40] Banham went on to remark that this was something that "McLuhan undoubtedly understands." Indeed, Banham's own thinking was clearly McLuhanesque at times: assumptions about the global village underpin a range of ideas from the radicalism of "A Home Is Not a House" to the tribal mobility of the transistor radio.

The 1960s was a decade of increased academic study of popular culture in Britain, but much of it continued the thinking of the cultural critics of the 1950s; indeed, the "major contribution" of the likes of Richard Hoggart and Raymond Williams was duly acknowledged. In *The Popular Arts* (1964), for example, Stuart Hall and Paddy Whannel argued that there was "a sharp conflict between the work of artists, performers and directors in the new media, which has the intention of popular art behind it, and the typical offering of the media—which is a kind of mass art."[41] Mass art was to be despised: it "destroys all trace of individuality and idiosyncrasy . . . and assumes a sort of depersonalised quality, a no-style"; furthermore, "the element of manipulation is correspondingly high." Banham deplored this type of thinking that meant the criticism would always be prejudiced against the sort of mass art he welcomed.[42] He retorted that "the intense sophistication and professionalism of Pop design is something that many people find hard to take: they would prefer a kind of Hoggartish spontaneity."[43] The prejudices of the 1950s were alive and kicking a decade later, and Banham remained a distinctive voice in his type of criticism.

At times closer to Banham was Tom Wolfe, whose collected writings, under the title *The Kandy-Kolored Tangerine-Flake Streamline Baby*, were published in the United States in 1965, and in Britain a year later. Many of the essays were concerned with fashionable society and social etiquette, but the section of the book titled "The New Culture-Makers" contained half a dozen essays—among them the title essay on car customizing, Las Vegas signs, demolition derbys, the disc jockey Murray the K, and the enigmatic record producer Phil Spector—which showed a real understanding of youth cults and Pop taste. The first three were subjects that also attracted Banham, and the two authors shared both a sensibility and an attitude to their subjects. The second ever contribution made by Banham to *New Society* was a review of *Kandy-Kolored* . . . in which he described the title essay on customizing as "a model essay in the anthropology of affluence that raises, *en passant* (Varoom! Varoom!) some pertinent questions about Public Bromide Number One: 'defending the quality of culture.'"[44] Against the charges from the cultural critics that Wolfe was nihilistic, Banham found him "full of affirmation and belief," upholding the kind of unorthodox but vital cultural practices about which Banham himself also wrote.

Banham praised Wolfe's "total, panoramic, wide-screen knowledge" of his subjects, and responded warmly to his prose style. Wolfe's stated intention was to find an equivalent to the energy and zest of his subject matter. The final paragraph of the introduction to Wolfe's book is a flamboyant example of his style. In response to a Las Vegas sign maker's categorization of his aesthetic as "free-form," Wolfe writes:

Free form! Marvellous! No hung-up old art history words for these guys. America's first unconscious avant-garde! The hell with Mondrian, whoever the hell he is. The hell with Moholy-Nagy, if anybody ever heard of him. Artists for the new age, sculptors for the new style and new money of the. . . . Yah! Lower orders. The new sensibility—*Baby baby where did our love go?*—the new world, submerged so long, invisible, and how arising, slippy, shiny, electric—Super Scuba-man!—out of the vinyl deep.[45]

Wolfe's "New Journalism"—a combination of reportage and creative writing—answered the Independent Group's call for an "involved aesthetic" and could itself be described as Pop prose. His aspirations were always closer to the novel than were Banham's, and his style was more "Las Vegas"—excess and impact—than Banham's "Los Angeles," with its "sense of possibilities" and diversity. However, there may have been an influence of Wolfe on Banham's writing. From the time of his regular *New Society* contributions, Banham's style did become more informal, but this could be put down not to an influence of Wolfe so much as to the growth of Pop sensibility. A significant difference was the two writers' attitude to high culture:

Wolfe tended to debunk it in *The Painted Word* (1976) and *From Bauhaus to Our House* (1982), whereas Banham always valued it as highly as the "noisy ephemeradae" of popular culture.

Some dismiss the writings of Wolfe and Banham—both the subjects and the treatment of them—as superficial and trivial. In Banham's case, this misses the point, in as much as he was writing about the expendabilia of the Second Machine Age in a manner appropriate to the subject matter. He was not elevating it to the realm of high art, but treating it in the manner it merited, and it merited serious (but not earnest) attention because it was a manifestation of a dynamic, technological culture of innovation, leisure, and pleasure. The architecture of Le Corbusier, Bucky Fuller, or the Smithsons needed to be written about in one way; the latest car styling, TV program, or paperback covers needed to be written about in another—with a concentration on style and meaning, and in an energetic style of writing which conveyed the pleasure and impact of the subject. Weekly publications such as *Architects' Journal, The New Statesman,* and *New Society* were appropriate vehicles for this type of writing.

Banham was well aware of different readerships, pointing out in 1981: "Obviously, the readers of *Art in America* were very different to those of *The New Statesman,* but probably nothing like as different as those of *Architectural Review* (monthly, cosmopolitan, intellectual, elitist) from the subscribers to *Architects' Journal* (weekly, local, business-like, work-a-day)."[46] This has led to a situation in which some people know Banham for one type of writing and subject matter, and others, for another, and partly accounts for the diversity of views about his criticism. Banham, however, saw no problem or contradiction: both durable and expendable writing were legitimate and necessary expressions of the same culture; both made sense of the Machine Age. Indeed, sometimes the apparently flippant could capture the spirit of the time better than the heavyweight:

The splendour (and misery) of writing for dailies, weeklies or even monthlies, is that one can address current problems currently, and leave posterity to wait for the hardbacks and PhD dissertations to appear later. . . . The misery and (splendour) of such writing, when it is exactly on target, is to be incomprehensible by the time the next issue comes out—

the splendour comes, if at all, years and years later, when some flip, throw-away, smarty-pants, look-at-me paragraph will prove to distil the essence of an epoch far better than subsequent scholarly studies ever can.[47]

The Independent Group's "both/and" philosophy is perfectly illustrated in Banham's approach to writing. At its best, it makes him the undisputed "historian of the immediate future."

Vehicles of Design Writing

Banham's design criticism is most commonly associated with *New Society,* the weekly social science magazine to which he contributed on a (more or less) monthly basis from 1965 until his death. In all, Banham published 235 articles or reviews in the magazine during the twenty-four-year period. Prior to *New Society,* a regular column was published in the politically Left *The New Statesman* between 1958 and 1965. Over these eight years, 110 articles or reviews appeared. Largely alongside *The New Statesman* was a column in *Architects' Journal* from 1956 to 1964, with occasional contributions thereafter. The "Not Quite Architecture" column averaged about eight a year over the eight years following 1958, before dropping down to one or two a year from the mid-1960s to mid-1970s. Predating all three of these regular columns were his *Art News and Review* pieces between 1950 and 1955, totaling fifty over the six-year period. The statistics reveal just how prolific a writer Banham was. In all, he published over 750 articles and reviews in his life, ranging from the scholarly through the theoretical or polemical, to the entertaining and instantly expendable. The four regular columns—*Art News and Review, The New Statesman, Architects' Journal,* and *New Society*—amount to just under 500 of them.

The least typical of what Banham became best known for were the *Art News and Review* contributions. The vast majority were reviews of current art exhibitions. However, under the heading "The Shape of Things," he did discuss a handful of design topics, among them the Courage Brewery corporate redesign carried out by Milner Gray and the Design Research Unit.[48] The number of articles on design and popular culture increased once Banham established his regular columns in *Architects' Journal* and *The New*

Statesman. In his *Architects' Journal* columns, the most frequent subject was architecture: of the ninety or more pieces he contributed to the *Journal,* half were on (mostly contemporary) architecture or planning issues. Aspects of contemporary design (Ulm's design school, Sottsass's work for Olivetti, and transistor radios), car styling and racing (the design of the Jaguar Mark X, and Formula 3 racing) comprised nearly a quarter of his output. In the 1950s and 1960s, he also wrote about popular culture films (*Dr Strangelove*), TV programs (*That Was the Week That Was*), science fiction (its relationship to architecture), science and technology (the theories of Fred Hoyle, and early flight in Britain), and miscellaneous subjects (including camping and cycling).

During the time Banham wrote for *The New Statesman,* architectural subjects accounted for 80 percent of the articles and reviews. Contemporary topics included new buildings by Stirling and Gowan, Cedric Price, and the Smithsons; the achievements of Buckminster Fuller and CLASP; and analyses of Sheffield's Parkhill housing scheme, Coventry Cathedral, and revivalism. Historical topics went from Le Corbusier, through Antonio Gaudi, to Lord Burlington and even Stonehenge. About 10 percent of the articles were on aspects of contemporary design such as the renaissance of British graphics, packaging and magazine design, the redesigns of coffee bars and restaurants, the styling of radios, and the shortcomings of the Council of Industrial Design and British design education. Cars and other forms of transport were occasionally featured: "The End of Insolence" was accompanied by pieces on the Consul Cortina, the experience of watching racing at Brands Hatch, an attack on the vintage car cult, and enthusiasm for the Moulton small-wheeled bicycle.

It was with the commencement of his regular contributions to *New Society* in 1965, under the "liberal and encouraging" editorship of Paul Barker,[49] that design criticism became more central to Banham's output. We now remember the late *New Society* as typical of the decade in which it was founded—the first issue was in 1962. It was consistently Left-wing and "progressive" in most spheres but, unlike previous publications of that persuasion, at home with an inclusive view of culture that went beyond the conventional high/low hierarchy. Banham's articles appeared in the "Arts in Society" section of the magazine that included such other regular contributors as John Berger, Peter Fuller, and Angela Carter—all were nonconformists who challenged orthodoxies and the status quo. Banham and *New Society*'s relationship was mutually beneficial: his witty and provocative contributions were perfectly suited to the ethos of the magazine; he thought himself "privileged" to be able to write about whatever he wanted and to have a receptive audience for his ideas.[50]

As with his two other regular columns—which effectively stopped when Banham started to write for *New Society*—more than half of the subject matter was architectural. Contemporary subjects ranged from architectural stars such as James Stirling, Norman Foster, and Frank Gehry, through new buildings in London and the mid-1960s avant-garde including Archigram, to more unexpected subjects like inflatables, eccentric pubs, and the mundane delights of London's Balls Pond Road. Historical subjects—including Bramante, Sir John Soane, Le Corbusier, Wright, and the Fiat factory in Turin—outnumbered contemporary subjects from the time he moved to the United States.

Other changes followed the move in 1976: not only were there more American topics—as one would expect—but there were fewer articles on contemporary design. Indeed, the *New Society* articles for which Banham is best known appeared during the years 1965 to 1975—almost exactly the period when he was at University College, London, full-time. There were some serious pieces on aspects of Pop art and Pop culture, but it was in these years his "flip, throw-away, smarty-pants, look-at-me" prose "distil[led] the essence of [the] epoch" when London was the Pop capital of the world.

Furthermore, a sense of international jet-setting and exoticness was added by articles about subjects in Canberra, Oslo, Buenos Aires, Paris, Berlin, and various cities and places in the United States. In *New Society* between 1965 and 1975, he wrote about the design of banknotes, paperback covers, potato chips, the decoration of ice cream trucks and Argentine buses, chairs and "furniturisation," kitchen appliances, Polaroid cameras, sunglasses as fashion accessories, the Native American bolo, California surfboards, the desert, Los Angeles, camp, *Thunderbirds, Barbarella,* Carnaby Street, the intimacy of recorded sound, the excitement of drag racing, customized and gentrified Minis, fur interiors in cars, the Mustang, Oldsmobile, Transit, Maxi and Capri, and the kinesthetic experience of Spaghetti Junction, the motorway interchange near Birmingham.

Second Machine Age Goodies: The Car

As an example of a product type, the car is a subject that Banham wrote about as early as 1955, and as late as 1986. Mary Banham once wrote of her husband that "his curiosity [was] particularly aroused by the unexpected and the incongruous and most particularly by anything with wheels and/or an engine."[51] Not surprisingly, therefore, cars reoccurred in his design writing, and in this part of the chapter we can survey how and what he wrote about them because this will provide an indication of his design values. As an example of another Second Machine Age goodie, Banham's writings about radios will then be discussed before returning to some further aspects of his writing about cars, and thence on to other subjects which further illuminate his values.

Earlier in the chapter we saw that cars played a role in three articles published in 1955: "The Machine Aesthetic," which appeared in *Architectural Review* in April; "Space for Decoration: A Rejoinder," in *Design* in July; and "Vehicles of Desire," published in *Art* in September. Taken together, these cover the key points of Banham's design thinking, including technology and continual change, the "mechanical sensibility," diversity and taste cultures, and styling and "symbolic iconographies." We have also seen that he returned to some of these points in his 1960 article "The End of Insolence." The period of the "insolent chariots" was coming to an end at the turn of the decade: "car styling is dead Pop-Art at present; the Minis and compacts buried an epoch, and cars ceased to be Number One status symbol,"[52] he declared in *Motif* in 1962. But this did not mean Banham lost interest in cars themselves, only that they were no longer the best vehicle for illustrating an argument about design and taste in a fast-moving technological society.

A fast-moving society appropriately produced fast-moving cars—an icon which continually attracted him. He wrote about car racing half a dozen times, and motor bike and sidecar racing once, in *Architects' Journal* between 1956 and 1963. In the first, he emotionally described being "dazzled with the noise and speed"[53] of the cars—a wholly Futurist sentiment which expressed the "mechanical sensibility." Leaving the reader in no doubt about what he felt to be its significance, in 1960 he described motor racing as a manifestation of "a technological culture letting off its surplus head of emotional and inventive steam"[54]—racing was one of the purest forms of "science for kicks." It also had a definite class dimension: the sport changed after the war, when it "let in a crowd of men who, having won a war by all means permitted under the Geneva convention, applied equally total tactics to motor racing. Victory now went to the canny, the iron-nerved and the diligent, not to the flannelled fool with the latest snob-job from Italy."[55] From being an upper-class pasttime, racing was opened up to a rising technocratic meritocracy: "People like me can identify with them in a way we never could with the *monstres sacrés* of the blood-and-guts epoch."[56]

Banham's enthusiasm for racing remained, and he occasionally sang its praises in both *The New Statesman* and *New Society*. In the latter, the enthusiasm and praise extended as far as drag racing in California and stock car racing in Sussex. In both cases, the speed and noise remained a constant appeal—"quiet motor sport is about as much fun as low-proof whisky or coitus interruptus"[57]—but a change was evident in his growing appetite for the social marginality of the activities. The heroism of the technocrat was being superseded by the anti-heroism of the outsider as Banham seemed to be seeking a kind of motor-racing *autre*. Drag or "grudge" racing was a "delinquent sport in its origins. It must have started with one hot-rod-crazy coming up alongside another at the traffic lights and saying something disparaging about the other's car. James Dean stuff."[58] There was, he continued, an undoubted "resemblance of some aspects of drag racing to that ultimate ritual of masculinity, the Draw."[59] Its appeal to Hell's Angels served to confirm its delinquency in the eyes of "slavering, bug-eyed social moralists from the East Coast." Not only was Banham's hatred of the East Coast intelligentsia applied to design and popular culture, but he developed a liking for marginality because it was both an undermining of the "codes and conventions" of established practice—in a way the equivalent to the radical nature of *architecture autre*—and an affront to good taste with its class connotations.

The class aspect was most forcefully stated in a 1972 *New Society* article, "Rank Values." Banham describes the scene at the about-to-close-down track in Sussex that he had visited: "Around the 300 yards of track, 37 wrecks were now distributed, two upside-down, one on its side, one burned out, two still smoking, several hissing quietly as their split radiators emptied, three hooked on the cables of the safety fence, five locked together by tangled metal at one turn, two seemingly friction-welded in eternal deadlock at the other, most immobilised because they had run over parts of their own internals and were reduced to fuming frustration." This could be described as "rank," meaning "detached from the bottom of an accepted value system": stock car racing was "not the bottom end of British motoring sport, it doesn't even connect with the official hierarchy [such as] . . . the Royal toffee-nosed Automobile Club." He was appalled that the "powers-that-be accept football rowdyism as an inalienable right of the labouring poor," but reject stock car racing because, in his view, it "involves the use of automobiles—something that the powers-that-be have always begrudged the labouring-poor."[60]

Stock car racing was subversive because the crowd goes to see cars, "top goodies of the consumer society, and the glowing symbols of Sunday-supplement success, reduced to a coughing, leaking, geriatric impo-

Drag racing (courtesy National Motor Museum)

tence. . . . It's marvellous, and completely shameless, the ultimate sadoporn of a product-obsessed culture. It is the terminal subversion of the power of material things, far more subversive of the established value system than most political or philosophical railings against materialism because it is seen to *work.*" The irony—if not contradiction—is that Banham himself had been guilty of writing about cars as the "top goodies of the consumer society"[61] and, even when they ceased to be top in the early 1960s, they remained seductive goodies.

From the mid-1960s, as he traveled regularly to the United States, Banham was more easily able to write about American automotive culture. These pieces were usually published in *New Society,* and discussed the design of the car as well as its social and cultural meanings, which were conveyed less by the "symbolic iconographies" of their detailing than they had been by the "insolent chariots" of the 1950s, and more by the car's marketing and overall image. The Ford Mustang, written about in 1967, is a case in point: "As a product success story it is probably the nearest Detroit has got to the Volkswagen class, complete with a built-in product mythology that carries conviction in the teeth of common sense—like, I can see *myself* laying dollars by to rent a Shelby Mustang in Denver, Colorado, drive it up to Aspen, and down through Las Vegas to the Fun City, Los Angeles, itself."[62] The article goes on to discuss, largely, the status of the car and the fact that "suddenly the Leisure People of the Age of Fun had found their transport of delight." Banham writes with apparent insider knowledge about the Mustang's design, social significance, and cultural meaning, and he writes as an immersed critic to the point of acknowledging his own desire.[63] One cannot imagine Barthes writing about a car in this way.

Second Machine Age Goodies: The Radio

Nor can one imagine Barthes writing about the radio in a way similar to Banham. Indeed, no critics at the time discussed this Second Machine Age goodie in as revealing a fashion. For example, when Banham wrote about radio design in *The New Statesman* in the early 1960s, he did not initially focus on the styling, but provided a context for the design:

Ford Mustang, 1967 (courtesy National Motor Museum)

I strode over the darkling dunes, down the deserted and wind-swept beach until the sea was breaking over my legs, and then, alone in the universe and the roaring surf, I listened—to the *Egmont* overture coming out of my top pocket. If it hadn't been a Beethoven Prom that was being relayed, the thought would never have occurred to me. But transistor radios seem to be so precisely the last fulfilment of the Romantic dream (a private music, cosmic in scale, drawn from the ether) that, as I say, it was compulsive.[64]

This anecdote makes a point about the condition of technology in contemporary society: the transistor radio "fulfils the cultural promise of mechanised sound" that had taken music from a public, social experience to a domestic service, and then on to a private experience that enabled a person "at a map reference on the Norfolk coast to hear the proceedings in the Albert Hall without being encumbered by any apparatus larger than a tobacco tin."[65]

This pointed to the nomadic condition of the Third, rather than the Second, Machine Age, but the thinking of radio stylists had not gone beyond the First—they were "loaded down with furniture-trade prejudices," still designing cabinets. A radical rethink by designers would lead to radios being equated with "pipes and cigarette cases and lighters that ride around in the interstices of our clothes, and are held in the hand when taken out." This meant that ergonomic considerations had to be addressed. The Murphy B585, for instance, produced a good sound quality, but was

. . . visually unconvincing—typography has got the better of plasticity so that the end-product looks like a rectangular box in a paper wrapper—but this is less important than its uncomfortable performance in the hand. The controls are awkwardly placed . . . and most comfortable compromises between an effective grip and a clear view of the tuning strip seem to result in the aerial (over two feet long when extended) becoming horizontal and caught up in the surrounding landscape. Even more unfortunate, the plastic of its case is thin and deforms easily under thumb pressure, giving an impression of flimsiness that is not reassuring (it may be perfectly strong enough in fact, but subjectively it inspires no confidence).[66]

The furniture background of most British and, indeed, European companies seemed to prevent them from thinking radically, and it was manufacturers like Sony, from Japan, "where transistor manufacture is liable to be in double harness with camera-production, electric shavers and other hand-held equipment," that pointed the way forward. This is critical design writing that not only assesses the product in use, but also supplies a context for the product type. Radio design, Banham concluded, is a "rich field for ergonomic experiment." In another *New Statesman* article in 1961, he declared that "ergonomics is where good design begins."[67] Here was Banham at his most rational, clearly influenced by consumer testing magazines such as *Which?*, which commenced in 1957, and condemning of the Council of Industrial Design's tendency to view good taste as a substitute for sound performance and good design.[68]

Predictably, the editor of the Council's magazine, *Design,* when discussing new radio design, concentrated on formal aspects: "The vitality of this model comes from the direct contrast of two different textures"; and he described a plastic portable radio case in terms of its "consisting of a central blue band and two identical cream coloured end caps [which] accentuate its slimness. The sound hole is exploited as a decorative feature on both sides of the set."[69] This Modernist, inward, formal orientation that focused on the object itself and its material and aesthetic properties, was not confined to British criticism. In 1962, a writer in *Industrial Design* discussed Braun's RT-20 radio as if he were analyzing an abstract painting:

An imaginary horizontal joins the top slots of the grille on the left with the Braun signature in the middle and top edge of the dial on the right. Similarly, the bottom slots of the grille are aligned with the bottom row of knobs on another horizontal. In the other direction, the vertical centerpiece of the grille stands parallel with the vertical row of knobs in the middle and the two vertical edges of the dial on the right. . . . Interruptions of a plain surface and functional attachments and inserts are invariably placed so as to emphasize the alignment and parallelism.[70]

This was not an approach to which Banham was ever sympathetic.[71] He had maintained since his earliest writing that "abstract is not enough."[72]

He wrote in 1961 that ergonomics "seemed likely to push matters of taste and aesthetics well into the background," but by the end of 1963, the Pop explosion around music and fashion led him to move away from rationalistic solutions to design, toward a reengagement with "symbolic iconographies" in which good design was more about "the radical solution to the problem of satisfying consumer needs."[73] Radios aimed at the affluent teenage market by this time, as Banham remarked in "A Flourish of Symbols," were "flashy and vulgar without being coarsely detailed."[74] Their symbolism was all-important—"you can go right round the product noting details that have been craftily and judiciously exaggerated in order to secure the transference of esteem from any and every relevant source." An illustration in the article labeled the references and meanings: "Pull-out aerial: science fiction symbol"; "Massive buckle: army-surplus symbol"; "Magic-eye tuning: miracle-of-electronics symbol"; "Clip-on component: special-equipment symbol"; "Twin speaker outlets: stereo symbols"; "Black leather: virility symbol"; "saddle-stitching: quality-product symbol"; "Wave-band selector: racing gear-change symbol"; "Huge, shiny knob: scientific precision symbol"; "Optimistic register of stations: romance of communications symbol"; "Type name and number: Mediterranean and missile-technology symbol"; "Heraldic device: snob symbol"; "Carrying strap: get-up-and-go symbol."

This was the kind of criticism which had a direct influence on the next generation of design critics and even architectural theorists—Charles Jencks, in *The Language of Post-Modern Architecture* (1977), for example, uses the same method of visual deconstruction, but applies it to popular architecture[75]—and it can legitimately be defined as Post-Modern. Pop design itself can be similarly labeled because it represents a rejection of almost all the principles and values of Modernism. Pop was design for the *Homo ludens* of the Second Machine Age.

The changes that were occurring in Britain around the mid-1960s were, indeed, considerable. The twin impacts of consumerism and Pop culture—fashion, music, design, art, advertising, and television—were transforming the British design environment. Growing affluence, especially among the young, ushered in the first generation of newspaper color supplements. Fashion and design featured prominently, and the notion of "lifestyle"—design and consumer goods reflecting and expressing a person's individuality and way of life—became as much an approach to design as the rejection of decorum and "good taste." Modernist and previously fashionable Scandinavian design came under attack: "For years Scandinavia has been the dominating influence on our furniture and furnishings. We have come to accept mass produced perfection in china, glass and furniture. . . . What we need is an unexpected touch of salt; something not off the conveyor belt."[76] Rational approaches, including consumer testing, were also criticized: "Poor design has become a target for anyone with a brick to throw: good design is treated as a sort of sacred cow. The attitude to function is racing to the same level of absurdity; testing is turning into an obsession. There are times when one longs to buy something plumb ugly and utterly unfunctional."[77] Fashionability and impact became the key ingredients of Pop design in the mid-1960s. Banham's 1950s theorizing about the role of expendability and the condition of "massive initial impact, small sustaining power" had found its time.

The icons may have been ephemeral, but Pop had a lasting effect on design theory. By 1967 even the Council of Industrial Design was acknowledging that design theory needed to be revised. The Council's head, Paul Reilly, wrote: "We are shifting perhaps from attachment to permanent, universal values to acceptance that a design may be valid at a given time for a given purpose to a given group of people in a given set of circumstances, but that outside these limits it may not be valid at all. . . . All that this means is that a product must be good of its kind for the set of circumstances for which it has been designed."[78] Reilly seemed to understand the implications of Pop and the new consumerism: a universal value system needed to be replaced by a relative, plural set of value systems—the Independent Group's "plurality of hierarchies"—that would ensure diversity and relevance. However, acknowledging a changing situation is not the same as welcoming it, and Reilly closed his article with a rallying call for the importance of "moral judgements. The need is again for discipline, for function, for commonsense in the midst of nonsense."[79] This sounded like the "ex-officers and gentlemen" tone of the 1950s, and further reference to the requirement to "sift the contributors from the charlatans when confronted with the challenge of Pop" did little to suggest that there had been any post-Pop or even post-Banham rethinking.

Banham was, of course, dismissive of talk about discipline, order, and charlatans, preferring to believe that "the consumer in the street is now the most powerful patron bidding for design skill, and he will, in the normal operation of a market economy, get the best."[80] Furthermore, the visual sense of the public that had grown between 1951 and 1961 had positively blossomed between the early and mid-1960s. When the perspective was from the Second—or even Third—Machine Age, the growth was phenomenal: "A lot of things have happened to people since the Bauhaus was young, things like junk sculpture, hand-held movies, Batman, action painting, the Hell's Angels, Surrealism, custom car shows, Op art, Henry Moore, Cinerama, and the like. And, as a result, people have become sophisticated—remarkably so—and far less visually prejudiced."[81]

Banham's list reads like a collection of his *New Statesman/New Society* pieces, and indicates the inclusiveness of his cultural model, from the Establishment high art of Henry Moore, to the delinquent and shadowy world of the Hell's Angels. But the point here is not about his own cultural model; it is the widespread cultural and visual changes in the 1960s which had resulted in a public no longer "dull and uncritical" in design matters, but capable of distinguishing "stainless from spray chrome at fifty paces." That the public had become more design-conscious is not doubted, but a public which can recognize styles and their sources is not the same as a public which understands the underlying value system of design in society. In his design criticism, Banham can be justifiably accused of mistaking visual sophistication for something arguably more important.

This is a criticism that can be leveled at Banham's final article on radio design, which appeared in 1974 in *New Society* under the title "Radio Machismo."[82] The transistor radio, he points out, in spite of its aural function, "is about the most advanced piece of technology that is bought on impulse and must therefore—in a market economy—have maximum visual impact at point-of-sale." That immediately confirms its position as a product of popular culture, but there had been definite changes in the design since the period of "A Flourish of Symbols," when the "trannie" was relatively consistent in appearance, and was positioned against "the rest of the radio business which was settled, middle class and adult."

A decade later, the product type was firmly established, its market had fragmented, and so, too, had the styling options. Part of the reason for the fragmentation was the development of pop music broadcasting: top forty singles on AM and album tracks on FM: "As soon as the split in broadcasting appeared, a new style of transistor emerged too—the first FM models began to back up, cautiously, toward the 'Good Design' type of styling, [but] more sculptural and less boxy in shape," presumably to reassure the consumer about the sound quality. More interesting is the fashion end of the market, where the styling is "more weird, more instructive, more unsettling. A visit to your local radio shop will reveal not only trannies combined with cassette recorders, but trannies *pretending* to be combined with recorders, pretending to be walkie-talkies, or large costume jewellery, or abstract sculpture, or space-equipment."

At one extreme is a small radio by Sony which Banham terms the "un-radio," but its gimmick also means it "lacks the physical bulk to make any positive statements visually." At the other extreme are Panasonic's "fashion models"—one spherical on a chain, one a cylinder with corners on a chain, and one a lop-sided bracelet that twists apart to reveal the speaker in one exposed end and the tuning dial in the other—which are worn as fashion accessories and aimed at the "girlie-bopper market."

Equally vying for attention is "male-chauvinist trannie styling [which] runs to a proliferation of knobs, switches and controls . . . and, above all, sub-sidiary indicator dials with genuine moving pointers and calibrated scales, over and above the actual tuning display." He attributed the source to "what's been happening to male chauvinist car-instrument panels of late; rampant diallism and the matte-black/metal-bead frame [which] can be found in many recent Fords and in the kind of super-car interior that turns up in cigarette advertising. Much of the idiom, however, comes over from 'serious' electronic gear like medical apparatus and recording stu-dio consoles."

Popular design could still be understood by reference to symbolic iconog-raphies which referred to higher status technologies. The iconographically most interesting radio was the Panasonic GX300, which, Banham argued, went beyond a mere army surplus look, was "absolutely crammed with ad-vanced circuitry," and was "armour-plated," looking like it "would go on working under three feet of Mekong mud." It was the Vietnam War iconog-raphy that intrigued him: "That's not just any old Vietnam . . . the whole style suggests the good, clean, innocent early-Kennedy days in the Delta when it was not a question of mutinous GIs slogging it out waist-deep in ir-rigation ditches, but of chopper-borne 'advisers' bearing down on the local insurgency-manifestations with concentrated high-technology weaponry-expertise—and keeping their boots clean. Now that's pretty advanced nos-talgia." Banham's final sentence was a stab at professional, "good taste" designers: "Never suppose that real-life product-styling is the genteel exer-cise they teach you at the Royal College of Art"!

Use and Symbolic Expression

It is also quite typical of Banham's design criticism during his "purple" *New Society* period between the mid-1960s and mid-1970s. One of the reasons he was attracted to writing about design was because it dealt with "the problem of use as well as, or parallel with, or on top of or underneath, the problem of symbolic expression, or what ever else you would like to call it."[83] He offered this opinion in 1964, and it remained relevant for most of his design criticism. Indeed, the combination of "use" and "symbolic expression" explains much about his writing, yet it appears at first an unremarkable, and even conventional, pairing. Superficially, it might seem to echo Modernist pronouncements of the 1920s. In 1923, Gropius was writing about the responsibility of the Bauhaus designer "to educate men and women to understand the world in which they live and to invent and create forms symbolising that world."[84] This "symbolic expression" of the machine age, Gropius added in 1926, was to grow out of a concern with "use."

But for Banham, use was a decidedly social aspect of design, not just a quasi-ergonomic one in which an object's "nature"—by which Modernist designers tended to mean the graspability of a handle or pourability of a spout, for example—led to well-proportioned, even handsome, but usually abstract form. Modernists may have supposed that "symbolic expression" (when it was admitted) and "use" led, via "systematic research," to "type-forms" whose "characteristic, primary forms and colours" were "readily accessible to everyone," but for Banham, type forms were fundamentally meaningless, and signified little more than a grafting of a classical aesthetic onto the products of industry. As early as 1951, he had argued that "Aesthetic value is not inherent in any object, but in its human usage,"[85] a sentiment that links up with his comment about abstract not being enough: "It is not the ratio which matters, but the use which is made of it."[86]

Design was about the product being socially used: there was virtually no distinction—certainly not one of significance—between use and symbolic expression. The two coalesced in what we might term "cultural usage" or "cultural expression," in which "use" was not to be seen as something objective and ergonomic, but as something social, cultural, and, literally, meaningful. In the early years of the decade he had claimed that "ergonomics is where good design begins," but with the arrival of Pop culture, both ergonomics and conventional notions of "good design" seemed of relatively little importance compared to social expression.

"Radio Machismo" and similar articles[87] illustrate well Banham's belief that design criticism "depends on an analysis of content, an appreciation of superficial rather than abstract qualities, and an outward orientation that sees the history of the product as an interaction between the sources of the symbols and the consumer's understanding of them." Equally, they show the critic dealing in the "language of signs" and being immersed enough in his subject matter to be able to deconstruct the product's "symbolic iconographies."[88] Banham achieves all this with insight and wit—they are typically Banhamesque in their entertainment value, and confirm Banham as the prime historian of the immediate future.

Their limitation is one that applies to most of Banham's design writing— they are largely uncritical of the values in which design operates. His appetite for novelty—and desire to be astonished—could eclipse wider cultural, social, and political values. An acceptance of novelty and innovation can be seen as a way of being part of the technological culture of the Second Machine Age; equally, it can be part of a system of design that encourages materialism, waste, and social one-upmanship. The political dilemma Banham experienced in the 1950s in relation to enjoying American popular culture, yet being politically Left, was never fully resolved in his writing or, one suspects, in his thinking. Phrases in "Radio Machismo" like "market differentiation" and "splintering market" come out of marketing, a development in design in the 1970s which became a boom in the 1980s, and a tendency about which Banham had major reservations. He remarked in 1980 that "products have become less interesting": marketing had displaced "creativity and originality."[89] Product styling may still have been a genteel exercise in the 1970s, but as enterprise culture took hold in the 1980s, marketing became a conscious, indeed central, ingredient of designing and a major part of the designer's mental equipment.[90] Reflecting his loss of interest, the number of *New Society* articles Banham wrote on contemporary product or graphic design dwindled to half a dozen from the mid-1970s until his death.

Customization and the Consumer

Banham had always had some reservations about the power of producers, whether manufacturers or designers with their "Napoleon complexes,"[91] because producer-determined standardization and predictability could overwhelm consumer-involved creativity and originality. For example, the mainstream Bauhaus approach to standardization resulted in sameness of outcome—all products looked alike. Banham much preferred the Detroit approach, which offered not only symbolic iconographies and a regular model change, but also, on any one model, options and, therefore, a degree of consumer choice as an integral aspect of design. He had learned from the Smithsons' 1956 "House of the Future" that standardization need not result in Modernist repetition; Archigram confirmed the lesson in their "Plug-in City" and "Capsule Homes" to the extent that, by 1965, Banham had rejected the idea of standardization as "the relentless repetition of an invariable product,"[92] in favor of the Detroit approach of "interchangeable options (e.g. Chevrolet with a choice of 17 bodies and five different engines)."

A central part of Banham's perceptive "Unavoidable Options" article of 1969—an article which again shows Banham as the informed and immersed critic rather than the detached academic—contrasts the approach to options manifested in the design and marketing of the Austin Maxi and Ford Capri. The Maxi's advertising stressed that it was "the car that killed the options game" in an attempt to "bamboozle the notoriously gullible liberal-graduate division of the A/B market."[93] Conversely, "every Capri flourishes a boast that not only is it, like the Mustang, the 'car you design yourself' but also what *kind* of car you designed yourself." Options included engine size and engine tune, normal and high-performance running gear, interior fittings, and exterior trim. In practice, the options game signified the possibility rather than the actuality of consumer choice: this made it perhaps closer to the idea of the "controlled" rather than the "responsive" environment—the Capri, like the Mustang and Detroit autos before it, represented limited choice rather than full consumer participation.

Car customization epitomized active participation. Banham first wrote about it in 1961, when his subject was the American Warshawsky catalog,

Austin Maxi, 1969 (courtesy National Motor Museum)

Ford Capri, 1969 (courtesy National Motor Museum)

the Original Warshawsky & Co., 1916 So. State St., Chicago. Ill. 60616

hrome Plated Deluxe Full-Wheel Covers for All Cars

Page from Warshawsky catalog, 1960s (courtesy Mary Banham)

which was full of "the odds and sundries to mop up the difference between what Detroit supplies and what the heart desires—comfort cushions, safety-belts, car-snoozers, gear-lever extensions . . . outside tail-pipes, simulated spot-lights, fender skirts, Custom grille sets, leather jackets, forward-look rear-view mirrors (no kidding), back-window tigers with stop-light eyes, and the rest of it."[94] The Warshawsky catalog was nothing less than "a guide to the first folk-art of the do-it-yourself epoch," an epoch that Second Machine Age technology and affluence was bringing about. When the "kit-of-parts" approach of the catalog was combined with the Pop sensibility of *Homo ludens* and direct experience of the West Coast, car customization came to epitomize the potential of design in a "live technological culture."

The first manifestation was the 1966 article "Notes Toward a Definition of U.S. Automobile Painting as a Significant Branch of Modern Mobile Heraldry,"[95] a title which played on T. S. Eliot's *Notes Towards the Definition of Culture* (1948), which had been reprinted in 1962 and 1965. Banham was making a point about what constituted live culture, as opposed to the obsolete cultural forms and attitudes expounded by high cultural critics, and the article was written in a style which parodied an academic treatise. As well as continuing his interest in iconography, it also showed that the "paint jobs" on dragsters and hot-rodders were, as Tom Wolfe had argued, a popular and vital art form which demonstrated the nonprofessional's "creativity and originality" and ability to usurp the standardization of mass production. Other articles on vehicle customization for a decade from the mid-1960s made similar points, and ranged from the "baroque and peacock-hued vehicles of the imagination" (California custom cars), though customized Minis and the use of Velvetex (a sprayed-on, velvet-like material) as an external finish, to the decorative designs on English hand-painted ice-cream trucks and the decorativeness of Argentine buses (the country's "most original contribution to the world scene" of Pop art).[96]

Software Thinking

The most sustained argument for participation came in "Softer Hardware" an article of 1969 that appeared in the Royal College of Art's journal, *Ark*. Banham once again praised customized cars, but he made the point that their creativity and originality needed to be viewed in relationship to their

Paint job on dragster (courtesy National Motor Museum)

standardization. There was a danger of seeing hot rodding, for example, as a form of noble savagery, based on the misguided belief "that there should always be absolute originality of design as well as absolute craftsmanship."[97] However, in practice "the vehicles are largely assembled from selections permuted from a very wide range of ready made components, standardised (but highly specialised) accessories and ingenious bolt-on or drop-in adaptors." What was required was mental dexterity and creativity to synthesize the mass-produced and the hand-crafted. In Banham's judgment, the mixture of

. . . the personal and the prefabricated, the standard and the special has probably given more genuine self-expression and more self-fulfilment to more hot-rodders than any amount of totally original craftsmanship would have done. We aren't all endowed with absolute originality, we have different talents differently arranged: a situation like this enables you to concentrate on your areas of talent and get the rest done by experts. You can make up as much of an original life style as you want and conform where you feel the need.[98]

What Banham was describing was an extension of Eames's "off the peg" approach, modified by Cedric Price's commitment to change and adaptability and Archigram's "clip-on" and "plug-in" experimentation, with flexibility in projects such as "Control and Choice" that enabled the radicalism of the responsive environment in which software predominated over hardware.[99] "Softer Hardware" was an approach which fitted perfectly the "interdeterminate participatory open ended situations"[100] that were supposedly symptomatic of the anti-hierarchical culture of the late 1960s. Participation and involvement were symptoms of the new technological condition, manifested not only in design but also politics. The radicalism of late 1960s student politics was making its mark on Banham.

Banham could have explained the shift he was describing in terms of the dawning of a new Machine Age—the Third—but in "Softer Hardware" he explained it as a breaking out of the mental shackles of "the cast iron prison of the factory system," by means of "smaller, handier, less obstructive, more adaptable machinery," into "post-industrial society."[101] Design thinking had suffered historically from a "hardware" obsession: "so powerful has been the thrall of the factory system mythology that . . . we have praised the Bauhaus for designing light fittings that show complete alienation from the human user. Praised them for being cheap and simple to produce in the factory—but failed to damn them for producing intolerable glare in the home of the consumer."[102]

The criticism is similar to that made in the contemporaneous *Architecture of the Well-tempered Environment,* which also attacked the First Machine Age's concern with an object-centered notion of design, rather than as viewing objects as means of enablement. Even the "design classics" of the Second Machine Age, although less symptomatic of the factory aesthetic, had the same type of limitation: "designed objects no longer have the impact they did a decade ago when an Eames chair, a Braun mixer, a Citroen DS 19 looked like manifestations of a future golden age."[103]

The reason "we are alienated even from these classic objects" was partly a result of their "perfect boring reliability": they may have been beautiful, but they were also predictable. The fault may not be with the products, but with the thinking behind them: "the classic approach to industrial design is no longer valid: whether that classic approach was, say, an Ulm student refining a product until it was indistinguishable from any other Ulm product, or Harley Earl restyling a Buick right round the bend, the approach was still simply the reworking of a given product. . . . Both visualized a giant industrial mechanism, remote from the life and control of the ultimate consumer, with the designer or stylist acting as an intermediary or interpreter between the two."[104]

Banham himself had, of course, upheld this system in the 1950s and first half of the 1960s, but the changed cultural climate was revealing its limitations. The conventional design process made consumers too passive: designers needed to take account of human participation, and design for the "ingenious adaptability of the human user"[105] in the way that Price and Archigram had posited in their middecade projects. Furthermore, designers had to break loose from their rationalistic method: "we still proceed by the classic method, which I suppose goes back to Descartes, in some way, of isolating a function, devising a mechanism to serve that function, and then progressively refining that mechanism." This results in "a proliferation of re-fined and highly specialised single function objects."[106]

In the liberating, open-ended mood of the late 1960s, people have begun

... to rediscover the reunifying virtues of the footloose flow of time in motion. ... Hence the fascination of temporarily rallying structures—Archigram's walking city or an inflatable dome—which mark the point in time where we meet to participate in this or that, and then move on. Or, to turn from the collective to the individual, the fascination of the customised car, which binds time and technology ... in a personal statement which is, in some vital though often hidden essential, as unique as its maker; symbol of our growing but barely understood capacity to shift the whole balance between men and their objects, to mould the world of equipment nearer to heart's desire.[107]

This quasi-Futurist/Situationist/Pop sentiment, if translated into an ap-proach, had as radical an implication for design as *The Architecture of the Well-tempered Environment* had had for architecture—it would be a move toward recasting design in terms of creating "fit services for hu-man activities."

Banham's radical rethinking about "fit environments" had started in the early 1960s. Arguably, his design radicalism stretched back even further. As early as 1956, he had contrasted the established Platonic approach to de-sign, with its belief in universality, timelessness, and the absolute beauty of primary forms, with Moholy-Nagy's imperative, expressed in an aphoristic-like statement, that "man, not the product, is the end in view."[108] It was a key quote for Banham, and reappeared in his writing on several occasions.[109] In his 1956 article, he had dismissed the Platonic approach in design as "in-human," whereas Moholy-Nagy's approach established a healthy distinc-tion between means and ends.

Just before he wrote "Softer Hardware," and at the time of its fiftieth an-niversary, Banham reassessed the reputation of the Bauhaus. His main the-sis was that our understanding was formed too much by the texts and objects the masters produced, which tended "to freeze a single flash-bulb image of moments in time, and leave in darkness most of what happened before and all of what came after."[110] The texts had been allowed to become definitive statements rather than evolving ideas-in-progress, and the objects had become crystal-clear visions:

> . . . the task of a design school is to produce designers, not objects. To create a particular thing, say a smooth hemispherical lampshade, might represent a tremendous educational experience to a student whose previous training had been in Expressionist decoration, but might simply be lazy intellectual self-indulgence to another who had already got the Bauhaus message. The end-products of design tasks were merely the vessels of the educational programme: the proof of the pudding is not the dish.[111]

Banham's own witty analogy is as instructive as Moholy-Nagy's, but the latter's aphorism is again evoked as a way of encapsulating an approach to design which Banham summarized as "No longer a more cultured or refined version of an object already existing—a more beautiful coffee pot, a more efficient light-switch—but more the provision of a service to satisfy a human need. That might be coffee, or light, or guidance for the blind, or a shelter in underdeveloped economies, but the material objects were the means, not—as in European design—the end."[112] This was radical thinking about design and design education, and countered cultural traditions, lores, and conventions. It parallels his ideas about architecture and "fit environments," explored in chapter 4, and continued his rejection of the "selective and classicising" approach which inevitably emphasized form as an end in itself. Banham's pudding test meant that a designed object is a means to some specified and personal end, such as, in the case of a customized car, "winning races, or picking up girls, or astounding your friends, or enraging the middle aged," as he put it in "Softer Hardware."[113]

The custom car may be the solution to relatively specialized needs. The standard family car could also be thought of in software terms. In his important 1965 article "A Home Is Not a House," he presents the car as a component in the "expanded field" of architecture; furthermore, it "could play the role of a travelling power plant," and it had already become an "essential component in one non-architectural anti-building that is already familiar to most of the nation—the drive-in movie house. Only the word *house* is a manifest misnomer—just a flat piece of ground where the operating company provides visual images and piped sound, and the rest of the situation comes on wheels. You bring your own seat, heat and shelter as part of the car."[114]

This represents a different way of thinking about the car. In his Independent Group days Banham had seen it in terms of the meeting of a symbolic iconography with an expendable aesthetic which, together, could become that "means of saying something of breathless, but unverbalisable, consequence to the live culture of the Technological Century." A decade or so later, he was no longer gazing *at* the car, but viewing it as an enabling device and standard-of-living package—as software. It was typical of Banham's "both/and" approach, however, that one way did not exclude the other, and so the software approach did not wholly *replace* an interest in symbolic iconographies, or new models, or customization, or the Futurist experience of drag racing.

Software thinking did, however, *displace* Banham's former thinking in the later 1960s. There are several reasons for the change. Primarily, it was a consequence of the "expanded field" approach which transformed the underlying values of *Theory and Design in the First Machine Age* into *The Architecture of the Well-tempered Environment*. It was also part of the "direct-participation, real-space, real-time involvement-aesthetic"[115] sympto-

Customized car (courtesy National Motor Museum)

matic of Late Pop culture and the commitment of architects like Price and Archigram to flexibility and change.

The effect of the student radicalism of 1968 had also made an impact, and so when Sir Kenneth Clark's *Civilisation* was broadcast in 1969, Banham attacked it vehemently in *New Society* for its "obsession with elaborately wrought objects," for being "thing-stricken."[116] Clark represented a culture, "now in rejection and disarray," which cared more for "material objects . . . than human values" because "things, being in infinite supply, are always much more predictable than ideas (which are what civilisation used to be thought to be about)." Banham's criticism applied not just to Clark's connoisseurship, but also to the "well intentioned Bauhaus rubbish"[117] which arose from object-centred, "hardware" thinking. Finally, he admitted he was finding products "less interesting. The kind of build-up of creativity and originality which their styling exhibited before 1968 burnt out in the aftermath of that year."[118] For someone who happily admitted that he "enjoys being astonished,"[119] design ceased to be sufficiently astonishing, certainly from the mid-1970s.

One of Banham's most entertaining and radical articles from the late 1960s that attacked "things" is "Chairs as Art," which appeared in *New Society* in 1967. He invented the word "furniturisation" to describe "how previously unselfconscious and virtually invisible domestic items suddenly become great, monumental objects which demand attention, dusting and illustration in colour supplements."[120] Seating had suffered from the process to the extent that "the area worst blighted by furniturisation lies right under the human arse. Check the area under yours at this moment. The chances are that it is occupied by an object too pompous for the function performed, over-elaborate for the performance actually delivered, and uncomfortable anyhow."[121] The process started from the flawed premise—an "infantile malady of design"—that for "the function 'sit' there had to correspond a separate 'sit-thing' to serve it." One of the major limitations of this process is that is was reductivist, and led designers to think of chairs just as things for sitting on, when "that is the very least of the things that happens to a chair. Most chairs are so little sat in that they could never justify themselves economically on that score." He went on to list their other uses:

Not only are they bought to be looked at as cult-objects, they are also used for propping doors open or (in French farce) shut. They are used by cats, dogs and small children for sleeping in: by adults as shoe-rests for polishing or lace-tying. They are used as stands for Karrikots and baby baths; as saw horses; as work benches for domestic trades as diverse as pea-shelling and wool winding; and as clothes hangers. If upholstered and sprung, they can be used for trampoline practice; if hard, as bongo drums. They are persistently employed as stepladders for fruit-picking, hedge-clipping, changing lamp bulbs and dusting cornices. And, above all, they are used as storage shelves for the masses of illustrated print that decorate our lives. . . . And the more a chair is anatomically well-designed for sitting in, the less use it is the other 95 per cent of the time.[122]

Banham may have been entertaining, but he was also making a point. Designing could become a very linear process which left all sorts of inductions unquestioned. The radical designer, the designer of the "fit services for human activities," would avoid object fixation and think more in terms of an expanded function and performance: "If rational inquiry were to prevail, it would show that chairs are simply detached units of a commonwealth of horizontal surfaces on which any number of objects, including the human fundament, can be parked." A radical approach would lead to a series of horizontal surfaces of varying degrees of softness, but this lateral solution would not be adopted because "we are a thing-struck culture" in which we accord precedence to "appearance over performance, form over function." Hardware dominated software when, in fact, the better solution would have been "a service, not thing."

Banham acknowledged that the chair "has been a symbol for as long as there has been western civilisation . . . loaded with overtones of westernisation . . . of white man's justice, of corporate power . . . of godliness, of episcopacy, electrocution, elegance (as in the sedan-chair) and, chiefly, of aesthetic self-expression second only to the fine arts."[123] This might reasonably have led him to accept the inevitability and, perhaps, necessity of cultural symbolism but, typically, he merely regretted that "cultural habit prevails over technology" and predicted that "pure technology would probably bring furniture to an end, or at least render it invisible,"[124] if only we could make the "mental breakthrough." Expressed in this way, we can see that "software" thinking, like the appeal of Moholy-Nagy's aphorism, was another way of maintaining a fundamental distinction between architectural and technological "habits of thought," as he had defined them in "Stocktaking" at the beginning of the 1960s, and as he had concluded in *Theory and Design.*

The Politicization and Academicization of Design Writing

A disillusionment with certain aspects of design could also be detected in "Household Godjets," a brilliant *New Society* article of 1970. As in "Chairs as art," Banham contrasted the increasing objectification and aestheticization of design, which he viewed negatively, with a technological approach which emphasized 'service" rather than "things." Writing about the contemporary fascination with household appliances, he mused:

. . . symbolic they certainly are; powerful ju-jus of the electronic jungle that daily encroaches on the civilised clearings that have been made by oppressing women, enslaving the servant classes, and maintaining western values generally. Not for nothing are domestic appliances symbols of "affluent futility," second only to the automobile. They represent one of the more embarrassing collisions between traditional art-culture, and the demotic culture of the way we actually live, and are often set up as symbols of the two-culture clash in much more general terms than that. So when someone raises a small cheer for technology, he will be ridiculed by the guardians of European culture (architectural division) as a "defender of the Frigidaires."[125]

The reference in the last phrase goes back to 1959 and, as we saw in the introduction, Banham's attack on Italian Neo-Liberty and Ernesto Rogers's spirited reply. It provides a reminder of the continuing "Stocktaking" "two-culture" context of technology in opposition to aesthetics and professional lores and conventions. Banham, as one would expect from previous texts such as "The Great Gizmo" of 1965, was fully in favor of appliances and the way they help to transform the environment (whether the wilderness or the home), but deplored the application of the classical aesthetic—"good design"—to these "household gods of the Eurobourgeoisie": "Good Design is the style you use when you want to sell something to the educated, culture-seeking A/B top end of the market—which is visibly where the main commercial action still is in appliance manufacture." He was intrigued by what happened when "Good Design, [which] in its abstraction and Platonic idealism and aloofness and classicism relates to the most central and elevated concepts of established western culture" confronts the domestic reality of use: "is a power-whisk lying on the floor in a pool of spilled mayonnaise among the shards of a glass mixing-bowl a beautiful object? Is a skillet crushed with the mortal remains of bubble and squeak? Or a toaster with a miniature mushroom cloud of blue smoke hovering over it?" His conclusion was that

The cost of bringing the Absolute into the kitchen is to soil it. . . . [T]he pretensions of Good Design require us to bring the noblest concepts of the humanistic tradition into direct confrontation with scrambled egg and soiled nappies, and that's not the sort of thing humanism, historically speaking, was designed to cope with. The big white abstractions must be devalued, ultimately, by these associations with dirt and muck and domestic grottitude. Congratulations, then, Ladies of Taste and Leisure, you could be doing a better job of lousing up western culture than was ever achieved by deriding great art or making rude signs at philosophers! [126]

Here, once again, is Banham the anti-classicist, making a serious point about the meaning and associations of the classical aesthetic in an undeniably witty way. With its dig at the "Eurobourgeoisie," there is also a class element in the piece, and there is certainly a more positive gendered perspective than had been usual in his writing. Banham's belief in the progress of technology and the benefit of appliances was passionate:

When I remember how my old rural relations and acquaintances had to cook (in wall ovens that made the kitchen an inferno) or do the laundry (over a steaming copper that rotted the linings of nose and throat) even in the 1940s, I would defend the delivery of a workable gas-cooker or electric washing machine . . . against the claims of any three masterpieces of modern architecture you like to name. And when I read (in the Architectural Association *Quarterly,* where else?) that "these gadgets are so numerous, so complex and so difficult to repair that the life of the American housewife is increasingly at their mercy . . . and room for unstructured free behaviour becomes increasingly small," I have to acknowledge that there is at least one kind of blithering silliness that only my own sex can perpetuate—no woman could write such rubbish.[127]

This critical, gendered perspective was new in Banham's writing, and shows some influence of the women's movement in the post-1968 years. However, the perspective was not the one most typical of feminist thinking in the 1970s. For example, in *Housewife* (1974), Ann Oakley reported that "the amount of time housework takes shows no tendency to decrease with the increasing availability of domestic appliances, or with the expansion of women's opportunities outside the home."[128] Indeed, she cited an increase of seven hours a week in a 1971 survey from one carried out in 1950. Nevertheless, few would argue that the chores themselves were as physically strenuous and exhausting as those performed during the First Machine Age, the measurement implied by Banham.

The politicization of design theory and history was beginning in the 1970s. Indicative of the changing time was Tomás Maldonado, who forsook the progressive rationalism he had preached at Ulm, for *Design, Nature, and Revolution: Toward a Critical Ecology,* as his book was titled when translated into English in 1972. Works on gender and design followed.[129] Banham did not contribute to this tendency beyond, arguably, "Household Godjets,"[130] but continued—in his *New Society* pieces—to write the sorts of entertaining and insightful essays for which he had become known.[131] He wrote very few pieces on aspects of design history after the mid-1970s, preferring to concentrate on architecture and the United States.

Given his passionate involvement in architectural polemics and history, and his great interest in design, it is surprising—and certainly regrettable— that Banham did not produce a book on design in the 1970s or 1980s, especially because the early 1980s was a mini boom time for serious and scholarly publications on design and design history, among them Jeffrey Meikle's *Twentieth Century Limited: Industrial Design in America, 1925–1939* (1979), John Heskett's *Industrial Design* (1980), Adrian Forty's *Objects of Desire* (although published in 1986, it had been completed in 1980), Penny Sparke's *Consultant Design: the History and Practice of the Designer in Industry*

(1983), and Arthur Pulos's *American Design Ethic: A History of Industrial Design* (1983). Banham had reservations about the growth of design history as an academic subject, commenting in 1986 that "after a mere decade or so, [it has] begun to enclose itself within a wall of canonical works in which to exercise increasingly Byzantine hermeneutics."[132]

Banham's own "book" contribution was restricted to a representative collection of thirty of his architecture and design essays and articles titled *Design by Choice*, edited by Penny Sparke and published in 1981. Sparke's essay offered a *résumé* of Banham's career that, unintentionally, gave the impression of something at an end. A foreword, written by Banham himself, also looked back but did contain a justification for his design criticism and journalism:

Never having believed that journalism is a waste of talents and energy that ought to be reserved for more serious matters, I have treated whatever has come my way, not with levity (as some have claimed) but with the enjoyment of finding things out, and gratitude for having an audience to tell them to. Offence has been taken, I know, by those who insist that profound matters must be discussed only in "serious" language, but having seen the mess that a Marx, a Mumford, a Levi-Strauss, a Galbraith or a Freud (let alone a Hoggart) can make by trying to handle light matters with heavy equipment, I felt I had license to do the other thing—and a better chance of being understood.[133]

His concern about being understood expressed an anxiety about the "academicization" of design theory and history with which he felt no sympathy.

Banham's feelings about design writing in the 1980s are expressed most clearly in a *New Society* review of Ralph Caplan's *By Design* (1983), a book developed from essays which had appeared in publications such as *Industrial Design* and *Design*. Caplan was a contemporary of Banham's and a former editor of *Industrial Design*, as well as a director of the Aspen conference. They shared similar outlooks and values, and what Banham writes of Caplan, to a great extent applied also to himself. The review starts with Banham issuing a warning that "there is a risk this book could miss that section of academe that needs it most: design historians—it's not written in Barthes-Marx, so they'll claim it's incomprehensible."[134] This jibe is followed by a statement about the book which applies equally to many of Banham's *New Statesman* or *New Society* pieces: "Caplan, however, does not set out to write history or theory, simply a book 'about design'—itself a period concept weighty with unacknowledged ideology." However, the historicizing does not lead to a major criticism—such as Caplan's writing now being anachronistic or irrelevant—but to an assertion that "it is the unacknowledged ideology of what begins to look like the most important period in design history so far: the last quarter century of professional corporate design."

In what follows, "Caplan" could be replaced by "Banham": "Once aboard this trend . . . he rapidly absorbed the value-system on which it operated (known at the time as 'common-sense') but added to it an illuminating capacity for smart one-liners, remembered anecdotes and telling instances. . . . Caplan's value in this context was the ability to go beyond simple anecdotage into the wild blue yonder—the intellectual vacuum where a body of theory ought to have been but wasn't." A quote from a Caplan article on the chair—a parallel approach to Banham's "Chairs as Art"—elicits the judgment that these "40-odd words say as much on that topic as do the four *thousand* words and scholarly apparatus of Joseph Rykwert's celebrated essay on 'The Sitting Position' . . . [because] to say it again, his line is not scholastic but worldly-wise and pragmatic. In pursuing it, he reveals a body of professional lore that suddenly begins to look like some kind of historically coherent whole. It is riddled with inconsistencies (that's life) and practical self-deceptions (the price of survival in the trade)."[135]

The final essay in the book deals with the design of Charles and Ray Eames. Banham criticizes it because Caplan does not explain the Eameses' design process: this might be due "either to the ineffability of genius—or (and?) that intellectual cavity where a theory of praxis might have been looked for. But before the dialecticians run off shouting 'We told you so,' they should have a good look at what Eames achieved, and what this book has to set forth; for both show, to salutary effect, how far that generation of designers could get on a combination of professionalism, prejudice and pragmatics—known at the time as common sense."[136] The proof of the pudding, as

Banham might have put it, is not a Marxist-Structuralist discourse on bourgeois eating habits!

It is design's great loss that Banham did not weave together the elements of design theory that he elucidated between 1955 and 1970—expendability, pleasure, symbolic iconographies, cultural usage, participation, customization—into a coherent and developed "common sensical," immersed, and socially embedded Post-Modern theory of design. An emphasis on cultural usage and "Softer Hardware" could have led to a radical book which, supplemented by case studies, would have been a significant and timely contribution to design thinking.

On reviewing an anthology of *New Society* articles, Peter Conrad attacked Banham, in his contributions to the book, for showing "an aesthete's indifference to politics. Ravished by appearances, enchanted by form and scornful of function, the aesthete has an interest in preserving things as they are."[137] Conrad may be right about the aesthete, but he is wrong about Banham. Anything more than a superficial reading of his design criticism reveals Banham's human-centeredness: Conrad wrongly equates a fascination with the visual, with Formalism—the visual as an end in itself. However, the criticism of indifference to politics does appear plausible, especially from the perspective of the increasing politicization of academic writing. The capacity to be astonished could lead to brilliant insights, passionate enthusiasms, and compelling prose; it could also lead to an uncritical acceptance of the new as if it is an inevitably good and natural spin-off of a politically neutral technology. "Re-equipping," scrapping, and obsolescence are seen solely as technological issues, not as ecological, political, or ethical ones. This could make Banham appear reactionary, and a consumer capitalist lackey.

But one should not lose sight of Banham's major achievement in design writing: embedding design in a social and cultural context—its "outward orientation," which brought into play reception, if not more than creation and production—and his emphasis on cultural meaning which opens up into deconstruction and the "expanded field" of visual culture, as opposed to previously defined boundaries relating to hierarchically perceived disciplines such as product design, graphics, film, auto sports, and so on. It

resulted in an approach that has become an established Post-Modern discourse, and is widely practiced in cultural studies.

However, two aspects distinguish Banham from much of today's visual culture writing. First is his belief that value judgments are an integral part of a
critic's role. In the same paper as the quotation which commenced this chapter, Banham asserted that "Much as one may say that criticism is to explain,
to make clear how and why the building has got to be the way it is, evaluation is a very important function at the moment."[138] He tended to think the
same about design criticism, sometimes explicitly reaffirming his belief in a
plurality of hierarchies in which judgment was possible and necessary—for
example, when discussing borax styling in the mid-1950s, he pointed out
that it was "a design language which can be used badly or well."[139] Explicit
judgements became fewer from the late 1960s, but they were usually still
implicit, and it is seldom difficult to work out Banham's own position.

Second, whereas recent and contemporary design writing can be overly
academic and "scholastic," Banham's evident "enjoyment of finding things
out," relishing the excitement and uncertainty of the present, and belief
that "man, not the product, is the end in view" ensured not only that he became the "historian of the immediate future" but also that there was in his
writing a fully human and deeply humanistic presence which reminds us
that design is not about mere objects, or even objects and their "symbolic
iconographies," but objects as part of human use and social activity in a living, even vital, culture.

CONCLUSION
Changing His Mind or Having It Both Ways?

CONCLUSION
Changing His Mind or Having It Both Ways?

We have discussed Banham's writing and ideas, which ranged through his revisionist *Theory and Design in the First Machine Age* (1960) and *A Concrete Atlantis* (1986); his Futurist sensibility and attitude with its promise of a "profound orientation towards a changed world"; belief in playing "science for kicks" as part of a quest for an *architecture autre;* the radical *Architecture of the Well-tempered Environment* (1969), which supposedly produced "fit environments for human activities"; Independent Group theorizing about the Second Machine Age and popular culture; the impact of Pop culture and the "sense of possibilities" which culminated in *Los Angeles* (1971); and his preferences and prejudices about such matters as conservation, revivalism, and low tech. The conclusion focuses further on the significance of Banham's values, including those relating to technology and class, and considers the role he ascribed to the historian, as well as assessing his performance in that role. It is instructive to position his ideas in relation to two key architectural historians with whom he was directly involved: Nikolaus Pevsner and Charles

Jencks—Banham wrote his Ph.D. dissertation under Pevsner; Jencks wrote his under Banham. This line of descent of historians born in 1902, 1922, and 1939 enables us to trace both continuities and changes of value and attitude across three generations.

Pevsner: Love and Hate for the Lieber Meister

Banham's relationship to Pevsner has been clearly visible at several points in this book. Chronologically early was Banham's proclaimed sense of "betrayal" after the War when Pevsner threw his weight behind the Picturesque faction, supported the Victorian revival, praised the Festival of Britain, and espoused the virtues of an Englishness that Banham saw as parochial and self-regarding. In the mid-1950s to early 1960s there was Banham's rejection of Pevsner's bias toward "selective and classicising" *Sachlichkeit* Modernism with the latter's claim of its historical inevitability and assumption of moral superiority. A "Second Machine Age" major disagreement between them was whether James Stirling's Leicester Engineering Building represented "wilful Expressionist idiosyncrasy" (Pevsner) or was "one of the most extraordinary spectacles" in contemporary architecture (Banham).

Banham greeted the publication of *The Sources of Modern Architecture and Design* (1968) with the criticism that "the narrowly cultural approach to its history established by historians of Pevsner's generation now begins to look *simpliste* and skimpy." That generation seemed to be as obsolete as a generation-old Futurist house: "*My* generation of historians," concluded Banham, "has quite a job to do."[1] Indeed, away from the realm of high culture, they held diametrically opposed responses to pop culture, an opposition typified by the 1950s American auto, which, for Pevsner, was vulgar, crude, "un-British [and] un-European," whereas for Banham, it was an "expendable, replaceable vehicle of popular desire."

There would have been even greater disagreement on individuals such as Bucky Fuller, Cedric Price, Archigram, and Frank Gehry had Pevsner considered it not beneath his historian's dignity to write about them. Los Angeles would have appalled Pevsner and represented the demise of all that was good about the First Machine Age—collectivism, restraint and universality rudely replaced by individualism, Pop exuberance, and the freedom of choice: egalitarianism dreams overturned by the hedonist nightmares that money could buy.[2] For Banham, Pevsner represented the dangers of never changing your mind—a comprehensive and absolute position hardened into a rigid and predictable orthodoxy that failed to adapt to changing circumstances and new conditions.

In the wake of the strong disagreements about "post-Modern anti-rationalism" and the "neo-Expressionist" architecture of James Stirling—around 1966 to 1968—the low point in their professional relationship occurred in *The Architecture of the Well-tempered Environment*. Banham chastised Pevsner for ignoring the Belfast Royal Victoria Hospital in his *Pioneers* "in spite of the fact that in all except the purely stylistic sense it was far more modern and far more pioneering then anything that had been designed by Walter Gropius, the hero figure of the book, before 1914."[3] He went on to attack Pevsner for failing to "draw attention to the environmental innovations in one of the buildings that he does emphatically find worthy of mention," Mackintosh's School of Art in Glasgow. These criticisms, Banham was at pains to point out,

. . . are raised not out of hostility to Pevsner . . . but as a complaint against the general design-blindness of the whole generation of historians of modern architecture whose writings helped establish the canons of modernity and architectural greatness in the present century. . . . Narrowly pre-occupied with innovations in the arts of structure, they seem never to have observed that free-flowing interior spaces and open plans, as well as the visual interpenetration of indoor and outer space by way of vast areas of glass, all pre-suppose considerable expense of thermal power and/or air-control, at the very least.[4]

He berates Pevsner—and his generation, including Sigfried Giedion—for this major flaw. Here is Banham at his most radical in terms of method and value, and at his greatest distance from Pevsner.

But there are two qualifications that must be made. First, Banham's method, values, and position in *The Architecture of the Well-tempered Environment* are not typical of his more general revisionist position, as expounded in books from *Theory and Design* and *Guide to Modern Architecture,* via *The New Brutalism* and *Megastructure,* to *A Concrete Atlantis* and the unfinished *High Tech.* Second, his criticism conceals the important underlying assumptions about modernity held by not only Pevsner but also by Banham himself. For example, both abhorred architectural historicism because it did not express the technological age: to revive, as Banham put it, is to "abdicate from the Twentieth Century." He warned against the "infantile regression" of Neo-Liberty in 1959; two years later Pevsner was voicing his concern about the "Return of Historicism," thanking Banham for bringing a number of worrying cases of what the latter termed "historicist defeatism" to his attention.[5] Both held fundamentally Modernist values about technology and its relationship to architecture progress and the zeitgeist.

Pevsner's belief in the zeitgeist was an orthodox Modernist one, reflected in his statement in *Pioneers* that Gropius's buildings before the First World War—the model factory and the Fagus factory of 1911—"mark the fulfilment of the style of our century; [they are] entirely representative of the spirit of today."[6] Banham's attitude to the zeitgeist is more complex—as well as less consistent over time. The "early" Banham of the 1950s interpreted it as one of the "art-historical miasmas [which we can put] back where they belong, and recognise that they are the cloaks of ignorance. Ideas do not bumble about in the abstract, looking for somewhere to settle. They are formulated in the minds of men, and communicated from man to man. The zeitgeist is primarily a record of our ignorance of the communications that took place in any particular epoch."[7] This anti-Pevsnerian, even anti-Modernist account is rationalistic and reductivist to the point of ignoring the commonality of values and the significance of iconology. However, this was not an opinion Banham seemed to hold for long. He did not subscribe to Pevsner's exclusive notion: indeed, there should be "multiple aesthetics"—perhaps shaped by a pragmatic, radical, or Pop approach—legitimate so long as they resulted from an open-minded attitude. Ideally, they involve a "profound reorientation towards a changed world" and, quintessentially, reveal a deep commitment to the "technological century," a belief that bound together Banham and Pevsner, however different their architectural versions of the zeitgeist.

Pevsner and Banham's disputes and disagreements may have revealed major differences, but they were *relative* differences; oppositions within Modernism. A perspective on this is provided by the historian David Watkin, who in his book *Morality and Architecture* (1977) refers, in passing, to the Royal Victoria Hospital that featured in Banham's *Architecture of the Well-tempered Environment.* Banham's argument had been that the hospital's "dismally and irrevocably" old-fashioned appearance belied its technologically advanced design, thus revealing the schizophrenia and inconsistency of the age in which it was built. Watkin may have agreed with Banham that "the point we should note is that the sophisticated system of air conditioning was conceived as part of a building designed in a wholly traditional Victorian style," but concluded, significantly, quite otherwise: "the presence of advanced technology need not determine the form of the building which contains it. The architect can certainly decide that he wants his building to look like a building that contains advanced technology, but that is an aesthetic decision which we should be free to accept or reject as we wish."[8] Here was a fundamental opposition to Banham's (and Pevsner's) belief that a building should express something of the technological condition of its age.

In the introduction to the book, Watkin informs the reader that *Morality and Architecture* "grew out of a lecture that I first gave at Cambridge in 1968"[9]—a significant year and a significant place in terms of the reception of British Modernism in general and Stirling's History Faculty in particular. The book was published just after Banham had left for the United States, an occurrence that could be seen as symbolic and even symptomatic of the shift of power and changed agenda of the British architectural scene. Almost as a parallel to Pevsner's *Pioneers,* which started with Morris and ended with Gropius, *Morality and Architecture* commences with a discussion of Pugin and leads on to Pevsner. In fact, a third of the book is devoted to Pevsner (under whom Watkin, like Banham, had studied), concluding that the "substantive views expressed by Pevsner" were "praise of industrialism while disliking capitalism; desire for egalitarian uniformity; dislike of any avowal of aesthetic criteria; belief in 'Hardness' and in 'Honesty' with nothing deliberately aiming at beauty."[10] These closely resemble the sort of criticisms Banham himself had made of Pevsner. Watkin makes the criticisms in the context of generous praise for Pevsner's "prodigious learning, energy, and enthusiasm for his subject"[11] in the same way that Banham, in *The Architecture of the Well-tempered Environment,* had made it clear that his own criticisms were "raised not out of hostility to Pevsner."

Yet Banham's lengthy review of Watkin's book in the *Times Literary Supplement* was almost wholly damning. He in fact agrees with Watkin that "there is nothing inherently improper or repellent about Watkin's intention to censure Pevsner for Whiggish historicism in imputing direction and purpose to history, and importing morality into architectural judgement. . . . We have all had our difficulties in not tittering at his insistence that . . . discovering a *Zeitgeist* in every single period [is] misleading, constricting and often glibly rhetorical, and have been dismayed by his persistent blindness to the importance of some kinds of architecture and design."[12]

Banham continues by picking up a number of relatively minor points in Watkin's text—consistency on dates, for example—then moves into his major criticism. That essentially centers on two words: totalitarianism and historicism. Watkin had drawn attention to Pevsner's use of "totalitarian"— Pevsner, in the last paragraphs of *Pioneers of the Modern Movement,* writes that the "new style of the twentieth century . . . because it is a genuine style as opposed to a passing fashion, is totalitarian"[13]—and claimed it related to beliefs about political totalitarianism. What Pevsner meant by it was "universal"—a word he substitutes in the 1949 edition of *Pioneers* and in subsequent editions.[14] Watkin is right to draw attention to the relatedness of political and cultural values, although Banham points out that it "might not have meant exactly what Allied wartime propaganda and Joe McCarthy had made it mean twenty years later."[15]

The second term—"historicist"—exercised Watkin more. Pevsner and Banham, as was customary in midcentury architectural circles, used it to mean "period revival"; Watkin introduces the philosophical meaning, via Herbert Butterfield and Karl Popper, of "holistic and pre-occupied with the future."[16] Historicism encourages, Watkin argues, "moral relativism because of its belief that the spirit has a totally new and homogeneous expression in each epoch, which thereby renders obsolete the cultural, religious, moral, and political patterns of previous epochs."[17] Pevsner's historicism undermines "our appreciation of the imaginative genius of the individual and . . . the importance of artistic tradition";[18] furthermore, his employment of the term is a "misuse."[19]

Banham was hostile to Watkin's strictures, and responded with characteristic gusto:

In Watkin's single-valued world . . . it seems that words can only have one meaning ever, and for this reason Pevsner's next worst crime after that "totalitarian" has to be his use of the word "historicism" in a sense different to that intended by Karl Popper. It has always been perfectly clear what Pevsner means by the word, and it is difficult to find a more convenient label to describe what he is discussing when he uses it, and it nowhere impinges on its other meanings, including those used in discussing historiographical techniques, but Watkin responds with the kind of epistemological seizure exhibited by Levi-Straussians when someone uses the word "structural" to describe the way a building, not a mythology, is put together.[20]

At the level of language and terminology, he made his point effectively, demonstrating a literalness in Watkin's criticism that concentrates on the letter rather than the spirit. However, the substantive point is one that Banham can only—in an understated way—acknowledge to be true, remarking that "Pevsner's kind of historicism in its English context is part of everybody's Pevsner-problem, not just Watkin's."

Banham's Watkin problem was that *Morality and Architecture* reduced history to texts and words: Watkin is being a bad historian for not conveying a sense of living history, but only its carcass; and, furthermore, for not acknowledging Pevsner's considerable achievement in identifying the legitimacy and influence of *Sachlichkeit* Modernism when he did: "Never mind whether that particular style is 'legitimate' or 'totalitarian': it remains an observable fact that, increasingly, throughout the whole of the two middle quarters of the present century, it has become the visibly dominant style of 'our times' and will continue so for some while, since there is no sign of an

effective replacement for it yet." Therefore, it was "historically irresponsible" for Watkin to pretend that the architecture promoted by Pevsner
"has not encapsulated the architectural ambitions of our powers-that-be as
surely as High Gothic, or Anglo-Palladian, or any other dominant style carried the equivalent ambitions of the bishops, earls, kings or princes of their
times." All this reveals that, for Banham, history was not just about method
and objectivity, but a compelling and passionately held argument:

> The relative blackness of pots and kettles is not the point at issue here: Pevsner's per-
> formance is. He got it right. . . . It behooves any of us who disapprove of his method-
> ology, or dislike his particular favourites and are concerned at his omission of *our*
> particular favourites, to recognise that he produced a picture of the architecture of
> his own time which was useful, applicable, and has had demonstrable predictive power.
> If it was Whiggish historicism, or the kind of moralising that comes naturally to a self-
> made Lutheran, that made it possible to do that, then so much the worse for Butterfield
> and Popper.[21]

    Banham rejects the relatively easy option of some form of political (or the-
oretical) correctness, and goes for judgment and persuasion. At least, he remarks, "a good Popperian" would approve of Pevsner for having offered a
"falsifiable hypothesis about the main style of twentieth-century architecture in the Western industrialised world, and having seen that hypothesis
resist falsification for forty years"! And as for whether Pevsner recognized
his own historicism: "The matter, I suspect, is one of indifference to Pevsner;
he might even be pleased to be a historicist in that sense. He has never, that
I can remember, denied his intention to push certain views of history."[22]
    Thus Banham disapproves of Watkin for two reasons. First, that he is a
type of historian concerned with method at the expense of a vital historical
sense: he is more interested in form than content, and more inward- than
outward-looking. Banham describes the historian as someone who can

> . . . cut through the glitter and confusions of "the Brownian movement of random
> events" to reveal patterns (true or false) that lie within. The discovery and delivery of such
> generalising patterns is one of the services that historians render to the lay members of

society. Indeed, the ability to generalise convincingly and usefully is one of the tests of a great historian, and is also one of the reasons historians' reputations are so perishable, since changing circumstances will undermine the conviction and utility of any generalisation.[23]

This shows, as in *The Architecture of the Well-tempered Environment,* an appreciation of historical relativism that was not Banham's most consistent virtue. But one suspects that his main disapproval was his suspicion of Watkin's own position, in particular the latter's complaint in *Morality and Architecture* about the exclusion of Lutyens from Pevsner's *An Outline of European Architecture* (1943) and his subsequent evaluation of Lutyens as "one of the two or three most brilliant and successful architects England has ever produced."[24] Banham comments that "Pevsner (like me) would find [this evaluation] preposterous."[25] As far as Banham was concerned, Watkin was one of the "lunatic core of the New Architectural Tories" who were discussed in chapter 5, and thereby an enemy of modernity and Modernism along with others such as "the present editors of the *Architectural Review* [and] Charles Jencks and the 'Post-Modernists.'"

The difference in age between Watkin (born 1941) and Banham is almost exactly the same as that between Banham and Pevsner. However, the differences in architectural values between Watkin and Banham are undeniably greater than those between Banham and his *lieber Meister.*[26] Pevsner and Banham may have had major differences of opinion from the early 1950s to the late 1960s, but in the post-Modern era, Banham seemed to realize major differences were not synonymous with opposing sides, and he became increasingly aware of what he shared with Pevsner. When he half-jokingly announced in 1961 that "I am a 'Pevsnerian' by 15 years' constant indoctrination,"[27] it had been truer than he realized, not just because of the sentimentalism of affection for his "first admiration among historians,"[28] but because, for all his disagreements with Pevsner, both shared Modernist, historicist assumptions about architecture and did not sufficiently question their own values.

Jencks: Hate and Love for the *Enfant Terrible*

Banham's relationship with Charles Jencks was also a revealing one, as we saw in chapter 5, and there is no need here to rehearse Banham's opinions about Jencksian Post-Modernism. However, the issue of historicism and Modernist values had arisen in an interview Jencks had conducted with Banham in 1975.[29] Jencks expressed his reservations about what he saw as the "tired," if not anachronistic, values of the recently published *Age of the Masters,* the update of the 1962 *Guide to Modern Architecture.* Jencks rather naughtily asked whether the new section on power—added to the sections on function, form, construction, and space—meant political power as opposed to mechanical services, as might befit the contemporary situation. In other words, Banham's *Masters* carried the values of a pre-1968 text and took no account of the sort of material that Jencks had included in his own *Modern Movements in Architecture,* published in 1973.

But Banham was adamant that he was writing about something which could still be defined as "Modern Architecture (with a capital M and a capital A)." The sort of crossovers and hybrids that interested Jencks did not lead Banham to rethink his categories: "although I do see plenty of blurred lines, I still think hard-line modern is something else." Jencks encouraged him to expand on some of his underlying historicist values: "Anyone who knew me could deduce a good deal of autobiography from the book, obviously the weight put on Mies for instance, the relative weight put on the German tradition generally which I think shows my training and background, and also the period in which I grew to understand modern architecture in the first place." However, it seemed that, as for Pevsner, Banham was indifferent to the accusation of historicism and might also have been "pleased to be a historicist in that sense." Without apparent regret or concern, he admitted that "I don't think I am sufficiently transparent to myself, I'm not Philip Johnson for instance, to be able to discuss my own taste in a manner that would be profitable."[30]

Banham's love/hate for his *lieber Meister* has obvious overtones of a son's relationship to his father. As a father figure—albeit an academic one—Pevsner's reserve and restraint must have been difficult to take for an adventurous, academically freewheeling and Pop-inclined seeker of "science for kicks." But wouldn't these characteristics make him an ideal father figure for an equally adventurous (etc.) son?

Of course, the main problem is that the son did not follow in his father's footsteps, forsaking the solid and eternal verities of Modernism for the show-off clevernesses of Post-Modernism. Banham's misgivings started not with Jencks's *Modern Movements in Architecture*—which is not wholly surprising, given his involvement with Jencks's Ph.D.—but with *Adhocism* (written with Nathan Silver), which, although published in 1972, Banham discusses in 1976. Thus, this first tiff predates the searing attack on *The Language of Post-Modern Architecture* by over two years. What Banham dislikes about *Adhocism* is what he sees as the false distinction between the technocratic (Modernist) engineer and the bricoleur, the improvisator taken from Lévi-Strauss's *La Pensée sauvage* whom Jencks and Silver presented as a model of post-Modern participation and direct action. Banham, no doubt with his own engineering background in mind, rejects the distinction as false: "the Lévi-Strauss engineer, conceiving and procuring everything specially for the project, may possibly exist in exam papers at the Ecole Polytechnique, but nowhere else in engineering as generally understood."[31] The bricoleur, taken out of context from Lévi-Strauss, is being trumpeted by Jencks and Silver as "the patron saint for their 'new' gospel of improvisatory design."

Banham finds it hard not to be condescending—not that he tries particularly hard—about the bricoleur as a Third World noble savage, "pottering around in his *bidon* in the *barriada,* improvising, as like as not, a wheelchair out of Coke cans and dismembered roller-skates—so that his neighbour, legless and blinded after the attentions of the local junta, can get to his begging pitch outside the Hilton Hotel"! What offended him even more was that the bricoleur was a new model of the designer who has "also come in patron-handy to ecomaniacs and alternative technologists, to architectural dissidents reacting against the sophisticated rigor mortis of 'system building,' to Popperian proponents of piecemeal planning as against comprehensive redevelopment."[32] Not only was Banham unconvinced by the argument; he also—rightly—interpreted the bricoleur as a further attack on Modernism.

An exchange of letters followed Banham's review. The first, from Jencks, made the substantive point that Banham was writing about technology in terms of the engineer in the laboratory apparently working in an improvisatory way, and not addressing the macro scale: "Does Banham really believe that the managers, researchers and inventors involved in the technostructure are really creating new combinations of off-the-peg parts every day?"[33] Jencks, accurately, emphasized the point that most of our technology is specialist and specific, and ended the letter with a jibe: "As Banham used to write in exasperation in the margin of my thesis, when I was his student, 'get it right!'" Banham, in his reply a week later, maintained that technological innovation developed "*not* with the all-new design, but by bricolating the tried and trusted ones already to hand."[34] This still overlooked the level of the technostructure, concentrating on the adhocism of invention rather than the specialization of production.

A final reply by Jencks explained further the grounds of his convincing argument, pointing out to Banham that "even his mini-cycle is Purist, integrated, and made by specialised parts. Look downwards, sirrah, you are sitting on the truth everyday!"[35] Banham was being beaten at his own game and in his own style. The last word, given to Banham and following on from Jencks's letter, weakly noted that the difference in their interpretations, "as Charles has often noted before, is one of 'changing the caption under the picture'—at which he is such an adept." In passing, one might argue that changing the caption is a more creative act than ignoring it, as Banham had claimed to do when scrutinizing books by the likes of Moholy-Nagy around the time of the war.

The *Adhocism* review and letters show something of the inflexibility of Banham's thinking about technology, and possibly even something of the way he had assimilated engineering's lores and conventions. It also shows, like his review of Watkin's *Morality and Architecture,* that he might appear reactionary or, at least, old-fashioned to a new generation of historians and critics.

Banham was indiscreet about Jencks in a review of the latter's *Late-Modern Architecture* and *Skyscrapers-Skycities* in 1980. He says little of substance about the books—*Late-Modern* has a "slightly dated flavour" and

Skyscrapers "is one of those pretty picture books . . . which no amount of learned prefaces can save from its own pretensions"[36]—but concentrates instead on Jencks's reputation. There is a predictable fatherly rebuke when Banham complains that it is

. . . infuriating . . . for me to discover that the only direct quotation from my writings in *Late-Modern* is wrong! Still, "Get it right, Charlie" is an old song now, and none of us is perfect, and he will almost certainly write a stiff letter to the editor pointing out that he has been misinterpreted again—or perhaps he won't this time, because he really doesn't need to be so nit-pickin' paranoid about his reputation any more. He is one of the fixed stars of the critical firmament now, almost certainly doomed to receive an AIA medal and—dammit—he's 42![37]

There is a feeling that Jencks is today's architectural historian, and Banham yesterday's, and a reputation had been handed on: "The life of an *enfant terrible* is tough—I know, I used to be one. Quite apart from the constant pressure to be more and more terrible (or infantile), there is the certainty of being over-run from behind by younger and more terrible *enfants* before you've had the time to enjoy the role. This is widely believed (among close watchers of the game) to be the impending doom of Charles Jencks, the Man Who Gave You Postmodern."[38]

J. M. Richards testified in his obituary to Banham's "carefully cultivated image of the *enfant terrible*,"[39] and there can be little doubt that he found the idea and image appealing. In describing his friend James Stirling as a "plain blunt Liverpudlian *enfant terrible*" whose "bloody-mindedness" and "dumb insolence" threatened the genteel, conservative establishment, there are resonances of characteristics that also apply to Banham himself.[40] It raises the question, too, of the extent to which he consciously thought of *himself* as an enfant terrible or Angry Young Man in his younger days. The enfant who grew up to be an Angry Young Man became the independent-minded, nonconformist, anti-Establishment, radical, Pop academic in the 1960s—a true man of his time with many of the strengths and weaknesses and virtues and vices of that decade. Banham goes on to question whether Jencks's standing as an enfant terrible has "already been overwhelmed by the all-new British antimodern polemicist, David Watkin of Cambridge, author of the sternly sententious *Morality and Architecture*."[41] However tongue-in-cheek the suggestion, there is a serious point here that history is not just texts and scholarship, but about personalities, power, and position. Jencks is of the opinion that Banham subscribed to a kind of "apostolic succession" regarding historians—except that the holy orders could be amended or even overturned by the succeeding interpreters of the faith.[42]

Banham seemed to be worried that, however immaculate his conceptions, "Watkin's relentlessly holier-than-thou approach is the true wave of the future." This thought brought a sense of proportion to Banham's criticism of Jencks, just as Watkin's criticism of Pevsner helped put Banham's own relationship with his "beloved teacher"[43] in perspective. Criticism turns to praise: for all his fundamental disagreements over Post-Modernism and architectural values, Jencks is

. . . by preference an instant commentator on current events, an addict of novelty, a compulsive trend-spotter, a historian of what happened between his last two heart beats. In a ponderous and slow-moving art like architecture, anyone who is tolerably up to date is apt to be mistaken for a mad visionary by the 99.999 per cent of the profession who did not have this morning's brainwave. Much of what he said first needed saying anyhow, and he occasionally gave himself time to do the research before saying it. And every word of it was said by a man who loves architecture and gets his main kicks in life from talking/writing about it.[44]

This outpouring of affection and respect not only seemed genuine, but could almost be interpreted as autobiographical, for it virtually perfectly describes Banham and, presumably, how he himself would like to be remembered (apart from the aside about the thoroughness of the research!).

There is, therefore, ambivalence in Banham's relationships with Pevsner and Jencks. Ultimately, however, he can be seen as conceptually closer to Pevsner, given his fundamental revisionism of his teacher's Modernist values, and closer in terms of attitude to the "post-68," Post-Modern Jencks—Banham wholly identified with his student's "love-it-all pursuit of the new."[45]

The Anti-Establishmentarian and Class

Part of the identification with the enfant terrible was the scope it allowed for opposing the Establishment. In the 1950s, the Establishment had been represented by Pevsner, the "Picturesque faction," and even the *Architectural Review* or, alternatively, by Herbert Read and the ICA, which generated among the Independent Group a ". . . hostility to what seemed to be established lines of political/architectural patronage and the stuff that flowed from the '51 Festival of Britain."[46] Symptomatic of what the Group despised about the British cultural establishment, Richard Hamilton recalled the time when, at a tribunal to hear Victor Pasmore's appeal to be a conscientious objector, Kenneth Clark adjudged that Pasmore was "one of six best artists in England." It was the idea, Hamilton explained, that "an establishment of this kind could be so precise about what English art was." This was "anathema" to those who sought a dynamic, innovative, and progressive culture.[47]

Furthermore, in Banham's mind, the progressivism of culture was a class issue. The year 1964 was important for him in this regard. With the growing confidence of Pop culture that year, following the "youthquake" the year before, Banham published his "Atavism of the Short-Distance Mini Cyclist," which directly addressed his cultural background and ideals in relation to class, and also compared two architectural schemes—the designs for the Roundhouse and Fun Palace—which encapsulated attitudes to class.

Banham defined his background as "working class": "I've had for what I thought the best reasons in the world to describe myself in print as a 'scholarship boy' to define my position for people who don't know the English social scene."[48] The culture in which he recalled he grew up in Norwich was not a sophisticated, "capital C" one, but was

. . . American pulps, things like *Mechanix Illustrated* and the comic books (we were all great Betty Boop fans), and the penny pictures on Saturday mornings; I know the entire Chaplin canon back to front and most of the early Buster Keatons, not through having seen them at the National Film Theatre under "cultural" circumstances with perfect air-conditioning, but at a 1d or 2d whack, in a converted garage (practically next to Nelson Street Primary School which was the rest of my cultural background, not to mention the speedway). I was a bob-ender in the days when a bob-ender meant a certain class of person doing a particular kind of thing on a Saturday night).[49]

Banham was not simply being nostalgic in stating this, but was making the point that "the thing about this background is that it really was the live culture of a place like Norwich at that time in the thirties." Thus, the mass media boom in the 1950s meant that "we were natives back home again."[50] As we saw in chapter 2, this put Banham and his ilk in opposition to the British cultural Establishment, who, generally brought up within high culture, could assume only that this enthusiasm for Pop was an example of "sophisticated people meddling in unsophisticated matters," as Banham had remembered Basil Taylor's phrase.

But it was important to acknowledge that "the English educational system, as you get towards the top of the academic pyramid, cuts certain people off from their origins, their ability to remember what they were like. I am not talking about people who don't have Pop origins—I'm talking about people like myself who have come up the educational ladder hand over hand."[51] A danger here would be to sentimentalize one's cultural background, and this is what Banham accused writers such as Richard Hoggart of doing: they romanticized traditional working-class culture and were antithetical to the Americanized popular culture that Banham had enjoyed since the 1930s. According to Banham, what was happening in the 1960s was that the working class was gaining power and influence, but this was a double-edged sword:

The rise of the working classes to political power has rested upon someone equipping them with the right kind of responses to social and political situations, manipulative responses. The desire to do something about the situation had to be attuned to basically middle class systems of government, both at the national and even more at the local level, in order to give the working class, not the automatically defeatist response of regarding government as "they," but the traditional "we own the joint" middle class response of regarding government as "us."[52]

So, as well as remaining "sentimentalised" as a form of noble savagery, the working class was also in danger of becoming "culturalised" into middle-class modes of operating, partly because "the Left is culturally still in the grip of traditional conservative institutions such as universities." In both cases, the Establishment was controlling the identity of the working class.

Banham cast the Pop movement of the 1960s as the dynamic alternative for working-class culture: it represented "the day of the outsider" and "the revenge of the elementary school boys" (and girls), as he described it in 1965.[53] The Establishment had not come to terms with the new cultural wave, but "progressive people, the people who are going to have to make social action, have got, somehow, to learn to ride with the real culture of the working classes as it exists now. It's no good these well-meaning people deluding themselves with trad jazz and Morris dancing and reed thatching and all that. It is time for them to try to face up to pop as the basic cultural stream of mechanised urban culture."[54] "Well-meaning" people included architects: "There are certain aspects of pop culture which architects find extremely hard to take. The most obvious one is expendability."[55] This takes us on to the comparison of the Roundhouse and the Fun Palace as class-related designs—designs in which "two radically different conceptions of a live popular culture are on offer and they are genuinely incompatible."[56]

A resonance of the "days when socialism was something done on the working class from a great height" infected the approach of the supposedly progressive Centre 42—the arts center founded by the playwright Arnold Wesker.[57] Wesker had acquired the Roundhouse in north London, a large railway shed that has "the accolade of inclusion in J. M. Richards's 1958 *The Functional Tradition* (the industrial revolution decontaminated by Georgian Group sentimentality) and its location on the ground is a perfect topographical symbol of hand-out culture: up the hill are the eggheads of Hampstead, east and south are the deprived ethnic minorities of Camden and Kentish Towns." The location may have been symbolic; so, too, was the building—it was, Banham thought, an overly expensive and unfunctional building for its purpose: any organization that was willing "to lumber itself with a bandaged-up load of Victoriana needs its head examined. . . . [A] clear site . . . would give them twice as much usable accommodation for half the money, and a chance to square up to the real problems of the working class without a chorus line of Knights and Dames confusing the issue by viewing it through Ivy-coloured spectacles."[58]

Centre 42's approach had "confirmed everyone's worst suspicions" that the project was run by "Establishment types doing culture on the poor, by deciding to immure themselves in that made-over, makeshift monument from an OK period in the past." The cultural contrast was with Joan Littlewood's Fun Palace project, which was given decidedly nonmonumental form by Cedric Price, whose "kit of parts" was an entirely appropriate solution to a progressive and dynamic culture: "What matters is that the various activity-spaces inside the Fun Palace will not be fossilised in a single architectural schema that may become functionally out of date in five years and is out of fashion already, like Centre 42's theatre-in-the-roundhouse." Banham eagerly looked forward to a "gigantic junk-playground for sophisticated grown-up people to whom the handling of mechanical tackle is nowadays as natural as breathing."[59]

In 1967 there was an occasion when Banham's wish for a creative playground for the classless society seemed to have been fulfilled. The irony is that the venue was the Roundhouse. The occasion—or rather, series of occasions—was the Underground, avant-garde, infamous, and celebrated "Million-Volt Light and Sound Raves":

The aim was total saturation of audio-visual experience—a full 360 degree sweep of projections ranging from abstract art to films about drug-addiction and patterns of moving liquid, synchronised to music amplified to well above the threshold of pain. But it is the (literally) surrounding ironics that give the Raves their unique flavour. . . . [T]he building in whose indoors it took place belongs to Centre 42, the last outpost of the subestablishment proposition that the function of Socialism is to hand down that "ancient aristocratic aesthetic" from the educated classes to the lower orders. . . . But the giant irony embracing all others is that the building which conceals the Rave from the well-educated eyes of Hampstead and Regent's Park . . . is the Chalk Farm Roundhouse, a structure whose qualities as architecture, as engineering, as a monument of the Functional Tradition and the Great British Nostalgia for Steam (and its merely being more than one hundred years old) all combine to ensure that any attempt to tamper with it will provoke a storm of militant preservationism.

The battle lines were drawn: monuments, preservation, nostalgia, and the Establishment versus facilities, innovation, progressiveness, and the young, classless generation:

We thus appear to be within sight of a situation in which, for instance, charabanc-loads of Labour party loyalists might be brought to see *Son-et-Lumière* histories of British Rail (scripted by John Betjeman and L. T. C. Rolt) projected on the outer walls of the Roundhouse, while Raves of mobile teenagers immersed themselves in audio-visual psychedelic happenings within. So, it would be a fair epitome of our present faltering transition from a culture based on aristocratic taste to one based on free-form self-fulfilment.[60]

No quote could better encapsulate the cultural polarities that Banham identified, and their relationship to class and the Establishment; nothing could better show that Banham's predilections were related to a political view of society. Here was "science for kicks," and all its youthful, liberatory potential, in practice. He knew which side of the "generation gap" of the 1960s he identified with, even if he did not belong to it chronologically! Banham's new, young, progressive working class had, it appeared at the time, become classless—they had been emancipated by the technological society. This is where Banham's attitude to class was wholly in keeping with the mood of the time. Harold Wilson's speeches of late 1963 and 1964—the time of Banham's greatest reflection of the relationship of class and culture—are full of references to the ills of the Establishment, the need for a vital and classless society, and the key role of science and technology.

The Technological Optimist

Banham was passionate in his optimism for technology: he may have regarded the 1960s as "the high summer of technological optimism,"[61] but it was a season created by the winds of technological change and a sympathetic climate. He viewed technology almost as a "naturalised" part of the Second Machine Age, and even beyond politics. "Technology," he wrote in

1962, "is morally, socially and politically neutral . . . [and] does not distinguish between recordings of John Glenn heard through the ionosphere, and recordings of Cliff Richard heard through an echo-chamber."[62] This was a naive technocratic belief that completely glossed over issues of control, ownership, content, and context. Banham had his critics. Manfredo Tafuri described him as the "paladin of technological orthodoxy";[63] Martin Pawley coined the term "technological superhumanists" for the likes of Bucky Fuller, Archigram, and Banham;[64] and Malcolm MacEwen, attacking Modernist technological assumptions, complained that Banham's ideas represented the "extreme of technological blindness."[65] It was his optimistic, wholehearted, and, at times, uncritical commitment to technology that makes aspects of his writings now seem dated and as much a part of their times as Pevsner's *Pioneers* appeared from the perspective of the late 1960s.

Banham did, however, acknowledge two dilemmas arising out of his attitude to technology. The first was the political dilemma we saw in chapter 3: the conflict he identified between his (and others associated with the Independent Group) "admiration for the immense competence, resourcefulness and creative power of American commercial design with the equally unavoidable disgust at the system that was producing it." As he put it in 1964, "we had this American leaning and yet most of us are in some way Left-orientated, even protest-orientated." Banham's justification was that it was technology they were celebrating, and it was only a historical coincidence that the best current technology was American. He "resolved" his dilemma by dislocating technology—and its spin-off, pop—from the society that produced it: "Pop is now so basic to the way we live, and the world we live in, that to be with it, to dig the pop scene, does not commit anyone to Left or Right, nor to protest or acceptance of the society we live in. It has become the common language . . . by which members of the mechanised urban culture of the Westernised countries can communicate with one another in the most direct, lively and meaningful manner."[66] Like pop, technology was, for Banham, universalist, a form of Esperanto: the dilemma was speedily "resolved" and we were back to technology's essential neutrality.

Technology and Architecture: Changing His Mind?

The second dilemma about technology was its relationship to architecture. This became clear in chapters 3 and 4, and reveals a serious discrepancy in Banham's thinking, certainly throughout the 1960s. On the one hand, he argued at the beginning of the 1960s, in both *Theory and Design* and "Stocktaking," that "technological habits of thought are hostile to architectural habits of thought." Furthermore, "technology will impinge increasingly on architecture in the next ten years," and thus architecture would have to run with technology. This was his "radical" attitude to technology, and it led to the Fulleresque "A Home Is Not a House" (1965) and continued with *The Architecture of the Well-tempered Environment* (1969), which restated some of the conclusions of his 1960 "technological habits of thought" mode.

On the other hand, Banham remained attached to architecture and its *cultural* associations. He sang the praises of Frank Lloyd Wright, Le Corbusier, Mies van der Rohe, and Rudolph Schindler and the "masterpieces" they created, even if he felt they were not full solutions to the Second Machine Age. He regarded Renzo Piano and Richard Rogers as first-rate architects, and their flamboyant Pompidou Centre was not just historically significant; it was also "a place that is unlike anywhere else on the earth's crust." Rogers's Inmos factory was "sensuously pleasing," even "beautiful"; Piano's Menil Gallery achieved "ethereal beauty" and "put the magic back into Functionalism."[67] James Stirling, let it be remembered, was celebrated not only for his "bloody-mindedness" at Leicester and Cambridge, but also for his "sustained inventiveness and poised wit" at Stuttgart.

These architects were "making architecture," to coin a phrase Banham used on several occasions in the 1980s. In fact, his last article, written during his final days and published posthumously in 1990, returns to his theme of "fundamental modes" of architectural designing, as opposed to, for example, Post-Modernism, which is "in the same relation to architecture as female impersonation to femininity. It is not architecture, but building in drag."[68] The "*modo architectorum,*" which was essentially timeless, did not guarantee good buildings or even "good design," but it was still, he believed, recognizable, even in the work of an architect such as Lutyens.[69]

There was undoubtedly a conflict here between all that Banham thought good about the *modo architectorum,* and all that he thought bad about "architectural habits of thought" with their conservative lores and conventions. In 1963 he admitted to being aware of the conflict in his thinking. Discussing Fuller's radicalism, Banham mused: "What I can't be sure about is whether Bucky's rules and the rules which govern architecture as we know it are mutually exclusive. When I wrote *Theory and Design,* I was convinced it was an either/or situation. . . . I am currently in a half-and-half position: radical technology like Fuller's will *dis*place architecture even if it doesn't *re*place it."[70] It was not clear from his characterization of "half and half" whether he envisaged that "either/or" would become "both/and," in the sense that a technologically determined architecture could emerge with elements of *both* radical technological thinking *and* architectural quality.

This was a plausible scenario. It would mean that "A Home Is Not a House" could be interpreted as one of the last outpourings of his "either/or" phase, which was being superseded by his research into the technology of mechanical services, culminating in *The Architecture of the Well-tempered Environment,* and moving him toward a "both/and" situation in which technology was *displacing* architecture. Most of the buildings included in that book could be described as "architecture," even if they were largely examples of architecture for and of a technological age. High Tech buildings could then be seen as a major achievement of the *dis*placement of architecture by technology in order to reinvigorate the "mechanical sensibility" in the Second Machine Age. Some of the solutions might be radical, but they were still "architecture" in terms of its *modo architectorum.*

This line of argument may have been plausible—and it was one that Banham occasionally recommended—but it was not the one he invariably took.[71] An either/or approach may have better suited his rhetorical and polemical style, but it often led to inconsistencies and, possibly, having it both ways. In *Theory and Design,* Banham waxed lyrical about buildings such as the Villa Savoye and Barcelona Pavilion, claiming that "Their status as masterpieces rests, as it does with most other masterpieces of architecture, upon the authority and felicity with which they give expression to a view of men in relation to their environment. They are masterpieces of the same order of the Sainte Chapelle or the Villa Rotunda."[72]

Yet in *The Architecture of the Well-tempered Environment* he attacked the same architects—even the same buildings—but on markedly different grounds. Architects like Le Corbusier were severely reprimanded for subjecting their clients "to a Gestapo-style luminous environment, with light streaming from bare, or occasionally opalescent, bulbs and tubes and glaring back from white walls."[73] This change of judgment might be explained away by a legitimate changing of his mind from the beginning to the end of the decade, but as we have seen in chapter 3, Banham continued to praise Le Corbusier and Mies in the late 1960s on the same grounds as he had praised them in *Theory and Design.* It is less a case of a changed mind than of being of two minds, and apparently of having two conflicting views simultaneously, with each seeming to be held passionately and exclusively.

Just as he could adopt different responses to technology—pragmatic, radical, and Pop—so, too, Banahm could posit "revisionist" and "radical" positions in a "half and half"—or possibly even "both/and" and, arguably, schizophrenic—way. The value system of each might be relatively exclusive, but both were valid options. A contradiction existed across texts, but sometimes one existed *within* a particular text. In *Theory and Design* there is the concluding commitment to running with technology and creating an "entirely radical" *architecture autre,* but also an obvious (and contradictory) appreciation of buildings which constitute the canon of Modernism. In *The Architecture of the Well-tempered Environment* the radicalism of the attack on architecture sits uneasily alongside revisionist Modernist values (Futurism and Scheerbart remain as heroes) or even conventional values, such as the dismissal of the Royal Victoria's revivalism when, compared to the real issues of environmental design at stake, the styling is almost wholly irrelevant. It seems that however much the polemic is that we should ditch architecture and its traditions, it is architecture and its traditions—the *modo architectorum*—to which Banham remains committed and emotionally attached.[74] An *architecture autre* never exists for long without *vers une architecture.*

A genuine Independent Group approach to "both/and" would acknowledge and respect a "plurality (or duality) of hierarchies" which were, potentially, equal—a radical approach could exist alongside a revisionist one. Banham, however, was sometimes guilty of inconsistently applying an "either/or" approach in which one value system was presented as better, even when he also subscribed to the other. In 1963 he may have dismissed "either/or" in favor of "half and half," but in a 1971 interview he was reiterating that "architecture and technology are two radically different ways of thinking about things." He went on to say that "One of the things that still makes architecture interesting is the difficulty of keeping any position between the two; between the engineering problem-solving attitude and the more general cultural concern which comes from the design tradition side."[75]

It was not, of course, a binary issue: another value-related issue became apparent with what Banham described as the "problem that forever haunts American architecture at large: just what is the relationship of the grand old art of architecture, with its liberal and aristocratic traditions, to a consumer-capitalist society that is anti-aristocratic, dubiously liberal, and not terribly bothered by traditions."[76] It was a relationship which could also be said to have applied to Banham himself, who could equally convincingly argue for consumer goodies and Pop, technology and *architecture autre,* or the *modo architectorum.*

The Problem of "Values"

With his apparent inclusiveness and tolerance, it is hard to understand why Banham took such a publicly hostile position to the *modo architectorum* "half" of his professional enthusiasms in an article in which, initially just in passing, he attacks George Baird and his semiotic approach to architectural value. The article—"Flatscape with Containers" (1967)—and further comments by Banham in 1969, serve as a way of focusing on some of his explicit and implicit values. "Flatscape" describes the way in which dock design was changing from monumental buildings associated with the nineteenth century to large, flat, empty areas in which sealed containers were delivered and collected: architecture by architects was being replaced by well-serviced

anonymity, "perfectly adequately designed by engineers without any interference from architects." The article expounded his "fit environments" thesis, and it was significant that Banham cited Cedric Price as the only architect
likely to come up with this kind of solution, on the grounds that he "applied
container technology, near enough, to university teaching in his Thinkbelt
project." This led Banham on to attacking the detractors of Price, those "intellectual dead-heads" who did not include, in this case,

> . . . some doddering old architectural knight, but . . . one of the profession's most es-
> teemed younger intellectuals, George Baird, arch-priest of the cult of "values" (rather
> than human service) in architecture. According to Baird, the Thinkbelt's avoidance of
> showy monumentality (for which "structuralism" is the current flip synonym) will lead
> to practically every fashionable evil in the book, from contemptuousness to bureaucracy
> (read all about it, if you can stomach the prose "style," in the June issue of the *Journal
> of the Architectural Association*).[77]

Banham's own attack, as one can read, was not dispassionate, but resembled his emotional reaction to Post-Modernism. Coincidentally, it was Jencks
who, as coeditor of the *Journal* issue on architectural semiotics, replied to
Banham's comments, provoking an exchange of letters in a tone similar
to the response to *Adhocism*.[78]

Baird's article—"'La Dimension Amoureuse' in Architecture"—was reprinted, along with Banham's "Flatscape with Containers," and commentaries by the authors and other contributors, in *Meaning in Architecture*,
edited by Jencks and Baird (1969). The commentaries revealed that no one
had changed his position. The main point of Baird's thesis was that a se-
miological approach to architecture could produce an architecture that
communicated, and that the public understood. In arguing his case, Baird
used Eero Saarinen's CBS building in New York and Cedric Price's Potteries
Thinkbelt: the former is remote and overwhelming; the latter, no more en-
riching than a coffee-vending machine. Baird was positing a theory of architecture which was to develop into Post-Modernism, an architecture that
communicated and worked *in* experience and memory, rather than *above*
or *outside* it.

Banham's reaction was evenly vehement but unevenly convincing. He was at his most convincing when he commented that "Far from treating the occupants of [the Thinkbelt] as 'objects,' Price pays them the compliment of treating them as independent-minded adults capable of ordering their own environment"[79]—a point related to his belief that culture was moving toward a condition of greater "free-form self-fulfilment." Baird had misunderstood Price's values, which, Banham pointed out, "could easily have been discovered . . . through personal conversation during the years he was in London," but Baird retorted that what he was criticizing was not Price's intentions, but his "misconception" of architecture. Only architectural technocrats would "read" Price's design in Banham's way: the majority were more likely to perceive it as "the most concrete symbolisation there has yet been of bureaucracy's academic equivalent, the 'education factory.'"[80] This, in effect, reintroduced the issue of historicism and the extent to which Banham had normalized the values of a progressive, technocratic society, and was unable to perceive its architectural manifestations as value-laden.

Banham was at his least convincing on the issue of values. In "Flatscape with Containers" he had described Baird as the "arch-priest of the cult of 'values' (rather than human service) in architecture." In his letter, Jencks rightly criticizes Banham for not accepting that "human service is a value and part of communication," and for misunderstanding completely that Baird was not arguing in favor of "showy monumentality," but rejecting it as "bankrupt"—this was the point of the Saarinen example. The Thinkbelt was criticized for not making values explicit enough. Banham's letter was confused and dogmatic. First, in reaction to the phrase "showy monumentalism," Banham asserted that "showy in some sense architecture must be if it is to communicate values, since this requires some sort of ostensible symbolism. A monument it will become if these values enjoy social approval." In reply to the point about human service being a value, Banham exasperatedly declared, "if that is what [Baird] means, then the ineffable superficiality of the whole approach is revealed. Human service is the prime and only reason why buildings get put up. Period. Not a value or a part, but the whole reason why architecture exists at all."[81]

To confuse Price's version of "human service" with a broader one having to do with function would seem to be willful, and certainly simplistic and re-ductivist, ignoring significant differences between, for example, revivalism and the Thinkbelt. To decry the symbolic role of public buildings through-out the history of architecture is a regrettable oversight, if not professional amnesia, because Banham had very recently heaped praise on (ironically) Saarinen's TWA terminal because of the way the architect solved its "physi-cal and its *symbolic* (or psychological) functions" (my italics).[82] Banham in-deed wrote of the importance of the "symbolic expression" in Stirling's Leicester building and, throughout his career, he referred to the role of sym-bolism in design with its "symbolic iconographies."[83] And to assume that to communicate values, some sort of "showiness" is necessary, again seems to be a travesty of what Banham had written previously in relation, say, to the architecture of Le Corbusier, Mies, or Eames—or even Albert C. Martin and Associates' Water and Power Building in Los Angeles.

The conclusion to *Theory and Design* overtly praised the architecture of the First Machine Age because it was "rich in the associations and symbolic values current in their time"[84] although, in *The Architecture of the Well-tempered Environment,* he was regretting the First Machine Age's tendency to see technology as a "portentous cultural problem, rather than something that the architect could use to make houses 'perfectly sanitary, labour-saving . . . where the maximum of comfort may be had with the minimum of drudgery.'"[85] In the mid-to-late 1960s, when he increasingly saw the United States as the place where technology and pragmatics ruled the day, he criticized the European intelligentsia because they assumed that "ques-tions which are susceptible of straight-forward physical investigation are nudged up to the 'higher' plane of cultural problems."[86] This would seem to apply not just to the prophets of the First Machine Age, but also to contem-porary writers such as George Baird and Charles Jencks.

As part of his commentary in *Meaning in Architecture,* Banham recorded his dissatisfaction with "the overpermanence of exclusive value-systems; what I find admirable about advanced technology is the number of em-balmed 'meanings and identities' that it threatens."[87] Banham's problem with values was twofold. First, he was deeply suspicious of "values" (in quotation marks), which, in his opinion, were academically conceived, consciously pursued, and held by "card-carrying reactionaries," like George Baird, who were part of a "cult." This suspicion was to become a major part of his criticism of Post-Modernism—values were something which "belonged" to the humanities, not technology, and which, in his celebrated 1965 remark, resulted in intellectuals being "isolated from Humanity by the humanities." Second, his unwillingness to historicize his own values made him partially value-blind, so he, like the model technocrat of the time, saw "human service," "well-serviced anonymity," or "fit environments" as, like technology, "neutral" and value-free. Or, to be precise, "almost value-free," as he put it in "Flatscape."[88] However, even his acknowledgment of the existence of values was not convincing: "The absence of 'values' identifiable by historical or philological techniques does not in fact produce a value-free architecture; the absence of those academic values can in itself be a 'value' if it frees the environment from cultural clutter."[89]

To set up a contrast of "cultural value/clutter" and an alternative that is supposedly almost free of them, is naive about the baggage and underlying assumptions of the latter. But, in Banham's view, "human service" buildings, with their "nearly value-free and self-effacing" properties, leave "their occupants in peace to go about their business." They are free of "*gratuitous values*" (italics added), and so allow the users themselves "to discover and impose their own values on their buildings." Paralleling the way he often dealt with technology, Banham could be accused of dealing with values at the micro level of personal choice rather than the macro level of cultural meaning and allied questions of power and control.

The Third Machine Age?

Banham's emphasis on the micro level of personal choice largely derives from his characterization of the Second Machine Age in *Theory and Design*. If the First Machine Age had been about technology that was transforming life at the basic level of reducing drudgery and making tasks less laborsome, technology in the Second Machine Age was often about the dreams that money could buy. First Machine Age universalism, collectivism, and notions of the common good (however paternalistic) gave way to Second

Machine Age individualism, consumerism, excitement, and fun. At the level of the city, New York may have been "the first, last, and only genuine Futurist city,"[90] but Le Corbusier's 1925 "plan Voisin" for Paris most comprehensively expressed the Modernists' aims and ideals of the First Machine Age. However, it was Los Angeles, that essentially consumerist, individualistic, creative playground of *Homo ludens* that lacked a significant public realm, which encapsulated the values of the Second Machine Age most convincingly.

Banham's normalization of technology meant that he interpreted the "breathless consequences" of consumer capitalism in the 1950s and 1960s as the *natural* outcome of a technological progression that was historically destined in the same way that high Modernist architects and writers had believed the precision and order of machines was part of an inevitable progression in the First. Discussing the different outlooks of Banham and Colin Rowe, a mutual friend recalled that Banham's enthusiasm for the consumer capitalism of the Second Machine Age "enrages Colin, absolutely turns him into a fury by his simple buoyancy and his simple optimistic belief that properly applied science and free enterprise will simply deliver the goods and provide a free for all, a Californian free for all."[91] Thus, when some of the manifestations and even premises of technology were questioned in the post-1968 period, it was no surprise that Banham was unsympathetic with the new mood to the point of intolerance, and failed to appreciate why his great passion and belief needed to be challenged in this way.

One of the consequences of the new sensibility was that the role and status of technology *as imagery* changed as we entered what might be the Third Machine Age.[92] Although technology remained the basis of Western society, it was no longer necessary to *respect* its imagery (as the First Machine Age had done), let alone *celebrate* it (as Second Machine Age designers from Detroit to Archigram had done). Of course, this did not mean an end to technological imagery—the rise of the personal computer ensured the continuation of the gray box phenomenon, the increasing sophistication of hi-fi was manifested the black box phenomenon, and flamboyant or cool High Tech demonstrated the excitement of an architecture of technology. But no longer was the imagery of technology dominant or central. It may not have been *re*placed, but it had been *dis*placed by other forms of imagery—for example, the greater emphasis on meaning and association evidenced by different forms and styles of revivalism and the languages of Post-Modernism.

Technology was questioned at several levels in the post-1968 period, and one of the most favored design and architectural solutions was to assume a certain level of functional or environmental technological performance "as given," but to find the dominant visual imagery in other forms and sources, from revival through retro to anthropomorphic. David Watkin's point about advanced technology not determining the form of a building was becoming intellectually and morally an orthodoxy. *The Architecture of the Well-tempered Environment* may have been radical, but it was so only within established Modernist terms and values. The shift from structure to mechanical services still emphasized "internal" or formal/technical elements, and was no more likely to communicate with the public than its earlier version had been.

Banham may have supposed a "deep intellectual and moral need . . . to be able to see the difference between the structure . . . and the services," but he represented a small clan. Post-Modernism was far more radical in its reorientation away from abstraction and toward one derived from broader or "external" social and cultural languages and modes of reference. In the Third Machine Age, the machine aesthetic lost its aura and the idea of a zeitgeist was no longer tenable. There were now genuinely multiple aesthetics. Banham somewhat grudgingly acknowledged this, but he was not sympathetic to it, in spite of the Independent Group's invention of a model of "multiple elites, multiple aesthetics." In effect, he accepted multiple aesthetics only *within* a range of technologically progressive options—genuine pluralism arrived with a younger, Post-Modern generation. Nor did Banham appear to entertain the possibility that the changes he was witnessing were part of the dawning of a Third Machine Age.

Like Modernists before him, Banham sought the New World, hoping that he would find there old attitudes to technology. Modernist Masters like Le Corbusier, Adolf Loos, and Erich Mendelsohn had looked toward the United States for its technological sophistication or, at least, honesty; the Independent Group had been seduced by the aesthetics of abundance; and Banham had saluted the country's unbridled enthusiasm for technology and its evident unwillingness to see technology as a cultural problem. Independent Group members, as we read in chapter 2, were criticized for romanticizing America, and Banham himself could be accused of doing the same. In "A Home Is Not a House," he had praised Americans as if they were noble savages, on the grounds that, when "left to their own devices . . . [they] do not monumentalise or make architecture,"[93] but also bemoaned the fact that, in practice, the majority reverted to architectural solutions, presumably "out of some profound sense of insecurity [or] a persistent inability to rid themselves of those habits of mind they left Europe to escape."[94]

In *Meaning in Architecture* Baird picked up on this discrepancy to underline his point about the need for architectural meaning as a form of "environmental symbiosis,"[95] and Banham's response to it is instructive: "there will be no chance of the kind of environmental symbiosis that interests people of my psychological type and cultural background if the world is cluttered with Baird's values cast in irremovable concrete." Apart from what appears to be an assumption that, somehow, the United States is still the home of the independent Wright/Whitman frontiersman mentality, the reference to type and background is telling because it is in some small way an equivalent to Banham historicizing himself: he is acknowledging that his particular makeup leads him toward certain types of preferences or solutions—he is admitting that he is not "value-free" or even "almost value-free"! The effect of this within the context of the article and discussion is to weaken Banham's position—an apparently general and generalizable argument suddenly has attached to it a "for me . . ." caveat, and that reduces the authority and force of the previous polemic.

The Language of the Ill-tempered Polemicist

"Polemic" is a key word in understanding Banham's writing. He believed in being polemical rather than dry or esoteric because theory and criticism, like history, were not just texts, but individuals with passions, prejudices, and positions. He wrote in a tone suited to the type of publication, and so there is greater formality in his books than in articles for professional architectural journals, and far greater still than in his informal *New Society* pieces.

However, the unbuttoned tone of the latter does not mean they are not to be taken seriously. As we have found throughout the preceding chapters, many of Banham's important arguments, positions, and values were expressed or explored in his magazine articles. Banham was able to convey enthusiasm for architecture and design in every type of publication. Equally, he could convey his condescension about, for example, the "frightened men" who were critical of Stirling's architecture, or the "the lunatic core of the New Architectural Tories" behind the Lutyens revival.

It is interesting to compare his writing about Lutyens with Pevsner's. The latter's article of 1951 is a model of moderation, scholarship, and balanced judgment compared to Banham's polemical tirade which is overshadowed by the political and social connotations of the revival. This is almost Banham at his opinionated worst—it runs a close second to his review of Jencks's *Language of Post-Modern Architecture* as an example of a substandard text which fails to engage the salient points of the book and theory being reviewed. A reader discovering Banham through his reviews of Jencks's *Post-Modern Architecture* or *Adhocism* would be likely to dismiss him as old-fashioned and intellectually intransigent to the point—ironically—of being unable to change his mind.

There is also, occasionally, an anti-intellectual tone—certainly an anti-academic tone—which comes to the fore in his attack on Baird's intellectualism. Banham detected what he described as "scholasticism" or "academicism" in much Post-Modernism, as we saw in chapter 5, which wrongly encouraged architects to "trumpet their erudition." Equally, with disdain, Banham lambasted "the self-righteous cant of New York academe represented by Kenneth Frampton,"[96] including his phrase "an architecture of resistance." The irony here—if not contradiction—is that Banham had himself been accused of intellectualism and esoteric language. On more than one occasion he was accused of "impenetrable prose";[97] making a "plethora of words" cover "very few ideas";[98] or obfuscating his subject "by thinking he was on to something new."[99] Even when he wrote densely, as in *Theory and Design,* he seldom wrote obscurely; more commonly, he wrote clearly and exoterically.[100]

The academic may write about communication, but does not always practise it, whereas Banham reaped the benefits of writing journalism for an intelligent lay audience. Doubtless, some academics would dismiss Banham's history writing because he "lowered" himself by writing accessible criticism; others might argue that his history was little more than criticism with historical flavoring. However, now that what he would term "scholasticism" is so firmly established in academe—with whole planeloads of academics snobbishly mistrusting anything written clearly as being intellectually substandard—Banham's writing is a delight to behold. He had the ability to engage his reader by conveying a sense of both enthusiasm and immediacy through his vibrant prose, whether he was writing about a contemporary building or a "masterpiece" from the First Machine Age. He was, in the words of the architectural historian Robert Maxwell, "a damned good writer," partly because he was, according to Paul Barker, "bullshit-free."[101]

That is not to deny that Banham was sometimes guilty of "journalese," employing unnecessary and irritating neologisms such as "Corbusiast," "Mendelsohnian" and "Boccionisms," whether in *New Society, Architectural Review,* or *Theory and Design.*[102] Or of using unprofessional, sexist terms like "dolly-birds," "bird-life," and "gorgeous Art Nouveau popsies"![103] On the one hand, domestic technology was "woman-controlled";[104] on the other, "boys [were] sent to do a man's job" when "*men* with trained minds, *men* with organised bodies of knowledge, have been the *men* whom architecture has most needed" (italics added).[105]

But it would be a mistake to think of Banham as especially sexist—the above quotations are symptomatic of the period in which they were written. The implication and conventional wisdom were that modernity liberated women, both in the home and from the home. Some of them may have become architects, but—with the exception of Alison Smithson—we are not introduced to them in Banham's writing, nor are the important and consequential relationships of gender to architecture or technology raised. Architecture was a man's world. Indeed, it was a world for the "tough-minded." In *Theory and Design* alone, Banham makes a dozen references to *toughness,* and this conventionally male attribute was presumably something that Banham identified with his own "psychological type."

His psychological type, anti-establishmentarianism, and "tough-minded-ness" combined to make Banham a powerful and independent voice who liked to be identified with a movement, cause, or group if it was adequately radical. We have seen that he found that sense of purpose with the New Brutalism, *architecture autre,* "fit environments for human activities," Cedric Price, and Archigram. These movements and so on were invariably in opposition to the architectural mainstream, and one suspects that, temperamentally, Banham enjoyed the notoriety and sense of being someone who was, among students, accorded guru-like status like Fuller's. His role as critic in chief to the avant-garde gave him an interesting position within architectural culture. His academic reputation, based on seminal publications such as *Theory and Design in the First Machine Age* facilitated access to the mainstream; his avant-garde reputation, derived from his polemical writing and lecturing, ensured that he had "street credibility" and knew what was going on in architectural gangland.

Banham held a "half-and-half" position and was able to look two ways, and thus appreciate *both* the mainstream *and* the "other." It was a position that enabled him to mix and gossip with the major players, yet simultaneously berate the profession for their inadequacies. The advantage of the position was that he could write about architecture in different ways while maintaining his credibility; the disadvantage was that he wrote about architecture in different ways, and therefore sometimes seemed to be contradicting himself. A danger of his position with one foot in the mainstream and one in the avant-garde is that it is potentially uncomfortable if you try to face both ways at once: if you turn one way, you might miss some important action. That Banham seldom missed out on what was new or interesting is a credit to his sense of judgment, timing, and appetite.

The Outsider-Insider Historian

However, the two-way approach did lead to inconsistency about what he argued to be the function of the historian. Sometimes Banham was the radical outsider historian, sometimes the revisionist insider. At the time of the publication of *Theory and Design,* he not surprisingly saw the historian as a revisionist figure who countered the First Machine Age generation of historians who had spent their time establishing the pedigree to ascertain "what glorious bearings may be quartered into the blazons of Modern architecture."[106] The idea of the historian being, "like Giedion, the servant of a faction" was not to be entertained.[107] Banham's generation of historians had to be part detective, part psychiatrist, and part technocrat: they had to find out "what really happened" and conduct a "psychiatric enquiry into the springs of action, the grounds of inhibition." But the historian, in keeping with his commitment to technology and management, needed also to be regarded "more and more as a sort of specialist consultant, like an acousticist," and so stand "firmly on a specialist qualification that proves his grounding in an orderly method, that proves an objective attitude towards the evidence."[108]

There is a heroism in his conviction that this "appointment of historians to a cure of souls, to the guardianship of the conscience, even the sanity, of the profession, places upon their shoulders a responsibility that they have not been asked to carry before." Furthermore, architecture's break with tradition meant that "it cannot regain its Vitruvian innocence. Without the ballast of an equivalent millennial tradition, architecture will have to be consciously trimmed and steered as it proceeds, and someone will have to plot its course continually. That someone is the historian," whose first job, Banham declares, "will be to pass judgement on the tendency . . . to modern movement revivalism." This romantic notion offers the model of the historian as a kind of technocratic sage or project manager. But, in 1962, Banham was warning against direct involvement with contemporary debates: "The price that historians have had to pay for . . . meddling in contemporary affairs has been the debasement of their own stature as purveyors of fact."[109]

Yet Banham did not heed his own wisdom, and not only meddled in contemporary affairs, but could also have been accused of being the "servant of a faction" on more than one occasion. By the mid-1960s he was admitting in *The New Brutalism* that the book had "a built-in bias toward the British contribution to Brutalism: it is not a dispassionate and Olympian survey, conducted from the cool heights of an academic ivory tower. I was there, involved."[110] He even acknowledged that one of his contemporary articles was not really representative of the architects' intentions, but "reveals only too clearly my attempt to father some of my own pet notions on the movement." This is hardly in keeping with the historian as sage and objective guide. Nor was Banham's involvement with Archigram, which provided him "with the kind of ringside view of a Movement that every critic or historian should experience at least once for the sake of his education."[111] Banham's polemicism rapidly overtook any claims to dispassionate objectivity or, like Pevsner, worries about being historicist. In the end it was taking a position with passion that mattered:

. . . extreme viewpoints are illuminating; animus has long been the very breath of life to historians for as long as the tribe has existed. We may complain about Whig historians and Maoist historians and pop historians and structuralist historians, but the bias which they all exhibit is their point. . . . Such bias is essential—an unbiased historian is a pointless historian—because history is an essentially critical activity, a constant rescrutiny and rearrangement of the profession.[112]

This confirms his own disregard for being historicist because the continual process of critical dialectics and apostolic succession would ensure that biases were countered, thus keeping the discipline robust and vital.[113] However, it does not justify his unwillingness to discuss his own values or make them more explicit. Equally logically (and possibly more responsibly), he could have argued that because bias is always present, the historian has a duty to identify his or her own biases. The probable reason for not doing this, as I have suggested before, was Banham's temperament and love of assertive polemic.

The combination of being an outsider and being an insider suited Banham's style, and throws light on his ambivalent relationship with the architectural history Establishment. His anti-establishmentarianism, including his class politics, explains his happiness with being an outsider. However, there would appear to be some psychological factors which drew him toward being accepted by the same Establishment. In interviews he refers to experiences which would be likely to have induced a feeling of failure—a failed HNC[114] and suffering from stress at the engineering company he was working for during the war. These experiences obviously had left their mark.

Banham recalled that "I decided to recycle myself as an intellectual," but in 1959 he referred to his "prophet-without-honour-in-own-country complex" when he was treated as a "VIP" during a visit to the Hochschule at Ulm.[115] As late as 1980 he was still recalling that the visit was the occasion on which he had met "a community of intellectuals who treated me seriously. In Britain, people would pat me on the head and say 'Marvellous—now get lost.'"[116]

His temperament and background, therefore, may have made Banham ambivalent about the architectural Establishment. Though he reveled in his radical outsider status, there was also obvious delight in his 1987 appointment to the Sheldon H. Solow chair of the history of architecture at the Institute of Fine Arts at New York University. Publicly, in his posthumously published, undelivered inaugural lecture, he states that it represented "the crown of my career in architectural history." Privately, with enormous pride and with no hint of an outsider's feeling of incorporation, his leaving announcement to colleagues and friends at the University of California and elsewhere proclaimed his new post to be "North America's most consequential professorship in architectural history outside the professional schools of architecture."[117] Reflecting on Bucky Fuller's Institute of American Architects citation in 1960, Banham had noted how the Establishment "tolerates a few peripheral radicals": this may have been how he saw himself, although any estimation would have to challenge an assumed peripheral status. Perhaps the outsider-insider was one of the most impressive achievements of a "both/and" approach.

The Rhetoric of Presence

Banham's Solow address dealt principally with the writing and character of his predecessor in the post, Henry-Russell Hitchcock.[118] Hitchcock was, according to Banham, "an 'observational' historian, like my master Nikolaus Pevsner and—I hope—myself. . . . This kind of history of architecture has been called, by Robert Maxwell of Princeton, a 'rhetoric of presence.' I have been there and seen for myself, and that is my licence to speak."[119]

This was of crucial importance to Banham, and it partly accounts for his distrust of any writing which he thought of as being too academic. We have seen how Banham's own writing was frequently based on his direct experience of a building—the Fiat factory in Turin, Stirling's Cambridge History Faculty and Stuttgart Staatsgalerie, and Gehry's Santa Monica house are good examples. Had he approached, say, the Stuttgart complex via photographs or a critic's text, his response might have been very different from the full-bodied one of being "almost knocked out" by the quality of the experience. "Being there" enabled him to make his judgment about the relative (in)significance of the stylistic issues compared to the space-time experience of the *promenade architectural.*

Not "being there" was a source of danger to the historian, who might perpetuate errors or even myths. For instance, Banham ticks off Vincent Scully for basing some of his judgments about American industrial buildings on *Vers une architecture* (which was itself based on illustrations used by Gropius) when Le Corbusier was not averse to doctoring both facts and illustrations.[120] Scully, "a half century later . . . could easily have access to photographs of real-life examples from close at hand,"[121] and could even have visited the structures themselves to make his judgment. Had he visited them, he might have noticed other things, such as the condition of the flat roofs— Banham proposed that one of the sources of the European Modernists' fondness for the flat roof was that, more often than not, the American buildings they were influenced by had similar roofs. Given the functional problem of the flat roof on European buildings, how could the American industrial architects, he wrote in *A Concrete Atlantis,* "be so suicidally perverse as to prefer a roof form that contradicted the norms of rationality, economy, and profitability by leaking?"[122]

The answer, based on his direct experience and observation, was that the American ones did not leak, "and some I have examined still do not, eighty or more years after their construction."[123] The reason was that if the European ones leaked, "they must have had some source outside local, current, and commonsense building practices."[124] And that reason was that too many of the roofs were "purely formalistic imitations of structures that had never been studied firsthand. Their designers had not seen the originals and had no opportunity to examine and understand how they should be designed, detailed, and constructed." So there was a moral in "being there" not for only the historian, but for the architect, too.

"Being there" was the basis for the rhetoric of presence. Banham wanted to *experience* the actuality of architecture to satisfy his emotional as well as his intellectual involvement. *A Concrete Atlantis* combines the academic argument and the personal response superbly. One example of the combination will suffice. Recording his response to the grain elevators in Minneapolis, he writes:

What one sees are those "beautiful forms, the most beautiful forms" praised by Le Corbusier, pure and uncluttered but black against the green of the summer grass and scrub—or, more sensationally yet—black against white fresh-fallen snow in winter. Wilhelm Worringer's concept of the geometrical and abstract as a mark of the primitive in all arts and cultures—the source of Walter Gropius's belief that American engineers had retained some aboriginal *Sinn für grosse, knapp, gebunden Form* (feeling for large, sparse, compact form) fresh and intact, and that their work was therefore comparable to that surviving from ancient Egypt—all that European superstructure of aesthetics and cultural sensitivities begins to look like good sense when one sees these blunt abstract forms in high contrast against the equally abstract surface of the snow. If Worringer's later sneering reference to some "ultimate Metaphysic of Form" to be found in North America has a metaphor of substance for me, it is in the sight of these grudging, lower-

Grain elevator, Minneapolis, Minnesota, 1901 (courtesy Mary Banham)

ing shapes crouched under a leaden winter sky, unlovable but compelling respect, the Protestant work ethic monumentalised.[125]

The "rhetoric of presence" and academic authority are, at their best in Banham's writing, mutually reinforcing.

The "rhetoric" also gives greater credibility to judgents about what is "good" as opposed to merely "interesting"—why, for example, he preferred to write about Frank Gehry rather than Post-Modernism. The silos and so on of *A Concrete Atlantis* were "buildings of great quality and power. They were as good as their European admirers had supposed."[126] And making a judgment about a quality architectural experience provided by, for example, the Washburn-Crosby elevators in Buffalo, New York, Schindler's house in Los Angeles, or the Centre Pompidou, was something Banham felt was a natural and necessary thing to do. He did not think of his response as just a subjective and personal one, but as a way of arriving at a judgment about whether a particular building was ordinary, good, or, exceptionally, a "masterpiece" and could, therefore, be admitted to the Modernist canon.[127] One of the reasons for making judgments is that they require—and thus promote—critical rigor. Just because a building is by Frank Lloyd Wright does not mean it should be preserved: "to denounce the

General Mills (formerly Washburn-Crosby) Elevators, Buffalo, New York, 1903 (courtesy Mary Banham)

demolishers of a Wright building without having visited it in the flesh, without knowing whether or not it was a *good* building by the master, seems to me irresponsible."[128] To save everything by the Master would indicate that, "as usual, the cognoscenti have chosen to believe the name on the label, not the quality of the specific product." Judgments should never be assumed, but continually argued over and revised.

The rhetoric of presence operated in two other ways in Banham's writing. First, in addition to the personal response and judgment about a particular building, Banham clearly enjoyed writing an "I-was-there" kind of history in books such as *The New Brutalism, Megastructures,* and, from the way he had planned it, *High Tech.* This was Banham the involved and partisan historian with an axe to grind and not averse to using it; in Jencks's phrase, it is Banham the "war correspondent,"[129] broadcasting his dispatches of the history of the immediate future. Second, whereas Pevsner's *Pioneers* foregrounds its metanarrative, and Jencks's *Language of Post-Modern Architecture* foregrounds his illustrated (by text and photographs) theory, *Theory and Design* (in particular) and *The Architecture of the Well-tempered Environment* allow the architects and designers to "speak" and "be present" by means of direct quotations. Robert Maxwell comments accurately that, in Banham's writing, "quotations speak with the vibrancy of key people interviewed on television. . . . Far from deadening the narrative, they sustain it and give it life". . . and presence.[130]

The exercising of judgment; a belief in the importance of the canon; the authorial presence . . . Banham was hardly the model new historian of the post-1968 period. Post-Structuralism and deconstruction, in theory and in practice, did not greatly impinge on his method or values. In 1972 he had perceptively noted that, like architecture itself, architectural history was changing: "We have had a good run for our money and there has been a lot for us to do, and I suspect that the bulk of it is for the moment done. The attention of historians will wander away from architecture, even in the architecture schools, into previously ignored fields like patronage, finance, land ownership, the internal sociology of the profession."[131] These were not, of course, developments which he himself desired to pursue, and in the 1980s he produced two of his most compellingly "observational" books—*Scenes in America Deserta* (1982) and *A Concrete Atlantis* (1986).

We have already discussed *A Concrete Atlantis*. *Scenes in America Deserta* merits attention at this point. It was written after his move from Buffalo to California, which gave him the opportunity to explore the deserts such as the Mojave, partly because of his relative disillusionment with contemporary architecture in the United States, but mainly because he had become a self-confessed "desert freak."[132]

Architecture features in the book but certainly does not dominate it. It ranges from Frank Lloyd Wright's Taliesin West and Paolo Soleri's Arcosanti, through religious and colonialist landmarks such as San Xavier del Bac and commercial enterprises like "Scotty's Castle," to vernacular settlements including Taos Pueblo and archaeological sites like Kuaua. Several pages are devoted to the Kitt Peak solar telescope near Tuscon, Arizona, which he describes as "a supreme product of the culture to which I belong—the culture of scientific enquiry, technological enterprise and engineering precision. I identify with it . . . because it belongs to my generation and people, the clever folks who came out of World War II determined to make over Western Culture according to a different rationality, however terrifying some of its by-products might be."[133] This passage is part of a chapter titled "Marks on the Landscape," a title which indicates that he is discussing interventions by humans in the desert environment, rather than the works detached from place. The desert "on its own" did not particularly attract Banham: what did, was

. . . the works of men [which] always interest me as much as the landscape in which they are wrought. The tire tracks in the sand, the old *arastra* by the gold mine's mouth, the grove where the station used to be, the shiny power pylons marching over the horizon, the old windmill in the canyon and the new telescope repeater on the peak, the Indian pictograph and the anti-war graffiti, the trailer home parked in the middle of nothing, the fragment of Coalport china found in the sand at the bottom of the wash. One of the reasons why the Mojave is my prime desert is that there are more traces of man to be seen, traces more various in their history and their import.[134]

Paolo Soleri, Arcosanti, Arizona (courtesy Mary Banham)

San Xavier del Bac, near Tuscon, Arizona (courtesy Mary Banham)

These traces underline the extent to which the desert is usually an *un*fit environment for human activities, and human existence often operates at a marginal level there—sometimes, indeed, at a perilous and, occasionally, a fatal level. The book takes the idea of environments for human activities and spends some time on the nature of those activities in a particular type of environment. In this sense it is his last—and most—"radical" book and sits alongside his last "revisionist" work, *A Concrete Atlantis,* continuing his "both/and" approach.

Looking back on his writing in the early 1980s, Banham remarked that "my consuming interest, through thick and thin, hardback and limp, is what happens along the shifting frontier between technology and art."[135] I find this a misleading description, partly because he was always troubled by art's function, its lack of "purpose whose absence cripples so much modern art."[136] Closer to the essence of his interest was what he identified in *Scenes* as the interrelationships of "man, machine, and wilderness," which I think can be generalized as "humans, technology, and environment."[137] The in-terrelationships include the social and, of course, the cultural, and so the definition covers not only the scope of *Scenes in America Deserta,* but also *The Architecture of the Well-tempered Environment* and *Theory and Design in the First Machine Age.*

Kitt Peak solar telescope, near Tuscon, Arizona (courtesy Mary Banham)

Scenes contains many rhetorics of presence. For all his fascination with the deeply humanistic "marks on the landscape," it is "the eye of the beholder" which engages Banham most. He recounts how "mine eyes [were] dazzled, my sensibility was transfixed, [and] my consciousness transformed"[138] by the "indelible visions" and "extraordinary luminescences" that he witnessed; he recalls the sheer "visual pleasure" of "the desert's ultimate splendour," which gave him "the consuming compulsion to return." His response provoked the need for self-examination: "it brings me hard up against my inner self, and forces me to ask what are, for me, difficult questions; like what is the nature of natural beauty?"[139] Weighing and setting aside explanations which ranged from Modernist aesthetics, through science fiction and cowboy associations, to the heaths of his Norfolk childhood, he concluded:

Deprived of the ancient categories of Picturesque and Sublime, dubious as to whether the deserts may be Beautiful in any equally ancient sense; knowing that I came into America Deserta culturally naked and ill-prepared; aware that I return to these landscapes in order to feast my eyes on visions that I am prepared to term addictive, I find myself driven closer than ever in my life to the idea that some scenes may be perceived as, simply, "beautiful." . . . There does seem to be something out there that communicates more directly to the pleasure centres of my brain than anything else I have ever encountered.[140]

This statement, like many others in the book, arises from the sort of question Banham admits he found "difficult because I thought I had them tidied up and understood, until I saw the Mojave and knew that my art historian's generalisations were confronted with a situation they could not handle."[141] This is Banham at his best: experiencing a situation (or building/artifact); responding directly to it; and working out his position accordingly. Whereas most academics would be strongly guided by their "art historian's generalisations" and subsequently fit the new experience into their preconceived categories, Banham had the confidence, independence, and strength to "change his mind" and contradict some previously held opinion or position. We have seen that this was not always so—sometimes Banham's opinions remained unchangeable in spite of contrary evidence—but, "as one who

The "extraordinary luminescence" of desert light (courtesy Mary Banham)

enjoys being astonished,"[142] he was always willing to take himself by surprise, so to speak, and allow experience and his considered response to shape judgment. Not only does this reveal integrity, but it also accounts for the vitality of his writing because of the way in which he explored the implications of his own responses. It enables him to challenge lores, conventions, and received wisdom, as we have seen not only in *Scenes,* but also *Los Angeles, The Architecture of the Well-tempered Environment,* and *Theory and Design.*

The Rhetoric of Pragmatism

Banham once revealingly wrote of his preference for "English pragmatism" over "continental systematics."[143] The latter represented to him too much of a theory-led position and resulted in inflexibility ("selective and classicising" Modernism, for example) or academicism (Baird's semiotics or Post-Modernism). Robert Maxwell, in an analysis of his criticism, pointed out that

Banham seemed to believe that "pragmatics are, or can be, independent of ideology. The pragmatic is his base for the criticism of architectural ideologies, and the fact that it is always identified by a concrete instance obscures the critical role it plays as a category."[144] The point is well made and sheds light on Banham's technocratic assertion that some architecture was "almost value-free."

However, acknowledging this important qualification, pragmatism—whether Anglo-Saxon or Anglo-American—facilitated variety, flexibility, choice, a "sense of possibilities," "fit environments," the "style for the job," "both/and," "non-Aristotelian" anti-idealism, open-mindedness, and changing your mind. Pragmatism and its associated values underlay Banham's architectural thinking and freed his mind from the sort of dogma that had infiltrated much Modernist thinking. Explicating Modernist thinking and communicating the "profound reorientation towards a changed world" is one of Banham's major achievements. Maxwell concludes that "it is his performance, not his promise, that has us in thrall,"[145] but this greatly underestimates what Kenneth Frampton describes as his "seminal scholarship"—particularly of Futurism and certain Expressionists such as Scheerbart—and "interpretative sensitivity."[146]

Because he referred to it when discussing two important historians, one suspects that Banham would equally want to be remembered for his *love* of architecture. In his Solow address, he recalled that Hitchcock "loved buildings—that was transparent to anyone who ever exchanged more than two words with him."[147] And while disagreeing with Jencks's Post-Modernism, he acknowledged that "every word of it was said by a man who loves architecture and gets his main kicks in life from talking/writing about it."[148] Whether his writing is in or out of fashion, Banham's love for his subject will be remembered—with enormous gratitude—and continually appreciated by generations of his readers.

NOTES

Preface

1 Reyner Banham, *Theory and Design in the First Machine Age* (London: Architectural Press, 1960), 9.

2 Reyner Banham, "Rubbish: It's as Easy as Falling off a Cusp," *New Society* (August 2, 1979): 252.

3 According to Martin Pawley in his *Theory and Design in the Second Machine Age* (Oxford; Basil Blackwell, 1990), Banham apparently believed we had already entered the Sixth or Seventh Machine Age by the mid-1980s (ix). My own ideas about Machine Ages are outlined in Nigel Whiteley, "Webbed Feat," *Art Review* (May 2000): 60–61.

Introduction

1 Interviewed by Martin Pawley, "The Last of the Piston Engine Men," *Building Design* (October 1, 1971): 6. Banham writes, in passing, about his forebears and their jobs in the gas industry in "Natural Gasworks," *New Society* (January 9, 1969): 41–42.

2 According to John Hewish, a contemporary at Bristol, Banham was "something of a star even then: he had an award from the Society of British Aircraft Constructors giving him a choice of firms to study with. Students at the Bristol Aeroplane Company's Engine Division mixed theory with spells on the shop floor. Encountered straight from school this environment of high-grade mechanical engineering was a heady experience" (from an obituary in the *Architectural Review* [May 1988]: 10).

3 Interview with John Maule McKean, "The Last of England?—Part 1," *Building Design* (August 13, 1976): 8.

4 Quoted in Pawley, "Last of the Piston Engine Men," 6.

5 At the end of the war, he moved back to Norwich and, among other things, taught adult education classes and wrote art exhibition reviews for the local newspapers. He continued to write art reviews, principally for *Art News and Review,* between 1950 and 1955, while he was studying at the Courtauld. Details of these publications are contained in the bibliography in Mary Banham, Paul Barker, Sutherland Lyall, and Cedric Price comps., *A Critic Writes: Essays by Reyner Banham* (Berkeley: University of California Press, 1996).

6 He was known to friends and colleagues as "Peter." The name "Peter Banham" appeared on his published writing only by mistake—much to his annoyance. "Reyner" was a professional version for his writing, adopted in its standard form at the time he recieved his undergraduate degree. Up to that point, in his *Art News and Review* pieces, he sometimes wrote his name "Reyner-Banham" (i.e., hyphenated); other early reviews were signed "P.R.B."

7 "The Atavism of the Short-Distance Mini-Cyclist," *Living Arts* no. 3 (1964): 92.

8 "Who Is This 'Pop'?" *Motif* no. 10 (Winter 1962/1963): 13.

9 "The Atavism . . . ," 91.

10 "WORLD, the; Book to Change, a," *Architects' Journal* (December 8, 1960): 809. A mild irony is that Banham was Banister Fletcher Visiting Professor in Architectural History at the University of London in 1982.

11 Ibid., 810.

12 This is the title of the lecture, reprinted in *Architectural Review* (April 1989): 89–92.

13 "The Bauhaus Gospel," *The Listener* (September 26, 1968): 390.

14 "1960 4: History Under Revision," *Architectural Review* (May 1960): 327.

15 Lawrence Alloway, "The Development of British Pop," in Lucy Lippard, ed., *Pop Art* (London: Thames and Hudson, 1976), 32–33.

16 "The Bauhaus Gospel," 391.

17 "1960 4," 327.

18 "WORLD," 809.

19 Quoted in Pawley, "Last of the Piston Engine Men," 6.

20 Nikolaus Pevsner, "Postscript," in Michael Farr, *Design in British Industry* (Cambridge: Cambridge University Press, 1955), 317.

21 Interview with Penny Sparke, "The Machine Stops," *Design* (December 1980): 31.

22 "WORLD," 809.

23 Quoted in McKean, "The Last of England?" 9.

24 Banham married Mary Mullett, artist and teacher, in 1946.

25 Quoted in McKean, "The Last of England?" 8.

26 *Theory and Design in the First Machine Age* (London: The Architectural Press, 1960), 47.

27 "Revenge of the Picturesque: English Architectural Polemics, 1945–1965," in John Summerson ed., *Concerning Architecture: Essays on Architectural Writers and Writing Presented to Nikolaus Pevsner* (London: Allen Lane, 1968), 265.

NOTES TO INTRODUCTION

28 The fact that Banham had major reservations about Pevsner's *Pioneers* was counter-balanced by their joint commitment to the Modern Movement, as we will see in the conclusion. The Pevsner material that Banham was referring to was thought by him to be *anti*-Modernist.

29 "Revenge of the Picturesque," 267. See, for example, Banham's "Painting and Sculpture of Le Corbusier," *Architectural Review* (June 1953): 401–404.

30 Herbert Read, *Art and Industry* (rev. ed.; London: Faber, 1956), 7.

31 Pevsner, in Michael Farr, *Design in British Industry,* 314.

32 "The Style: 'Flimsy . . . Effeminate'?," in Mary Banham and Bevis Hillier, eds., *A Tonic to the Nation* (London: Thames and Hudson, 1976), 191.

33 Pevsner, in Michael Farr, *Design in British Industry,* 319.

34 Mary Banham, *A Tonic to the Nation,* BBC Radio 4 (November 29, 1976).

35 "The Style: 'Flimsy . . . Effeminate'?," 194.

36 *Architectural Review* articles included "Mendelsohn" (August 1954): 84–93; "School at Hunstanton, Norfolk" (September 1954): 153–158; "Machine Aesthetic" (April 1955): 224–228; "Sant'Elia" (May 1955): 295–301; and "The New Brutalism" (December 1955): 354–361. "Vehicles of Desire" appeared in *Art* (September 1, 1955): 3; and "Industrial Design and Popular Art" was published in Italian in *Civiltà delle machine* (November/December 1955): 12–15.

37 See McKean, "The Last of England?," 8–9.

38 Examples are "Simplified Vaulting Practice" (September 1953): 199–202; "Howard Robertson" (September 1953): 160–168; and "Royal Trains" (June 1953): 401.

39 These include "Footnotes to Sant'Elia" (June 1956): 343–344; "Ateliers d'Artistes: Paris Studio Houses and the Modern Movement" (August 1956): 75–83; "Wright Anthology" (October 1956): 264; "Ornament and Crime: The Decisive Contribution of Adolf Loos" (February 1957): 85–88; "The One and the Few: The Rise of Modern Architecture in Finland" (April 1957): 243–248; "Mondrian and the Philosophy of Modern Design" (October 1957): 227–229; "Tridon" (April 1958): 229–231; "The Glass Paradise" (February 1959): 87–89; and "Futurist Manifesto" (August 1959): 77–80.

40 Nikolaus Pevsner, "Modern Architecture and the Historian or the Return of Historicism," *RIBA Journal* (April 1961): 230.

41 Ibid.

42 *Theory and Design,* 48

43 *The Architecture of the Well-tempered Environment* (London: The Architectural Press, 1969), 83.

44 *Mechanical Services,* unit 21, course A305, "History of Architecture and Design 1890–1939" (Milton Keynes: The Open University, 1975), 19.

45 "1960 1: Stocktaking—Tradition and Technology," *Architectural Review* (February 1960): 96.

46 "Neo-Liberty: The Italian Retreat from Modern Architecture," *Architectural Review* (April 1959): 235.

47 Ibid., 232.

48 Ibid., 235.

49 Ibid.

50 Ibid.

51 *Casabella* no. 228 (June 1959): 2–4; a translation appears in Joan Ockman, ed., *Architecture Culture 1943–1968: A Documentary Anthology* (New York: Rizzoli, 1993), 301–307.

52 Ibid., 306.

53 Ibid., 303.

54 Ibid., 307.

55 Ibid., 300.

56 *The New Brutalism: Ethic or Aesthetic?* (London: Architectural Press, 1966), 127.

57 *Architecture of the Well-tempered Environment,* 242.

58 "Vehicles of Desire," 3.

59 "Beyond Sir's Ken," *New Society* (April 17, 1969): 600.

60 "The Embalmed City," *New Statesman* (April 12, 1963): 529.

61 Ibid., 530.

62 Ibid., 529.

63 Ibid., 529–530.

64 Ibid., 528.

65 Ibid., 530.

66 Ibid., 528.

67 Ibid., 530.

68 Ibid., 528.

69 Ibid., 530.

70 Ibid., 528. Banham's radicalism and anti-preservationism comes into sharpest focus when he berates those who complain about what the car is doing to the city: "Only once in a while does someone like Cedric Price have the guts to get up and counter-deplore what our towns are doing to cars" (ibid., 530).

71 Harold Wilson, "Labour and the Scientific Revolution," in *Annual Conference Report* (London: The Labour Party, 1963), 140.

72 Related to this was his *Mechanical Services.*

73 Stephen Bayley, "View from the Desert," *New Society* (August 13, 1981): 276.

74 See "Counter-Attack, NY," *Architects' Journal* (May 4 1961): 629–630.

75 *A Critic Writes,* 47.

76 Banham was, understandably, appointed editor of *The Aspen Papers: Twenty Years of Design Theory from the International Design Conference in Aspen* (London: Pall Mall, 1974).

77 He had been Benjamin Sonnenberg Visiting Professor there in the autumn of 1985.

78 The 1980s was the decade when Banham received international honors. They included an honorary doctorate from the Otis Parsons Institute in Los Angeles (1983), an honorary fellowship from the Royal Institute of British Architects (RIBA) (1983), Institute Honors ("for twenty years of architectural writing") from the American Institute of Architects (1984), and an honorary D.Litt. from his hometown University of East Anglia in Norwich (1986). He had also received the Prix Jean Tschumi of the Union Internationale des Architectes in 1975.

79 Mary Banham, in *A Critic Writes,* 149.

Chapter 1

1 "The Glass Paradise," *Architectural Review* (February 1959): 89.

2 "Machine Aesthetic," *Architectural Review* (April 1955): 225.

3 Ibid., 226.

4 Nikolaus Pevsner, *Pioneers of the Modern Movement* (London: Faber, 1936), 202.

5 Ibid.

6 Ibid., 179–180.

7 Ibid., 206.

8 Quoted in Frank Whitford, *Bauhaus* (London: Thames and Hudson, 1984), 38.

9 Walter Gropius, *The New Architecture and the Bauhaus* (London: Faber, 1935), 48.

10 Ibid., 53.

11 "1960 4: History Under Revision," *Architectural Review* (May 1960): 326.

12 Ibid., 331.

13 Ibid., 332.

14 "Machine Aesthetic," 227.

15 Or, in addition, the belief that simplicity and smoothness were aesthetically sophisticated, and thus represented cultural progress. This is something he discusses in "Ornament and Crime: The Decisive Contribution of Adolf Loos," *Architectural Review* (February 1957): 85–88.

16 "Machine Aesthetic," 227.

17 Ibid., 228.

18 Ibid., 226.

19 Ibid., 228.

20 Ibid.

21 "The Glass Paradise," 88.

22 Ibid., 87.

23 Ibid., 88.

24 Ibid., 89.

25 "Mendelsohn," *Architectural Review* (August 1954): 85.

26 Ibid.

27 Ibid., 89–90.

28 Ibid., 86.

29 There is a similar analysis of Finnish architectural aesthetics in "The One and the Few: The Rise of Modern Architecture in Finland," *Architectural Review* (April 1957): 243–248.

30 Quoted in John Maule McKean, "The Last of England?—Part 1," *Building Design* (August 13, 1976): 9. *Theory and Design in the First Machine Age* was dedicated, in part, to André Lurçat, Ernö Goldfinger, Pierre Vago, Rob van t'Hoff, Mart Stam, Walter Segal, Marcel Duchamp and Artur Korn "for the use of their memories or their libraries." Most of one section of the book is "in debt to the personal memoirs of survivors of the period" (265).

31 "Mendelsohn," 92–93.

32 Ibid., 93.

33 Ibid.

34 Ibid. This is, in fact, a topic Banham had discussed in "The Voysey Inheritance," *Architectural Review* (December 1952): 367–371.

35 "Mendelsohn," 86.

36 "The Glass Paradise," 88.

37 Lewis Mumford, *Art and Technics* (New York: Columbia Press, 1952), 54.

38 F. T. Marinetti, "The Founding and Manifesto of Futurism" (1909), in Umbro Apollonio, ed., *Futurist Manifestos* (London: Thames and Hudson, 1973), 22. The manifesto is discussed by Banham in "Futurist Manifesto," *Architectural Review* (August 1959): 77–80—an article to mark the fiftieth anniversary of its publication.

39 Marinetti, "Founding and Manifesto," 21.

40 Sant'Elia, "Manifesto of Futurist Architecture" (1914), in Ulrich Conrads, ed., *Programs and Manifestoes on 20th Century Architecture* (Cambridge, Mass.: MIT Press, 1970), 36.

41 Ibid., 38.

42 Banham updates the Sant'Elia research in "Footnotes to Sant'Elia," *Architectural Review* (June 1956): 343–444, claiming that his own article "proved to be the first swallow of a Santelian summer, in the course of which large and valuable contributions were made to the published material both on the architect himself and on

Futurist architecture in general" (343). Further historical research on the "Manifesto" is in "Futurism and Modern Architecture," *RIBA Journal* (February 1957) 129–139, and is summarized in *Theory and Design,* 127–131.

43   Conrads also differentiates between Sant'Elia's text, which had accompanied his "New City" exhibition, and the additions by Marinetti and Decio Cinti. See Conrads, *Programs and Manifestoes,* 34–38. According to Banham, Sant'Elia's statement was, in part, written by Ugo Nebbia, who claimed it adhered faithfully to Sant'Elia's ideas. See *Theory and Design,* 129.

44   "Sant'Elia," *Architectural Review* (May 1955): 300.

45   Ibid., 301.

46   This is part of the third proclamation of the "Manifesto." See Conrads, *Programs and Manifestoes,* 38.

47   "Sant'Elia," 301.

48   "Futurism and Modern Architecture": 129–139. The arrival of Futurism at the RIBA was itself a sign that the architectural establishment was beginning to accept that old certainties were no longer unchallengeable—Peter Smithson commented at the end of the lecture that Banham lecturing at the RIBA was like finding Jelly Roll Morton in the Library of Congress! (137).

49   Ibid., 131.

50   *Theory and Design,* 134.

51   Ibid., 131.

52   Ibid., 129. Banham maintained this position, as a letter from him in the *RIBA Journal* (May 1973): 247 confirms.

53   *Theory and Design,* 129.

54   Ibid.,132.

55   Banham discusses Futurism in relation to contemporary culture in "Futurism for Keeps," which will be discussed in chapter 3.

56   *Theory and Design,* 11–12.

57   Ibid., 10.

58   Ibid.

59   Ibid., 11.

60   Ibid.

61   Ibid., 99.

62   Ibid., 109.

63   Ibid., 183–184.

64   Ibid., 283.

65   Pevsner's *The Anti-Rationalists,* edited with J. M. Richards (London: Architectural Press, 1973) was a collection of essays on Romantics and outsiders by various authors, including Banham.

66   *Theory and Design,* 97.

67   Ibid., 95.

68   Ibid., 47.

69   Ibid., 45. Banham also uses the term "gossamer aestheticism" to describe Scott's contribution. See "Apropos the Smithsons," *New Statesman* (September 8, 1961): 317.

70   *Theory and Design,* 48.

71   Ibid., 66.

72   Ibid., 224.

73   Ibid., 241.

74   Ibid., 159.

75   Gleizes, quoted in ibid., 206.

76   *Theory and Design,* 245.

77   Ibid., 320.

78   Ibid., 324.

79   Ibid.

80   The incorporation of the car into the design of the plan posed a number of problems and possible solutions. These are outlined by Tim Benton in *The Villas of Le Corbusier* (New Haven: Yale University Press, 1987), but none could be claimed as an "inversion."

81   *Theory and Design,* 325.

82   Ibid.

83   Ibid., 321.

84   Ibid., 325.

85   Ibid., 12.

86   "Sant'Elia," 301.

87   In *The Anti-Rationalists,* Pevsner writes: "The book was originally called *Pioneers of the Modern Movement;* for there was then a Modern Movement, and I was of it, even if not as much as Sigfried Giedion. But a believer I certainly was" (1).

88   Pevsner, *Pioneers of Modern Design* (London: Pelican, 1960), 17.

89   Ibid., 211.

90   Ibid., 217.

91   See, for example, "All that Glitters Is Not Stainless," *Architectural Design* (August 1967): 351.

92   Frampton, in a letter to the author dated January 12, 2000.

93   See review by Jonathan Barnett, *Architectural Record* (August 1960): 84.

94   See, for example, a negative review by Harry H. Hilberry, *Society of Architectural Historians Journal* (December 1963): 241.

95   Review by Paul Goodman, *Arts* (January 1961): 20.

96   Review by Sibyl Moholy-Nagy, *Progressive Architecture* (April 1961): 200.

97   Review by Alan Colquhoun, *British Journal of Aesthetics* (January 1962), reprinted in Joan Ockman, ed., *Architecture Culture 1943–1968: A Documentary Anthology* (New York: Rizzoli, 1993), 343.

98   "On Trial: 6. Mies van der Rohe: Almost Nothing Is Too Much," *Architectural Review* (August 1962): 125–128; and "The Last Professional," *New Society* (December 18, 1969): 986–987.

99   "The Last Formgiver," *Architectural Review* (August 1966): 97–108; and "Le Corbusier," *New Society* (September 14, 1967): 353–355.

100   "Master of Freedom," *New Statesman* (April 18, 1959): 543–544; and "The Wilderness Years of Frank Lloyd Wright," *RIBA Journal* (December 1969): 512–519.

101 "Missing Persons," *New Statesman* (June 25, 1965): 1020.

102 "Hermann in Eden," *New Society* (December 9, 1971): 1154–1155.

103 "The Reputation of William Morris," *New Statesman* (March 8, 1963): 350–351.

104 "Painters of the Bauhaus," *The Listener* (April 19, 1962): 679–680; and "The Bauhaus Gospel," *The Listener* (September 26, 1968): 390–392. Both of these articles continue Banham's praise for those at the Bauhaus who were committed to change and innovation. They included Johannes Itten whom Banham describes as one of the Bauhaus's "greatest glories." "The Glass Paradise," *Architectural Review* (February 1959): 89.

105 Individual buildings are discussed in his *Guide to Modern Architecture* (London: Architectural Press, 1962) "as monuments to the creative skill of men in a particular situation—our present situation—not as demonstrations of philosophy or justifications of any theory" (10). *Guide* was revised and updated as *Age of the Masters: A Personal View of Modern Architecture* (London: Architectural Press, 1975). Neither of these books adds anything to the issues discussed in this chapter, and are essentially popularizing books for "architecture fans" (*Guide,* 9).

106 "Modern Monuments," *New Society* (November 14, 1986): 12–14.

107 "Nostalgia for Style," *New Society* (February 1, 1973): 248–249. All quotes from 249.

108 "The Tear-Drop Express," *Times Literary Supplement* (July 23, 1976): 907.

109 Pevsner, *Pioneers* (1960), 211.

110 "The Teardrop Express," 907.

111 "Machine Aesthetic," 228.

112 "Ornament and Crime," 85.

113 *Theory and Design;* 325. In *Age of the Masters,* Banham acknowledges that streamlining "as a *national* style and a serious style never made it. Johnson Wax alone survives as a testimony to what might have been" (105). It is interesting to note that he uses the word "serious."

114 Pevsner, *Pioneers* (1960), 210.

115 Sigfried Giedion, *Space, Time and Architecture* (London: Oxford University Press, 1971), 610.

116 Gropius, *New Architecture,* 92.

117 "Rudolph Schindler," *Architectural Design* (December 1967): 578.

118 Ibid., 579.

119 "Woman of the House," *New Society* (December 6, 1979): 555–556, is a respectful and affectionate tribute to Schindler's wife, who had continued to live in the Schindler Chase house.

120 *A Concrete Atlantis: U.S. Industrial Building and European Modern Architecture, 1900–1925* (Cambridge, Mass.: MIT Press, 1986). A related cassette/slide set was titled *Mythical Vernacular Monuments* (London: Pidgeon Audio Visual, 1982).

121 *A Concrete Atlantis,* 3.

122 Ibid., 7.

123 Named after, Banham points out, Francis Bacon's *New Atlantis,* in which "he describes an island in the ocean some long way to the west of Europe and specifically compares it to 'the Great Atlantis (that you call America),' though only to differentiate the real place from the imaginary." *A Concrete Atlantis:* 8.

124 Ibid., 19.

125 Ibid., 18.

126 Ibid., 53.

127 Ibid., 227.

128 Review by Nicholas Adams, *Times Literary Supplement* (October 10, 1986): 106.

129 *A Concrete Atlantis,* 68.

130 Banham also discusses the building in "Fiat: The Phantom of Order," *New Society* (April 18, 1985): 86–87.

131 *A Concrete Atlantis,* 237.

132 Ibid., 239.

133 Ibid., 247.

134 Ibid., 247–248.

135 Ibid., 236.

136 Marinetti, quoted in ibid., 246.

137 *A Concrete Atlantis,* 242.

138 Ibid., 243.

139   Ibid., 242.

140   "Futurism and Modern Architecture," 134, 135. See also *Theory and Design,* 193.

Chapter 2

1   The most notable is by Anne Massey, *The Independent Group: Modernism and Mass Culture in Britain, 1945–59* (Manchester: Manchester University Press, 1995). Other recent, more general texts on the Group include David Robbins ed., *The Independent Group: Postwar Britain and the Aesthetics of Plenty* (Cambridge, Mass.: MIT Press, 1990); and The Institute for Contemporary Art, *Modern Dreams: The Rise and Fall and Rise of Pop* (Cambridge, Mass.: MIT Press, 1988).

2   *Fathers of Pop,* film/video (London: Miranda Films, 1979). On the mythologizing of the group, see Massey, *The Independent Group,* chapter 8.

3   There is undoubtedly mythologizing in Banham's accounts of the Group. With one exception, he does not name the Independent Group in his articles in the 1950s, tending to refer—for example when discussing the Smithsons in 1956—to those who "have been involved in recent studies at the Institute of Contemporary Arts into the way in which advertising reflects and creates popular aesthetic standards" ("Things to Come?," *Design* [June 1956]: 28). In 1957, even an article on Lawrence Alloway makes no reference to the Independent Group, instead commenting that Alloway is the most successful of "a whole generation of junior pundits raised in that nursery of promise, *Art News and Review . . .*" ("Alloway and After," *Architects' Journal* [December 26, 1957]: 941). This may be because Banham thought of what was going on as a series of informal meetings taking place at the ICA rather than as the activities of a group defined by a name and identity.

   The exception to the absence of naming in the 1950s is "Industrial Design e arte popolare," *Civiltà delle macchine* (November/December 1955): 12–15 in which four footnotes refer to some of the lectures and discussions "del Gruppo Indipendente dell'ICA" between 1953 and 1955. The translation of this text as "A Throw-Away Aesthetic" (*Industrial Design* [March 1960]: 61–65) did not include the notes, and so no reference is made to the Independent Group. More surprisingly, given the parallels he was drawing between Futurism and contemporary society, Banham does not mention the Independent Group in "Futurism for Keeps" (*Arts* [December 1960]: 33–39), even though he remarks how Richard Hamilton and he "came down the stairs from the Institute of Contemporary Arts those combative evenings in the early fifties . . . into a London Boccioni had described" (37–39). In 1961 Banham refers to "the ICA's investigations into Pop culture" ("Apropos the Smithsons," *New Statesman* [September 8, 1961]: 317) and "pop-art polemics at the ICA" ("Design by Choice," *Architectural Review* [July 1961]: 44), and not to the Independent Group.

   In mid-1962, referring to the "pioneering studies of Borax styling . . . ," Banham still wrote of the ICA rather than the Independent Group ("Towards a Pop Architecture," *Architectural Review* [July 1962]: 43). But by the end of that year, he was naming the Independent Group and its members as "those who have helped to create the mental climate in which the Pop-art painters have been able to flourish in

England (there is a direct line from the Independent Group to Peter Blake and the Royal College) and the New American Dreamers in the USA" ("Who Is This 'Pop'?," *Motif* no. 10 [Winter 1962/1963]: 13). Soon afterward, he was criticizing "the Smithsons and Eduardo Paolozzi and people like that [who] have been calling rather necrophilic revivalist meetings of the Independent Group to try and clear their names of being responsible for the present pop art movement in England. It's now become necessary for them to revise their own immediate back-history and autobiography, almost in the Le Corbusier manner" ("The Atavism of the Short-Distance Mini-Cyclist," *Living Arts* no. 3 [1964]: 96).

Banham's own "back-history" of the Group commences around 1965, when he describes himself as "the only historian who was even remotely concerned with the original conception of the pop movement ten years ago." The Group was now being written firmly into history with the claim that, "by the time pop painting finally emerged . . . all the interested parties in England were able to discuss the pop product with a good deal of sophistication and the Independent Group's vocabulary" ("Pop and the Body Critical," *New Society* [December 16, 1965]: 25). The Pop artists themselves were less convinced of the significance of the Group's influence. Allen Jones in 1965 claimed that the activity of the Independent Group "was just a little beach in the blackness and it wasn't known outside a very small community. It wasn't enough to generate the kind of response that would create its own critical self awareness and out of that, the critics." And Richard Smith stated that "their views were influential but primarily for their sociological implications." See Bruce Glaser, "Three British Artists in New York," *Studio International* (November 1965): 175–183.

An interesting claim for the IG's significance appears in Banham's "Towards a Million-Volt Light and Sound Culture" (*Architectural Review* [May 1967]: 331–335), in which he compares the IG and Tom Wolfe in terms of class opposition to the establishment. The *Fathers of Pop* film (1979) completed Banham's own "back-history" of the Group.

4   See Massey, *The Independent Group,* 109–110.

5   In *Fathers of Pop.*

6   "Futurism for Keeps," *Arts* (December 1960): 33.

7   "The New Brutalism," *Architectural Review* (December 1955): 356.

8   A full list of topics with abstracts is in Massey, *The Independent Group,* 139–141.

9   In 1954 Banham chaired an Independent Group series of lectures titled "Books and the Modern Movement," also based on his contemporary research into Modernism.

10   Massey, *The Independent Group,* 140.

11   Ibid.

12   John McHale (1977), quoted in ibid., 77.

13   See ibid., appendix 2, 142–144.

14   Richard Hamilton, *Collected Words* (London: Thames and Hudson, 1983), 18.

15   He also reviewed "Man, Machine and Motion," *Architectural Review* (July 1955): 51–53.

16   Alison Smithson (1983), quoted in Massey, *The Independent Group,* 79.

17   Lawrence Alloway, introduction to *This Is Tomorrow* (London: Whitechapel Gallery, 1956), unpaginated. The phrase was borrowed from David Riesman's *The Lonely Crowd* (New Haven, Conn.: Yale University Press, 1950), an influential text in Independent Group circles for its analysis of changing social conditions.

18   "Space, Fiction and Architecture," *Architects' Journal* (April 17, 1958): 557–559.

19   "Space for Decoration: A Rejoinder," *Design* (July 1955): 24.

20   "The Atavism . . . ," 95.

21   Richard Hamilton remarked that, at the time of the IG activities, "there was no such thing as 'Pop Art' as we now use it." The use of the term by the IG referred "solely to art manufactured for a mass audience. 'Pop' is popular art in the sense of being widely accepted and used, as distinct from Popular Art of the handicrafted, folksy variety" (*Collected Words,* 28). The change in the common usage of Pop came in the early 1960s with the emergence of young artists on both sides of the Atlantic who incorporated the graphic imagery of popular culture—for example, pin-ups of film stars or jukebox graphics—into their work. This heralded the arrival of Pop art as an art historical movement.

22   Lawrence Alloway, "The Development of British Pop," in Lucy Lippard, ed., *Pop Art* (London: Thames and Hudson, 1966; 1974 ed.), 31–32.

23   "Vehicles of Desire," *Art* (September 1, 1955): 3 (all quotes).

24   "Who Is This 'Pop'?," 13.

25   Lawrence Alloway, "Personal Statement," *Ark* 19 (1957): 28.

26   Basil Taylor, "Art—Anti-Art," *The Listener* (November 12, 1959): 820.

27   "Pop and the Body Critical," *New Society* (December 16, 1965): 25.

28   Richard Hoggart, *The Uses of Literacy* (London: Chatto and Windus, 1957; 1958 ed.), 340.

29   Ibid., 343.

30   Ibid., 345.

31 "The Atavism . . . ," 93.

32 Ibid., 92.

33 Ibid., 93.

34 "A Flourish of Symbols," *The Observer Weekend Review* (November 17, 1963): 21.

35 "The End of Insolence," *New Statesman* (October 29, 1960): 646.

36 "A Flourish . . . ," 21.

37 Ibid. Banham refers to Hoggart several times in his articles, always in a derisory way, such as "sentimental Hoggartry," to describe outmoded assumptions about working-class architecture. See "Coronation Street, Hoggartsborough," *New Statesman* (February 9, 1962): 200–201.

38 Lawrence Alloway, "The Long Front of Culture," *Cambridge Opinion* 17 (1959): 25.

39 Hoggart, *The Use of Literacy,* 340.

40 Alloway, "The Long Front of Culture," 25.

41 John McHale, "The Expendable Ikon—1," *Architectural Design* (February 1959): 82.

42 Lawrence Alloway, "Notes on Abstract Art and the Mass Media," *Art* (February 27-March 12, 1960): 3.

43 "Who Is This 'Pop'?," 13.

44 Ibid.; Lawrence Alloway, "Artists as Consumers," *Image* 3 (1961): 18.

45 "Persuading Image: A Symposium," *Design* (June 1960): 55.

46 Alloway, "The Development of British Pop," 32.

47 Alloway, "Notes on Abstract Art . . . ," 3.

48 "The Atavism . . . ," 22.

49 Alloway, "Personal Statement," 28.

50 Alloway, "Notes on Abstract Art . . . ," 3. Banham made a related point in 1967: "With one eye [the Independent Group] saw a distant culture, remote beyond two thousand miles of water and the distortions of a common language. They thus had psychological distance and a sense of perspective that most American students of Pop culture never had. But with the other eye they saw something so close, and so familiar for much of their conscious lives, that it was more real than the humane learning they had acquired at grammar-school." "Towards a Million-Volt Light and Sound Culture," 332.

51   "Representations in Protest," *New Society* (May 8, 1969): 718.

52   "The Atavism . . . ," 92.

53   "First Master of the Mass Media?," *The Listener* (June 27, 1963): 1081.

54   Lawrence Alloway, "Technology and Sex in Science Fiction," *Ark* 17 (1956): 20.

55   Hoggart, *The Uses of Literacy,* 344.

56   Lawrence Alloway, "The Arts and the Mass Media," *Architectural Design* (February 1958): 34.

57   Herbert Read, *Art and Industry* (London: Faber, 1934; 1956 ed.), 17.

58   John McHale, "The Fine Arts in the Mass Media," *Cambridge Opinion* part 17 (1959): 28.

59   Alloway, "The Long Front of Culture," 25.

60   T. S. Eliot, *Notes Towards the Definition of Culture* (London: Faber, 1948; 1962 edition): 31.

61   Alloway, "Personal Statement," 28.

62   This was a claim being made around this time by Barbara Jones, whose book, *The Unsophisticated Arts,* was published in 1951 (London: Architectural Press), the same year as her "Black Eyes and Lemonade" exhibition at the Whitechapel Gallery, a part of the Festival of Britain.

63   Alloway, "Personal Statement," 28.

64   Alloway, "The Long Front of Culture," 25.

65   Lawrence Alloway, "Dada 1956," *Architectural Design* (November 1956): 374.

66   Alloway, "Personal Statement," 28.

67   John McHale, "The Plastic Parthenon," in Gillo Dorfles, ed., *Kitsch: The World of Bad Taste* (London: Studio Vista, 1969), 101.

68   McHale, "The Fine Arts . . . ," 29.

69   Hamilton, *Collected Words,* 151.

70   This is the term I employ in *Pop Design: Modernism to Mod* (London: The Design Council, 1987), 225–226.

71   "Design by Choice," 48.

72   "Vehicles of Desire," 3.

73   "A Throw-Away Aesthetic," *Industrial Design* (March 1960): 65. This article is a translation of "Industrial Design e arte popolare," 12–15.

74   "Vehicles of Desire," 3.

75   "Who Is This 'Pop'?," 12.

76   Ibid.

77   "Vehicles of Desire," 3.

78   "Space for Decoration: A Rejoinder," 24.

79   Ibid., 25.

80   Peter Blake, comments on "Space for Decoration: A Rejoinder," ibid.

81   Roy Sheldon and Egmont Arens, *Consumer Engineering: A New Technique for Prosperity* (New York: Harper and Brothers, 1932), 54.

82   Ibid.

83   *Theory and Design in the First Machine Age* (London: The Architectural Press, 1960), 9.

84   Ibid.

85   Ibid., 65.

86   Ibid., 64–65.

87   J. Gordon Lippincott, *Design for Business* (Chicago: Paul Theobold, 1947), 14.

88   Ibid.

89   Ibid., 15.

90   Ibid., 16.

91   Harley J. Earl, quoted in J. F. McCullough, "Design Review—Cars '59," *Industrial Design* (February 1959): 79.

92   "Design by Choice," 45.

93   Harley J. Earl, "What Goes into Automobile Designing?," *American Fabrics* 32 (1955): 78.

94   Eric Larrabee, "The Great Love Affair," *Industrial Design* (May 1955): 98.

95   George Nelson, "Obsolescence," *Industrial Design* (June 1956): 88.

96   Ibid., 82.

97   Banham praises Larrabee's contribution to design thinking in "Design by Choice," 44.

98   Ibid., 43.

99   Richard Hamilton, "*Hommage à Chrysler Corp.*," *Architectural Design* (March 1958): 121.

100   See Hamilton, *Collected Words,* 28.

101   John McHale wrote two articles titled "The Expendable Ikon," which appeared in *Architectural Design* (February 1959): 82–83, and (March 1959): 116–117.

102   *This Is Tomorrow,* unpaginated.

103   "Not Quite Architecture, Not Quite Painting or Sculpture Either," *Architects' Journal* (August 16, 1956): 63.

104   "This Is Tomorrow," *Architectural Review* (September 1956): 187.

105   Ibid., 186.

106   Ibid., 188.

107   Ibid.

108   Ibid., 187.

109   Alison and Peter Smithson, "Thoughts in Progress," *Architectural Design* (April 1957): 113.

110   Alison and Peter Smithson, "Statement" (1955), reprinted in *Without Rhetoric—An Architectural Aesthetic* (London: Latimer New Dimensions, 1973), 2.

111   "The New Brutalism," *Architectural Review* (December 1955): 355–361.

112   Michael Tapié, *Un Art autre* (Paris: Gabriel Giraud et Fils, 1952).

113   Jackson Pollock, "Statement" (1951), in Herschel B. Chipp, ed., *Theories of Modern Art* (Berkeley: University of California Press, 1968), 548.

114   "Futurism for Keeps," 39.

115   *The New Brutalism: Ethic or Aesthetic?* (London: Architectural Press, 1966), 61.

116   Ibid., 62.

117   "Machine Aesthetes," *New Statesman* (16 August 1958): 192.

118   Smithson and Smithson, "Statement," 2.

119   Banham draws a parallel between the "Angry Young Men" of English literature, and the New Brutalists in "Machine Aesthetes," 192. The former, a loose grouping of writers and critics that included John Osborne, Kenneth Tynan, John Wain, Lindsay Anderson, and Colin Wilson, were of the same generation as Banham and IG members, and gained notoriety and much publicity in 1957 with the publication of *Declaration.* However, Banham argued that the link was superficial because the Angry Young Men were "as dated as last week's [soccer] pools coupons [whereas] the Brutalists are not parochial."

120   See *The New Brutalism,* 10; and "The New Brutalism," 356–357.

121   Smithson and Smithson, *Statement,* 2.

122   Ibid.

123   "School at Hunstanton, Norfolk," *Architectural Review* (September 1954): 152.

124   Ibid., 153.

125   See "The Style for the Job," *New Statesman* (February 14, 1964): 261, and Banham's introduction to *James Stirling* (London: RIBA, 1974).

126   Rudolf Wittkower, "Architectural Principles in the Age of Humanism," *Studies of the Warburg Institute* XIX (1949); and Colin Rowe, "The Mathematics of the Ideal Villa: Palladio and Le Corbusier Compared," *Architectural Review* (March 1947): 101–104.

127   Philip Johnson, introductory statement in Banham's, "School at Hunstanton," 151.

128   Smithson and Smithson, "Thoughts in Progress," 113.

129   Ibid.

130   Alison and Peter Smithson, "Cluster City," *Architectural Review* (November 1957): 333.

131   When discussing topology, Banham advises that, for "a handy back-entrance . . . without using the highly complex mathematics involved, the reader could not do better than acquire a copy of *Astounding Science Fiction for* July, 1954" ("The New Brutalism," 361).

132 Ibid., 359.

133 Ibid., 357.

134 Ibid.

135 Ibid., 361.

136 Ibid.

137 Ibid.

138 Ibid., 356.

139 *The New Brutalism,* 68.

140 Ibid., 65.

141 See their special edition of *Architectural Design,* titled "The Heroic Period of Modern Architecture" (December 1965): 590ff.

142 See Peter Smithson, "Theories Concerning the Layout of Classical Greek Buildings," *Architectural Association Journal* (February 1959): 194–209.

143 *The New Brutalism,* 67.

144 However, in an article of 1961, Banham praises the Smithsons for their consistency toward imageability: "in spite of their stylistic variability, or because of it, they care deeply about what their buildings look like, and their aim is always to create an image that will convince and compel. When they demand that every building must be a prototype, an exemplar, for the cities of the future, they intend this not only to be read functionally, but visually too." Even their anti-Brutalist Economist Building is included in this notion of image-prototype, providing "a sort of sample of what future developments in central areas should look like." "Apropos the Smithsons," 317–318.

145 *The New Brutalism,* 69.

146 Alison Smithson, quoted in Thomas L. Schumacher, "Architectural Paradise Postponed," *Harvard Design Magazine* (Fall 1998): 82.

147 Alison and Peter Smithson, "But Today We Collect Ads," *Ark* (November 1956): 50.

148 Smithson and Smithson, "Thoughts in Progress," 113.

149 Smithson and Smithson, "But Today We Collect Ads," 49.

150   Ibid., 50.

151   "Things to Come?," 28.

152   Alison Smithson and Peter Smithson, "The Future of Furniture," *Architectural Design* (April 1958): 177.

153   Alison Smithson and Peter Smithson, "Talks to Fifth Year Students," *Architects' Journal* (May 21, 1959): 782.

154   "Things to Come?," 28.

155   Ibid., 25.

156   "A Throw-Away Aesthetic," 62.

157   "Design by Choice," 43.

158   Ibid., 44.

159   "Who Is This 'Pop'?," 12.

160   Stated in a letter to the author, dated August 12, 1980.

161   Banham also had concerns about the quality of the Smithsons' work "in this genre—the whole house tends to degenerate into a series of display niches for ever-changing relays of hire-purchased status-symbols." "Design by Choice," 46.

162   "The New Brutalism," 358.

163   "Who Is This 'Pop'?," 5.

164   Alloway, "The Arts and the Mass Media," 34.

165   Alloway, "The Development of British Pop," 32–33.

Chapter 3

1   *Theory and Design in the First Machine Age* (London: Architectural Press, 1960), 12.

2   Ibid., 9.

3   Ibid., 10.

4   Ibid.

5   "Vehicles of Desire," *Art* (September 1, 1955): 3.

6   *Theory and Design,* 9–10.

7   "Futurism for Keeps," *Arts* (January 7, 1960): 37–39.

8   Ibid., 37.

9   Ibid.

10 *Theory and Design,* 132.

11 "Sant'Elia," *Architectural Review* (May 1955): 301.

12 "Futurism for Keeps," 39.

13 "On Trial 1: What Architecture of Technology?," *Architectural Review* (February 1962): 97. Attacking the architectural profession was a perennial activity for Banham. Around this time he also attacked it because "In a century that has carried communications . . . from the electric semaphore to colour television, architects have achieved the equivalent of improving the appearance of the electric semaphore" ("The Small Revolution," *New Statesman* [October 17, 1959]: 504). In "Eighteen Thousand Marbleheads" (*Architects' Journal* [January 14, 1960]: 37–39), he complains that architects "design in almost total ignorance of the facts of life compared to the engineer" (39).

14 *Theory and Design,* 329–330.

15 "Machine Aesthetes," *New Statesman* (August 16, 1958): 192.

16 Ibid., 193.

17 "Le Corbusier," *New Society* (September 14, 1967): 355.

18 Ibid., 354.

19 Ibid., 355.

20 "The Last Professional," *New Society* (December 18, 1969): 987.

21 "On Trial 6. Mies van der Rohe: Almost Nothing Is Too Much," *Architectural Review* (August 1962): 126.

22 Ibid., 128.

23 Ibid., 126.

24 See "Casa, Scuola, Palazzo dell'Arte," *Domus* (December 1960): 11–12.

25 "On Trial 4: CLASP—Ill Met by Clip-joint?," *Architectural Review* (May 1962): 352.

26 Banham had earlier devoted a whole *New Statesman* column to a CLASP school just after its award ("A Gong for the Welfare State," *New Statesman* [January 6, 1961]: 26–27). He describes its authority, which comes "from the sustained application of experienced imagination to the resolution of every problem, however fundamental, however superficial," and, as in his more sustained "On Trial" essay, concludes that its achievement is that it represents "'*une architecture autre,*' something different from the architecture to which we have been accustomed since the Renaissance" (26–27). Banham also likens CLASP architecture to something akin to a consumer product: "The idea that architecture of this quality should be rolling off the production line, almost like cars or fridges, was just too much for some people" (26). This rather fanciful parallel with the *House of the Future* is not something Banham took further.

27 He discusses the Eames approach to designing in "Tridon," *Architectural Review* (April 1958): 231, and describes the Eameses' "open-minded, experimental, hands-on, improvisatory [and] quirky" approach (186) in "Klarheit, Ehrichkeit, Einfachkeit . . . and Wit Too!," in Elizabeth A. T. Smith, ed., *Blueprints for Modern Living: History and Legacy of the Case Study Houses* (Cambridge, Mass.: MIT Press, 1989), 183–195.

28 *Guide to Modern Architecture* (London: Architectural Press, 1962), 28.

29 *Age of the Masters: A Personal View of Modern Architecture* (London: Architectural Press, 1975), 77.

30 "On Trial 6," 128.

31 "On Trial 1. What Architecture of Technology?," *Architectural Review* (February 1962): 99.

32 Ibid.

33 See "On Trial 2. Louis Kahn: The Buttery Hatch Aesthetic," *Architectural Review* (March 1962): 203–206.

34 "On Trial 1," 98.

35 Ibid.

36 *Guide to Modern Architecture,* 64.

37 "On Trial 6,"128.

38 "1960 1: Stocktaking—Tradition and Technology," *Architectural Review* (February 1960): 94.

39 *Theory and Design,* 326.

40 The full text is published as "Influences on My Work" (1955), in James Meller, ed., *The Buckminster Fuller Reader* (London: Pelican, 1972), 44–68.

41 There is a passing reference to Fuller in the first chapter of *Theory and Design,* in which Banham calls him "an engineer" (20).

42 "Thought Is Comprehensive," *New Statesman* (August 15, 1959): 188–189. See also "The Dymaxicrat," *Arts Magazine* (October 1963): 66–69.

43 Fuller, "Influences . . . ," 64.

44 Marshall McLuhan, "Buckminster Fuller Chronofile" (1967) in James Meller, ed., *The Buckminster Fuller Reader* (London: Pelican, 1972), 30.

45 *The New Brutalism: Ethic or Aesthetic?* (London: Architectural Press, 1966), 69.

46 "1960 1," 94.

47 Philip Johnson, "Where We Are At," *Architectural Review* (September 1960): 175.

48 "Futurism for Keeps," 39.

49 *Theory and Design,* 327.

50 Ibid., 382.

51 "1960 1," 94.

52 Banham quoted in Ann Ferebee, "Home Thoughts From Abroad," *Industrial Design* (August 1963): 78.

53 Banham, with A. C. Brothers, M. E. Drummond, and R. Llewelyn Davies, "1960 2: The Science Side," *Architectural Review* (March 1960): 190.

54 Ibid.

55 Buckminster Fuller, "The Architect as World Planner" (1961), in Ulrich Conrads, ed., *Programs and Manifestoes on 20th Century Architecture* (Cambridge, Mass.: MIT Press, 1970), 180.

56 Hannes Meyer, "Building" (1928) in Ulrich Conrads, ed., *Programs and Manifestoes on 20th Century Architecture,* 120.

57 Banham does reevaluate Meyer somewhat in "Missing Persons," *New Statesman* (June 25, 1965): 1020. He refers to him as "a sort of *beau idéal* of the modern architect of 1928: scientific, geometricising, socially committed," and praises him for his attitude to change at the Bauhaus.

58 See Ulrich Conrads, ed., *Programs and Manifestoes on 20th Century Architecture,* 117–20.

59 Ibid., 119.

60 *Theory and Design,* 306.

61 "1960 1," 95.

62 "Pop and the Body Critical," *New Society* (December 16, 1965): 25.

63 Banham, J. M. Richards, Nikolaus Pevsner, Hugh Casson and H. deC. Hastings, "1960 5: Propositions," *Architectural Review* (June 1960): 381–389. See also the comments following "The History of the Immediate Future," 252–269.

64 "1960 1," 96.

65 "Things to Come?," *Design* (June 1956): 27.

66 Hugh Casson, in Banham et al., "1960 5," 385.

67 Nikolaus Pevsner, ibid.

68 Banham, ibid.

69 "Space for Decoration: A Rejoinder," *Design* (July 1955): 25.

70 "1960 5," 388.

71 Ibid.

72 Ibid.

73 "On Trial 5. The Spec Builders: Towards a Pop Architecture," *Architectural Review* (July 1962): 43.

74 Ibid., 44.

75 Opening statement, *Archigram Paper One* (May 1961): unpaginated.

76 Peter Cook ed., *Archigram* (London: Studio Vista, 1972), 8.

77 Ibid., 16.

78 Ibid.

79 *Archigram 3* (1963): unpaginated.

80 Cook, *Archigram,* 15.

81 Ibid., 11.

82 *Megastructure: Urban Futures of the Recent Past* (London: Thames and Hudson, 1976), 17.

83 Peter Cook, "Responses," *Architectural Association Journal* (December 1966): 140.

84 Editorial, *Archigram 4,* reprinted in Cook, *Archigram,* 27.

85 "A Clip-on Architecture," *Design Quarterly* 63 (1965): 30.

86 Banham's last completed book, finished a month before his death, was also Archi-gram-related, a study titled *The Visions of Ron Herron* (London: Academy Editions, 1994).

87 "A Clip-on Architecture," 5.

88 Ibid., 9.

89 Banham first used the term "clip-on" in "Without Mercy or Metaphor," *The Listener* (November 13, 1958): 775–776 when discussing robot detectives in science fiction.

90 "A Clip-on Architecture," 9.

91 Ibid., 10.

92 Ibid., 11.

93 Ibid., 30.

94 Ibid., 11.

95 Ibid., 30.

96 See Nigel Whiteley, *Pop Design: Modernism to Mod* (London: The Design Council, 1987), chapter 5.

97 Cook, *Archigram,* 5.

98 Ibid.

99 *Megastructure,* 100.

100 Ibid., 100–101.

101 Warren Chalk, quoted in Priscilla Chapman, "The Plug-in City," *Sunday Times Colour Supplement* (September 20, 1964): 33.

102 Harold Wilson, "Labour and the Scientific Revolution," *Annual Conference Report* (London: Labour Party, 1963), 140.

103 Priscilla Chapman, "What the Kids Are Doing," *Sunday Times Colour Supplement* (August 30, 1964): 42.

104   "Bulge Takes Over," *Town* (September 1962): 43.

105   Quant, *Quant by Quant* (London: Cassell, 1966), 74.

106   Harley J. Earl, "What Goes into Automobile Designing," *American Fabrics* 32 (1955): 78.

107   "Zoom Wave Hits Architecture," *New Society* (March 3, 1966): 21 (for all quotes).

108   "Futurism for Keeps" is the most obvious example. Also, in "Futurist Manifesto," *Architectural Review* (August 1959): 77–80, Banham outlines the contemporary relevance of the manifesto.

109   Banham makes a similar point about the Bauhaus: it is its attitude to a live, and therefore changing, outlook, and to a belief in "continuous development"—not the collection of forms or theories—that is its greatest legacy. See "The Bauhaus Gospel," *The Listener* (September 26, 1968): 392.

110   Statement in *Megascope* 3 (November 1965): unpaginated.

111   Le Corbusier, *Towards a New Architecture* (London: Architectural Press, 1927; 1970 ed.), 269.

112   Buckminster Fuller, extract from lecture, *Megascope* 3 (November 1965): unpaginated.

113   Stated as early as 1960 in "1960 1," 93.

Chapter 4

1   Banham uses the phrase in "1960 1: Stocktaking—Tradition and Technology," *Architectural Review,* (February 1960): 93, and links it to *architecture autre.*

2   Rosalind Krauss, "Sculpture in the Expanded Field" (1979), reprinted in Hal Foster, ed., *Postmodern Culture* (London: Pluto Press, 1985), 31–42. These quotes, p. 31.

3   Ibid., 38.

4   Ibid., 39.

5   Buckminster Fuller, lecture extract, *Megascope* 3 (November 1965): unpaginated.

6   "A Home Is Not a House," *Art in America* (April 1965): 70.

7   The historical phase Banham is recounting is when the cost of mechanical services for a wide range of public buildings becomes significant. There were earlier excep-

tions, such as Broadcasting House, which Banham discusses in "The Fully Conditioned Interior," in *Mechanical Services,* unit 21 of A305 (Milton Keynes, U.K.: The Open University, 1975), 18–20.

8 *The Architecture of the Well-tempered Environment* (London: Architectural Press, 1969), 252.

9 Ibid., 249.

10 Ibid.

11 The book most commonly cited in connection with Banham's theme was Sigfried Giedion's *Mechanisation Takes Command* (Oxford: Oxford University Press, 1948). Banham was dismissive of its reputation as "a new and revealing study of American technology," stating in the main text of *The Architecture of the Well-tempered Environment* that "It proved, however, in no way to deserve such a reputation. . . . The true fault of the book lay in its reception. Awed by the immense reputation of its author, the world of architecture received *Mechanisation Takes Command* as an authoritative and conclusive statement, not as a tentative beginning on a field of study that opened almost infinite opportunities for further research. In the ensuing twenty-odd years since its publication, it has been neither glossed, criticised, annotated, extended nor demolished" (13, 14–15).

12 *The Architecture of the Well-tempered Environment,* 12.

13 Ibid., 120.

14 Ibid., 12.

15 Ibid., 171.

16 This is part of the title of a biography of Carrier. Ibid., 172, note 2.

17 Ibid., 175.

18 Ibid., 178.

19 Ibid., 187.

20 Ibid., 192.

21 Ibid., 242.

22 Ibid., 76.

23 Ibid., 82–83.

24 Ibid., 83.

25 Further research confirmed Banham's judgment about the building's significance, but his attribution of the mechanical services part of the design has been questioned. See John Tovey, "Ventilating the Royal Victoria Hospital," *RIBA Journal* (October 1981): 8–9.

26 *The Architecture of the Well-tempered Environment,* 83.

27 Ibid., 83–84.

28 See Adolf Loos, "Cultural Degeneration" (1908), in Yehuda Safran and Wilfried Wang, eds., *The Architecture of Adolf Loos* (London: Arts Council, 1987), 99.

29 Le Corbusier, *Towards a New Architecture* (London: Architectural Press, 1927; 1970 ed.), 42.

30 *The Architecture of the Well-tempered Environment,* 70.

31 Ibid., 86.

32 Ibid., 90.

33 Ibid., 92.

34 Ibid., 91.

35 *The Architecture of the Well-tempered Environment,* 2nd ed. (Chicago: University of Chicago Press, 1984), 305.

36 *The Architecture of the Well-tempered Environment* (1969 ed.), 92.

37 Ibid., 27.

38 Ibid., 112.

39 Ibid., 124.

40 Ibid., 134.

41 Ibid., 148.

42 Ibid., 130.

43 Herbert Read, *Art and Industry,* rev. ed. (London: Faber, 1956), 7.

44 *The Architecture of the Well-tempered Environment* (1969 ed.), 129.

45 It actually seems more like Sir Reginald Blomfield, a staunch and intolerant traditionalist. It is hard to imagine someone more opposite to Banham in his views, but Blomfield's infamous book, *Modernismus* (London: Faber, 1934), includes a condemnation of Modernism because it is "a conscious and deliberate pose, based on mistaken sociological theories and on arbitrary psychological assumptions" imported from Europe, especially from Germany (168–169). This appears not wholly different from Banham's criticism.

46 *The Architecture of the Well-tempered Environment* (1969 ed.), 121.

47 Ibid., 123.

48 Ibid., 122.

49 Ibid., 162.

50 Ibid., 162–163.

51 Ibid., 170.

52 "1960 1," 94.

53 "A Home Is Not a House," 75.

54 Ibid., 80.

55 See Philip Johnson, "House at New Canaan, Connecticut," *Architectural Review* (September 1950): 152–159.

56 *The Architecture of the Well-tempered Environment* (1969 ed.), 231–232.

57 Ibid., 233.

58 "A Home Is Not a House," 79.

59 Le Corbusier in *Precisions* (1930), quoted in *The Architecture of the Well-tempered Environment* (1969 ed.), 159.

60 *The Architecture of the Well-tempered Environment* (1969 ed.), 160.

61 Ibid., 274.

62 "A Home Is Not a House," 79.

63 Ibid., 73.

64 Ibid., 75.

65 Ibid.

66 Ibid., 73.

67 Ibid., 75–76.

68 "The Great Gizmo," *Industrial Design* (September 1965): 49.

69 Ibid., 49–50.

70 Ibid., 52.

71 Ibid. Banham writes of Evinrude: "So ideal, and so American is this solution, that other one-shot aids to the back-porch technologist have proliferated—to cite only one, the adapters that make it possible for any hot-rod-crazy to fit any engine to almost any gearbox and transmission. Warshavsky's [*sic*] current catalogue has three pages of them" (ibid.). We will return to Warshawsky, and the design approach it represents, in chapter 6.

72 "A Home Is Not a House," 79.

73 "Softer Hardware," *Ark* (Summer 1969): 11.

74 Cedric Price, quoted in Jim Burns, *Arthropods* (London: Academy Editions, 1972), 58.

75 Cedric Price, "Fun Palace" (1965), reprinted in *Cedric Price: Works II* (London: Architectural Association, 1984), 56. (Exhibition catalog).

76 "People's Palaces," *New Statesman* (August 7, 1964): 191.

77 Ibid., 191–192.

78 Ibid., 191.

79 Cedric Price, summary of "Planning for Pleasure" (1964), quoted in *Cedric Price: Works II*, 61.

80 Price, quoted in Banham, "The Open City and Its Enemies," *The Listener* (September 23, 1976): 359.

81 Banham refers to the significance of John Huizinga's *Homo Ludens* in *Megastructure: Urban Futures of the Recent Past* (London: Thames and Hudson, 1976), 60.

82 Lawrence Alloway, "Notes on Abstract Art and the Mass Media," *Art* (February 27–March 12, 1960): 3.

83 Peter Cook, "What of the Future?," in Ella Moody, ed., *Decorative Art and Modern Interiors 1966–7* (London: Studio Vista, 1966), 6.

84 Peter Cook, "Control and Choice," reprinted in Peter Cook, ed., *Archigram* (London: Studio Vista, 1972), 68.

85 Peter Cook, *Archigram* 8 (1968): unpaginated.

86 Cook, *Archigram,* 74.

87 Peter Cook, quoted in "Pneu World," *Architectural Design* (June 1968): 259.

88 "Monumental Windbags," *New Society* (April 18, 1968): 569.

89 Ibid., 570.

90 Arthur Quarmby, *The Plastics Architect* (London: Pall Mall, 1974), 114.

91 Paul Scheerbart, *Glass Architecture* (London: November Books, 1914; reprinted 1972), 41.

92 "Monumental Windbags," 570.

93 A number of strands of Banham's thought at this time—the controllable, responsive, and soft environments; *Homo ludens* and the Pop sensibility; and the new cultural conditions—coalesced in another article of 1968, "Triumph of Software" (*New Society* [October 31, 1968]: 62). It acts as a bridge between the idea of architecture in the expanded field, and the wider scale of the city.

94 Cook, *Archigram,* 38.

95 Peter Cook, Ron Herron, and Dennis Crompton, "Instant City," *Architectural Design* (May 1969): 277.

96 Banham wrote of "light-sound raves" in "The Eleclit Undersound," *Interior Design* (November 1967): 48–50. His contention was that these events depend upon "a recent combination of affluence and portable technology [such as] overhead projectors, baby spots, tape decks, movie projectors, amplifiers, strobes and whatnot . . . [which are] fairly easy to buy, rent or scrounge, fairly easy to set up if you have fifteen amp power outlets, and very easy to operate. . . . This do-it-yourself potential helps psychedelic consumers believe that in some way they have done it themselves, are involved as communicants rather than as customers. Overt professionalism is suspect" (48).

97 Peter Cook and Ron Herron, "Instant City," *Architectural Design* (November 1970): 567.

98 Ibid.

99 Fuller had anticipated what was, in effect, the Instant City: "autonomous facilities and helicopter transport will make possible the initiation of utterly new civil centres requiring neither sewage, water nor power mains. This independence of means will permit overnight air dropping of complete towns at new sites." "Continuous Man" (1960–1963), in James Meller, ed., *The Buckminster Fuller Reader* (London: Pelican, 1972), 365.

100 Cook, Herron, and Crompton, "Instant City," 280.

101 Tom Wolfe, "Las Vegas (What?) Las Vegas (Can't Hear You! Too Noisy) Las Vegas!!!" (1965), in *The Kandy-Kolored Tangerine-Flake Streamline Baby* (London: Mayflower, 1972), 18.

102 Robert Venturi, *Learning from Las Vegas* (Cambridge, Mass.: MIT Press, 1972), 1.

103 Robert Venturi and Denise Scott Brown, "A Significance for A&P Parking Lots, or Learning from Las Vegas," *Architectural Forum* (March 1968): 37–43.

104 Venturi, *Learning from Las Vegas,* 87.

105 Wolfe, "Las Vegas (What?) . . . ," 19; Venturi and Scott Brown, "Significance . . . ," 52.

106 *The Architecture of the Well-tempered Environment* (1969 ed.), 269–270.

107 Scheerbart, *Glass Architecture,* 72.

108 *The Architecture of the Well-tempered Environment* (1969 ed.), 270. This was something he did not change his mind about. In his 1975 *Age of the Masters: A Personal View of Modern Architecture,* he made a similar point: "It may sound strange, almost blasphemous, to say so, but it is in Las Vegas that one comes nearest to seeing gross matter transformed into etherial substance by the power of light" (62).

109 *Los Angeles: The Architecture of Four Ecologies* (London: Pelican, 1971), 124.

110 Ibid., 21.

111 Ibid.

112 Ibid., 22.

113 Ibid., 23.

114 Ibid., 24.

115 Ibid., 99.

116 Ibid., 173.

117 Ibid., 201.

118 Ibid., 36.

119 This is the title of a film Banham wrote, directed, and presented for the BBC, broadcast in 1972.

120 Adam Raphael, *The Guardian* (July 22, 1968), quoted in *Los Angeles,* 16.

121 "Encounter with Sunset Boulevard," *The Listener* (August 22, 1968): 235.

122   *Los Angeles,* 243.

123   Ibid., 185.

124   Ibid., 134.

125   The concept of critical regionalism is developed by Kenneth Frampton, "Towards a Critical Regionalism: Six Points for an Architecture of Resistance," in Hal Foster, ed., *Postmodern Culture* (London: Pluto Press, 1985), 16–30.

126   *Los Angeles,* 139.

127   Ibid., 123–24.

128   Ibid., 129.

129   "The Art of Doing Your Thing," *The Listener* (September 12, 1968): 331.

130   Ibid., 330.

131   Ibid.

132   *Los Angeles,* 222.

133   Ibid., 22.

134   Ibid., 88–90.

135   "Roadscape with Rusting Rails," *The Listener* (August 29, 1968): 268.

136   See Ulrich Conrads, ed., *Programs and Manifestoes on 20th Century Architecture* (Cambridge, Mass.: MIT Press, 1970), 36.

137   *Los Angeles,* 214–215.

138   Ibid., 216.

139   Banham was largely dismissive of the smog criticism: "On what is regarded as a normally clear day in London, one cannot see as far through the atmosphere as on some officially smoggy days I have experienced in Los Angeles. Furthermore, the photochemical irritants in the smog . . . can be extremely unpleasant indeed in high concentrations, but for the concentration to be high enough to make the corners of my eyes itch painfully is rare in my personal experience, and at no time does the smog contain levels of soot, grit, and corroding sulphur compounds that are still common in the atmospheres of older American and European cities." Ibid., 215–216.

140   Ibid., 222. It may also be significant that Banham had only recently learned to drive: "like earlier generations of English intellectuals who taught themselves Italian in order to read Dante in the original, I learned to drive in order to read Los Angeles in the original" (Ibid., 23). Perhaps Banham was enjoying the novelty of being able to drive—something that he had learned only in 1966, at the age of forty-four. See "Unlovable at Any Speed," *Architects' Journal* (December 21, 1966): 1527–1529.

141 *Los Angeles,* 210–211.

142 Ibid., 236.

143 Ibid., 243.

144 Ibid.

145 Ibid., 36.

146 See Anne Massey, *The Independent Group: Modernism and Mass Culture in Britain, 1945–59* (Manchester: Manchester University Press, 1995), app. 2, 142–144.

147 "The ceaseless irregular motion of dust particles which is observed in liquids and gases." Alan Bullock and Oliver Stallybrass, eds., *The Fontana Dictionary of Modern Thought* (London: Fontana, 1977), 79.

148 Lawrence Alloway, "The Long Front of Culture," *Cambridge Opinion* no. 17 (1959): 25.

149 "The Art of Doing Your Thing," 330.

150 "Beverly Hills, Too, Is a Ghetto," *The Listener* (September 5, 1968): 298.

151 Ibid.

152 "Roadscape with Rusting Rails," 267. Banham does not discuss the social problems of Watts in Los Angeles, making only a passing reference (173).

153 Richard Austin Smith, "Los Angeles: Prototype of Supercity," *Fortune* (March 1965), quoted in *Los Angeles,* 17.

154 *Los Angeles,* 248.

155 Ibid., 203.

156 Ibid., 238–240.

157 "Roadscape with Rusting Rails," 267.

158 *Los Angeles,* 75.

159 Ibid., 23.

160 "Encounter with Sunset Boulevard," 236.

161   *Los Angeles,* 23–24.

162   Ibid., 237.

163   Ibid., 137.

164   Ibid., 237.

165   "Pop and the Body Critical," *New Society* (December 16, 1965): 25.

166   *Los Angeles,* 244.

167   Review by John Donat, "Drive-in City," *RIBA Journal* (May 1971): 218.

168   Review by John S. Margolies, *Architectural Forum* (November 1971): 10.

169   Review by Thomas S. Hines, *Journal of the Society of Architectural Historians* (March 1972): 76.

170   Peter Plagens, "Los Angeles: The Ecology of Evil," *Artforum* (December 1972): 76.

171   Hall was professor of geography at the University of Reading; Barker, editor of *New Society.*

172   "Non-Plan: An Experiment in Freedom," *New Society* (March 20, 1969): 436.

173   Ibid., 442.

174   Ibid., 442–443.

175   A rare example of "spontaneity and vitality" in Britain was the Windsoc pub, written about by Banham in "Immoral Uplift," *New Society* (February 24, 1972): 405–406.

176   "Non-Plan," 443.

177   Quoted in "The Open City and its Enemies," 359.

178   *The Plan for Milton Keynes,* vol. 1 (Milton Keynes, U.K.: Milton Keynes Development Corporation, 1970), xi.

179   "The Open City," 359.

Chapter 5

1   Peter Cook, "The Electric Decade: An Atmosphere at the AA School 1963–73," in James Gowan, ed., *A Continuing Experiment: Learning and Teaching at the Architectural Association* (London: Architectural Press, 1975), 142.

2 Nikolaus Pevsner, "Architecture in Our Time—1," *The Listener* (December 29, 1966): 954. Pevsner made it clear in the introduction to *The Anti-Rationalists: Art Nouveau Architecture and Design,* coedited with J. M. Richards (London: Architectural Press, 1973), that he had still not changed his mind.

3 Nor, indeed, was his relationship to Pevsner, which will be discussed in the conclusion.

4 Quoted by Penny Sparke in an interview with Banham, "The Machine Stops," *Design* (December 1980): 31.

5 See "Le Corbusier," *New Society* (September 14, 1967): 355.

6 Pevsner would have been hard pressed to deny an aesthetic element of his zeitgeist justification, attacking the "fervent avoidance of lightness, of anything that could be called elegant" ("Architecture in Our Time—1" 954) in the contemporary architecture of which he disapproved. Not all "new materials" produced an architecture that was intrinsically light and elegant.

7 "1960 1: Stocktaking—Tradition and Technology," *Architectural Review* (February 1960): 96–97.

8 Nikolaus Pevsner, "Architecture in Our Time—2," *The Listener* (January 5, 1967): 7. Pevsner was still attacking Stirling in 1973 in the introduction to *The Anti-Rationalists,* 2.

9 "The Style for the Job," *New Statesman* (February 14, 1964): 261; "The Word in Britain: 'Character,'" *Architectural Forum* (August–September 1964): 118–124.

10 "The Word in Britain: 'Character,'" 119.

11 Ibid., 123–124.

12 Ibid., 121.

13 Ibid., 123.

14 Ibid., 121.

15 The friendship dated back to the beginning of the 1950s when Banham met, and became friendly with, Stirling as well as Colin St. J. Wilson, Robert Maxwell, Alan Colquhoun, the Smithsons, Richard Hamilton, Eduardo Paolozzi, Nigel Henderson, Bill Turnbull, and Sam Stevens. Banham remarked that "most of my indoctrination into the Modern Movement in architecture came from the Sam Stevens/Bob Maxwell/Jim Stirling/Sandy Wilson network" in which "Sunday morning coffee *chez Banham* became almost [a] religious rite." Banham, quoted in John Maule McKean, "The Last of England?—Part 1," *Building Design* (August 13, 1976): 8.

16 "The Word in Britain: 'Character,'" 119.

17 Ibid., 124.

18 "The New Brutalism," *Architectural Review* (December 1955): 357.

19 "The Word in Britain: 'Character,'" 121.

20 *The New Brutalism: Ethic or Aesthetic?* (London: Architectural Press, 1966), 134.

21 Ibid.

22 "Plucky Jims," *New Statesman* (July 19, 1958): 83.

23 See Kenneth Frampton, "Towards a Critical Regionalism: Six Points for an Architecture of Resistance," in Hal Foster, ed., *Postmodern Culture* (London: Pluto Press, 1985), 16–29.

24 Pevsner, "Architecture in Our Time—1," 953.

25 "History Faculty, Cambridge," *Architectural Review* (November 1968): 329.

26 Ibid., 330.

27 Ibid., 330–331.

28 Ibid., 331.

29 Banham devoted a whole column to Finagle's Law in *Architects' Journal* (October 22, 1959): 373–375.

30 "History Faculty, Cambridge," 330.

31 "Play Power," *New Society* (January 7, 1971): 26.

32 "History Faculty, Cambridge," 330. There is perhaps an irony here that Stirling is related to Expressionism, given Pevsner's attack on the "neo-Expressionism" of his Leicester building.

33 Nikolaus Pevsner, *The Buildings of England: Cambridgeshire,* rev. ed. (London: Penguin, 1970), 217.

34 "History Faculty, Cambridge," 332.

35 Ibid. Banham deals with the History Faculty building within the context of Cambridge architecture more fully in "Cambridge Mark II," *New Society* (September 26, 1968): 454–455.

36 Banham's writings on Stirling were almost invariably full of praise. However, a more critical piece is "Coronation Street, Hoggartsborough," *New Statesman* (February 9, 1962): 200–201, in which Banham wonders whether, although Stirling and Gowan, in their working-class housing scheme in Avenham, Preston, may provide "a functional and visual setting for much that is valuable in proletarian culture *at the moment,* they are prepared to accept a visual style that may leave a developing working class lumbered with an unsuitable functional environment 20 affluent years from now" (201).

37 "Cambridge Mark II," 454.

38 Ibid.

39 "History Faculty, Cambridge," 332.

40 Gavin Stamp, "Stirling's Worth: The History Faculty Building," *Cambridge Review* (January 30, 1976): 79.

41 "Machine Aesthetic," *Architectural Review* (April 1955): 228.

42 Gavin Stamp, "The Durability of Reputation," *Harvard Design Magazine* (Fall 1997): 55.

43 Stamp, "Stirling's Worth," 81.

44 Stamp, "The Durability of Reputation," 57.

45 Stewart Brand, *How Buildings Learn* (London: Viking Books, 1994), 58.

46 David Watkin, *Morality and Architecture* (Oxford: Oxford University Press, 1977), x.

47 Stamp, "Stirling's Worth," 77.

48 Sorbonne students quoted in Theodore Roszak, *The Making of a Counter Culture* (London: Faber, 1969), 22.

49 Quoted in Anne Corbett, "Building Architects," *New Society* (February 19, 1970): 298.

50 Peter Hodgkinson, "Drug-in City," *Architectural Design* (November 1969): 586.

51 Michael Middleton, "The Wider Issues at Stake," *The Designer* (February 1970): 1.

52 Hasan Ozbekhan, quoted in "Technology: Good Servant or Errant Monster?," *Design* (October 1969): 56.

53 Statement by the French Group in Reyner Banham, ed., *The Aspen Papers: Twenty Years of Design Theory from the International Design Conference in Aspen* (London: Pall Mall, 1974), 208.

54 Malcolm MacEwen, *Crisis in Architecture* (London, RIBA Publications, 1974), 22. A similar attack can be found in Brent C. Brolin, *The Failure of Modern Architecture* (London: Studio Vista, 1976).

55 Stamp, "The Durability of Reputation," 56.

56 Banham, quoted in John Maule McKean, "The Last of England?—Part 2," *Building Design* (August 27, 1976): 26–27.

57 *The Aspen Papers,* 222.

58 "History Faculty, Cambridge," 332. Harvey Court was a hostel for Caius College designed by Leslie Martin and Colin St John Wilson.

59 Patrick Cormack, *Heritage in Danger* (London: Quarter Books, 1978), 15–16.

60 Christopher Booker, *The Seventies* (London: Penguin, 1980), 271.

61 "Only an Academic Flywheel?," *RIBA Journal* (August 1972): 338.

62 "Preserve Us from Paranoid Preservers," *The Observer Magazine* (October 21, 1973): 15.

63 "Slight Agony in the Garden," *New Society* (December 17, 1981): 507.

64 "King Lut's Navy," *New Society* (November 12, 1981): 285.

65 Nikolaus Pevsner, "Building with Wit," *Architectural Review* (April 1951): 217–225.

66 "King Lut's Navy," 284.

67 "The Thing in the Forecourt," *New Society* (July 28, 1983): 138.

68 "King Lut's Navy," 284.

69 Cormack, *Heritage in Danger,* 14.

70 Gavin Stamp, letter in *New Society* (November 19, 1981): 339.

71 "King Lut's Navy," 285.

72 "The Writing on the Walls," *Times Literary Supplement* (November 17, 1978): 1337.

73 Charles Jencks, *The Language of Post-Modern Architecture,* 2nd ed. (London: Academy Editions, 1978), 8.

74 "The Writing on the Walls," 1337.

75 "Vehicles of Desire," *Art* (September 1, 1955): 3.

76 "The Purified Aesthetic," *New Society* (June 26, 1975): 788. This was written at the time of the growing interest in and appetite for decoration as a reaction against Modernist plainness. It incorporated movements like the Crafts Revival and

Memphis. For an account of this tendency, see Robert Jensen and Patricia Conway, eds., *Ornamentalism* (New York: Viking, 1982).

77 "The Purified Aesthetic," 788.

78 Letter from Charles Jencks, *Times Literary Supplement* (December 1, 1978): 1402.

79 "The Purified Aesthetic," 788.

80 It is interesting to note that what Ernesto Rogers had been damned for in 1959—the hybrid mixture of "eclecticism, regionalism and modernism"—was what Post-Modernism was claiming as its strength by the late 1970s (see Jencks, *Modern Movements in Architecture* [London: Pelican, 1973]: 326). Banham also refers to the strong influence of Japanese architecture on emerging Post-Modernism. See "The Japonization of World Architecture," in Hiroyuki Suzuki, Reyner Banham, and Katsuhiro Kobayashi, *Contemporary Architecture of Japan 1958–1984* (London: Architectural Press, 1985), 21–22.

81 Robert Venturi and Denise Scott Brown, *Learning from Las Vegas* (Cambridge, Mass.: MIT Press, 1972). The book was developed from their 1968 article.

82 *The Architecture of the Well-tempered Environment* (London, Architectural Press, 1969), 270.

83 *Age of the Masters: A Personal View of Modern Architecture* (London: Architectural Press, 1975), 62. There is one reference to Venturi, and it is an interesting one. He remarks that "The masterworks of architects both great and small may be simple, but never simple-minded; their complexities and contradictions (as Robert Venturi called them) make them perceptually rewarding and perennially unclassifiable" (65). This makes Venturi's "complexity and contradiction" phrase far more inclusive than Venturi intended, and is used by Banham to include the Modernist works that Venturi felt lacked those very characteristics. Banham also writes on Las Vegas in "Europe and American Design," in Richard Rose, ed., *Lessons from America: An Exploration* (London: Macmillan, 1974), 67–91; and "Mediated Environments or: You Can't Build That Here," in C. W. E. Bigsby, ed., *Superculture: American Popular Culture and Europe* (London: Paul Elek, 1975), 69–82.

84 "The True False Front," *New Society* (December 2, 1976): 473.

85 Tom Wolfe, *The Kandy-Kolored Tangerine-Flake Streamline Baby* (London: Mayflower, 1972), 14.

86 "The True False Front," 473.

87 "Vehicles of Desire," 3.

88 "The True False Front," 473.

89 *Age of the Masters,* 62.

90   "The Writing on the Walls," 1337.

91   "The Ism Count," *New Society* (August 27, 1981): 362.

92   "AT&T: The Post Post-Deco Skyscraper," *Architectural Review* (August 1984): 27.

93   "Santa Cruz Shingle Style," *Architectural Review* (May 1983): 35.

94   "The Ism Count," 362.

95   "1960 1," 94. For an account, see "Revenge of the Picturesque: English Architectural Polemics," in John Summerson, ed., *Concerning Architecture* (London: Allen Lane, 1968), 267–270.

96   "Santa Cruz Shingle Style," 35.

97   "The Purified Aesthetic," 788.

98   "The Academic Arrival of Postmodernism," *AIA Journal* (August 1984): 81.

99   Ibid.

100   "Building Inside Out," *New Society* (July 24, 1987): 12. Banham had judged Gehry's late 1960s work in Los Angeles in terms of the "continuing validity of the stucco box" within an Angeleno context, and as being in the lineage of Schindler (*Los Angeles: The Architecture of Four Ecologies* [London: Pelican, 1971], 198). Also to his liking, because of avoiding "cleverness" while making historical references, were the architects of the Santa Cruz Shingle Style. See "Santa Cruz Shingle Style," 34–38.

101   Charles Jencks, "Deconstruction: The Pleasures of Absence," in Andreas Papadakis, Catherine Cooke, and Andrew Benjamin, eds., *Deconstruction: Omnibus Volume* (London: Academy Editions, 1989), 120.

102   Ibid., 119. Gehry is one of the central architects in Jencks's account. He was also one of the seven architects featured in the Museum of Modern Art's Deconstructivist Architecture exhibition (1988).

103   "That *Interesting* Play," *Times Literary Supplement* (June 30, 1986): 673.

104   "Building Inside Out," 13.

105   Charles Jencks, *The Language of Post-Modern Architecture,* 4th ed. (London: Academy Editions, 1984, 163.

106   "Stirling Escapes the Hobbits," *New Society* (October 4, 1984): 16.

107   Charles Jencks, *The Language of Post-Modern Architecture,* 3rd ed. (London: Academy Editions, 1981), 136.

108   "Stirling Escapes the Hobbits," 16.

109   Jencks, *The Language of Post-Modern Architecture,* 3rd ed., 138.

110   Letter from Charles Jencks, *Times Literary Supplement* (December 1, 1978): 1402.

111   "Stirling Escapes the Hobbits," 16.

112   *Megastructure: Urban Futures of the Recent Past* (London: Thames and Hudson, 1976), 216.

113   "The Academic Arrival of Postmodernism," 79.

114   Ibid., 79–81.

115   This appears in a review of Gavin Macrae-Gibson's *The Secret Life of Buildings* in "That *Interesting* Play," 673.

116   "The True False Front," 473.

117   Venturi and Scott Brown, *Learning from Las Vegas,* 128.

118   A "decorated shed" is not, therefore, synonymous with "decorated construction." For Banham, the latter has some *architectural*—as opposed to some other form of— value; the former does not.

119   Jencks, letter to *Times Literary Supplement* (December 1, 1978): 1402.

120   *Megastructure,* 8.

121   Ibid., 76.

122   Ibid., 17.

123   Ibid.

124   Ibid., 116.

125   Ibid., 197.

126   Ibid., 9.

127   Ibid., 92.

128   Ibid., 96.

129   Ibid., 10.

130   Ibid., 13.

131 Ibid., 70.

132 Ibid., 105.

133 Ibid., 168.

134 Ibid., 169–170.

135 Ibid., 170.

136 Ibid., 117.

137 Ibid., 208.

138 Ibid., 10.

139 Ibid., 209.

140 Ibid., 203.

141 Ibid., 208.

142 Ibid., 84.

143 Ibid., 211.

144 Ibid., 212.

145 Ibid., 214.

146 "La megastructure è morta" was the title of a lecture given in Naples, reported in *Casabella* (March 1973): 2.

147 "Enigma of the Rue du Renard," *Architectural Review* (May 1977): 277.

148 Ibid.

149 "Art-Space Angst," *New Society* (January 24, 1986): 152, 153.

150 "Enigma of the Rue du Renard," 277.

151 "Art-Space Angst," 152.

152 Ibid., 153.

153 "Enigma of the Rue du Renard," 278.

154 "The Quality of Modernism," *Architectural Review* (October 1986): 56.

155   Le Corbusier, *Towards a New Architecture* (London: Architectural Press, 1927), 16.

156   Ibid., 140.

157   See "Grass Above, Glass Around," *New Society* (October 6, 1977): 22–23.

158   "The Quality of Modernism," 55. The special issue of *Progressive Architecture* on Foster's Hong Kong building (March 1986) contains an interview with Banham about High Tech (75–77).

159   See "Introduction," *Foster Associates* (London: RIBA Publications, 1979), 4–8. Banham had possibly taken to heart an attack by Lance Wright, the editor of the *Architectural Review,* who had written to *New Society* (in response to Banham's article on Foster's Willis Faber building), complaining that "it is an article of faith with Reyner Banham that if you use high technology in building you simply can't go wrong" (October 20, 1977: 144). Banham, in a follow-up letter (November 10, 1977: 318), vigorously disagreed.

160   "Art and Necessity," *Architectural Review* (December 1982): 35.

161   Joan Kron and Suzanne Slesin, *High Tech: The Industrial Style and Source Book for the Home* (New York: C. N. Potter, 1978).

162   "Art and Necessity," 35. Banham looked at these "smart sheds" in both "Art and Necessity" and "Silicon Style," *Architectural Review* (May 1981): 283–290.

163   Banham rated highly Piano's work, which he happily termed High Tech. See "In the Neighbourhood of Art," *Art in America* (June 1987): 124–129, and "Making Architecture: The High Craft of Renzo Piano," *Architecture and Urbanism* (March 1989): 151–158. He also explores the influences on Piano, Rogers, and Foster—and on High Tech in general—of the California case study houses of the 1950s. See "Klarheit, Ehrichkeit, Einfachkeit . . . and Wit Too!," in Elizabeth A. T. Smith, ed., *Blueprints for Modern Living: History and Legacy of the Case Study Houses* (Cambridge, Mass.: MIT Press, 1989), 183–195.

164   *Foster Associates,* 5.

165   Banham credits James Gowan with its invention, and applies it to Stirling and Gowan's work in "The Style for the Job," *New Statesman* (February 14, 1964): 261. Banham had earlier used it in relation to Saarinen in "The Fear of Eero's Mana," *Arts Magazine* (February 1962): 73.

166   "Art and Necessity," 34.

167   Ibid., 37.

168   Ibid., 38.

169 Ibid. The Greenough quote comes from "Relative and Independent Beauty" (1853), reprinted in Horatio Greenough, *Form and Function* (Berkeley: University of California Press, 1947), 69–86. Banham, in his RIBA address on the occasion of Rogers's receipt of the Gold Medal (June 25, 1985), declared that "sensuous pleasures do not derive from ornament, erudite or invented. They derive from the right fashioning and elegant assembly of what must necessarily be." Typescript in Reyner Banham: Papers 1951–1989 archive, no. 910009, box 9, Getty Research Institute.

170 "Making Architecture," 154.

171 "Art and Necessity," 35.

172 "The Quality of Modernism," 55.

173 Ibid.

174 The *Architectural Review* (June 1982): 22–35 contains articles and photographs of Bofill's work.

175 "The Quality of Modernism," 55.

176 "Hong Kong Bank: Interview with Reyner Banham," *Progressive Architecture* (March 1986): 75.

177 "Art and Necessity," 38.

178 "The Quality of Modernism," 55.

179 "The Thing in the Forecourt," 139. Mies had also belonged to "that grand old constructive tradition [which] . . . for the three millenniums of Man's technological infancy . . . has served us well." "The Last Professional," 987.

180 *Foster Associates,* 5.

181 Ibid.

182 *Megastructure,* 209.

183 "On Trial 5: The Spec Builders—Towards a Pop Architecture," *Architectural Review* (July 1962): 42.

184 "The Sage of Corrales," *New Society* (March 17, 1983): 431.

185 His *Guide to Modern Architecture* (1962), reprinted in 1963 and 1967, was revised as *The Age of the Masters* in 1975; both versions were aimed at the "intelligent lay person." Banham recounted that "When the book started life in the 1960s it had no title because what it actually said on the contract was a 'pop book on modern architecture.'" See Charles Jencks, "In Undisguised Taste," *Building Design* (May 16, 1975): 12.

186   *The Architecture of the Well-tempered Environment,* rev. ed. (Chicago: University of Chicago Press, 1984), 286.

187   Ibid., 305.

188   Ibid., 286.

189   Ibid., 312.

190   Ibid., 269.

191   Ibid., 288.

192   Ibid., 279. Banham goes on to stake a half-claim for Paolo Soleri's "perpetually un-finishable Arcosanti project" in Arizona as an "impressive monument." In "The Mesa Messiah" (*New Society* [May 6, 1976]: 307) he describes it as "a fabulous place to be" but is ambivalent about the underlying architectural and social concepts. He provides an extended discussion of Soleri in *Megastructure,* 199–201.

193   *The Architecture of the Well-tempered Environment,* rev. ed., 312.

194   Ibid., 13. There is no real evidence for this. The most negative review at the time appeared in 1969; see Martin Pawley, "Loneliness of the Long Distance Swimmer," *Architectural Design* (April 1969): 184. Seldom do reviews appear more than two years after publication. An exception was one by Kenneth Frampton in *Oppositions* (Winter 1976/1977): 86–89. Frampton attacks Banham for what he sees as his apolitical (lack of) perspective about technology–a different point.

195   "The Japonization of World Architecture," 20.

196   McKean, "The Last of England?—part 2," 27.

197   *Los Angeles,* 242.

198   He also provided an introduction to *Buffalo Architecture: A Guide* (Cambridge, Mass.: MIT Press, 1981).

199   In an interview with Neil Jackson, "Thoughts of the Well-Tempered Reyner Banham," *Building Design* (May 9, 1980): 20.

200   Ibid.

Chapter 6

1   "Convenient Benches and Handy Hooks: Functional Considerations in the Criticism of the Art of Architecture," in Marcus Whiffen, ed., *The History, Theory and Criti-*

cism of Architecture: Papers from the 1964 AIA-ACSA Teacher Seminar (Cambridge, Mass.: MIT Press, 1965), 91.

2   "Machine Aesthetic," *Architectural Review* (April 1955): 227.

3   "Futurism for Keeps," *Arts* (December 1960): 39.

4   Walter Gropius, *The New Architecture and the Bauhaus* (London: Faber, 1935), 92.

5   Both phrases were used by Banham to describe the attitude in the postwar to mid-1950s period. The first is from "The Style: Flimsy . . . Effeminate," in Mary Banham and Bevis Hillier, eds., *A Tonic to the Nation* (London: Thames and Hudson, 1976), 197; the second, from "A Tonic to the Nation," (BBC Radio 4, November 29, 1976).

6   The CoID was founded in 1944 as a government-funded body to "promote by all practical means the improvement of design in the products of British industry." Its name was changed to the Design Council in 1972. Its magazine *Design* was introduced in 1949.

7   Michael Farr, *Design in British Industry: A Mid-Century Survey* (Cambridge: Cambridge University Press, 1955), xxxvi.

8   Read, speaking at the National Union of Teacher's conference, in *Popular Culture and Personal Responsibility* (transcripts of proceedings) (London: NUT Publications, 1960); 155.

9   "H. M. Fashion House," *New Statesman* (January 27, 1961): 151.

10   "The End of Insolence," *New Statesman* (October 29, 1960): 646. In his address at the 1966 Aspen conference, Banham dated what he described as the tradition of "art worry" back to the nineteenth century and "that loveable Victorian nut A. W. N. Pugin." The legacy is that improving the public's taste and fighting for good design are part of the "great progressive do-gooder complex of ideas based upon the proposition that the majority is always wrong, that the public must be led, cajoled, sticked and carrotted onward and upward." "All That Glitters Is Not Stainless," *Architectural Design* (June 1967): 351.

11   "The End of Insolence," 646.

12   "A Flourish of Symbols," *The Observer Weekend Review* (November 17, 1963): 21. The Design Centre was the showroom where objects from the Design Index—and those which had received the Duke of Edinburgh's Award for Elegant Design—were on display to the public.

13   "The End of Insolence," 644.

14   Ibid., 646.

15   Ibid., 644.

16   A parallel can also be drawn with the use of classicism by the New Brutalists (see chapter 2) as just another option within multiple aesthetics.

17   "The Cult," *New Statesman* (November 17, 1961): 755.

18   "The End of Insolence," 644.

19   *Theory and Design in the First Machine Age* (London: Architectural Press, 1960), 10.

20   "Who Is This 'Pop'?," *Motif* (Winter 1962/1963): 12.

21   "Design by Choice," *Architectural Review* (July 1961): 46.

22   Ibid., 48.

23   "The End of Insolence," 644.

24   "Vehicles of Desire," *Art* (September 1, 1955): 3.

25   "Space for Decoration: A Rejoinder," *Design* (July 1955): 24.

26   "A Throw-Away Aesthetic," *Industrial Design* (March 1960): 65.

27   "Space for Decoration: A Rejoinder," 24.

28   "A Throw-Away Aesthetic," 65.

29   "Machine Aesthetic," 228.

30   Ibid.

31   "Vehicles of Desire," 3.

32   Deborah Allen, "The Dream Cars Come True Again," *Industrial Design* (January, 1957): 103.

33   Deborah Allen, "Guide for Carwatchers," *Industrial Design* (January 1955): 89.

34   Roland Barthes, *Mythologies* (London: Granada, 1973), 89.

35   "Pop and the Body Critical," *New Society* (December 16, 1965): 25.

36   Ibid.

37   "Towards a Million Volt Light and Sound Culture," *Architectural Review* (May 1967): 331.

38   Marshall McLuhan, *The Mechanical Bride* (reprinted London: Routledge and Kegan Paul, 1967), v.

39   These are terms used in Nigel Whiteley, *Pop Design: Modernism to Mod* (London: Design Council, 1987), chapters 5 and 8.

40   "The Message Is a Monkee," *New Society* (February 23, 1967): 284.

41   Stuart Hall and Paddy Whannel, *The Popular Arts* (London: Hutchinson, 1964), 68.

42   An interesting example of Banham arguing in favor of some of the characteristics that Hall and Whannel (et al.) opposed is "Top Pop Boffin," an article about the role of the "creative technician"—in this case, the record producer and former Independent Group member Frank Cordell (*Architects' Journal* [February 20, 1958]: 269–71).

43   "A Flourish of Symbols," 21.

44   "Kandy Kulture Kikerone," *New Society* (August 19, 1965): 25.

45   Tom Wolfe, *The Kandy-Kolored Tangerine-Flake Streamline Baby* (London: Mayflower, 1972), 14.

46   Preface in Penny Sparke, ed., *Design by Choice* (London: Academy Editions, 1981), 7.

47   Ibid.

48   "The Shape of Things: Take Courage," *Art News and Review* (January 27, 1951): 6.

49   From a letter to the author dated April 4, 1981.

50   According to Mary Banham, in Mary Banham, Paul Barker, Sutherland Lyall, and Cedric Price, comps., *A Critic Writes: Essays by Reyner Banham* (Berkeley: University of California Press, 1996), 149.

51   Ibid.

52   "Who Is This 'Pop,'?" 7.

53   "1,2,3,4 . . . Green!," *Architects' Journal* (May 10, 1956): 467.

54   "So This Is FJ?," *Architects' Journal* (January 7, 1960): 1.

55   "The Descent of F3," *Architects' Journal* (August 27, 1959): 75.

56   "Brands Hatch," *New Statesman* (July 17, 1964): 98.

57   "Rank Values," *New Society* (September 14, 1972): 511.

58   "Grudge Racing Tonight," *New Society* (February 3, 1966): 21.

59   Ibid., 22.

60 "Rank Values," 510.

61 Ibid.

62 "Horse of a Different Colour," *New Society* (November 2, 1967): 637.

63 A similar approach is evident in a piece on four-wheel drives, "The Four-Wheel Life," *New Society* (August 18, 1977): 350–351; and in "Stretch City," *New Society* (March 7, 1986): 413–414.

64 "Transistorama," *New Statesman* (September 1, 1961): 281.

65 Ibid., 282.

66 Ibid.

67 "H. M. Fashion House," 151.

68 See "Handsome Doesn't," *New Statesman* (May 19, 1961): 806.

69 Farr, *Design in British Industry,* captions to plate XXXI, illustrations 2 and 3.

70 Richard Moss, "Max Braun," *Industrial Design* (November 1962): 39–40.

71 His sharpest attack on Braun and the classical aesthetic of appliances is "Household Godjets," *New Society* (January 15, 1970): 100–101.

72 "On Abstract Theory," *Art News and Review* (November 28, 1953): 3.

73 "The End of Insolence," 646.

74 "A Flourish of Symbols," 21.

75 See Charles Jencks, *The Language of Post-Modern Architecture* (London: Academy Editions, 1977), 63–66.

76 Adrianne Carstaing, "Peasant Props, Glazes and Glitter," *Sunday Times Colour Supplement* (January 6, 1963): 17.

77 Janice Elliot, "Design + Function," *Sunday Times Colour Supplement* (April 15, 1962): 26.

78 Paul Reilly, "The Challenge of Pop," *Architectural Review* (October 1957): 256.

79 Ibid., 257.

80 "A Flourish of Symbols," 21.

81 "All That Glitters Is Not Stainless," 351.

82   "Radio Machismo," *New Society* (August 22, 1974): 494 (all quotes).

83   "Convenient Benches and Handy Hooks," 91.

84   Walter Gropius, "The Theory and Organisation of the Bauhaus" (1923), in Tim Benton and Charlotte Benton with Dennis Sharp, eds., *Form and Function* (London: Granada, 1980), 127.

85   "The Shape of Everything," *Art News and Review* (July 14, 1951): 2.

86   "On Abstract Theory," 3.

87   For example, "Shades of Summer," *New Society* (June 29, 1967): 959. See my discussion of it in Nigel Whiteley, "Olympus and the Marketplace," *Design Issues* (Summer 1997): 24–35.

88   "A Space for Decoration," 24.

89   Quoted in an interview with Penny Sparke, "The Machine Stops," *Design* (December 1980): 31.

90   See Nigel Whiteley, "Design in Enterprise Culture: Design for Whose Profit," in Russell Keat and Nicholas Abercrombie eds., *Enterprise Culture* (London: Routledge, 1991), 186–205.

91   Quoted in "Persuading Image: A Symposium," *Design* (June 1960): 55.

92   "A Clip-on Architecture," *Design Quarterly* 63 (1965): 6.

93   "Unavoidable Options," *New Society* (September 18, 1969): 446 (all quotes).

94   "On First Looking into Warshawsky," *Architects' Journal* (July 26, 1961): 111.

95   "Notes Toward a Definition of U.S. Automobile Painting as a Significant Branch of Modern Mobile Heraldry," *Art in America* (September 1966): 76–79.

96   "The Art of Doing Your Own Thing," *The Listener* (September 12, 1968): 330–331; "Anti-technology," *New Society* (May 4, 1967): 645; "Gentri-Mini Mania," *New Society* (November 28, 1974): 555–556; "A Fur-out Trip," *New Society* (February 4, 1971): 200; "Sundae Painters," *New Society* (April 11, 1974): 82; "Bus Pop," *New Society* (September 5, 1968): 343–344.

97   "Softer Hardware," *Ark* 44 (1969): 6.

98   Ibid., 6–7.

99   There was something, too, of an anticipation of Jencksian "adhocism" and the bricoleur (see conclusion). Charles Jencks claims to have been working on his theory of adhocism in 1968, and may therefore have influenced Banham. See Charles

Jencks and Nathan Silver, *Adhocism: The Case for Improvisation* (New York: Anchor, 1973), 9.

100   "Softer Hardware," 11.

101   Ibid., 7.

102   Ibid., 2–5.

103   Ibid., 11.

104   Ibid., 6.

105   Ibid., 10.

106   Ibid., 9.

107   Ibid., 11.

108   "Industrial Design and the Common User," *The Listener* (May 3, 1956): 550.

109   For example, in *Theory and Design,* 314, 319.

110   "The Bauhaus Gospel," *The Listener* (September 26, 1968): 391.

111   Ibid., 392.

112   Ibid.

113   "Softer Hardware," 6.

114   "A Home Is Not a House," *Art in America* (April 1965): 76.

115   "Monumental Wind-bags," *New Society* (April 18, 1968): 570.

116   "Beyond Sir's Ken," *New Society* (April 17, 1969): 600.

117   "Softer Hardware," 5.

118   Quoted in Sparke, "The Machine Stops," 31.

119   *Scenes in America Deserta* (London: Thames and Hudson, 1982), 166.

120   "Chairs as Art," *New Society* (April 20, 1967): 566.

121   Ibid., 567.

122   Ibid., 568.

123 Ibid., 567.

124 Ibid., 566. It recalls Moholy-Nagy's contemporary at the Bauhaus, Marcel Breuer, predicting that "in the end we will sit on resilient columns of air." This future form of seating followed from the Bauhaus experiments between 1921 and 1925 that Breuer illustrated in 1926. See the exhibition catalog *Bauhaus 1919–1928* (New York: Museum of Modern Art, 1938, reprint 1975), 130.

125 "Household Godjets," 100.

126 Ibid., 101.

127 Ibid., 100.

128 Ann Oakley, *Housewife* (London: Penguin, 1976), 6.

129 For example, Dolores Hayden, *The Grand Domestic Revolution: A History of Feminist Design for American Houses, Neighbourhoods and Cities* (Cambridge, Mass.: MIT Press, 1981); Caroline Davidson, *A Woman's Work Is Never Done: A History of Housework in the British Isles* (London: Chatto and Windus, 1982); and Ruth Schwartz Cowan, *More Work for Mother: The Ironies of Household Technology from the Open Hearth to the Microwave* (New York: Basic Books, 1983).

130 One might include *The Aspen Papers: Twenty Years of Design Theory from the International Design Conference in Aspen* (London: Pall Mall, 1974), which he edited and for which he provided some commentaries.

131 For "classic" Banham writing, see "The Crisp at the Crossroads," *New Society* (July 9, 1970): 77; "Power Plank," *New Society* (June 28, 1973): 762; "Paleface Trash," *New Society* (February 22, 1973): 426; "Sex and the Single Lens," *New Society* (December 19, 1974): 763; and "Faces of Time," *New Society* (February 9, 1978): 323.

132 Unpublished review of Forty's book in Reyner Banham: Papers 1951–1989 archive, no. 910009, box 11, Getty Research Institute.

133 Foreword, in Sparke, ed., *Design by Choice,* 7.

134 "Old Designers' Tales," *New Society* (May 19, 1983): 274.

135 Ibid.

136 Ibid., 275.

137 Peter Conrad, "The Scientists of Camp," *Times Literary Supplement* (October 21, 1977): 1237.

138 "Convenient Benches and Handy Hooks," 101.

139 "Machine Aesthetic," 228.

Conclusion

1   "Flower Power Mark 1," *New Society* (June 6, 1968): 846.

2   As well as those articles cited in previous chapters and above, Banham also wrote about Pevsner in "World, the; Book to Change, a," *Architects' Journal* (December 8, 1960): 809–810; "England His England," *New Statesman* (September 28, 1962): 27; "Pevsner de Luxe Model," *Architects' Journal* (December 11, 1968): 1378–1379; and "A Real Golden Oldie," *New Society* (December 13, 1973): 666–667.

3   *The Architecture of the Well-tempered Environment* (London: Architectural Press, 1969), 84.

4   Ibid., 85–86.

5   Nikolaus Pevsner, "Modern Architecture and the Historian or the Return of Historicism," *RIBA Journal* (April 1961): 230, 233.

6   Nikolaus Pevsner, *Pioneers of the Modern Movement* (London: Faber, 1936), 202.

7   "Ornament and Crime: The Decisive Contribution of Adolf Loos," *Architectural Review* (February 1957): 85.

8   David Watkin, *Morality and Architecture* (Oxford: Oxford University Press, 1977), 10–11.

9   Ibid., 2.

10   Ibid., 104.

11   Ibid., viii.

12   "Pevsner's Progress," *Times Literary Supplement* (February 17, 1978): 191.

13   Pevsner, *Pioneers of the Modern Movement,* 206.

14   Nikolaus Pevsner, *Pioneers of Modern Design* (New York: Museum of Modern Art, 1949), 135; (London: Pelican, 1960), 215.

15   "Pevsner's Progress," 191.

16   Watkin, *Morality and Architecture,* 111.

17   Ibid., 104.

18   Ibid., 115.

19   Ibid., 110.

20   "Pevsner's Progress," 191.

21   Ibid., 192.

22   Ibid., 191.

23   Ibid.

24   Watkin, *Morality and Architecture,* 114.

25   "Pevsner's Progress," 191.

26   This is how he first describes Pevsner in "England His England": 27.

27   Pevsner, "Modern Architecture and the Historian," 237.

28   "Flower Power Mark 1," 846.

29   Interview with Charles Jencks, "In Undisguised Taste," *Building Design* (May 16, 1975), 12–13.

30   Ibid., 13.

31   "Bricologues à la lanterne," *New Society* (July 1, 1976): 25.

32   Ibid.

33   Charles Jencks, letter to *New Society* (July 15, 1976): 141.

34   Letter to *New Society* (July 22, 1976): 195.

35   Charles Jencks, letter to *New Society* (July 29, 1976): 251.

36   "Two by Jencks: The Tough Life of the *Enfant Terrible,*" *AIA Journal* (December 1980): 50.

37   Ibid., 51.

38   Ibid.

39   Obituary by J. M. Richards, *Architectural Review* (May 1988): 10.

40   "England and America," *Journal of the Society of Architectural Historians* (December 1977): 263.

41   "Two by Jencks," 50

42   Jencks, in conversation with the author, November 24, 1999.

43   "Only an Academic Flywheel?," *RIBA Journal* (August 1972): 339.

44   "Two by Jencks," 51.

45   Ibid., 50.

46   This quote is attributed to Sam Stevens in John Maule McKean, "The Last of England?—Part 1," *Building Design* (August 13, 1976): 8. Thomas "Sam" Stevens had been director of historical studies at the Architectural Association.

47   Richard Hamilton, in *Fathers of Pop* film/video (London: Miranda Films, 1979).

48   "The Atavism of the Short-Distance Mini-Cyclist," *Living Arts* no. 3 (1964): 91.

49   Ibid., 92.

50   Ibid., 91.

51   Ibid., 96.

52   Ibid., 94.

53   "Pop and the Body Critical," *New Society* (December 16, 1965): 25.

54   "The Atavism . . . ," 97.

55   Ibid., 95.

56   "People's Palaces," *New Statesman* (August 7, 1964): 192.

57   Banham loathed paternalism and described what he saw as Lord Reith's "moral elitism" at the BBC in the 1930s as typical of this attitude. *Mechanical Services,* unit 21 of A305 (Milton Keynes, U.K.: The Open University, 1975), 18.

58   "People's Palaces," 191.

59   Ibid., 191–192.

60   "Towards a Million-Volt Light and Sound Culture," *Architectural Review* (May 1967): 335.

61   "The Japonization of World Architecture," in Hiroyuki Suzuki, Reyner Banham, and Katsuhiro Kobayashi, *Contemporary Architecture of Japan 1958–1984* (London: Architectural Press, 1985), 20.

62   "On Trial 5. The Spec Builders: Towards a Pop Architecture," *Architectural Review* (July 1962): 43.

63   Manfredo Tafuri, *Theories and History of Architecture* (London: Granada, 1976), 14.

64   Martin Pawley, *Architecture Versus Housing* (London: Studio Vista, 1971), 113.

65   Malcolm MacEwen, *Crisis in Architecture* (London: RIBA, 1974), 23.

66   "The Atavism . . . ," 97.

67   "In the Neighbourhood of Art," *Art in America* (1987), reprinted in Mary Banham, Paul Barker, Sutherland Lyall, and Cedric Price, comps., *A Critic Writes: Essays by Reyner Banham* (Berkeley: University of California Press, 1996), 273, 275.

68   "A Black Box," *New Statesman and Society* (October 12, 1990): 22–23.

69   Given what he had written previously about Lutyens (see chapter 5), it is surprising to find Banham stating that "architecture is often conspicuously present—*in the work of Lutyens for instance*—in buildings that are pretty dumb designs from other points of view." Ibid., 23. (My italics).

70   Banham, quoted in Ann Ferebee, "Home Thoughts from Abroad," *Industrial Design* (August 1963): 78.

71   In an interview with Martin Pawley in 1971, Banham remarked that "one of the ways we handle . . . problems is by making them apocalyptic and assuming radical, militant, polarised positions and then deciding the outcome on a sort of knock-down drag-out fight basis. This doesn't appeal to me at all because once you've po-larised a situation it becomes an either/or matter and the third solution—which is probably the right one, and which might well not be a compromise between the other two at all—never even gets discussed" ("The Last of the Piston Engine Men," *Building Design* [October 1, 1971]: 6).

72   *Theory and Design in the First Machine Age* (London: Architectural Press, 1960), 325.

73   *The Architecture of the Well-tempered Environment,* 129.

74   Martin Pawley makes a similar point in his review of the book. See "Loneliness of the Long Distance Swimmer," *Architectural Design* (April 1969): 184–185.

75   Interview with Martin Pawley, "The Last of the Piston Engine Men," 6.

76   "The True False Front," *New Society* (December 2, 1976): 473.

77   "Flatscape with Containers," *New Society* (August 17, 1967): 232.

78   Letter from Jencks, *New Society* (August 31, 1971): 302; letter from Banham, *New Society* (September 7, 1967): 338.

79   Banham, comment on George Baird, "'La Dimension Amoureuse' in Architecture," in Charles Jencks and George Baird, eds., *Meaning in Architecture* (London: Barrie and Jenkins, 1969), 81

80   George Baird, "'La Dimension Amoureuse' in Architecture," in Charles Jencks and George Baird, eds., *Meaning in Architecture* (London: Barrie and Jenkins, 1969), 93.

81   Letter from Jencks, *New Society* (August 31, 1971): 302; letter from Banham, *New Society* (September 7, 1967): 338.

82   "Convenient Benches and Handy Hooks: Functional Considerations in the Criticism of the Art of Architecture," in Marcus Whiffen ed., *The History, Theory and Criticism of Architecture* (Cambridge, Mass.: MIT Press, 1965), 104.

83   Ibid., 103.

84   *Theory and Design,* 325.

85   *The Architecture of the Well-tempered Environment,* 121.

86   Ibid., 123.

87   "The Architecture of Wampanoag," in Charles Jencks and George Baird, eds., *Meaning in Architecture* (London: Barrie and Jenkins, 1969), 118.

88   "Flatscape with Containers," 232.

89   "The Architecture of Wampanoag," 101.

90   "Old Futuropolis," *Architects' Journal* (August 31, 1966): 503.

91   Sam Stevens, quoted in McKean "The Last of England?—Part 1," 9.

92   This terminology is open to debate. I define the Third Machine Age differently in Nigel Whiteley, "Webbed Feat," *Art Review* (May 2000): 60–61.

93   "A Home Is Not a House," *Art in America* (April 1965): 73.

94   Ibid., 79.

95   Baird, "'La Dimension Amoureuse' in Architecture," 118.

96   "A Black Box," 25. An "architecture of resistance" is, in effect, (as I have argued before), how Banham was interpreting New Brutalist architecture and the work of James Stirling. He even referred to "Brutalist gestures of defiance" in 1972. Introduction, *The Architecture of Yorke Rosenberg Mardall* (London: Lund Humphries, 1972), 5.

97   See letter from Hugh Johnson in *Architectural Review* (July 1967): 6.

98   See, for example, comments following his lecture "The History of the Immediate Future," reprinted in *RIBA Journal* (May 1961): 260.

99   See "Hair-Cut, You!," *Architects' Journal* (October 4, 1956): 469–471.

100 This is a distinction made by J. K. Galbraith in his memoirs, *A Life in Our Times* (Boston: Houghton Mifflin, 1981), 24, between that which is addressed to one's academic peers but is impenetrable to a lay readership, and that which is aimed at the latter. Galbraith acknowledges he borrowed the terms from Thorstein Veblen.

101 Robert Maxwell, "The Plenitude of Presence," in Demetri Porphyrios, ed., "On the Methodology of Architectural History," *Architectural Design* 6/7 (1981): 57; Paul Barker, letter to the author, April 23, 2000.

102 "Le Corbusier," *New Society* (September 14, 1967): 354; "Mendelsohn," *Architectural Review* (August 1954): 93; *Theory and Design:* 133.

103 See "Zoom Wave Hits Architecture," *New Society* (March 3, 1966): 21; "Monumental Wind-Bags," *New Society* (April 18, 1968): 569; "First Master of the Mass Media?," *The Listener* (June 27, 1963): 1080.

104 *Theory and Design,* 10.

105 "Historical Studies and Architectural Criticism," *Transactions of the Bartlett Society* 1 (1962–1963): 36.

106 "1960 4: History Under Revision," *Architectural Review* (May 1960): 331.

107 Quoted in George Kassaboff, ed., "The Value of History to Students of Architecture," *Architects' Journal* (April 23, 1959): 640.

108 "1960 4," 332.

109 "Historical Studies and Architectural Criticism," 44.

110 *The New Brutalism: Ethic or Aesthetic?* (London, Architectural Press, 1966), 134.

111 Banham, in Peter Cook, ed., *Archigram* (London: Studio Vista, 1972), 5.

112 "Only an Academic Flywheel?," 339.

113 This is confirmed by Banham's favorable response to Jencks's "History as Myth" (in Charles Jencks and George Baird, eds., *Meaning in Architecture* (London: Barrie and Jenkins, 1969), 244–265). From a conversation with Jencks (November 24, 1999).

114 McKean, "The Last of England?—Part 1," 8.

115 "Lecturing at Ulm," *Architects' Journal* (April 16, 1959): 587; for his comments about design at Ulm, see "Cool on the Kuhberg," *The Listener* (May 21, 1959): 884–885.

116 Interview with Sparke, "The Machine Stops," 31.

117 Leaving announcement contained in Reyner Banham: Papers 1951–1989 archive, no. 910009, Getty Research Institute.

118 In 1968 Banham had written about Hitchcock: "Professor Hitchcock was much culti-vated by the younger generation at this time, partly as an 'antidote' to Pevsnerian influence. His frequent and continued presence in England was assured by the preparations for his contribution to the (Pevsner-edited) Pelican *History of Art, Ar-chitecture: Nineteenth and Twentieth Centuries.* When this finally appeared in 1958, it was greeted with almost universal disappointment by his younger support-ers." "Revenge of the Picturesque," in John Summerson, ed., *Concerning Architec-ture* (London: Allen Lane, 1968), 269.

119 "A Set of Actual Monuments," *Architectural Review* (April 1989): 89. Actually, Ban-ham was misquoting. Maxwell's phrase was "the plenitude of presence," but Ban-ham is perhaps varying his dictum so that "the only way to prove you've got a mind is to misremember things occasionally"! See Maxwell, "The Plenitude of Presence,": 52–57.

120 Conversely, he praises Leonardo Benevolo's writing about Gropius's Fagus factory because he "clearly had seen the plant with his own eyes, because he describes its site as only an eyewitness could have done." *A Concrete Atlantis: U.S. Industrial Building and European Modern Architecture* (Cambridge, Mass.: MIT Press, 1986), 184.

121 Ibid., 225.

122 Ibid., 17.

123 Ibid., 17–18.

124 Ibid., 18.

125 Ibid., 136.

126 Ibid., 19.

127 Banham contradicts this in 1986 when writing about the Maison de Verre: "It is surely a contradiction of the intentions and nature of Modernism for its products to stand around long enough to become monuments anyhow. . . . I still get a funny feeling whenever I write a phrase like 'the modern tradition' even though I know it stands for something real, and I think that at least one of the reasons why we have been having the 'crisis of modernism' that gets academics so excited at conferences is that we are faced with the problem of forcing a lot of anti-historical material into historical categories that it was deliberately designed not to fit. . . . Could it be . . . that the 'permanent masterpieces' of modern architecture operate under a differ-ent rule book in which the canon is almost irrelevant . . . ?" ("Modern Monuments," *New Society* [November 1986]: 14). I find this quasi-Futurist, certainly High Mod-ernist pronouncement a throwback to the period of his "Stocktaking" articles.

128   *A Concrete Atlantis,* 169.

129   Jencks, "History as Myth," 262.

130   Maxwell, "The Plenitude of Presence," 57. Jencks points out that Banham's method is "closer to the tradition of humanist scholars than any other historian; he seeks to connect the stated intentions of an architect with his design, whereas most historians . . . are more interpretative." "History as Myth," 257.

131   "Only an Academic Flywheel?," 339.

132   *Scenes in America Deserta* (London: Thames and Hudson, 1982), 11.

133   Ibid., 188.

134   Ibid., 199–200.

135   Preface, *Design by Choice* (London: Academy Editions, 1981), 7.

136   *Scenes in America Deserta,* 188.

137   Ibid., 92.

138   Ibid., 11.

139   Ibid., 18.

140   Ibid., 221.

141   Ibid., 18.

142   Ibid., 166.

143   "Pop and the Body Critical," 25.

144   Maxwell, "The Plenitude of Presence," 56.

145   Ibid., 57.

146   Kenneth Frampton, "On Reyner Banham's *The Architecture of the Well-tempered Environment,*" *Oppositions* (Winter 1976/1977): 88.

147   "A Set of Actual Monuments," 89. It was also published in *Art in America* (October 1988): 173–177, 213, 215. Interestingly, and accurately in Banham's case, the sentence is followed by "And next to buildings, he loved gossip, which is the other essential for a good architectural historian"!

148   "Two by Jencks . . . ," 51.

BIBLIOGRAPHY

The following texts have been overlooked in the almost comprehensive bibliography of Banham's writings that appears in *A Critic Writes.*

1951
"The Shape of Things: '. . . Take Courage.'" *Art News and Review* (January 27, 1951): 6.

1952
"Walker's Galleries" and "I.C.A." *Art News and Review* (December 13, 1952): 2.

1953
"Royal Trains." *Architectural Review* (June 1953): 401.
"ICA Dover Street: Collectors' Items from Artists' Studios." *Art News and Review* (August 22, 1953): 4.
"Photography: *Parallel of Life and Art.*" *Architectural Review* (October 1953): 259–261.
"Paul Klee." *Art News and Review* (November 28, 1953): 7.

1954
"Klee's *Pedagogical Sketchbook.*" *Encounter* (April 1954): 53–58.
"Collages at ICA." *Art News and Review* (October 30, 1954): 8.

1955
Contributions to *Man, Machine and Motion.* London: Institute of Contemporary Arts, 1955. Exhibition catalog.

1956
"Introduction 2." *This Is Tomorrow.* London: Whitechapel Art Gallery, 1956. Exhibition catalog.
"The House of the Future." *Design* (March 1956): 16.

1959
"The City as Scrambled Egg." *Cambridge Opinion* no. 17 (1959): 18–24.

1960
"Balance 1960." *Arquitectura* (February 1960). (Unpaginated).
"A Throw-away Aesthetic." *Industrial Design* (March 1960): 61–65. Translation of "Industrial Design e arte popolare" (1955).

1962
"The Role of Architects." *Domus* part 36 (1962): 6–7.
"Historical Studies and Architectural Criticism." *Bartlett Society Transactions* 1 (1962–1963): 35–51.

1963
"Symbols and Servants." *Architectural Review* (May 1963): 353–356.

"Keeping Down with the Jones's." *Architects' Journal* (September 11, 1963): 505–507.

1964
"Introduction." In *Umberto Boccioni: An Arts Council Exhibition of His Graphic Art,* 3–5. London: Arts Council, 1964. Exhibition catalog.

1965
"Convenient Benches and Handy Hooks: Functional Considerations in the Criticism of the Art of Architecture." In Marcus Whiffen, ed., *The History, Theory and Criticism of Architecture: Papers from the 1964 AIA-ACSA Teacher Seminar,* 91–105. Cambridge, Mass.: MIT Press, 1965.
Statement in *Megascope* no. 3 (November 1965). (Unpaginated.)

1966
"BOAC at JFK." *Architects' Journal* (April 28, 1966): 1088–1089.

1967
"The Future of Art from the Other Side," *Studio International* (June 1967): 280–282.

1968
"Revenge of the Picturesque: English Architectural Polemics, 1945–1965." In John Summerson, ed., *Concerning Architecture: Essays on Architectural Writers and Writing Presented to Nikolaus Pevsner,* 265–273. London: Penguin, 1968.

1969
"The Architecture of Wampanoag." In Charles Jencks and George Baird, eds., *Meaning in Architecture,* 100–103. London: Barrie and Jenkins, 1969.
Blue Stockings and Black Stockings: Changing Patterns in Art Education. London: Ravensbourne College of Art and Design, 1969.

1971
"At Shoo-Fly Landing." *Architectural Design* (January 1971): 60–63.

1972
"Introduction." In *The Architecture of Yorke Rosenberg Mardell 1944–1972,* 4–7. London: Lund Humphries, 1972.
"A Comment from Peter Reyner Banham." In Peter Cook et al., eds., *Archigram,* 5. London: Studio Vista, 1972.

1974
"All That Glitters Is Not Stainless." In Reyner Banham, ed., *The Aspen Papers,* 155–160. London: Pall Mall Press, 1974. 1966 address.
"Introduction." In *James Stirling, RIBA Drawings Collection,* 5–14. London: RIBA, 1974.
"Europe and American Design." In Richard Rose, ed., *Lessons from America: An Exploration,* 67–91. London: Macmillan, 1974.

1975

"Mediated Environments or: *You Can't Build That Here.*" In C. W. E. Bigsby, ed., *Superculture: American Popular Culture and Europe,* 69–82. London: Paul Elek, 1975.
"Memoirs of a Reluctant Juryman." In James Gowan, ed., *A Continuing Experiment: Learning and Teaching at the Architectural Association,* 173–175. London: Architectural Press, 1975.
"Under the Hollywood Sign." In *Edward Ruscha: Prints and Publications 1962–74.* London: Arts Council, 1975. Exhibition catalog.

1976

"Detroit Tin Re-visited." In Thomas Faulkner, ed., *Design 1900–1960: Studies in Design and Popular Culture of the 20th Century,* 120–140. Newcastle upon Tyne: Newcastle upon Tyne Polytechnic Press, 1976.
"The Style: 'Flimsy . . . Effeminate'?" In Mary Banham and Bevis Hillier, eds., *A Tonic to the Nation: The Festival of Britain 1951,* 190–198. London: Thames and Hudson, 1976.

1977

"Happiness Is a Warm Pistol Grip." In *Leisure in the Twentieth Century,* 10–13. London: The Design Council, 1977.

1979

"Introduction." In *Foster Associates,* 4–8. London: RIBA, 1979. Exhibition catalog.

1984

"Comments on John McHale and His Work." In *The Expendable Ikon: Works by John McHale,* 37–43. Buffalo, N.Y.: Albright-Knox Art Gallery, 1984.
"The Price Is Right." In *Cedric Price: Works II,* 98. London: Architectural Association, 1984. Exhibition catalog.

1987

"*La Maison des hommes* and *La Misère des villes:* Le Corbusier and the Architecture of Mass Housing." In H. Allen Brooks, ed., *Le Corbusier: The Garland Essays,* 107–116. New York: Garland, 1987.

INDEX